MODERNITY
An Ethnographic Approach

MODERNITY
An Ethnographic Approach

*Dualism and Mass Consumption
in Trinidad*

Daniel Miller

BERG

Oxford/Providence

First published in 1994 by

Berg Publishers

Editorial offices:
221 Waterman Street, Providence, RI 02906, USA
150 Cowley Road, Oxford, OX4 1JJ, UK

Library of Congress Cataloging-in-Publication Data
A catalogue record for this book is available from the Library of
Congress.

British Library Cataloguing in Publication Data
A catalogue record for this book is available from the British Library.

ISBN 0-85496-916-0 (cloth)
      0-85496-917-9 (paper)

Cover photograph courtesy of *Express Newspaper*, Trinidad and Tobago.

Printed in the United Kingdom by Short Run Press, Exeter.

For David

Contents

Preface

No one teaching within the social sciences can have been able to ignore the plethora of books on the topic of modernity and post-modernism that dominated publications in the late 1980s. Faced with the extensive description and evaluation of what are assumed to be the key characteristics of living within the condition of modern or postmodern life, I suspect not a few people retain one major and sceptical question. Are these traits merely the symptom of a particular academic trajectory, an internal debate about the works of several important but highly academic theorists, or do they describe and help us understand the actual experiences of what would purport to be literally billions of people?

This scepticism towards theoretical debate is probably related to another evident phenomenon within publishing at the present time. In many of the most dynamic and forward looking of the new forms of academic study within this domain – areas such as Media Studies, Gender Studies and Cultural Studies – there are numerous recent books which argue that ethnographic enquiry provides some kind of next stage in the development of their concerns. The appeal is not usually to anthropology *per se* which is seen as tainted by colonial links in the past, but, in as much as this call for ethnography is associated with a generalising and comparative use of ethnographic data, then it is contemporary anthropology which is best placed to fulfil this prescriptive 'solution'.

The title of this book is intended to indicate that I share these current concerns. I feel that there are grounds for asserting that Caribbean ethnography provides an ideal opportunity to juxtapose the premises and assumptions behind these models of 'modern' life against the generalised observations of particular communities as represented through ethnography. The emphasis

1

within this book is on the literature devoted to modernity rather than to postmodernity since I find the former both empirically more plausible and theoretically sustained.

I recognise, however, that there may be other grounds by which readers may find the ethnographic materials of interest or significance, and I have tried to be gentle with my presentation of a particular theoretical concern. I hope that the substantive materials are amenable to other forms of interpretation and appropriation than that which I have advocated, in recognition that the production of a text should also be an invitation to creative consumption. This book can therefore be read from two directions. I hope that for the anthropologist the relevance of these writings on modernity will emerge from the ethnography of Trinidadian society, and the arguments given within the book that alternative and more obvious approaches to account for these observations are insufficient. By contrast, for those principally interested in modernity, I hope that the same ethnographic sections will evoke the more familiar abstract debates about modernity such that the direct relationship between these phenomena may be then drawn out in detail.

This is certainly not the book I set out to write when I embarked on this project in 1987, or even when I returned from fieldwork at the beginning of 1989. At that time I had recently published a largely theoretical book on the nature of mass consumption, and was concerned to apply the ideas developed therein through ethnographic work. I considered working in Fiji but a combination of the *coup* there, and reading about the oil-boom in Trinidad on the prompting of Philip Burnham, suggested that the latter might be a better choice. I felt that there was a gulf between books that concentrated upon consumption such as Bourdieu's *Distinction* (1984) and the many available studies of production and distribution. I also hoped that an island the size of Trinidad would allow me to study production, distribution and consumption and the articulation between them.

I am now in the process of writing a volume which deals with the fieldwork I carried out on commerce and consumption in Trinidad – working with transnational companies, advertising agencies, marketing and retail establishments. This, however, is now designated as a second volume – a sequel to the present book. The genesis of the present book derives from a well-established characteristic of anthropology: that the phenomena which is to be studied is most commonly approached through an ethnography of the society which provides its context. In carrying out such work the ethnographer needs to spend at least as much time trying to understand this general context as in focusing upon the intended domain of inquiry. Since returning from the field I have become increasingly absorbed by this struggle to appreciate the larger framework posed by the heterogeneous and complex society that I encountered in Trinidad. Furthermore, I have become increasingly convinced that this project might be of particular significance in so far as it sheds light on some theoretical and abstract academic issues as to the nature of modernity.

I initially encountered these issues through my colleague Michael Rowlands who taught a course on modernity, and these debates about modernity and postmodernism subsequently became pervasive in the teaching of social science where I work in London. I was already dissatisfied with the voluminous and apparently ever-increasing literature that has emerged on this topic, precisely because of the tendency to generalise without much sense of whether the supposed characteristics would have actually emerged from the study of any particular society.

In no sense, therefore, is this book the result of an attempt to prove or disprove a hypothesis. I am well aware that the material lends itself to other perspectives and interpretations, and that the ethnography is partial in both senses of that word. Nevertheless, the sheer discrepancy between the intended work and the actual book is, I believe, largely a result of the constraints imposed by the actual observations made, as against my expectations. The book represents a commitment to an anthropological perspective both in terms of its forms of fieldwork and in the sense that a comparative perspective has helped ease me out of assumptions born of the parochial experience of consumption in my own society through the dissonance created by the experience of these phenomena within another regional context.

I fully acknowledge that I use my material to illustrate my point and perspective, that I come closest therefore to the idea of ethnography as 'apt illustration'. There are few inclusions that are intended to disrupt or negate my argument; the material is used to exemplify, not confront. I also assume, however, that my work is both empirically informed as of a qualitative science but also inextricably infused with moral and interpretative direction. A bias may also be noted as emergent from my background in material culture studies rather than social anthropology. I am more concerned to examine observed practice, while treating language more as a level of legitimation by informants than as privileged access to explanation. I also attempt to construct my observations more as ordering taxonomies which, in the tradition of Durkheim and more especially Bourdieu, are used by individuals but not necessarily best constituted as individual subjectivities.

In methodological terms I regard myself as a 'kitchen-sink' ethnographer, happy to incorporate any information that comes my way. Most of the evidence which emerged from studies of commerce and consumption will be used in the second book (as also certain topics deleted for the purpose of minimising overlap between these books such as food and drink and music). Nevertheless, I found that commerce was also a useful source of information about ordinary social life which might not have been so readily available from more direct enquiries. Following the same logic I often found it useful to talk to doctors, nurses, lawyers, teachers and other professionals, as well as to people working in shops, behind bars or in domestic service, about their relationship to the public. I reviewed the media daily, cutting out articles from newspapers and making audio and video cassettes from the radio and television respectively. I also searched for attitudes to consumption from institutions such as the Church, government bodies and educational authorities.

The fieldwork on consumption was carried out in four communities which are described in Chapter 1. These were selected to be representative of the new kinds of housing estates which are pointers to developments in Trinidad and were also roughly in proportion to the ethnic make-up of the island as a whole. The town of Chaguanas was chosen for its commercial development. I found also that there is a degree of difficulty in getting to know people from different ethnic communities and class backgrounds within a single community, and having four centres helped me to interact with different groups each within their own milieux.

I carried out a survey of forty households in each community, chosen on the basis of house form with the intention of including some diversity of income and ethnicity, but without any formal sampling criteria. I also obtained information through forming friendships and through the networks of people I employed (for example for typing transcripts). I made considerable use of direct tape recording of conversation, the results of which may be found in the direct quotations which appear in the text. I soon found that for many areas of consumption it was women who were likely to be the most important informants, and my fieldwork was considerably enhanced by the fact that I was working as part of a family unit. This meant not only the presence of my wife Rickie Burman, who is a trained anthropologist, but also that I was categorised as a family man rather than a single man which I felt made my presence less problematic for many of the women with whom I worked. I was assisted by two research assistants, one for six weeks and the other for eight months, both female. In retrospect I feel that my self-consciousness about being a male working on a subject where the expertise is largely seen as female may have led to a kind of over-compensation on my part. On the whole I feel my desire to construct empathetic links with women may have led to a neglect of male perspectives and subsequently it is probably the material I collected from men in which I now have less confidence.

There are other aspects of this work about which I continue to have doubts. Other things being equal I would not have focused upon sexuality, being aware of the sensitivity of a topic which has been instrumental in the development of racial stereotypes as they pertain to this region. I have been led to this topic, as I perceived it to be a dominant idiom for other concerns that I had intended to focus upon. I now feel it might be better to attempt to account for and interpret these issues, rather than trying to impose a self-censorship in the interest of some post-colonial angst about what liberalism should or should not allow as the frame of enquiry. Given the complexity of these issues I have no firm idea of what would be the 'right' or the 'wrong' policy to follow, and I have therefore followed what I take to be the integrity of the academic programme in the hope that the result is not irresponsible.

My son David was born three months into the fieldwork and this occasioned a major shift in the acceptance of my family in the communities (as well as creating a sentimental bond to the island within myself). Compared to the anonymity of North London, where our first child was born, there was a dovetailing here of my pleasure as parent with the much greater social acknowledgment of the event and the anthropological goal of expansion of my networks. The needs of a family also provided for considerable participation in consumption! My involvement in each community tended to develop around what I took to be the major forms of sociality. In one this meant attending religious and life-cycle events, in another it meant regular participation in parties and *fêtes*. Since one community was more lively at night and another in the day, this sometimes seemed to require almost twenty four hour fieldwork! I also allowed my particular interests to develop as vehicles for social interaction. These ranged from a quickly established love of soca music, to which I am now firmly addicted, to attempts to improve my skills in cake decoration through advice from the many Trinidadians who are far more accomplished in this art than myself. Perhaps most important has been the development of friendships which three years after fieldwork continue as a major legacy of the experience, through visits of Trinidadians to London and of my family to Trinidad. My experience of Trinidad was overwhelmingly positive; I have never been treated with such hospitality and friendship. I have probably also never had as much fun or felt so relaxed. I have found that this sometimes makes people sceptical of my academic commitment, but I do not feel that my research suffered unduly from the fact that I enjoyed it.

Acknowledgments

Above all I owe a considerable debt to my wife Rickie Burman who sacrificed a year from her own work in order to become the companion of mine and constantly suggested approaches or topics for observation which I had missed. I am extremely grateful and obligated to the many people who helped me in my research in Trinidad but I will not name them individually in order to preserve at least some prospect of the anonymity which I always insisted would be theirs. Instead I would issue a general thank you to the literally hundreds of Trinidadians who gave their time and indulgence and often their sincere friendship during this endeavour. I hope I did not spoil too many 'limes'.

I gratefully acknowledge the assistance of those who helped in the logistics of organising the fieldwork, including the family of Moonilal Dass and (now sadly the late) Polly Dass, Renita Griffiths, Jackie Lewis, Esmond Ramesar and Angela and Joe Pulchas. I also owe a great deal to my two research assistants, Alana Nathanal and Shanaz Mohammed. Various people have helped through commenting on parts of this book or related articles in preparation, including Bridget Brereton, Peter Jackson, Kim Johnson, Brad Lander, Patricia Mohammed, Dennis Singh and R.T. Smith. Lise Winer, as an excellent linguist, must have suffered terribly when faced with my dreadful use of language, but overcame this to do far more than just correct my use of dialect. If I may single out three people in London to whom I am greatly in debt, I have benefited from continual discussion with Stephen Frosh and Mike Rowlands, while Philip Burnham has altruistically spent much time on advising the 'writing up'.

Grants towards the fieldwork in Trinidad between 1987 and 1989 and a return trip in 1990 were funded by: The British Academy, The Central Research Fund of London University, The Nuffield Foundation and The Wenner-Gren foundation for Anthropological Research, to all of whom I am very grateful.

DANIEL MILLER
London, 1993

Chapter 1

Trinidad and Modernity

Introduction

There is one clear precursor to a book on the relationship between the ethnography of a Caribbean society and general writings on modernity. This is *Crab Antics* (Wilson 1973), which argues on the basis of an ethnography of a small Caribbean island for an observable cultural dualism in the region which could best be understood by reference to dialectical theories of modernity. But before undertaking fieldwork I had been sceptical about this book, partly because of its representations of gender. In particular, I felt suspicious about Wilson's reading of history out of which he proposed a positive male egalitarianism arising from the people and a negative female hierarchy as the legacy of colonial doctrines. While his book seems to rest largely upon ethnographic studies centred around the activities of men, my own ethnography, focusing upon consumption, was based largely upon the lives of Trinidadian women.

My own sense of a powerful dualism arose not from this domain of gender, but from observations on the manner in which imported ideas and goods seemed to bifurcate when they reached the shores of Trinidad. I wondered why in the main road near where I lived there was one shop for items devoted to the car exterior and another for the car interior, or why there seemed to be such a clear distinction between the kind of people who were expected to be concerned with new fads that directed attention to the outside appearance of the body, as in body building, and others whose keep-fit fashions directed attention to internal health. Finding my study of consumption permeated by such distinctions I started to look for other areas in which this relationship of surface to interior might achieve greater clarity and found this in the clear opposition between the values which were expressed in the two key festivals of Christmas and Carnival. It also seemed that the dualism which was projected as the opposed qualities of goods was also commonly applied to persons, in this case forming the major ethnic stereotypes.

I also realised that if I was ever to engage in any kind of empathetic analysis of this dualism I had to dismiss all those assumptions which are rendered by the use of the term 'superficial'. This meant that many of the current debates on modern society which focus on the term postmodern were unlikely to be of much assistance. The literature on this topic, which is represented by the critique of postmodernism associated with the writings first of Baudrillard (1981) and latterly Jameson (1991) and which has had some influence upon anthropology and cultural studies, is largely based upon an uncritical reliance on the semantic linkage between the derogatory term 'superficial' and the manifestation of images on the surfaces of peoples and things. This did not seem a promising starting point for an analysis of consumption within which the sense of style figured prominently.

As with perhaps the majority of anthropologists conducting fieldwork I found disconcerting complexities to the application of a set of ideas I had developed previously in more abstract terms. For example, I had expected that the degree to which Trinidad was dependent upon imported goods would be a source of a sense of dependency and alienation which would have to be overcome, but, as the material presented in Chapter 4 demonstrates, in some instances it was the contrary situation which was encountered. In such cases imported goods were far less problematic than the appropriation of locally produced materials. These experiences, which challenged my expectations, helped also to sunder me from any simple representation of Trinidad as a 'traditional' society confronted by a modernity which was represented by imported goods, images and behaviours. It also suggested that the centrality of the concept of 'authenticity' to the ideologies which lay behind anthropological and other theories of social self-construction, as well as to the design of consumer goods (see Orvell 1989) might not apply in this particular context, and there were instead other blocks and difficulties which threatened the sense of national self-worth.

In some cases there were worrying discrepancies between different kinds of information. Conversation and self-representation were constantly dominated by a concern over ethnicity and this accorded with most contemporary writings about Trinidad in which ethnicity is the key variable. By contrast, in my first and most systematic survey of material culture – the contents of the living room in 160 households – I found that ethnic distinctions were of minimal importance to the selection of objects and their juxtaposition in home design. This was the first of many cases where the desire to respect one's informants' views, as against my own self-critique of expected biases and assumptions, came into conflict with what seemed the evident discrepancies between what people expressed in language and what they seemed to value in action.

This finding was also important in that ethnographic analysis of Trinidad has hitherto been dominated by the topic of ethnicity and there is a clear temptation to reduce most observable cultural difference to ethnic distinctions. It was perhaps fortunate that this survey which demonstrated the intractable nature of everyday material culture, with respect to a reduction to social relations of this kind, was one of the earliest features of my fieldwork. As a result the 'logic' of such analytical procedures was increasingly reversed and it was the factors which seemed to be manifested in material culture which also appeared to explain the manner by which social distinctions were experienced. The appeal of the more abstract literature on modernity was precisely that it provided a generalised account of cultural contradictions which might give rise to these observable patterns in material culture and social distinction.

I recognise, however, that for many readers of this book the approach is likely to be from the opposite direction: that is, coming to ethnography from a reading of works on modernity. The book listings of academic publishers are replete with titles which include the terms 'modernity' and 'postmodernity'. Indeed, the desire to characterise these phenomena seems to involve a considerable proportion of contemporary academic research in the social sciences and humanities. Much of this spills over into aesthetic concerns and the conflation of modernism and modernity, with works devoted to film, literature and so forth. The terms have also had a considerable recent impact on disciplines such as history, politics and psychology. Much of this literature is about the relationship between modernity and some phenomena such as 'modernity and the state' or 'postmodernity and the body'. There is also what might be called a 'core' tradition of works which, at the risk of reifying the terms, are devoted to the problem of characterising modernity in and of itself, as a contemporary experience of the world. Recent examples on modernity would include Lash and Friedman's (1992) collection of essays or two recent books by Giddens (1990, 1991), while on postmodernity there is Harvey (1989) and Jameson (1991).

A nagging doubt that I suspect affects many readers of this genre of academic literature is the sense that most of the contributors tend to project the attributes they locate on to the population at large. A particular source of anxiety exemplified in some psychological crises, or crises of representation, becomes the crisis of modernity itself with implications for us all, as by definition living within modernity. So whether we are London train-drivers or Brussels secretaries we are all consumed with anxiety as a result of 'space-time' compression. What remains questionable is whether a social group which was not being examined or considered with this particular perspective in mind would exhibit the various concerns and forms of experience which are assumed to be intrinsic to the condition of modernity. Indeed, books on postmodernity with their concern for global transformation seem even more inclined to talk about 'late capitalism' or cultures of inauthenticity as though they represent in their effects the psychic states and generalised experiences of most of contemporary humankind.

The universalising tendencies of theories of modernity do not easily juxtapose with the relativising imperative of ethnographically informed anthropology. For anthropologists, Trinidad could never be the pure ideal type to the characterisation of modernity. It could only ever be an apt illustration of the kind of tendency to which the contradictions of modernity give rise. Nevertheless the particular here may well be the means by which the general theory is best subject to critique and refinement. Indeed, although narrowed and constrained by such a focusing down on the particular, it may come as some relief that there is at least some corner of the globe within which all this outpouring of academic concern has some actual bearing and pertinence! Ironically, it may then become the literature on modernity and postmodernity itself which comes over as parochial, in failing to account for the diverse contexts within which the dilemmas of modernity are manifested (though see Friedman 1992).

In the remainder of this chapter I will first propose that the Caribbean is indeed a particularly suitable area for examining these questions of linkage, and then introduce the ethnographic setting for the investigation which provided the material which is being considered in the light of these debates over the nature of modernity. I recognise, however, that merely making the claim of relevance is insufficient. The argument in this chapter is that given the particular history of the region, its peoples come up against the problematics of modernity with a particular jolt, having had stripped away many of the traditions and structures which would mediate this relationship elsewhere. I do not want this, however, to become an argument of historical determinism: that given this history such an encounter has to become the key to the formation of modern identity. Instead this book presents the argument for the relevance of modernity directly from the representation of its ethnography of contemporary society.

The organisation of the subsequent chapters follows from this initial establishment of possible linkage. In a book which purports to be about a topic as diverse as modernity it is necessary first to establish which version of the current usages of that term is intended. Given the plethora of writing on modernity and the postmodern, there are a host of possible models of these phenomena that might provide the core to the theoretical contribution of this volume. It makes little sense, however, simply to pluck out one particular version of these models of modernity and as it were 'test it out' against the ethnography. Only the most die-hard exponent of naturalism in the social sciences can still believe in hypothesis testing of that kind. Most social scientists will regard social and cultural phenomena as far too contingent and unpredictable to warrant such an approach. For most anthropologists, a generalised abstract 'modernity' does not exist except as a necessary objectification within the process of accounting for specific social practices. The intention in Chapter 2 is therefore not to adjudicate on some abstract grounds between alternative representations of modernity but to enunciate that approach which seems most apt for the particular ethnographic encounter which follows. The chapter therefore provides an indication as to which aspects of the modern condition may indeed be illuminated by this particular ethnographic enquiry. The model of modernity used is derived from a reading of Hegel by Habermas, and refined through a consideration of recent writings which attempt to list the key traits of being modern, and finally a brief consideration of the historical development of mass consumption that provides a comparative instance to the main analysis of Trinidad.

The core to this model of modernity is a transformation in temporary consciousness and it is this aspect of contemporary Trinidadian life which emerges most forcefully from the consideration of the subject of Chapter 3: that is the festivals of Christmas and Carnival. These are the two major festivals that dominate a considerable part of the Trinidadian year and are clearly acknowledged as fundamental to Trinidadian's conceptions of themselves. It will be argued that, as is commonly the case, ritual events of this kind are able to represent with relative clarity relationships which otherwise are submerged in the pragmatic concerns of everyday life. Indeed, it follows that the very importance of these festivals lies in the degree to which they are used to objectify[1] the fundamental and paradigmatic principles upon which most Trinidadians structure both their ideologies and their social practices. The chapter concludes by abstracting from the systematic opposition between the values expressed by the two festivals as an underlying dualism.

The advantage of festivals, from the perspective of clarity of analysis, is also their disadvantage from the perspective of an ethnography which intends to situate itself also in the mundane and everyday life of the peoples among whom the ethnographer lives. The contents of Chapter 4 are therefore the necessary complement to Chapter 3. The festivals demonstrate in ritual form the presence of two systematically opposed principles, one orientated towards the event, and the other determined to reduce the vicissitudes of events by subsuming them within a long-term perspective oriented both to the past and future. The task of Chapter 4 is to document the pervasive importance of these principles in Trinidadian social relations. Chapter 4 therefore starts with a focus upon kinship, which anthropologists generally assume to be a core institution and idiom for everyday social relations. It goes on to argue that a focus on kinship in and of itself would not be appropriate in this case. Instead the chapter highlights the domains of property and sexuality which emerged ethnographically not only as core domains in which social relations are objectified and experienced but also as key symbolic idioms by which many other aspects of Trinidadian life are encompassed, including kinship. The contents of Chapters 3 and 4 should therefore be considered in relation to each other. Our understanding of the values and expressive concerns found in Christmas and Carnival is considerably extended when these festivals are found to crystallise certain ordering principles which can now also be perceived within the more diffuse setting of the social relations constructed during 'ordinary' time.

These two chapters provide the argument and evidence for a central dualism which rests upon two opposed temporal orientations but extends to many other dimensions of Trinidadian life and imagery. In attempting to account for contemporary Trinidad, however, one is almost overwhelmed by the traumatic events of the last two decades which are termed 'oil-boom' and 'recession'. Even where it might be granted that there are paradigmatic cleavages in 'traditional' Trinidadian society, it is generally assumed that Trinidad was swamped during the oil-boom by foreign influences: in particular, the arrival of mass commodities and mass media. It might then be assumed that any resonance with the sense of modernity is merely an effect of very recent changes which have demolished the specificity of what previously had been relatively autonomous developments and homogenised Trinidad within a 'global' experience of modernity or postmodernity. Chapter 5 provides the evidence to reject these expectations and assertions. Rather it is argued that in many respects the arrival of these new material facilities and images were employed more to complete ideological projects that had already been formulated in the more traditional institutions outlined in Chapter 4. In many cases, therefore, the influences from outside bifurcate on their arrival in Trinidad to provide exemplary instances of these established cultural projects but also to extend and clarify them.

In the ethnographic detail presented in Chapters 3 to 5, gender, class and ethnicity are certainly mentioned and utilised in the description. But an anthropologist may perceive an almost wilful refusal systematically to relate the analysis of cultural institutions and patterns to social distinctions or even social relations. The patient/frustrated anthropologist who has borne with this 'lacuna' for four chapters will hopefully find in Chapter 6 precisely what had been lacking so far: the systematic analysis of class, gender and ethnicity. In each case the argument is put that the dualism which has been revealed in the previous chapters can best be accounted for in relation to one of these dimensions. These arguments are derived from other ethnographies in the Caribbean which have put forward powerful claims that class and gender do indeed provide the proper grounds for any explanation of this phenomena, while the literature on Trinidad tends to start and end with ethnicity. In each case the arguments refer back to the history of slavery, indentured labour and colonialism and the formation of contemporary social distinctions in the light of this history. In Chapter 6 I attempt to refute these claims, at least with regard to Trinidad. In contrast, I argue that much of the literature on these social dimensions needs to be recast as an effect rather than a cause of dualism. It follows that while each is of considerable importance in understanding the specific manifestations of dualism in the region, none provide the best starting point for a more general explanation.

This is extremely important for the argument of the book as a whole. It is very likely that many readers, and in particular readers from Trinidad, will feel when considering the ethnographic detail that this book is 'really' about ethnicity. I have no doubt that when most Trinidadians conceive of their society as dualistic, the dominant image of dualism is that derived from ethnicity and the opposed stereotypes of ethnic groups. I hope, however, that when the ethnography of Chapters 2 to 4 is reconsidered in the light of the evidence and arguments put forward in Chapter 6, a convincing case will have been made that this pervasive dualism is not the result of ethnic difference but quite the contrary: that much of the specific content of ethnic stereotyping and the contemporary experience of ethnicity is the result of the use of ethnic groups to objectify a dualism whose source lies elsewhere.

My case is made first through a comparative anthropology which demonstrates that the same specific traits which are perceived as ethnic in Trinidad are conceived of as gender, class or even age in other Caribbean islands. This undermines the argument in each individual case that one of these dimensions is paradigmatic to contemporary cultural order. Second, there is the evidence from the previous chapters that both material culture and other aspects of Trinidadian culture quite often failed to support the expectations drawn from conversation in Trinidad that ethnicity will prove the dominant dimension of difference. Third, I argue that the history of ethnic groups in Trinidad reveals considerable and rapid changes in their supposed characteristics which suggests that they are being made to fall into line with some other imperative rather than being themselves the inspiration for the attributes they are presently held to possess. All this should force observers to raise their eyes from the descriptive and

interpretative detail of the immediate ethnography and scan a
wider horizon before completing an account of these phenomena.

In a sense this conclusion brings the book full circle, because
the failure of more conventional accounts, such as would be
derived from more conventional anthropological and sociological perspectives, becomes the grounds for justifying the concern
with modernity as outlined in Chapter 2, which provides precisely what other approaches have been missing. That is: grounds for
an understanding as to why culture and society in Trinidad
might manifest a pervasive dualism which then becomes objectified in social distinctions such as ethnicity.

In essence the argument is that a particular consciousness of
time may challenge customary morality and the given criteria by
which life is judged. This creates a new fragility in which people
become much more conscious of the processes of self-creation
and the creation of the principles by which they judge themselves. It is argued that while most of the literature on modernity emphasises the new sense of the ephemeral and fragmentary
or individualistic elements in culture, this same fragility also
underlies an equally prominent but opposed struggle for the
establishment of stable institutions, religiosity and concern for
the maintenance of descent. In the concluding chapter the implications of dualism are dissected, and then the relative contribution of theories of modernity to an understanding of
contemporary Trinidad, and in turn the contribution of an
ethnography to the study of comparative modernity. Finally it is
argued that consumption itself provides the key medium
through which the general possibilities posed by theories of
modernity become the significant condition of a particular
region.

It will certainly not follow from this ethnographic approach
that Trinidad can be viewed as somehow more truly 'modern' or
closer to some pure modernity than some other society. This is
precisely because an anthropological approach is unlikely to
privilege (some might say fetishise) an abstract model of modernity pitted against a concrete description of a society. It does
allow, however, for the study of comparative modernities, and
part of the intention of this book is precisely to propose such a
study which may be far more fruitful in furthering social science
than the kind of relentless and abstract theoretical debates which
have dominated to date. The advantages are drawn from both

ends. The observation of a paradigmatic structure to Trinidadian cultural order can be better understood in relation to theories about the fundamental nature of modern societies. I also hope that an illustration of how some of the characteristics attributed to modernity actually articulate in a given social context will help problematise some of the assumptions in the theoretical literature on modernity. The relativising of terms such as 'freedom', 'fashion', 'individualism' and 'superficiality' through an ethnographic approach is not intended to render theoretical debates irrelevant, but to give them relevance to social analysis. The more such terms become clichés about the state of postmodern society, the further they seem to drift from being descriptive categories which might enhance our understanding of the condition of being modern. An ethnography, or better still a range of comparative ethnographies, may force them back into becoming the refined instruments we so clearly need to describe and appreciate the circumstances and ideologies we inhabit.

Anthropology, Modernity and Trinidad

It is precisely because anthropology is most readily associated with the study of groups defined as 'non-modern' that the debates over modernity could be argued to have nowhere played a more central role than in the development of that discipline. Until recently anthropology has been almost synonymous with the portrayal of populations which are viewed as contemporary but not modern, and certainly in its popular role this remains almost the sole task of the discipline. Mauss, Malinowski and many others of the most influential figures in the development of twentieth-century anthropology devoted much of their writings to the construction of images of other populations which are defined almost by opposition to what are seen as the dominant traits of the modern, and especially of capitalist society. Whether the emphasis is on the gift, the use of metaphor, the relationship with the environment (or today 'nature'), the forms of kinship or ritual, anthropology has always existed in alterity with an often unexplicated image of the traits of modernity. Indeed, this split has been fundamental in retaining in a post-colonial world a distinction between anthropology and sociology, the latter's task being to explicate the attributes of modern societies.

For this reason the anticipated site for an ethnography of the modern tends to be cities such as New York or Paris, within countries otherwise designated as metropolitan. It may seem somewhat perverse, therefore, to be locating an ethnography of modernity within a region which is usually designated as peripheral to the metropolitan and where most ethnographies have looked for 'traditional' traits, for example, homogeneous East Indian villages or remnants of Yoruba religion[2]. The treatment of the Caribbean, however, has always been ambivalent, and this 'traditional'-style ethnography is matched by many comments by intellectuals and novelists who have acknowledged that the region exists in a particular relation to modernity (e.g. James 1962: 89; Naipaul 1962). I would therefore make no claims to originality in proposing this linkage[3] (for a recent academic comment see Hart 1989: 2–3). What is required is a more precise statement of the grounds for positing this relationship and the expectations that are thereby raised.

Until recently there was a fairly obvious model available for the construction of an argument that the contemporary population of the Caribbean is the best exemplification of modernity. This was provided by analogy with the work of Lukacs and, in particular, his *Reification and the Consciousness of the Proletariat* (1971). Lukacs, following the Hegelian logic embedded in Marx, argued that the most extreme example of rupture in human history ought to precede the most extreme resolution, that is communism should follow from capitalism, but that the instrument of the transition ought to be that element of humanity which was most clearly in a state of alienation. It was the proletariat whose position, virtually external to society, meant that they alone could provide the perspective from which the larger totality could be perceived and would construct the consciousness necessary for the vision and the achievement of the overthrow of capitalist society. This would place them in the vanguard of modernity.

There is an obvious case for substituting the proletariat with the African slave in the New World. Slavery, as Patterson (1982) has argued, amounts to a form of 'social death' whose starting point is the absolute alienation of the individual in a much more radical form than any proletariat. Moreover, the context for slavery in the Caribbean was the development of a plantation system which was set up specifically on the periphery to serve as the supplier of raw materials for the core metropolitan society. This was of considerable importance in the development of that aspect of nascent capitalist relations which has been described as a world-system. Mintz (1985a: 32–73) has argued that the sugar plantation was a clearer example of industrialisation than virtually any system of production in Europe of its time. The fact that sugar cane requires to be cut and processed at particular times made its manufacturers much more time-conscious and observant of 'efficient' practices than other industries, and more comparable to modern agro-industrial complexes. Mintz has also noted, along with many others, that it was the sugar plantation which saw the most oppressive treatment of slaves. In many parts of the Caribbean the native population was virtually exterminated and the population replaced by large-scale slave populations and a relatively small white slave-owning class.

As historians have noted (e.g. Higham 1979: 55) the slave-owners deliberately separated out the incoming slaves to prevent the emergence of groups which could retain identity from their local origins, and there were many strategies used to create the fullest sense of rupture and alienation. According then to the arguments furnished by Lukacs, slavery should provide fertile grounds for the emergence of the consciousness of modernity. No condition would be more conducive to the state of radical rupture, in which custom and ontological security is stripped away for a humanity reduced to merely an expendable 'machine' part.

The logic of such an argument is clear enough, but few academics today would accept its use of mechanical and teleological forms of history. The preference now is for history as a much more subtle and contingent representation of unfolding events. Within Europe itself the working-class has been shown to be quite capable of exemplifying reactionary as opposed to radical politics in various histories of the European nation. It is no longer acceptable to argue some historical necessity which allows us to project on to a population a propensity for achieving a particular vision of the world. Instead we need, in a rather more cautious and circumscribed examination of historical developments, to find evidence that a particular consciousness has actually emerged and can be seen to be associated with a relevant set of historical events. Even if the version of Lukacs' argument was acceptable as a logic of history, the specific history of the island of Trinidad would render it one of the less convincing candidates.

The island of Trinidad is the larger part of the state of Trinidad and Tobago. Tobago will not be considered in this book since it has a very different history, population structure and self-characterisation. Trinidad itself is 4,828 sq km, and lies in the south-eastern Caribbean 16km north-east of Venezuela. There is one major range of hills in the north, and today 50–60 per cent of land is forest. Trinidad's emergence into modern history is best situated at the end of the eighteenth century. Before that date the main feature is the decline of the original population of Arawak and Carib, following the arrival of Columbus in 1498, to the extent that although many people of mixed descent claim some aboriginal ancestry there is no identifiable pure Amerindian community today. Although the Spanish first colonised and ruled Trinidad, the numbers involved were always very small, such that Brereton in her history of Trinidad (1981) entitles her chapter on the period 1498–1783 'the Deserted Island'. By contrast, the last two centuries have witnessed the arrival of an abundance of peoples to produce the highly heterogeneous contemporary population. Slavery developed later in Trinidad than on other Caribbean islands such as Barbados and Jamaica, and it was also less dependent upon massive sugar plantations, with crops such as cocoa having a major influence. By the time a significant slave population of around 10,000 was established, the slave trade was being abolished and within 40 years there was the slave emancipation of 1834 (though this was complicated by the arrival of French Catholic planters and their slaves). Already at that time there was a significant urban population, and a higher proportion of slaves became familiar with this cosmopolitan centre than in most Caribbean contexts. The colonial population was also divided into a number of competing groups, essentially British by political control (as a Crown colony since 1802) but French-dominated numerically and culturally.

Trinidad continued to see the arrival of diverse populations during the nineteenth century. The largest immigration was of 143,939 South Asian indentured labourers brought in between 1845 and 1917 to replace slave labour on the sugar and cocoa plantations (Vertovec 1992: 66–130). Perhaps next most significant in population, though much less remarked upon by historians, is the migration of 'peons', a Spanish-speaking peasantry from nearby South America who have made a considerable impression on Trinidadian culture. A full list of immigrant sources would be impressive, including Chinese indentured labourers, Portuguese shopkeepers, French royalists and republicans, economic migrants from the Middle East (today known as Syrians), and others. Within the black population there is also considerable diversity of origins. Apart from the descendants of slaves, there are settlements of soldiers from the American War of Independence, free settlers from Africa, settlers from other West Indian islands (e.g. Barbados, St Vincent, Grenada), indentured labourers from Africa, etc. This complexity is then added to by the number of groups defined through mixed descent, such as the 'Dougla', defined by their mixed South Asian and African parentage, or the coloured population that creates a spectrum between the white and black populations.

This sense of creolisation and heterogeneity has been as much assisted by emigration in the twentieth century as by immigration in the nineteenth. Trinidadians have migrated in waves to London, Toronto, New York and Miami. The élite colonial population has seen its scions depart at various moments of political emancipation. This has included the establishment of the government by Eric Williams, leader of the People's National Movement (PNM) in 1956, Independence granted in 1962, or the black power struggles of 1970 when a combination of popular protests and demonstrations, together with a mutiny in the army, came close to overthrowing the government. Up to this period the government's economic policies had not been noticeably successful but, following the oil price rise of 1973, many people's incomes increased several times over, and Trinidadians speak of reversing the previous flow of remittances by sending money to their relatives abroad. Another wave of emigration followed with recession and 1988 saw a flood of emigrants to Canada, this time mainly of East Indian[4] descent. As a result of these movements an extraordinary number of Trinidadian families are in effect transnational. In a survey of 160 households (for details see below), I found that an extraordinary 101 could name a member of their immediate family (parents, children or siblings) living abroad, 38 mentioned more distant relatives and only 21 stated that they had no relatives living abroad. In 1990 the total population was 1,234,388. The number of people living in other countries and with other nationalities but who still see themselves as Trinidadian is unknown but likely to be large.[5]

The complexity of this history militates against the simple linkage of a slave population to modernity in the style of Lukacs.

But these very same factors which create difficulties for one argument become the main evidence for a more complex and contingent argument of association. What emerges from a brief perusal of Trinidadian history is precisely the plurality of contributory forces and the difficulty of fitting contemporary Trinidad with a clear set of 'roots'. Few can claim ancestry with an original population, and although there are links with countries of origin such as India, no single group can claim the kind of hegemonic dominance which would permit a single historical trajectory to be transposed into a genealogy for modern Trinidad. For example, when the calypsonian Black Stalin sang 'we all came in the same boat' in the chorus of his 1979 calypso, he evoked less a sense of unity than a storm of protest (Deosaran 1987).

Trinidad is then clearly a Creolised (or in some accounts pluralist) society, which continues to have to define itself as much by its relations to other lands as to its origins. If it is to construct a sense of being 'Trinidadian' it has to do so under conditions of extreme difficulty. It is a society which has a strong sense of rupture, a radicalisation of the present with the concomitant effect that it cannot rely on a clear sense of custom or a morality that is defended as mere custom.

There is, however, a kind of unity which centres around a second criterion for modern consciousness, a generalised sense of oppression. Although slavery itself may not have had quite the same impact as in other Caribbean islands, it still pervades the historical consciousness of the black population today as a collective ancestry and origin in extreme oppression, matched by a population of Indians some of whom still recall living under indentureship. This sense of the past is best understood in relation to the continuities since slavery. What has remained is a legacy of deep inequalities, within which virtually all contemporary groups feel aggrieved. Trinidad has always been an island divided between a population which was designated as white and ruling and a population designated as Black and Asian (or more often as 'nigger' and 'coolie'), which was ruled. Apart from the political disparities there were clear disparities in economic strength. The hegemonic pressures have created a culture of disparagement of the powerless and emulation of the powerful.

This continuity of oppression is important, since otherwise events in the early nineteenth century might have few consequences today. In Trinidad, however, continuity is very evident in the first sociological portrait of the country by Braithwaite (1975) which documents a clear amalgamation of racial and class inequalities, with a white ruling class mediated by a mixed middle class entrenched over a black and Indian working class. There are a number of differences between the emergence of social stratification in Trinidad as compared to class and racial divisions in other Caribbean islands such as Jamaica. Partly this is an outcome of the proportion of Indians in the population (which by the 1980 census had reached virtual parity with the African population). It has also been argued by Macdonald (1986) that as a result of oil revenues which even before 1930 were greater than sugar and cocoa exports combined, there is an older, and more influential middle class.

This legacy of alienation and oppression has been furthered also by the consciousness of Trinidad as a periphery with respect to the economy and culture of the world around it, a consciousness which is that much more potent given the high levels of education and actual international contact which are available to many Trinidadians. This factor has never been more poignant than during the one period when it suddenly found itself with genuine economic authority. Trinidad was led through its political independence of 1962 by Eric Williams, whose party, the PNM, dominated the political scene between 1956 and 1986 when it was replaced by the National Alliance for Reconstruction. Although there was internal alienation of ethnic groups (mainly East-Indian) who associated themselves with the political opposition, Eric Williams had the strong consciousness of colonialism and its legacy which could have fostered the emergence of a powerful sense of rebirth in an emancipated and positive vision of the post-colonial state. This was particularly the case after 1973 when, facilitated by the revenues of the oil boom and prodded by the disquiet of the black power movement of 1970, he attempted to assert Trinidad's emergence out of peripheral economic status through an explicit identification with heavy industry, the iron and steel and chemical works of the economic core.[6]

In retrospect, many of Eric Williams' policies of industrialisation, but also his antagonism to local agricultural production, seem to have been dictated less by economic sagacity than by the desire to assert something that had always been denied – the capacity for a developing country to manufacture materials generally associated with First World forms of industrialisation. This was, however, in the event, but a short period of assertive nationalism which came to a close with the oil price decline when the oil companies and the IMF returned to dictate the terms of existence for the contemporary Trinidadian economy.[7]

This historical sequence makes clear that from its inception Trinidad has been the creation of the global economy, and continues to have little protection from the buffeting of larger economic trends. This puts a particular complexion on the anthropological disquiet about applying images of modernity which have been derived from the particular history of Europe and the United States on to a region usually thought of as the developing world. Although it is true that as a peripheral region the Caribbean is rarely allowed to intrude upon this literature on modernity, this ignores the actual centrality of such areas to the development of modern Europe and largely perpetuates global inequalities. The Caribbean was itself the creation of a modernist scheme established with unusual clarity and completeness by Europeans, and today the IMF and World Bank continue to exert this peculiar rationality of economics, if in less extreme fashion.[8] As such a comparison between modernity as expressed in the experience of the people of this region with a literature developed in the European context may not seem an unreasonable exercise.

The Ethnographic Setting

For an insight into the nature of modernity most Trinidadians would probably turn to the capital city of Port of Spain and its expansion into almost continual urban settlement along what is called the 'East-West corridor'. It is, however, the small town of Chaguanas which has seen the fastest expansion in recent years, and which is the setting of the present study. Since my intention was to study mass consumption, I deliberately adopted a policy which I took to be the inversion of most previous ethnographers' desire for ethnically homogenised 'traditional' communities which would lend themselves to the traditional anthropological characterisation of 'culture' (though see Yelvington forthcoming for an exception). By contrast, I attempted to locate communities which appeared typical of current and likely future trends in residential housing, for example, the new style of suburbia, the consolidation of large-scale squatting and the new government housing schemes, such that three out of the four communities studied had not existed for more than 15 years. These are not then communities in the usual sense of the term, rather in at least three cases they are artificial constructions taking peoples from all over Trinidad with no pretensions to any sense of community roots.

Chaguanas itself presents a good starting point for examining a process of the modern self-creation of identity, since it is a highly self-conscious town which struggles against a history of non-recognition by the Trinidadian government. Chaguanas lies in the county of Caroni, the region usually referred to simply as 'Central': the region was traditionally important for agriculture, but was generally seen as backward, poor and associated largely with Indians. Today, however, Caroni is the fastest-growing region in population (up 25 per cent between 1980 and 1990), and Chaguanas is the symbol of this new development.

Although there was an early settlement of slaves in nearby Carapachaima, the area around Chaguanas is better known for its association with Indian indentured labour. Chaguanas, whose name is derived from the Amerindian tribe of Chaguanes, developed as a small, sleepy village largely through its position with respect to road and later rail development. There is little mention of the area in nineteenth-century maps and records except through the involvement of local sugar estates in troubles associated with the festival of Hosay, for example in 1865, 1881 and 1883. In the twentieth century the development of Chaguanas is most closely bound up with the rise in fortunes of one particular sugar estate at Woodford Lodge. In oral history the two become almost synonymous, as this was clearly the main employer. Interviewees portrayed the mill as an extremely harsh employer, undercutting local wages by importing labour from the smaller islands and trying to protect its use of child labour from legislative control. It was equally rapacious with its economic competitors, lending out money to smaller concerns and then bankrupting them in order to expand its own control over the local sugar industry. Extensive use was made of short-term Scottish overseers who (according to oral traditions) often took local mistresses.

Despite this emphasis on sugar, the more detailed oral accounts which I collected suggest that much of the local area was previously used for other crops such as citrus and especially cocoa production, which at the turn of the century would have been as important as sugar. There was also local rice and 'ground provision' (edible tubers) cultivation. While the majority of Indians remained cane-cutters after the end of their indentureship, some managed to establish themselves by the turn of the century in retail establishments and later expanded into construction and other enterprises, although they had rivals in the Chinese and the Portuguese who were involved in retail and in the latter case also a drink and essence factory in central Chaguanas. By the 1930s Chaguanas already had the aura of a central place and a market of increasing significance. Its importance is clear in its portrayal as 'Arawak' in Naipaul's *A House for Mr Biswas* (1961) and in its central role in the disputes over the influence of the Hindu reformist group the 'Arya Samaj' (Forbes 1984). As well as the development of Indian institutions, there was always a significant African presence especially as workers inside the factory section of Woodford Lodge and as carpenters and blacksmiths, in relation to which there developed several Masonic lodges (and numerous friendly societies), and a local Carnival tradition with associated stick-fighting.

More recently, Chaguanas has become as important as a symbol as it has as a settlement. The key to its symbolic power is the sense, shared by all the ethnic groups which inhabit it, that it has developed in the teeth of opposition, especially from the state. For most of this century there have been two towns contending for the dominant centre of the county of Caroni. Government reports make clear that it is Couva to the south west which has been favoured by the state. This was the site chosen for the major government offices, and the PNM government saw it as an integral part of its plan to develop the industrial complex of Point Lisas using the resources of the oil-boom. From 1962 to 1986 most central MPs were members of parties in opposition to the PNM government. Despite this, it is Chaguanas which has undoubtedly won this rivalry and established itself as the main regional centre, and this image of the self-made town meshes well with the importance of the self-made entrepreneurial skills which have been seen as the key factor in establishing the town's contemporary importance. Probably of greater significance was the advantage of Chaguanas in terms of transport, being sited on the country's main north-south highway. Despite all of this, government administrative classifications have for long resisted the acknowledgment of Chaguanas as more than a village on a par with much smaller and less substantial settlements.

Beyond this image of the self-made town is the specific symbolic role of Chaguanas with respect to the Indian population who have made it a kind of alternative ethnic capital of Trinidad. This act is in direct defiance of the dominant image of the Indian as the 'coolie'. For the last century and more, the Indians have been seen as primarily agricultural and rural, and therefore also as backward and unsophisticated compared to the considerable section of the African population located in Port of Spain and surrounding suburbs. The Indian presence in the capital is relatively small and they make up only a quarter of the second largest town of San Fernando despite the proximity of that town to major rural areas of Indian settlement. It is only Chaguanas, perceived by most Trinidadians as essentially an Indian settlement, which provides the potential image of an unambiguously urban Indian population.

As a result of this symbolic role, two tendencies arise. One is to exaggerate the affinity with a single ethnic group. Few would realise the actual demography of Chaguanas where the African population has always composed around 30 per cent of the population, dominated some of the major economic activities and in recent years increased their numbers through the incorporation of fringe settlements where they are numerically dominant. The second tendency is for people from the capital to exaggerate the peripheral nature of Chaguanas as a place 'somewhere in the South', which they could claim with evident pride never to have visited. A family who had recently moved to a middle-class suburb noted 'when my relatives come from Port of Spain they always say the same thing – "What! It only took 25 minutes, it's hard to believe..."'. The sense that I was writing a book about 'Trinidadian' culture based largely on an analysis of Chaguanas quite horrified informants based in Port of Spain, who would have had no problems with the idea that *they* should be taken as representative of the whole. In practice, the four communities used as the basis for this work reflect the ethnic proportions of the population as a whole, with approximately 40 per cent each of African and Indian populations and 20 per cent mixed and other, something which would be difficult to achieve in a study based in the capital.

Today Chaguanas is a bustling small town. Including settlements now incorporated as continuous housing, I would estimate the population as around 20,000. It is dominated by an extremely busy main street lined with banks and fabric shops leading to an extensive market, mainly for foodstuffs, but with some drygoods sections. The market is too big for the allotted space and often spills out into the main road. The main road literally bristles with advertising signs often brightly lit, and the pavements are crowded to overspilling through most of the day. There is a one-way traffic system through the main street and this traffic is constant and noisy. The sense of commercial vitality is enhanced by three shopping malls all within a five-minute walk. These are enclosed, two-storey shopping areas which include fast-food outlets such as pizzerias and one major supermarket in each. The mall closest to the main street is almost constantly full of school children who have considerable daytime leisure as some schools operate a shift system owing to a lack of space. A mall next to the highway, by contrast, attempts a more expensive and exclusive air.

At the western end of the main street lies the original centre of the town, now occupied by government offices such as the court and police station. This gives way to the ruins of Woodford Lodge. Further down one passes the Lion House, made famous as 'Hanuman House' in Naipaul's *A House for Mr Biswas* and now as the author's birthplace. There is, however, little tourism and indeed there is not a single place to stay for those without local friends or family. The road west then leads to some smaller settlements, the large village of Felicity and then the sea. There are a number of roads going north from the town which have their own residential districts and some have shopping parades. The eastern expansion of the main street ends with the flyover from the main north-south highway leading from Port of Spain to San Fernando.

One of the main changes in Chaguanas in recent decades is the way it has expanded across the highway to join up with a number of previously separate settlements. The main road continues, though in a much more restrained fashion, through the district of Montrose, which includes a small retail area and a minor industrial estate including a bakery and a small sweet-drink (soft-drink) bottling plant. Further down, the road divides between the southern main road, which was replaced as the major route to the north by the highway, but which provides an alternative route to Port of Spain past the sprawling settlements of Enterprise and then Cunupia. Alternatively, one continues eastwards past continuous housing to the village of Longdenville and further on into the countryside. An ethnographic account of an Indian village close to Chaguanas may be found in the site of Amity studied by Klass (1961, 1991) and Nevadomsky (1982, 1983). All around Chaguanas are smaller settlements occupied mainly by Indian agriculturalists who use Chaguanas as their urban centre. For them Chaguanas provides many services, government offices and retail outlets, but also cinema, clubs and paid fêtes or parties held at the malls. Chaguanas is clearly the centre for Indian culture, symbolically asserted with the annual Divali Nagar fair held in the parking lot of a mall, but the same site may be used for political meetings of the Indian dominated opposition party, for competitions of Hindi singing, and Indian 'orchestras' – the music varies from classical, religious and film musical genres to a Trinidadian form known as 'chutney'.

Most of the economic development was locally inspired and the building of the malls represented a kind of conspicuous display of the rivalry between successful local businessmen. Many national retail chains are evident in the malls, and by 1990 in the main street also. The attempted coup of 1990 which damaged the economy of Port of Spain only served to increase the importance of Chaguanas, and local businessmen claimed with pride to have overheard the Chaguanas banks telling how their local branch had the highest turnovers in Trinidad.

Four Communities

My fieldwork was not based upon the centre of Chaguanas itself except for that part which was devoted to commercial research. My intention was to look for communities which seemed to represent the contemporary trends of Trinidadian society. I therefore chose four communities, all on the periphery of Chaguanas, joined in each case to the town by continuous residential housing along the main roads and therefore but a short taxi ride from the centre. Each was seen as representative of a significant form of housing development. Their fictional names are: 'Ford' – part of an extensive settlements of squatters, one of a large number of such settlements scattered throughout the country; 'The Meadows' – a middle-class settlement and an example of what are termed 'residential areas' without which no semi-urban development in Trinidad would seem complete; 'Newtown' – an example of a number of settlements deliberately constructed by the government's National Housing Authority as part of its use of oil-boom resources; and finally 'St Pauls' – which is the only one of the four that existed more than 15 years prior to the study, and a village which has become increasingly incorporated as a suburb to Chaguanas during the oil-boom expansion.

None of these settlements exactly equate with units used by the government census, but an approximate view of their populations can be given through the use of census and other data.[9] Most of the research was conducted through the typical methods of participant observation, making friends and establishing contacts through their networks, becoming involved in local residential groups, sports days, and cultural, religious and life-cycle ceremonies and leisure activities. In addition to this, 40 households from each of the four areas were subjected to a more formal questionnaire-style survey. These were selected with a desire to reflect the approximate ethnic and income distributions of each community, but not as statistical samples. The answers given are certainly influenced by respondents' sense of a 'correct' reply, but I do not think they are as inaccurate a basis for generalisation as the government censuses and surveys in the area. In the main I have used them as part of a more qualitative descriptive survey, and in particular to illustrate the distinctions between the four communities studied. As well as suggesting a reasonable coverage of income levels and ethnicity, the answers to the question where people were born suggests that the population surveyed (and therefore this ethnography more generally) represents far more than just this immediate area, since there were some 58 persons from the area of Port of Spain and the east-west corridor region, and a further 55 persons from San Fernando and the south of the country. Indeed in Newtown only eight out of 67 respondents were originally from this region.[10]

St Pauls

The village of St Pauls will be described first since it provides the only guide to the longer-term history of the area.[11] The village, which developed in the mid-nineteenth century and is thus as old as Chaguanas itself, was surrounded by small estates of sugar, cocoa and coffee upon which its economy was based until the 1930s when first one and later another factory was established in the area to emerge as the main employers. It is generally regarded as a bit nondescript and local people see its development as having been largely suppressed by the longevity of the agricultural estates and the general low pay. It has nothing of the singularity and specific reputation which is presently enjoyed by the village termed Amity by Klass, and now the best-known ethnographic example of an Indian-dominated village.

The village is unusual in that Indians and Afro-Creoles, as well as French Creoles, were historically involved in estate ownership and the local élite who recall, for example, occupying the first-class sections of the train to Port of Spain, were therefore more ethnically representative than in most regions. Whites were mainly present as foreigners running the local factory (producing building materials) which seems to have been typically exploitative, paying low wages and contributing very little to the local community outside of its own meagre Christmas festivities. In the early stages St Pauls seems to have gone further than Amity in reconstructing traditional South Asian social organisation. There was a powerful *panchayat*[12] presided over by the local Indian estate owner which adjudicated on moral and social affairs within the community. As one informant recalled, 'there was a case where a man's daughter ran away with a villager so the *panchayat* was held in the savannah where there was a big tent and the entire village invited, and he said well look he couldn't speak much good English, well observed dey "frying" long time, actually meaning they were "friending" long time and the entire congregation bus (burst) out in a big laugh and what not and actually he was expelled from the group three months'.[13] Caste was clearly established, and at least in religious affairs the inter-caste obligations reminiscent of the Indian *jajmani* system seem to have been present. The village was, however, also unlike Amity in the continuous presence of an African section, numerically dominant in some streets, and the village had a reputation, if not renown, for its participation in Carnival and stick-fighting.

Traditionally the main festivals held were Christmas when the Chinese and Indian storekeepers and the estate owners provided luxuries such as cake and ice cream. There was also the Cropover festival on the sugar estates, the Muslim festival of Hosay which from early on saw extensive African participation, and the Hindu festival of Ram Lila which was also watched by the entire local community. Interethnic relations seem to have been generally good, marked by cordiality but separation. Oral accounts commonly recall the deleterious effect of the emergence of democratic politics in souring these ethnic relations. For example, one of the first taxi drivers in the village saw this (the late 1950s) as the time from which people might refuse a taxi if the driver was of the wrong ethnic group.

Here, as also in Chaguanas, oral histories stress the impact of the American presence during the Second World War, especially the airbase at Carlsen field to the south. The Americans paid significantly higher wages as a result of which the sugar estates (for which this period seems to have been the beginning of the end) found their workforce melting away. The money which came to the village provided the first sense of modernisation and the availability of new commodities. The village remained dominated, however, by its conservative elements, the traditions of mud-built (or *tapia*, that is earth and grass on a wooden frame) houses and earth ovens, and a clear social hierarchy, only gradually being transformed. Then in the mid 1970s came the oil-boom, during which this village, as most of Trinidad, experienced changes of extraordinary scale and velocity. Today, only one or two mud-built houses exist, acknowledged as relics of a past, as the village was rebuilt with substantial brick or concrete two-storey houses, often with terrazzo floors and a front yard enclosed by large iron gates. The new houses were replete with electrical appliances and a high standard of plumbing. 'When the first set of money came in this sort of area, people started to look for the car first, and then we had this TV first and video, and when this money did[14] start to come in those people who did have the black and white, when money started to flow people would tend to say – "me eh (don't) want black and white, I want colour".' From a small core of shops there are now small supermarkets, music and gift shops, hardware outlets, chemists, rumshops (and other kinds of bar). With the gradual expansion of the population the older social order has been challenged. New civil servants had incomes to match the once-affluent land owners, and traditions of caste and social distinction have gradually been replaced by other social divisions. Indeed, given the reputation of the village as a rather impoverished backwater, it provides among the best evidence for the penetration of oil-boom affluence to most sections of the population, at least for a few years. With recession there has been a return to agriculture with market gardens for vegetables and tobacco.

There is still a sense of the core village community which tries to impose its normative values, as was evident to a newcomer more used to urban ways. 'People around here are not friendly, they are friendly to their own people, the people who lived around here a long time, so I feel like an outsider, most of the people have been around here a long time. Around here they talk more about people business, they watch the neighbour, they might find you living too good for them, they might envy you and might not like how you are living, talking about you and you might hear about it and confusion start. They might make your husband beat you or the person you living with ... you get licks (beatings) for nothing.'

Today it is hard to talk of a single village since the area has become subdivided into clearly distinct regional sections with their own character. One area is based around a prominent Hindu temple which exerts considerable influence upon the neighbourhood. The people in that part of the village tend to a strong religiosity and are centred around family life and festivals. Temples of all religions tend to organise events such as family excursions, for example, to other religious institutions or to the beach. As is commonly the case in Trinidad, festivals are not restricted to the relevant religion; indeed the youth organisation that in 1988 organised the local Divali 'lighting up' displays were dominated by Indian Muslims and Christians. To a lesser extent the two mosques and the several local churches also create a kind of aura in their immediate neighbourhood which is settled by members of their congregation.

Another part of the village is dominated by 'liming'. This is one of the most important social institutions of Trinidad and today has expanded into a number of varieties, but in this case liming refers to the older sense of the term, which is where men of the area tend to hang around at particular street corners. Here they show off their clothes, smoke marijuana and heckle passing women, but most of all they look to exchange news and hope for some action or event they can participate in. Lieber (1981) provides an ethnography of this activity based in Port of Spain which, on a smaller scale, is replicated here (compare Wilson 1973: 188–214 on crews). The associated area then gains a negative reputation, as when a villager noted, 'by that junction, it have a place, only limers, they give trouble, they heckle you if they find you in the area too much, they watch you, na, I find so I doh (don't) like that spot'. This characterisation is particularly directed at conditions in the late 1980s when recession meant high unemployment. Ten years before, the atmosphere was much more positive. The local village council, dominated by patronage from the PNM government, had supplied facilities for a very active basketball court and sponsored other events. 'Every weekend the centre would have a dance, every monthend a big dance, it was a very fast way of life.' Today, paid fêtes run by the council are very rare, the function having been taken over by the malls in Chaguanas.

In the area as a whole, this kind of street-based lime was much less important than the car-based lime which had become the dominant form of liming during the oil-boom. The typical pattern for such a lime is for two men to meet on a Friday night and decide to drive around to a friend's; from there they might make a succession of visits picking up others as they went, and possibly also some women to accompany them. They might just go from house to house which was common for limers from Newtown, or visit several of the plentiful bars and rumshops in the area, occasionally frequenting the brothels mainly situated in villages and towns outside Chaguanas. They might go to a beach for a moonlight swim but, most commonly, especially for those in The Meadows, go into Port of Spain.

Limes in St Pauls, particularly during the oil-boom, were extensive, often lasting a weekend or more before the men turned up again at their homes or work. For some professions where work practices could be 'eased', for example, employees of the local councils with an obliging timekeeper, work groups might turn up at around 6.00 a.m., finish work around 8.30 a.m. and then lime through to around 2.00 or 3.00 a.m. the following day. The ideology of a lime is that it should be spontaneous and unlimited. During a lime, there will be many stories about how one only went to post a letter in one's slippers but then met a friend and ended up liming in the small islands[15] for four days. As one storekeeper remembered, 'you pack your car, you lime, you chill out, and I carry a few fellas, and is only when they start liming they realise that too late they can't come back. And fellas used to fraid me after that. When they see me Saturday night they pass me straight. They say "na boy you ent bringing me back home".' As is evident from this, there was often a conflict between the ideal of a lime and the sense of domestic responsibilities (for which see Eriksen 1990). In general, car-based liming in recession time was becoming increasingly reduced to a Friday night event.

A very different section of the village has recently established their own village council under the auspices of the NAR, thus bypassing the core village council which had been so closely associated with the PNM that it became defunct when NAR replaced PNM in government. This new council is trying hard not to replicate the strong identification of its predecessor with one ethnic group, the African population, and is active in areas such as running an unemployment register, setting up a nursery and asking government for improved utilities.

There remain a number of institutions which help to construct a sense of social solidarity. Sports continue to be important. There are at least six cricket teams as well as football, basketball, draughts and netball teams in the village. There are Indian orchestras and dancers who perform at religious events. In such villages, sports such as 'wind-ball' cricket and 'small-goal' football, which are less formal and require less capital outlay than the official versions, are popular. Recently there have been attempts to revitalise traditions associated with Hosay and Carnival, the latter with some success. Groups gathering money for such events may hold a communal barbecue or small bazaar.

For housewives two institutions have developed which create social contact. The most important is the *sou sou* (Levin 1973), a rotating credit system. Typically, about ten women will form a group and each gives a set sum of money per week or month. The resultant 'hand' will be taken by each member in turn and used for any larger capital expenditure. In some cases, the organiser takes a percentage of the whole, but also the risk from any defaulter. In the survey, thirty-eight persons noted that they were involved in a *sou sou* at that time, though many more mentioned having been involved at other times. The most common use of their 'hand' was for building materials followed by paying bills, but fixing the car, buying things for children and food were also mentioned. Of lesser importance, but significant over the last few years, has been the suitcase trade with Margarita and Caracas. Individual housewives take orders for goods from their friends and neighbours and then travel to Venezuela, where prices are considerably lower than in Trinidad, to purchase these items (and to take a commission).

The Meadows

The second fieldwork area is an example of an increasingly important category of housing in Trinidad. The formation of 'residential areas' has become the single most successful strategy for constructing a distinct and distinguishable middle class.[16] The deliberate intention has been to move away from complex settlements with considerable divergence of income and status, in order to create relatively homogeneous housing areas where one's presence is indicative of one's social position. This process started in Port of Spain but has become increasingly important in the rest of Trinidad during the oil-boom, and there are several such areas associated with Chaguanas. The Meadows is typical in having been created by a private company established by the landowners. They provided the basic infrastructure and then both built houses for sale and also sold off land in lots for leaseholders to construct their own houses. The contracts have many zoning stipulations, such as the minimum sum which must be spent on each house, its materials and limits on its form. People in the area are forbidden to engage in most forms of commercial activity and to advertise from home. Every leaseholder has been individually interviewed by the housing company to determine their suitability.

In practice many such stipulations are ignored, and with the recession commercial activity, in particular, is flourishing, if discrete. The desired effect has been achieved, however, and although the first set of houses built around fifteen years prior to fieldwork were relatively inexpensive, the overall high status of the area is undisputed. Although most of the houses built by the company were of two or three basic types, such is the penchant for 'renovations' (rebuilding and making additions) that the original house form is now very difficult to discern, except in some of the recent housing for rent where renovations are not possible. Despite the architectural diversity, an aura of homogeneity is evident. 'When you pass on a Saturday you see everybody cutting their lawns, and Sundays you pass, you see them washing their car and basically that's how it does be week after week.' This is part of its aura of respectability, its niceness said to derive from the fact it 'is people of the same age and the same position'. The housing was originally advertised as being half way between the first and second largest towns in Trinidad. It was successful in appealing to those who expected to be posted to different areas and did not want to have to move accordingly. Teachers are especially prevalent and along with civil servants dominate over business people. Teachers have a high social status and the status of the emerging area became its own attraction. 'I felt (The Meadows) were a bit above my class, so that it would encourage me to move up, and then mixing in the area and my children playing here would encourage them to move up still further.' As in St Pauls there is some evidence for internal distinctions: areas which were purchased for larger sums at the height of the boom distinguish themselves from the earlier areas which were purchased relatively cheaply and have been less grandly renovated. One of the several residents' associations which have developed seemed to consist largely of doctors and lawyers and was seen as self-selected and exclusive.

The housing itself is impressive. The general affluence is evident in the variety of architectural features, from mock towers and arches, to the wooden ceilings (which some saw as emulating Canadian patterns). Houses tend to be well-protected with high exterior walls and gates enclosing yards patrolled by Dobermans, Alsatians and Rottweilers, after which one gains access to houses in which all doors and windows are protected by metal grills termed 'burglar-proofing'. Outside it is quiet, since most people travel by car, except the schoolchildren passing through certain areas and the vendors or gardeners offering their services. There are exceptions and typically a newly settled section will have a lively street atmosphere based around the large number of children born within a few years of families settling in. In such areas teachers may put on special activities during school holidays for all the children in the street and there is a general sense that 'we're all uncles and aunts here'. There seems to be a distinctive developmental cycle, however, as in older areas people reminisce that 'we all lived like a family ... but now everybody is independent, it's changed because the children got bigger'. In these mature stages social interaction seems minimal. Most of the inhabitants of the area not only work in Port of Spain but also see the capital as the location for their social life. Their children may go to school in Port of Spain which is where they have their doctor and do their shopping. In some respects the focus of culture goes beyond the capital to places abroad. Many of the residents have frequent contacts in other countries, travel for business or governmental meetings and have family abroad. Many houses have furniture or decorations from Toronto or New York. Only three out of the forty households did not report household members as having travelled beyond the West Indian islands and Venezuela; thirty reported at least one visit to the United States. At social gatherings much of the news or the latest jokes doing the rounds are derived from abroad and the expected knowledge of things from 'away'. In turn there is a symbiotic relationship with less affluent relatives who are living in more rural areas. The residents may visit these on weekends and return with a car-trunk full of fresh vegetables and fruits, having dispensed information about how to deal with bureaucrats and school systems in return.

The exceptions are likely to be those with origins from this area, who are more likely to be involved in local philanthropic and social organisations such as Rotary or Lions. Other forms of local social activity may also develop. Recently the fashion for jogging has filled some streets in the early morning. Many of the sections tried to develop a Residents' Association in the initial period, partly to organise facilities such as playgrounds, which had been anticipated as part of the infrastructure but which have been cut back in the recession. These associations also hold barbecues, carnival dances and put up a crèche at Christmas, but several have closed down as the initial enthusiasm waned.

Residents of The Meadows will also lime, but that is because this term has spread its semantic field and can now be applied to almost any activity involving more than one person orientated towards relaxation outside the home and with an aura of at least potential spontaneity for growth or change. A family going to the seaside is a 'beach lime; either families or males as a group, may organise a 'river lime' in which they go up a river and make a fire on which they cook a chicken – 'make a cook'. This activity is even open to teetotal Indians who favour the slightly up-market variation of the 'duck lime' in preference to the chicken. Liming in The Meadows tended either to be orientated to drinking at local bars or associated with 'staying late at work' in town. In at least one area, a set of males engaged in limes based around the downstairs sections of houses built on pillars, which had been organised as a male preserve specifically for liming purposes. In general, however, any activities which might be considered to threaten propriety take place outside The Meadows. There is the general expectation that people will be discreet and considerable annoyance at families who bring any suspicion of 'bacchanal' to the area itself.

Ford

If The Meadows lies unambiguously at one pole of the spectrum of social hierarchy, the people of Ford are equally clearly at the other end, and each freely acknowledges its opposition. Squatting has played an important role in the history of Trinidad, from the early period of slave emancipation when many ex-slaves occupied area to which they had no formal rights. Today there are still many settlements without legal status, which then put pressure on government to regularise their position as *de jure* communities. A positive response to such requests is most commonly forthcoming just before an election. The extent of current squatting was suggested by an article which claimed that one eighth of the lands of Caroni (the name for the government sugar-estate company as well as for the region) was currently being squatted, of which 2,000 acres were residential (*Guardian*, 7 September 1988).

Ford is just one section of a very extensive squatting area, which aerial photographs reveal as one of the most densely inhabited areas around Chaguanas. There were a few residents in the area before the squatting, which had no specific date but seems to have accelerated about ten years before fieldwork and then continued at a more leisurely pace until the area has become virtually without unoccupied land. The inhabitants are of mixed origins. Some whole families moved into the neighbourhood: for example, within one small area there are six households of one family, the parents and five of their ten sons. Many others have moved in for particular reasons, such as a woman who had been driven out of Amity because of local feuding, or an Indian woman living with an African man who had found the pressure from her ethnic compatriots too great. Others had come from destitution and an inability to pay any rent in the recession. This was an area where men established 'deputies' (mistresses) during the oil-boom: 'If the men have the money they will build a portion, and if they could reach outside for betterment they gone, most of them bring the women and live with the women because it is a kind of hideout for them and a cheaper way of living, they could plant a little garden, push a little weed'. This practice has declined with the recession: 'The men who used to put out money on deputies don't do it any more, I believe they were much more promiscuous during the oil boom, now we are more or less sort of contented, I think AIDS made a lot of difference'. Although outsiders consider the area to be full of immigrants from the small islands of the Caribbean, in fact these make up less than twenty per cent of the inhabitants of Ford.

The housing is mainly of wood or the boxes which are used by the local car-assembly plants to import their parts. There are, however, a number of concrete houses which have developed using the oil-boom money and which could rival St Pauls or Newtown in the affluence suggested by their interior furnishings. The lack of legal ownership created some problems, such as people 'selling' land to which they had no rights. In general this has settled down and the borders between homes are, if anything, less subject to dispute than in St Pauls. There is a clear market in houses and land and present occupants can expect a small but significant price for their property whose change in ownership is recognised locally. As an example of pragmatic anarchism, the area is exemplary. Occasional problems still arise, however, such as a woman whose partner left her and proceeded to sell the house, forcing her to buy it back a second time from its purchaser.

The area is not particularly attractive for settlement: it turns to mud after heavy rain and has no proper drainage. Many prefer not to put on their shoes until they have reached the edge of the settlement. Over the years, some infrastructure has developed. Roads are gradually being given gravel surfaces to allow vehicular access; materials are supplied by political patronage and the work is done by local people. A few homes near the edge of the settlement have internal water supplies, though most have to use standpipes, often at some distance. Rather more houses have electricity, often tapped from a neighbour with an official supply. The government is starting to look more favourably on the supply of proper facilities for households which register their possession, though most people are very unclear about their rights and what procedures should be followed. Also 'a lot of smart men pass in, took people money, just ent do nothing and go their way'. Houses are increasingly fenced off in the manner of the other settlements, and many people keep chickens and grow a few vegetables. None of the four settlements have yards which are shared in the manner of traditional Caribbean settlement styles.

Two occupations seem to dominate employment: there are many masons who undertake building work where and when they can find it, and a number of vendors from the Chaguanas market, although with the recession unemployment is the most characteristic position of the inhabitants. Others work in shops, most commonly for a maximum of six months, after which the shops find an excuse to fire them before they gain legal entitlements. Also common is domestic work, for example, in The Meadows, or working as security guards in Port of Spain. An important source of income has been trading in drugs. During the height of the oil-boom, cocaine was very prevalent, and while a few made large sums, many more were impoverished by their own consumption of the drug. Today both use and dealing in cocaine is much reduced and there has been a return to the older trade in marijuana. There is also some, though not extensive, involvement in other illegal activities such as pickpocketing and petty larceny. There are few households with considerable stored assets, and there are a number with incomes which would have been classified as middle class but for the tendency to spend money with some rapidity. Fashion-consciousness is at least as important here as in the other three areas. There are also examples of unremitting poverty and houses which are little more than unfurnished shelters for children who soon learn to hustle for their food, usually presided over by women who gain no support from the children's fathers for their subsistence.

Given the general level of unemployment, the area is busy at all times. With the recession, many children have stopped going to school; parents may be embarrassed by their inability to afford school books and proper clothing and prefer to keep their children at home. This was particularly the case in late 1988 though by 1990 there had been a slight upturn in the economy and there were relatively few children at home. There are many liming spots, and the local sports ground is much used. Gambling is ubiquitous, the most common activity being 'all-fours', a card game with various elaborate signs passed between the participants. Almost as important is *'whe whe'*, a Chinese numbers game based on thirty-six numbers represented by marks with various symbolic significance. Punters can place bets twice a day and are heavily influenced by their dreams as to which number will come up. The bets are collected by 'markers' who take them to the 'banker' who pays out on the number chosen with the help of elaborate charts. Much less important is the betting on the horses, both from Trinidadian races and English races, at betting shops in Chaguanas.

Social life is lively in Ford. Village councils and self-help groups, intending to extract money from political patrons and divert it to the area, come and go with some frequency, since their leaders are almost invariably subject to suspicion of embezzlement or individual self-interest. There is a strong ideology of self-help and nationalist pride which, for example, may lead to the whole community raising funds for a Hindu festival such as Divali, or a children's Christmas party. Also used for fund-raising purposes are local fashion shows and excursions in which maxi-taxis are hired to take people to the beach. These are in effect limes with prodigious quantities of rum, coca-cola and ice consumed at all stages. People also gather for extensive pre-funeral wakes, and for house parties supplemented by larger paid fêtes both within the settlement and in Chaguanas. There are numerous small 'parlours' selling bread and soft drinks. There is also a nearby panyard for steelband practice, but few of the musicians are from this immediate area.

Above all, the area is characterised by the spirit of 'bacchanal', a term which carries positive connotations of enjoyment and spontaneity but also negative ones of disorder and confusion. Relationships are turbulent, with considerable social interaction, in borrowing, *sou sou* and general gossiping. Since houses are mainly of wood and board, and close together, and given that the low level of employment meant that people were often present at home, it follows that visiting patterns were easily discernible. Gossip was considerable and continuous, as is often commented upon by the inhabitants. Such gossip might lead to quarrels and then to a 'cuss-out' when a private quarrel would take the form of a public airing. Typically, an individual feeling aggrieved would stand in front of the person or house of the assumed guilty party and launch a loud verbal diatribe, starting with the specific complaint but quickly escalating, especially in the face of any spirited reply, into a general listing of accusations and gossip about the supposed bad behaviour of the accused. This may remain relatively small and private, but on occasion the 'cuss-out' becomes much more elaborate and the neighbourhood will gather around to enjoy the quality of the verbal invective. The battle of words could go on for hours or, it is said, even days, occasionally erupting into physical violence. Although there is violence, especially by men on women, people also pride themselves on their quick forgiveness and ability to re-establish relations.

Ford is conspicuous in comparison to the other three areas, in the development of individual 'characters', persons with strong local reputations for slightly eccentric habits, which are often systematically cultivated. Such individuals will often engage in slightly outrageous behaviour and tell tall tales of their achievements. Associated with the development of the character is the pervasive humour and jokiness of the settlement and the belief that humour can always bring down pretensions and disarm the opponent. Although 'cussing out' can lead to violence, this is regarded as a failure, since the better stories come of the barbed wit of the verbal invective. Because of the term 'bacchanal', it is hard to disagreggate a romanticisation of the 'culture of poverty' found in attitudes projected from other quarters, including academics, from the self-conception of the squatters themselves. Most are well aware of the conflicting stereotypes and reputations of such areas and more often attempt to live up to them than to repudiate them.

In a sense there is a continual discourse on the proper forms of sociality. On the one hand there are egalitarian pressures to be involved and to share: 'if you just run into a drinking friend, and say we does drink in the same rum shop, you have trouble, because one day he might tell you – come over by me instead of sitting down here, look I buy a bottle – so you gone by him. So next thing you hear Sunday morning you are ready to go to church and he come drink. If you tell him no you have an enemy.' There is also competition: 'around here it have a lot of women jealous and competition sometimes ... leh we say I have a black and white TV and I buy a colour TV, they would find I have no right to buy a colour TV and they would try everything in their power to get a colour TV'. The tension is often between social participation and self-imposed privacy: 'I think here is the founder for Bacchanal. One of the main things that cause confusion in this area here is that people don't like to stay in their house, and once you see people like going in people place and talking that is the beginning of confusion ... the woman who is staying with me is from the church and she is real cool, she doh have much friends, and she doh go by neighbours because we doh believe in doing that.' These negative comments on the area are common, but there is an equally strong pride in the openness and friendly nature of the settlement and a dismissal of people who don't mix as being 'social' (meaning aloof or anti-social). It is women who most clearly suffer from this ambivalence about social life: 'you can't discuss your problems with anybody because as you tell them they laughing at you and they only waiting to have a little argument to curse you and throw it in your face'.

In general, although there are people in the area devoted to their religion, there are rather more who have very little active involvement.[17] Although this does not come out in the government census, the dominant religion in the area is clearly the Spiritual Baptist church, and several houses carry the flags indicating the status of a church. Although formally this Spiritual Baptism is distinct from the worship of the syncretised African/Christian spirits known as *Orishas*, of which the best-known example is Shango, for local people both are versions of a general complex, and there are a number of homes in the area which will host Shango feasts. Both are also closely associated with the practice of *obeah* and forms of magical strategies by which people hope to solve various problems. A typical negative comment went: 'I ent know about Baptist because those people are bacchanal, they ent easy ... I think the mother (leader) in that church set it up probably for money, she gives excursion, dinners and other things so they make a lot of money, and people also come by who have problems, they fool a lot of people. Every day people outside will come here, as long as they see two flags they will come and say – well could you do something for me, and they will charge you for medicine. The most common things people will go for is like catching a man, or like they living with a man and they don't want him again and they want her to do something to keep him out, or they see somebody else they want.' This is of course only one view, and there are many committed Baptists whose relation to the religion is closer to that described by Glazier (1983) for Trinidad Baptist churches, and which is closer to conventional Christian belief and organisation. There is a strong Hindu and Muslim presence and increasing attempts by evangelical churches to penetrate the area, creating a counter-tendency in favour of extreme privacy and respectability, but few can maintain this stance for long. A more complex category is the Rasta, of which there are many in this area. Although many Trinidadians associate Rastafarianism with crime and indolence and complain about the associated loud music, there is a clear tendency for Rasta to develop into another version of the many variants of Christian churches with a considerable degree of religiosity, respectability and intense concentration on the minutiae of keeping the faith.

Newtown

One of the developments characteristic of the oil-boom was an extensive government-housing programme designed to help people move out of depressed areas. These National Housing Authority schemes are found throughout Trinidad, but one of the most extensive was planned for the Chaguanas area. The approximately 500 housing units which were actually built were only a fraction of the settlement which had been intended when recession cut short further development. The result was viewed with considerable suspicion in Chaguanas, since the newcomers were almost all African and assumed to be under direct PNM patronage. The project was viewed as a deliberate government attempt to change the demography of an area which was dominated by the Indian-led opposition. The fears were not allayed by the fact that a significant number of those given houses work in the army, police and coastguard.

The settlement was occupied in three phases, with a variety of methods of recruitment, including a lottery. Several occupants implied that specific political patronage was employed; indeed, one went so far as to identify various sections of the settlement with the politicians she believed had been instrumental in choosing the occupants. Each phase also has different proportions of renting and owner occupation. As a result there is a strong sense of distinction between the three phases which are seen as retaining the status given them by their method of selection.

The contracts with leaseholders have similar restrictions to those of The Meadows in terms of limitations on commercial activity, and there is a clear attempt to use the settlement to bring a section of the population into a higher class bracket. In some NHA settlements this has been spectacularly unsuccessful with estates gaining rapid notoriety as the sites of youth gangs, for example. In other settlements, including this one, the strategy has had considerable success, and the aura of Newtown is one of self-imposed quiet, in a generally collective effort to escape from the origins of many of the people through a generalised new respectability associated with home ownership. A major factor in this is the relatively high income of a settlement whose inhabitants often have secure government employment.

The recession meant that the original plans for schools and playgrounds have been shelved, and the local Residents' Association has had to fight for basic amenities such as lighting and to improve the inadequate water and sewage facilities. In general the government has found it difficult to maintain and upkeep its own housing stock and has had little success in collecting rents and mortgage payments. As a result there is a move to change the status of such housing. An article (*Guardian* 9 September 1988) noted that the government wanted to sell off all NHA properties since the arrears in rents were double the income from rents, and this income only covered a seventh of the cost of upkeep. In Newtown many of the houses which were originally given on the basis of mortgages were having to be drastically revalued downwards, as the original mortgages were created before the property slump associated with recession.

Most of the houses were built to two or three set patterns, but although most of the occupants had only lived there between two and four years the extent of 'renovations' was impressive. Of the thirty where this information was recorded, only three had made no changes. Twelve had made some alterations such as putting concrete foundations down, fencing off the yard, putting in cupboards, extending the garage or adding a porch. Fifteen had gone as far as adding additional rooms, typically adding a master bedroom with associated washroom and an extended kitchen at the back of the original house. There is considerable individualisation of the front areas. 'They say Trinidadians, even if you give them a palace will always have some renovations to do, that is what they're like. I think they live to show one another – well I could do this' ... 'So everybody trying to make it at least slightly different from their neighbour. So most people trying to make it as different as possible.' One man talked about how he carefully surveyed the other houses on the street before deciding to paint the front of his house in two tones, a feature not previously attempted (but which was then promptly copied by his neighbour).

Housing in Trinidad is typically constructed in stages, for example, in Ford one can often see a concrete foundation which has been laid, or some 'galvanise' (corrugated iron sheeting) roofing which has been stored, as each section of a house is completed when the resources are available. In Newtown it is rare for people to employ professional help except for specific technical tasks. Much more commonly employed is the system of 'gayap' whereby friends and relatives gather on an appointed day and collectively construct the section required, in return for generous food and drink and the expectation of reciprocal help in their own renovations.

What is particularly striking in Newtown is the development of the extraordinary pluralism of interests which frequently characterises the modern urban condition. One householder is firmly committed to Freemasonry and spends a considerable amount of time at meetings of the five secret orders to which she belongs. Another is devoted to Tupperware parties at which she attracts some twenty-five people from her neighbourhood. Several are heavily involved in evangelical churches, another is an aspiring calypsonian and has managed to make some records locally, while yet another spends his weekends with the scouting movement.

The diverse origins make the place: 'what I call a dormitory settlement, where people just come to sleep. Most people are lucky enough to have cars, but they jump in their cars and go back to wherever they came from.' The effect is exaggerated by the large number of men who work in the armed services such as the army and coastguards, where they are expected to be away for lengthy periods of time. Women predominate in the settlement and many of them have opted for an intense involvement in the evangelical churches and general respectability. 'That is the way it's supposed to be in this sort of housing scheme, so you find they kinda stay to themselves. Not that they are impolite or anything like that, if you should bounce them up face to face they would say hello and that's about it.' The intention is to get away from origins in a different social atmosphere: 'The people in Laventille where I come from are not very friendly, they like this bacchanal thing, they always fight for this and quarrel for that and they always have this killing attitude and is something if I have my children I would not grow them up like that. I like it here.' Such behaviour also causes resentment, however: 'some of the people here feel they more up than others, yes they have a big

shot attitude' ... 'people come in here and everybody aim to play
middle-class with this sort of standoffishness.' The degree to
which respectability does imply a lack of neighbourliness was
demonstrated by the survey which included a question asking
the last time when a household had paid a visit to each of its
neighbours. Visiting of neighbours was least frequent in The
Meadows, but Newtown had managed to achieve second place in
this regard.[18]

There are exceptions and some of the women will lime with
groups of women but, like the men, they tend to keep their more
exuberant leisure activities for places outside the immediate area,
and most especially for Port of Spain. Women-only liming is comparatively rare given the pervasive ideology of gender: 'men go
liming the whole week, I think that men would lime Monday to
Friday but we think about liming on weekends because tomorrow
is work, I have to set my hair for work I have to make sure my uniforms are ironed, you are a housewife of course, if you go liming
tonight, you have to get up early the next morning to pack lunch
for school and send your husband to work and things like that so
it's a hassle. But it's not like that with men, they lime anytime,
most of their liming is on the weekends, but there is nothing to
stop them from liming in the week, once it's a lime, no problem.'

The social activities found in the other communities such as
sou sou are also found here; there are people who exchange flowers as found in Ford and others who exchange video tapes as
found also in The Meadows. There is considerable involvement
in sports and locally held fund-raising events such as barbecues
and parties. Children may come together for birthday parties,
which, like all Trinidadian parties, are dominated by music and
dance, although the relationship between children is also one of
the most common sources of dispute between neighbours. Many
householders described their social relations in terms of who
they would and would not allow their children to play with.
There is some local commerce: small parlours have been set up,
seamstresses work from their homes, one house has a ceramics
factory in the back yard, another sells roses from the front yard.

The atmosphere of the settlement is much affected by its basic
contradiction which is that it is striving for respectability at a time
when recession makes this difficult. This creates a tension which
erupts as rivalry between the three phases. Youths from each
phase are known to engage in fights at fêtes in Chaguanas. The

annual Newtown sports day was a disaster in 1988 as disputes over the judging of events led to bitter recriminations between the three phases. 'The sports centred too much on rivalry between the phases, which was the exact opposite of what we set out to achieve, that is community spirit. There was no harmony between the phases, there was a lot of bickering with four-and-a-half pages of rules for a little sports that was supposed to create harmony.'

Newtown exemplifies the changes which has resulted from the establishment of all four communities. Traditionally in Trinidad social distinctions have not been well-marked in resi dential segregation. Clarke (1986) notes, for San Fernando, that despite the clear ethnic distinctions in social behaviour, these are not represented as residential segregation, and the same point might have been made for class, except in Port of Spain. In recent years, however, there has been a spate of housing construction in which each area aims to homogenise its occupants. In the case of Newtown and The Meadows this is deliberate policy, but it also affects a settlement such as Ford which then becomes a kind of 'sink' community or refuge for those who have difficulty in being accepted in other communities. Even St Pauls is homogenised by default, as some of its more ambitious and affluent households have moved to areas such as The Meadows and some of its less successful to places such as Ford.

It would be wrong, however, to speak too quickly of class relations in housing segregation, since the various quotations used in the description of the communities suggest that there are particular ideas held by Trinidadians about the nature of social hierarchy which may be diminished by appending the concept of class. The key term in judging social behaviour is 'bacchanal', which is almost synonymous with the concept of 'confusion' – a state which arises from gossip and mixing and is opposed to a form of respectability which focuses on privacy and aloofness. These attributes may be viewed either positively or negatively depending on who is making the judgement. Respectability can be denigrated as 'social' and a false façade, with bacchanal as a form of authenticity celebrated at Carnival. Equally, bacchanal can be viewed with disgust as uncontrolled and a corrupt immorality. There is a clear association with money and resources, and The Meadows, which most clearly avoids bacchanal, is the wealthiest settlement while Ford, which often celebrates bacchanal, is the least affluent. This relationship is complex, however, not least because there are very different attitudes to money itself and whether it should be stored or spent, which are interwined with the symbolic connotations of bacchanal. This relationship will be explored further and hopefully clarified in subsequent Chapters.

In Newtown, the atmosphere is probably the least relaxed of the four communities precisely because there is tension over the appropriate model for social behaviour, with many trying rather desperately to move their social status upwards through a transformation in their own behaviour, while others are still attracted by elements they are supposed to be repudiating. In all the communities apart from Ford, the problems are partially resolved by a strong distinction between 'inside' and 'outside': the former is concerned with the realm of the domestic and the residential community, the latter with the world of liming, the street and what can be permitted when one is away from home.

A Note on Ethnicity

In so far as this section is a descriptive introduction to the area of fieldwork it is impossible to proceed without an explicit discussion of ethnicity. This topic is probably the most extensively researched of any aspect of Trinidadian social relations and for more detailed accounts of the relevant debates reference should be made elsewhere (e.g. for a recent survey see Yelvington, forthcoming; Segal 1989). Ethnic terms will be used frequently throughout this book and I therefore wish to clarify what they do and do not connote.

For the largest group within the Trinidadian population there exists a general sense of a continuum which includes not only those who would see themselves as having pure descent from Africa and would be labelled colloquially within Trinidad as 'Negro', but also the spectrum of lighter-skinned groups resulting from mixed white and black ancestry often known by local terms such as 'red' or previously 'high-brown'. Within this spectrum there is considerable concern for micro-differentiation in descriptive terminology. For example, the term 'red nigger' is not necessarily pejorative but may refer to a person who lies ambiguously between the category red and that of Negro. Some Africans also attempt to apply this continuum in a manner which would incorporate Indians as a periphery which grades away from the core to which they ascribe their own identity. The term 'Creole' is often used by academics for the entire continuum (and is also sometimes so used locally, for example as opposed to Indian). I will use this term when referring to academic debate, the term African for descriptive and generalising purposes and the term Negro when referring to the use of that term in a local context. The academic term Creole is confusing since most Trinidadians use the term Creole to refer to Trinidadian whites, and French Creole to refer to a plantocracy which was dominated by the French.[19]

By contrast there are groups that are defined as homogeneous and without graded forms. These include the Indians, the Chinese, the Portuguese and the Syrians. A specific category of *Dougla*[20] has been created to describe the descendants of mixed African and Indian unions. The other ambiguous term is 'Spanish' which may refer to descent from Spanish, Amerindian or in rural areas simply mixed origins. The literature on the mixed population tends to concentrate on the gradation from Black-Brown-White, assuming a basis in the mixed mating of whites and blacks. In practice Indians working on the sugar plantations also seem to have produced an important gradation towards Whites. An Indian who as a taxi driver used to arrange the liaisons with white (mainly Scottish) overseers in the 1920s and 1930s enumerated many such genealogies, and oral history suggests that although marriage was rare, mating between Indian and Africans in the Chaguanas area was much more common than current ideologies would acknowledge. Given that all the original populations present considerable variety of physiognomy the result is, to say the least, cosmopolitan.

For most Trinidadians, the discourse of ethnicity is one of assumed expertise, which allows them to categorise in terms of origins and to predict future behaviour accordingly. The extent to which this is an essentialist view is made evident in the emphasis on the physiognomy of babies. This expertise is intended not only to establish (or more often to question) fatherhood on the basis of inherited characteristics but also attempts to place the character and future of the infant on the basis of these looks. When I first arrived in Trinidad, I was struck, like most other visitors, by the physical diversity of the population, but discourses can be powerful, and after about nine months I assumed I had learnt to make

'correct' placements, in the same way that I had learnt to understand 'dialect'. It was only at the end of the fieldwork when I was
conducting an experiment based on determining consumer
responses to advertisements that I sensed the false objectivism I
had relaxed into. As part of this work I asked informants to give
me the ethnic description of the persons in each advertisement.
Informants performed this task with ease and alacrity but their
answers were remarkably inconsistent, even allowing for the
deliberate policy of advertisers to select ambiguous models in
order to broaden their marketing appeal. Individuals I took to be
clear exemplifications of one ethnic category were strongly
asserted to be something quite different. This was a far cry from
the folk science of racial genealogy I had come to assume.[21]
Indeed I had reached the absurd position of biting my lip to
avoid telling individual informants that they were 'wrong' in
their identifications. By coincidence, another anthropologist
working in southern Trinidad at the same time, came to the same
conclusion by exactly the same technique of discussing television
advertisements with informants (Neil Sanpath, personal communication).

A similar problem arises with the interpretation of the 160-
household survey. I first tried to establish how the household
might be designated with regard to the census terms, and found
that the proportions of African (sixty-five) Indian (sixty-seven)
and Mixed (twenty-eight) were similar to those of the national census (though the census is concerned only with individuals). When
a more exacting question was asked with regard to the ethnic origins of the respondent's parents, the results showed that many
more of my informants could be taken as largely of mixed descent.
At this level only fifty-seven were found to be solely Indian, and
forty African, while sixty-three included some mixed elements.
These mixed elements were noted as follows: thirty-four Spanish,
ten Carib, seven White, five Chinese, five Portuguese, three
Scottish and two French Creole.

A similar conclusion is suggested by the government censuses
for Trinidad which for several decades have shown no increase in
the mixed population. This must imply that since there are forces
which produce greater mixing in conventional terms, there are
counter forces which lead people to oppose such a classification.
For Indians there is a clear imperative to see themselves as unambiguously part of the category since one tends either to be fully

incorporated in pseudo-kinship forms or excluded. Abdullah suggests that the decline in the mixed self-description, together with a rise in Africans in the census from 1960 to 1970, reflects the impact of Black Power at that time (1988: 446). By the same token many of those who might otherwise be seen as *Dougla* rapidly assimilate to the African population and define themselves accordingly. There are examples in Newtown who seem to assert their African roots more assiduously than those without mixed parentage.

Another finding of my own survey was the degree of endogamy among the mixed population. Of the twenty-eight households which categorised themselves as mixed, twenty-three included couples where both partners were either of mixed or Spanish origins, while only five consisted of one mixed partner and one who was solely Indian or African. This is partly an arte-fact of households which have only a small mixed element ignor-ing this in their self-classification, but also implies a strong element of endogamy. Some of these are clear categories, as when two persons of *Dougla* origin form a relationship, but the evi-dence suggested that people who saw themselves as generally of 'mixed' origin would also tend to associate with each other.

All this evidence does not detract from the viability of a clear set of descriptors based on ethnic labels which are used to self-designate and to categorise others and in turn to objectify moral and social norms and expectations. Although historical sources demonstrate the very varied origins of the African community (Brereton 1981: 96–100) from ex-slaves to demobilised American soldiers, this and the general gradation of colour designation is under pressure from the development of a central contrast of Negro and Indian, enhanced by the tendency of the former group to espouse the concept of 'Africa' as roots.

A long attempt to disaggregate the 'free coloured' society as a nascent middle class also seems to be surrendering to this larger classificatory imperative. As will be argued below, the shift in recent years is also one from a definition of African in opposition or assimilation with white, to an increasing concern to define the contrast between African and Indian. It is this contrast and in par-ticular the stereotypes and expectations which it generates which will be most commonly employed in the present book, since it is here that ethnicity seems to play a major role in objectifying the different forms of temporal consciousness with which this study is particularly concerned. The emphasis on this contrast is also in part an artefact of the field situation in Chaguanas where this process has perhaps gone furthest.

Notes

1. My frequent use of the terms 'objectify' and 'objectification' throughout this book follows from the definition given in Miller (1987: 19–82). Whereas the term 'symbol' implies a prior value or object which is reflected in the symbol, the term objectify refers to a dialectic in which that which objectifies and that which is objectified are creations of the same process which is known as objectification. This is particularly important given the considerable use made of material culture in this book, since such an approach rejects the usual privileging of subject over object common to such studies.

2. For Trinidad the work of Herskovits (1947) and Klass (1961), in particular, exemplify these concerns.

3. There is also a considerable literature on the more general claim that the black diaspora population has a specific relationship to modernity by virtue of its history. I have not attempted to address this literature but several recent presentations by Paul Gilroy suggest that his forthcoming book on this topic will enormously enhance our understanding of this relationship.

4. For the remainder of this book I will use the term Indian to designate the peoples who have come to Trinidad from South Asia, which conforms to local usage and is equivalent to African for the ex-slave population and other immigrants from Africa.

5. In a forthcoming ethnography, Olwig explores the case of Nevis where an even higher proportion of the population live on remittances as part of transnational families.

6. While Brereton (1981) provides the best coverage for the period leading up to Independence, the post-Independence period is best surveyed by Ryan ed. (1988) for political and economic change and by Ryan ed. (1991) for social and cultural change.

7. For the tensions between nationalist politics and the power of oil and other industrial corporations, see Hintzen (1989), Magid (1989) and Singh (1989).

8. For a useful and concise description of the general political and economic condition of Trinidad during the period of fieldwork, see Yelvington (1991).

9. By approximating census units with the areas covered in fieldwork a rough characterisation of some differences between some of these sites is obtained from the 1980 Census (although Newtown was built after the Census). This would suggest the following:

ETHNICITY

The census suggests that Africans comprise around 55 per cent of the population of Ford, but only 30 per cent of The Meadows. Indians comprise 50 per cent of the population in The Meadows but only 33 per cent of Ford. My own survey suggested that Newtown has very few Indians, but that St Pauls has a significant minority of Africans. Only The Meadows indicates any white population at 1.3 per cent. The national population is as follows:-

African	Indian	Mixed	White	Chinese
40.8	40.65	16.32	0.94	0.37

EDUCATIONAL LEVELS (stage at which left school by percentage)

	None	Kinder	Primary	Secondary	University
Trinidad	13.65	2.02	56.28	26.6	1.44
Ford	15.9	3.6	58.34	21.7	0.37
Meadows	12.7	3.47	37.26	39.0	7.4
St. Pauls	16.6	1.8	59.35	21.84	0.37

(information for Newtown was not available in the census)

POLITICS

In the 1986 election, all four areas gave more votes to the victorious National Alliance for Reconstruction than to the defeated Peoples National Movement, but in Ford and Newtown the vote was close, while in St Pauls and especially in The Meadows the victory was overwhelming.

RELIGION

The table below represents the combination of the census evidence for the relationship between ethnicity and religion for several census regions in and around the area of fieldwork (though not coincidental with it). My own survey suggested several major inaccuracies of this data. In particular, many of the people of Ford see themselves as Baptist but have clearly given different answers to the census questionnaire. There are also more Rastafarians in that area than is indicated by the category of 'Other'.

	African	Indian	Chinese	White	Mixed
Anglican	1141	37	4	21	150
Baptist	183	7	0	0	19
Hindu	3	2532	3	0	26
Jehovah W.	79	21	0	0	12
Methodist	160	10	0	1	13
Muslim	8	694	2	0	27
Pentecostal	164	95	0	1	55
Presbyterian	4	369	1	3	36
Roman Cath	1968	420	21	18	728
Seventh D.A.	111	39	5	0	20
Other	114	65	0	0	10
TOTAL	3935	4259	35	44	10

10. Four findings provide for an immediate means of distinguishing between the four settlements:
The following table indicates differences in declared household income per month in TT dollars.

	<1,000	1,000–2,500	2,500–5,000	5–8,000	>8,000
MEADOWS	0	8	15	8	9
NEWTOWN	2	11	18	9	0
ST PAULS	6	22	7	3	2
FORD	21	13	3	3	0

These figures are reinforced by the evidence for car ownership in the four communities (the difference in the relative wealth of St Pauls and Newtown may in part be an artefact of the amount of the differences in sources of income. Those in Newtown are mainly in the public service and may therefore declare a higher proportion of their actual income to a survey than those in St Pauls who are mainly in private business):

	TWO CARS	ONE CAR	NO CAR
MEADOWS	16	22	2
NEWTOWN	2	24	14
ST PAULS	3	27	10
FORD	0	7	33

The distribution of declared ethnicity of households in the survey was as follows:

	AFRICAN	INDIAN	MIXED
MEADOWS	14	18	8
NEWTOWN	28	2	10

ST PAULS	5	34	1
FORD	18	13	9

Finally the birthplace of those individuals who responded to this question indicates that only St Pauls represents a largely local population, since in the other three communities those born in the central region of Trinidad form a minority.

PLACE OF BIRTH	NEWTOWN	FORD	MEADOWS	ST PAULS
Chaguanas/Central	8	26	27	62
Port of Spain/ East-West Corridor	32	7	20	5
San Fernando/South	20	11	19	5
Rest of Trinidad	4	4	1	1
Abroad	3	8	0	0
TOTAL	67	56	67	73

11. Out of the 40 households surveyed in St Pauls only 3 arrived within the last 10 years, 5 more arrived between 10 and 40 years previous to the survey and the remainder are long-term residents.

Newtown is the most recent settlement, 5 arrived within the last year, 4 had been there 1 year, 8 for 2 years, 9 for 3 years, 13 for 4 years and only 1 for more than 4 years.

The figures for The Meadows and Ford are as follows:

	<5 years	5–9 years	10–14 years	15–19 years	>19 years
MEADOWS	5	8	7	17	3
FORD	4	18	8	2	2

(6 households in Ford did not respond to this question).

12. A council which adjudicates local disputes. This might relate to a village, but often in India it was specific to a particular caste.

13. He had meant to say that he had observed them friending for a long time, which means they were sexual partners but not necessarily living together.

14. Quite often in these quotes, informants attempt to 'hypercorrect' dialect terms back into formal English, because of my presence. In this case 'did' refers to the dialect term 'di' which is derived from did but is not quite synonymous. I am very grateful to Lise Winer for her advice on these problems of translation and dialect.

15. The small islands are the nearby West Indian countries. This was a type of lime which was remembered as a reflection of the oil-boom economy.

16. The term class is not very commonly used, though there are local equivalents such as 'big-shot' people. In the three communities who were questioned as to their class (Ford was not included), it was evident that it is the expression 'middle' class which dominates this self-conception, in that most people would describe themselves as 'less than middle' or 'not middle' rather than lower or working class. Taking this into account only one person in Meadows described themselves as upper-middle, twenty-two in The Meadows twenty-two in St Pauls and eleven in Newtown described themselves as middle class. two in The Meadows, five in St Pauls and fifteen in Newtown used terms implying lower-middle class, while eleven in The Meadows, five in St Pauls and five in Newtown used terms suggesting lower or working class.

17. The following table provides the responses to the question, 'When did you last go to church', for those Christians who answered this question:

	NEWTOWN	FORD	THE MEADOWS	ST PAULS
WITHIN WEEK	19	5	12	6
WEEK TO A MONTH	5	7	1	4
MONTH TO A YEAR	11	8	9	1
MORE THAN YEAR*	2	11	7	0
TOTAL	37	31	29	11

* INCLUDES DON'T GO

18. The following table indicates the replies to the question of when householders last visited their neighbour on either side. It was commonly pointed out that neighbour often communicated by talking over the fence or in the street, but the table suggests that actually entering into the neighbour's home is often a sign of greater intimacy which certain communities seek to avoid.

	NEWTOWN	FORD	MEADOWS	ST PAULS	TOTAL
NEVER	31	23	40	11	104
OVER 1 YEAR	8	15	15	19	57
OVER 1 MONTH	11	12	13	14	50
OVER I WEEK	11	8	6	11	36
LESS THAN 1 WEEK	12	15	4	23	54
TOTAL	73	73	78	78	302

19. Lise Winer notes that the term French Creole is now also used to refer to all local whites or indeed anyone in the lighter-skinned economic and social élite.

20. Lise Winer notes that *Dougla* was originally a Hindi-Bhojpuri (Trinidadian Hindi) word meaning bastard, but the pejorative aspect has been largely softened.

21. Compare Banton (1983: 19–22, 76–7) for the problem of 'appearance' more generally.

Chapter 2

Modernity as a General Property

An ethnographic approach to modernity requires the direct juxta-position of two elements: a theory of modernity and a descriptive ethnography. In the previous chapter it was argued in general terms that the Caribbean might have a particular resonance with those conditions which have been thought to pertain to modernity. Furthermore, the selection of the four communities which were studied was based on exactly the opposite criteria from that employed in an older tradition of anthropological enquiry. These were not traditional and bounded units, but mainly the artificial creations of the most recent transformations within Trinidadian society and housing. There are, however, many differences between the connotations of the term modernity as an analytical concept and merely the sense of an object of study as being recent or even vanguard. Indeed, modernity is not usually thought of as a contemporary condition so much as an historical process which has been developing over centuries. To warrant the direct analo-gy between these two requires not only a clear account of the con-text of ethnographic enquiry but also some clarity as to what aspect of modernity is being referred to in the use of this other-wise very general term.

What is Modernity?

There are few terms which seem to unleash such a flood of words and debates as that of 'modernity'. The term acts as a kind of goad to the academic, it seems to connote some central problem, some fundamental issue, a context for all other discussions, which must be addressed. Yet to be confronted with it, head on as it were, merely creates the sense that however important a concept, it is extremely hard to characterise its specific nature. Of course this very anxiety, born out of contradictory desires for ultimate or totalising explanation on the one hand and pragmatic concerns with more immediate issues on the other, is itself a typical example of those conditions which are often cited as characteristic of the experience of modernity.

In the context of this book, the aim is fortunately not to try and resolve the question of modernity, but, in the first instance, to describe an approach or model of the causes and consequences of modernity which seems pertinent to the ethnography of Trinidad. This lightens the burden somewhat since it would follow, at least from an anthropological perspective with its relativist suppositions, that an ethnography cannot be expected to describe more than an instance, one of the many possibilities, which are engendered by any central foundational elements to modernity as an historical process. The concern is not with whether Trinidad is the best candidate, or provides the more profound insights into modernity. The claim is merely that juxtaposing a description of Trinidad with a description of modernity may help to account for some of the specific features and contradictions found in the characterisation of both.

Before embarking upon an account of modernity, a peculiar problem must be acknowledged, which would arise in any attempt to juxtapose ethnography with the problematic of modernity. For a book whose presuppositions are largely, though by no means entirely, drawn from the disciplines of material culture and anthropology, there is an uncomfortable feeling in talking about anything modern with the connotation of 'unprecedented'. In the history of anthropology there is an unenviable legacy which assisted in the creation of a creature on the periphery of civilisation, 'the primitive', unchanging, immutable, thoroughly unmodern. This image was then used by colonialists to portray themselves as agents of the evolutionary advance of progressive humanity at the expense of redundant leftovers of past stages, or equally by romantics declaring noble savages as tokens of a purity and mysticism which has been lost in the modern world. It has taken quite some time for anthropology to come to terms with a humanity that is equal, that is universally dynamic and changing, possibly in different ways within different cultural projects, but which could not simply be sundered into the progressive and the traditional.

For this reason a return to the term modern has to be under-taken with eyes wide open as to its consequences. In this particu-lar instance, there is perhaps less likelihood of a falling back into primitivist assumptions, since the population which will be used to explore sometimes extreme forms of modernity is one which a previous variant of anthropology might well have categorised as on the other side of the boundary, as pre- or non-modern.

Habermas on Hegel on Modernity

The particular characterisation of modernity which will be used here is itself twice removed, since it is largely derived from an account of Hegel given by Habermas. I have selected this for two reasons. First, many alternative approaches and attempts to deal with the question of modernity tend to be largely descriptive of traits; indeed the second half of this chapter consists of just such an account of supposedly 'dominant' traits of the modern condi-tion. Alternatively they provide an historical description of the development of these same traits. What, however, would be required here is a theoretical model which rather than focusing upon this or that characteristic, identifies a foundational transfor-mation in human consciousness or circumstance that gives rise to these various modern traits. The ideas that follow provide such an analytical model. This means that while the account is derived from a particular historical trajectory and region, it can be appro-priated for the comparative purposes that an anthropological approach to modernity would necessitate.

The second reason for emphasising this particular approach is that it highlights certain features of modernity which constantly surfaced in my attempts to understand the dynamics of Trinidadian culture. It appeared to be particularly relevant to the descriptive ethnography which follows. This is then a selected juxtaposition: it is in no sense the testing of a hypothesis or a sci-entific (in the naturalistic sense) procedure. Finally, this is clearly a deliberate extraction of an academic debate with the intention of using it out of context. The very point of this work is that Trinidad is in many respects *not* similar (though as argued in the previous chapter possibly analogous) to the kind of conditions of eighteenth- to twentieth-century Europe from which most of our ideas about modernity are derived. Despite their specific origins, such theories have had pretensions to much wider relevance. This may well turn out to be justified, but the intention of the present book is by explicitly making this leap out of context to provide material such that others can form an opinion of just how valid a procedure this is. We are not then concerned with whether Hegel or Habermas derived their ideas from debates with this or that academic or within a given socio/political context, but whether by chance the resulting ideas may be useful in unintended contexts.

The first chapter of Habermas's book *The Philosophical Discourse of Modernity* (1987) is titled *Modernity's Consciousness of Time and its Need for Self-Reassurance*. The relation to time is complex but central. Habermas contends that Modernity is itself temporally located, it arose at a particular time and circumstance. It was the juxtaposition of three events, the Renaissance, the Reformation and the discovery of the New World, all of which are approximately dated to the early sixteenth-century. It has commonly been argued that for European history at least, this period did see a shift in temporal consciousness. For example, in the domain of art there is a gradual move towards a perspective based upon a sense of the present. In earlier painting, such as in the thirteenth-century, a portrayal of biblical events would be based on costumes and scenery of the thirteenth-century, but with Modernity there is the emergence of a sense of world-historical quality that is of the present in relation to history. From this time a classical picture might be given what is supposed to be a classical setting, a Biblical picture a projection of the environs of over a millennium before. There is then a new concept of presentness, one which takes its sense from an opposition to the past and the future. The present is then a moment of becoming and this in turn leads to connotations of advancement or even acceleration. A whole string of new terms and concepts thereby come into play, such as the notion of progress, or emancipation, of *Zeitgeist* or the spirit of the times. Habermas states: 'A present that understands itself from the horizon of the modern age as the actuality of the most recent period has to recapitulate the break brought about with the past as a *continuous renewal*' (1987: 7).

This implies a new consciousness about the present and its separation from the past. The significance of this distinction becomes apparent when one appreciates how much was dependent upon a previous seamless link between past and present.

This new rupture stands for the end of a sense of the customary, a given tradition or order which legitimates everything that is done today simply as continuity with the way things have always been. An obvious example of this break is secularisation, but it is not only religion which affirms moral principles as imminent and which becomes called into question through a process of disenchantment. There is also a decline in a wider sense of a customary 'habitus'[1] the power of the taken-for-granted sense of tradition.

In so far as the sense of the customary has also been the sense of legitimacy, it follows that this transformation of temporal consciousness has profound moral consequences. Habermas notes that, 'modernity can and will no longer borrow the criteria by which it takes its orientation from the models supplied by another epoch; *it has to create its normativity out of itself*' (1987: 7). As such, Modernity imposes a quite novel but crushing burden upon humanity, to forge for itself the criteria by which it will live. Even more burdensome, it has to forge these principles, knowing that this is what it is doing. Thus the second part of the chapter's title – modernity's need for self-reassurance.

Habermas argues that Hegel is the first to construct a philosophy around this transition, a philosophy which sees modernity as both a cause for celebration and the core problem for modern humanity. Hegel sees as his enemy what he projects as the premodern sense of tradition when that becomes the dead hand of mechanical repetition. Most particularly he takes his stance from his own background as a modernist whose domain was religion. He inveighs against what he sees as dead ritual or religion which is merely practised without consideration, and has the reformist zeal for reinjecting voluntarism and morality into religion as a living practice. This characterisation is rather different from those who have branded Hegel as a more conservative thinker, with a strong penchant for 'customary morality' (*sittlichkeit*). Certainly Hegel is not interested in revolutionary change for its own sake as are many later modernists. He also favoured a morality with some relativistic elements which looked favourably to regional traditions and customs. These were accepted, however, in so far as they could be continued as reflexive and dynamic criteria for life, and would be attacked if and when they regressed to the dead weight of mere 'positivity' (Wood 1990: 195). Indeed, what Hegel provides, with a sophistication which has rarely been followed, is the possibility of constantly dynamic reconciliation between the principles of reflexive thought, rationality and a morality grounded in custom.

Of course, anthropologists, at least those who reject a simple dichotomy between dynamic 'hot' and 'cold' societies, the latter unreflective and unchanging, would certainly reject the implied unreflective primitivism as a characterisation of pre-modern ritual and cosmology, but for Hegel the concern is essentially with the specific period of European history which preceded him, and his comments on 'oriental' or other societies may be discarded along with the teleological sequence of history.

Hegel welcomed elements of the changes which characterise modernity, but understood them in terms of the necessary contradiction of objectification. On the one hand modernity brings self-consciousness, a refusal merely to follow custom, and a desire for self-knowledge, but at the same time this brings alienation from the criteria by which we continue our lives, and at first, the knowledge that many of these criteria are indeed our own creation, rather than merely given by some external force, is a deeply unsettling one. Hegel attempts to provide the new criteria for assessing modernity, by demanding a resolution of subjective and objective elements in culture and insisting upon a humanity which injects its own rational concerns into the principles by which it lives.

In Habermas's representation of Hegel, it is as though Hegel goes through a whole series of possible candidates for the star role in resolving this contradiction, and each is considered in turn. The first candidate which is associated with Hegel in his youth is derived from the domain in which the problematic itself first emerges, that is religion. Hegel is represented as experiencing a dissatisfaction common to many of his colleagues at the German seminaries. This takes the form of a reformist desire, a legacy of the reformation and counter reformation, and a concomitant concern with a new subjectivity in which the key enemy is a sense of traditional religion as meaningless ritual performed by rote. A new reformed religion would express itself in civil life, and would reinject morality into ordinary life. This would be modern religion, chosen as reason, not simply given by custom, in which one's will is forged in the act of submitting to criterion by which life is to be lived.

The next candidate to emerge was one which Hegel again takes from his contemporaries, many of whom leave religion in

order to follow the new spirit of romanticism which was emerging in Germany at the time. Habermas looks to the work of
Schiller and others, who felt that art alone could provide the
image of totality and reconciliation which was lost in the disenchantment of custom. This aesthetic has dominated approaches
to modernity ever since, and developed as the main rival tradition to Hegel's own later position (see also Eagleton 1990).
Starting with romanticism the aesthetic approach receives its
most important boost from Nietzsche. For Hegel and later
Habermas there are, however, clear benefits to the enlightenment
and development of abstract rationality; the problem is taking
hold of them. But Habermas argues that for the aesthetic tradition, and for Nietzsche, the idea that we could fashion our own
criteria is neither possible nor desirable. What we need is immediate reconciliation in art and transcendence. Rationality distorts
and vulgarises the basic human aesthetic impulse, as against the
will to power.

Habermas launches a systematic critique of this whole tradition. From Nietzsche he turns to a wide range of thinkers:
Bataille's celebration of violence, the disorderings of sadism and
Heidegger's undermining of rationalism through a mystical
ontology, a kind of primitive being. Finally, this aesthetic tradition which sees no resolution except in immediacy is located in
the variety of post-structuralist and post-modernist writers. This
tradition concentrates on tragic loss, it constantly romanticises
the past as a holism, a natural primitivism. For the present it has
little to offer but despair and that from the lofty protected academic heights of assertions of pointlessness and vulgarity.

The third candidate for the resolution of modernity proposed
by Hegel, after religion and art, comes during what has become
known as the Jena period. Prior to writing the *Phenomenology*
Hegel worked, according to Habermas, with principles of reason
based in a kind of free intersubjective consensus, what one might
call the democratic imperative. This is precisely what Habermas
takes as his own point of departure in looking for a solution to
the problems of modernity and it is the focus of the last part of his
book. Habermas is a clear proponent of the necessity of rationality and its centrality to the models from which morality can be
constructed and sustained. As the author of articles such as
Technology and Science as Ideology (1970) he is also a powerful critic of a reified rationality which acts to suppress such morality.

The final candidate arrived at by Hegel, and the one he henceforth retained in the main part of his work, is that outlined in the *Phenomenology*, and the conceptualisation of the absolute which was used to bring that book to a close. It is a concept of rationality, but one which insists, in the idealist sense, that it is a given quality of the world which is to be approached through philosophical appreciation and abstraction. Habermas is fiercely critical of this attempt at a resolution and today it may appear to have relatively little support, given the criticisms which have been made of its translation though Marx into Communism and beyond.

All these issues arise out of the desire to reconcile and resolve the contradictions of modernity. An alternative perspective would, however, accept contradiction as intrinsic. One of the most instructive characterisations of modernity, that by Simmel, takes precisely this position. Simmel (1978) focuses upon one particular manifestation of this contradiction. On the one hand modernity is evident in the desire for abstraction expressed most clearly in money as pure exchange, which gives freedom from tradition and a manipulative ability in creating relations between previously separate spheres of value. But the same imperative gives rise to the opposing desire to retain a sense of the specific value of particular elements in life that had been previously given by their resistance to such abstraction and relativism. Simmel accepts the consequences of this contradiction and the simultaneous negative and positive consequences of the developments in modernity.

As already noted, most anthropologists would baulk at the idea of a specific trajectory of intellectual thought during certain periods of European history becoming generalised into a global historical shift between modern and pre-modern societies. Many ethnographies and histories might reveal comparable concerns with the criteria of legitimacy and the reproduction of culture in other times and places. It is possible, however, to talk of the unprecedented nature of modernity, when it is acknowledged that the continued significance attributed to these debates does not follow solely from their intellectual trajectory. Equally important is the degree to which they prefigure and then coincide with the emergence of tremendous changes in the world, which follow from the sequential industrial, scientific and communication revolutions of the last two centuries. It is these changes which are irrefutably unprecedented. It is they which finally transform the sense of change from something continuous and gradual to something accelerating exponentially, and create an overwhelming sense of the compression of space and time. It is the (selective incorporation of) objective changes in the world which give profundity to the intellectual discussions about the sense of loss, the experience of an extreme presentness and subsequent challenges to criteria of legitimacy.

At this point, the portrayal of an unprecedented contradiction comes into articulation with another still more fundamental source of contradiction that is not only precedented but universal. Even if one rejects the sense of the absolute which Hegel takes as the conclusion of the *Phenomenology*, we might still retain the basic characterisation of the process of human self-creation. I have previously attempted to generalise a version of these ideas around the term 'objectification'.[2] This process, which also has contradiction intrinsic to it, is not specific to modernity but exists in all societies including non-modern ones; it is merely accentuated and takes on a particular form within modernity. Essentially, culture is a process by which humanity creates forms in which it comes to have consciousness of itself and give meaning to itself. These may be historical forces generalised as cultural traditions but also more abstract institutions such as judiciaries or moralities. In so far as these are recognised for what they are, they may be appropriated in humanity's quest for self-understanding and self-creation.

The fundamental contradiction arises from the essential externality and abstraction of culture, which has an intrinsic tendency towards reification such that forces which were developed to enhance human understanding may become instead the reified goal of life and obfuscate and oppress their own creators. In this sense all historical societies are perceived as in some sense 'tragic' and bound in contradiction, Melanesian as much as European, historical as fully as contemporary. This is a potential of all culture but is not a necessary outcome. Neither a tribal elder in seventeenth-century East Africa nor a contemporary middle-class American can be assumed to be beset by a sense of angst or alienation. Either may be satisfied by the manner in which the cultural forms available to them are appropriated towards the moral and social goals of the group within which they live, and we cannot therefore merely presume a sense of loss or alienation.

Objectification is then entirely precedented and nothing new. In modernity, however, as portrayed by Hegel, the process of objectification as it were expands, and the gulf between the products of history and the subjects of history widens and becomes harder to reconcile through appropriation. The knowledge that culture is indeed our own construction becomes more evident and simultaneously more abstract and more difficult to deal with. The self-knowledge that one is modern proceeds through a rupture between the present and the past towards a new temporal consciousness enhanced by a transformation in our productive and communicative abilities.

This particular viewpoint may then merge with the 'classic' characterisations of modernity. For Durkheim, too, the problem is the end of custom, a reflective treatment of traditions which have lost their quasi-natural status. Modernity is the problem posed when morality appears as artifice, and yet is essential to sociality. Equally, one could incorporate Weber with his emphasis on the problem of rationality concretised in bureaucracy, abstraction and in capitalism, the threat of rationality as an iron cage.

If the sense of the unprecedented was claimed with respect to these arguments alone, however, the anthropological critique from relativism would be difficult to avoid. Habermas's version of Hegel might represent an argument with respect to the particular sense of change and academic debates in Central and Western Europe, but would it have any relevance to, for example, the transformation of Islam in South East Asia? Increasingly, academics have balked at the pretensions of a particular European tradition and history being assumed as the relevant account for areas as diverse as Latin America or Japan.

In response to this critique we again turn to the increasingly global nature of objective transformations in the world. This has become much more evident since the time of Hegel. The sense of unprecedented modernity comes from the industrial and scientific revolutions which provide a new consciousness of modernity with novel forms of objectification such that the sense of being modern is constantly reinforced by the 'evidence' of transience and innovation which are taken as characteristic of contemporary life. When we talk of a radical sense of presentness, then today this evokes images of the charity pop concert celebrating the freedom of Nelson Mandela or the television images of the Gulf War. The sense of time (and space) today is of television time (and space) (Wilk 1990), a very possibility of immediacy, and self-consciousness about the importance, artificiality and manipulation of images, which is undoubtedly unprecedented. There is little benefit in attempting to disaggregate the original meaning of theories of modernity from the actual sense we have of them in the knowledge and experience of radical changes in the media of objectification today. It is the combination of all these changes which we are concerned with when we consider the nature of modernity. As such, as long as the academic debate on modernity is grounded in these experiential changes and retains the dynamism that is found in the global environment of modernity, it may be relevant as a self-consciously 'global' academic debate.

Anthropology as an investigative quest could also assist in moving the debate over modernity from the specific trajectory of European traditions to the very distinct development of human societies in areas such as Japan or Brazil and examine key questions as to the balance between global transformations with homogenising consequences as against the localising of new commodities by the particularity given them within specific social and historical contexts. To achieve this role requires ethnography stimulated by a desire to determine the relevance of the characterisation of modernity for the diversity of contemporary experience.

Anthropology is certainly moving in this direction, and this book is likely to be one of several over the next few years which are explicitly concerned with comparative modernities, based in non-European contexts. Ironically, it is Europe itself which has seen conspicuously few attempts to ground the literature on modernity in the lived experience of ordinary populations. The preference has been a leaning towards aesthetic works with the resultant conflation of modernity with modernism. The following section, which attempts to summarise the supposed characteristics of modernity, is therefore in large part a reflection on the implications of theoretical models. I do not wish to imply any endorsement of the positions which will be briefly recounted, merely that these are typical of the kind of traits which writers on modernity who have been influential in anthropology have suggested characterise the modern world. This implies that although we may suppose, for example, that there is a radical compression of space-time consciousness, we may be ignoring the ability of large populations to refuse to have an opinion on the political events of far-off places (e.g. Bourdieu 1984: 397–465 on France), and instead appropriate television into local concerns through their response to particular forms such as soap opera.

Resulting Characteristics of Modernity

Perhaps the most influential book (or at least the most influential title) on modernity in recent years has been Berman's *All That is Solid Melts into Air* (1982). This quotation from Marx forms part of the book's project to emphasise the modernist element in Marx's writing. The spirit which is evoked is one of a systematic tearing at the roots, leaving a humanity in an increasingly unstable, fluid environment, which can be both exhilarating and frightening. On the whole it is the poets and artists such as Baudelaire who are used to describe the experience of living under such conditions. It is they who seem to have been set the task of formulating a perspective on the increasingly fragmentary and ephemeral nature of modern life.

From early on there has been a pronounced ambivalence and contradiction in response to this aspect of modernity. Baudelaire celebrates the new sensations of speed and anonymity but, as with Nietzsche and many others, tempers this with a desire for the event to be articulated with a sense of the eternal and the return. The modernists seem to want to shock with dissonance but are sometimes themselves easily shocked. For example, in a television interview Saul Bellow (1987: 19), a self-consciously modernist author, abhors the actual transience of contemporary teenagers who watch television by channel-hopping rather than following a narrative.

This idea of the spirit of modernity is most commonly articulated with both capitalism on the one hand and modernism on the other. Following Marx it is capitalism which is seen as the destructive force which removes traditional social context and relationships to leave us in an individualised amoral world as mere workers and consumers. Modernism as a movement in the arts is seen as either handmaiden or critic of these transformations. For example, there was a debate of now classic status in Germany in the late 1930s which focused on the proper role of art as both an expression of fragmentation and an attempt to transcend this with images of totality. Both these strategies assumed a given relationship between capitalism and the sense of transience and fragmentation. But while Benjamin and Brecht tried in different ways to evoke fragmentation and artifice, others such as Lukacs looked to realism both to expose the contradictions and provide a healing image of totalities lost (Jameson (ed.) 1977).

Out of this tortuous literature on modernism and aesthetic modernity we may wish to derive some consistent generalisations about modernity as underpinning the experience of ordinary people today. This is difficult since as Habermas notes, 'Nietzsche so directed the gaze of his successors to the phenomena of the extraordinary that they contemptuously glide over the practice of everyday life as something derivative or inauthentic' (1987: 339). Nevertheless an attempt may be made. We are assumed to be living in an increasingly unstable world, with a growing sense of speed and flux. A world whose earlier pretensions to totalities have given way to the experience of fragmentation. Within modernity, the attempt to inject significance into individual events and experiences is mocked by the sheer massivity and diversity in the world. While once it was death alone which mocked our pretensions to accomplishment, now the same derision is faced constantly in life.

Another perspective on these same changes has become grounded in descriptions of the twentieth-century developments in transport and communication. This is summarised as 'the compression of space-time' where everything has become literally more immediate. This concept plays an important role in recent attempts to characterise modernity by academics in Human Geography and Sociology (e.g. Giddens 1981; Harvey 1989) and represents a development of earlier work on the experience of urban life. Such authors link the experiential aspects of these new conditions with the new forms taken by power relations and issues of control.

An attempt to construct a stable sense of identity is held to be constantly undermined by the dynamics of this modern world. The stability of the division of labour is challenged by the industrial and subsequent communication revolutions. Identity is less easily established than in customary labour niches. The constant increase in material culture and its subservience to fashion and transience further undermines the anchoring of identity in possessions and in the visual environment. To cite an example, there are the effects on identity of the increasing importance of

Creolisation. As more people live in migrant status or with complex ancestry (Appadurai 1990) they challenge the imagined community of the nation (Anderson 1983). The growing heterogeneity of their own community is set against increasing awareness of the massivity and homogeneity of the global community (King (ed.) 1991).

These changes in the objective conditions for life are taken as instrumental in creating a variety of unprecedented forms of subjectivity. Campbell (1987), for example, argues that the traditional desires for pleasure and for new goods are transcended (via the effects of the romantic movement) by a quite new form of insatiable desire for new experiences and the restless dissatisfaction with the inability of objects to match up to expectations. One of the most consistent portrayals of the new subjectivity is of a humanity which responds by turning into itself with a new sense of the private. Sennett (1977) traces an historical sequence from a self which is judged by its appearance in public encounters to a sense of an authentic inner self separate from mere appearance but increasingly both the subject and goal of personal interest. The self becomes a refuge of personal idiosyncrasy against the universality of the global form. As portrayed by Lasch (1979) this leads finally to an extreme individualism and personal self-cultivation amounting to a narcissism.

The contributors to a recent volume (Lash and Friedman (eds) 1992) assert a wide variety of consequences for subjectivity in a modernity in which we find ourselves with ever more responsibility for self-creation. They also differ markedly in their moral interpretations of this new subjectivity, from, on the one hand, a celebration of the individual utilisation of a dynamic popular culture to, at the other extreme, despair at the reduction of the subject to a mere instrument in the reproduction of a triumphant capitalist-consumer culture. Relativising anthropology has provided ethnographic detail for a wide spectrum of differing concepts of the individual (or the lack of such as concept) (e.g. Carrithers, Collins and Lukes (eds) 1985), but is more hesitant in providing a portrait of plural forms of individualism within the conditions of modernity (though see Friedman 1992).

Each contributor to the debate tends to focus upon certain elements of this new subjectivity. Giddens (1991), for example, emphasises the element of reflexivity, and the issues of doubt, risk and trust in the construction of relationships, as well as a

brave attempt to point out the serious implications of plural possibilities implied in the term 'lifestyle'. Some books are clear as to
the limitations of these supposed traits. Frosh (1991), for example,
provides a useful survey of the linkages to a specific set of
debates on narcissism and Oedipal processes arising out of psy-
choanalysis. But in most cases there are no such boundaries.

In Hegel's own portrayal of the rise of modernity, a central role
is played by the quest for freedom, and this has maintained its
importance in subsequent accounts. Hegel's own concept of freedom was extremely complex and eschewed the ideal of mere freedom from constraint as something which would often detract
from the more profound sense of freedom as empowerment. In
philosophical discourses the relationship between 'freedom from'
and 'freedom to' continues to play a central role. These complexities are reduced in most accounts of the experience of modernity.
The colloquial expression of freedom emphasises only the narrower sense of freedom from constraints, in particular those historically constituted traditions and moral precepts which are
experienced as a limitation upon the scope of human action.

In the portrayal of modernity as experience, the sense of freedom is constantly reified as a goal in and for itself, and there is a
considerable focus on media such as music and dance which can
be used to express the 'feeling' of freedom. Certain domains have
also been taken as of particular significance in the struggle for freedom. The two paramount arenas that have emerged are first political emancipation in the public sphere, and second the struggle for
free sexuality within the private domain. There are contrastive
academic discourses as exemplified by Foucault (e.g. 1979) who
has excavated a powerful sense of control within what appeared to
be expressions of freedom, but these have impinged little upon the
more general continuing quest for freedom as a kind of purity.
This quest for the free subjective spirit may reinforce the previous
characterisation of individualistic self-absorption when, as Lasch
(1979) argues, we have nothing left to aim for but ourselves.

The next characteristic of modernity has been vividly portrayed as amounting to the 'disenchantment of the world'. The
conventional description is of the inexorable rise of abstraction
and social orders and images based upon abstracted rationalities.
This achieves its prime objectification in two forms: money and
bureaucracy. In both cases the specificity and particularity of
things are reduced in order to ensure absolute commensurability.

These are held as necessary for a new sense of efficiency and equality. All things may be valued against the common yardstick of currency, but by this same process there is a sense that in commodification, value as a qualitative form is reduced. This is part of a general rise of quantity over quality, as time and space also become subservient to efficient systems of planning and communication which reduce them to co-ordinates. The writing on such changes associated with classic figures in the social sciences such as Weber and Simmel is so voluminous and well-established as to require no summary here, merely evocation.

The sense of disenchantment refers to this loss of the qualitative, but also has connotations of the rise of secular society and the decline of metaphorical imagery. All systems of relations based upon the apparent qualities of natural juxtaposition are replaced by encoded knowledge of demonstrable and objective relations in the triumph of science over alchemy, medicine over mythology. There have always been counter instances of increasing religiosity, and at present there is the rise of holistic medicine with associated 'new age' beliefs (e.g. Coward 1989). Such phenomena evoke conflicting views. They might be seen as reactionary last gasps set against the inevitable trend, or alternatively as signs that the modern is finally being superseded by a new pluralist post-modern based on fundamental shifts in the political economy. The one area where there is postulated a more consistent re-enchantment is that of commerce and consumption. Writers from Walter Benjamin (1983) to Raymond Williams (1980) have emphasised the nature of the commodity as a new magical system, associated with concepts of lifestyle that are thought to be quite irreducible to these new abstract rationalities.

In works on modernity, there is considerable consistency in the assumed effect of these various changes, and this differs little whether the problem is seen more in terms of fragmented transience or a dominant techno-rationality. In each case the result is the sense of alienation. There are of course variants of this: the alienated may emerge as a sense of anomie in Durkheim, the blasé in Simmel, or as a general sense of angst and anxiety in the works of a multitude of novelists and film directors. Alienation, however, is assumed to be the quintessential modern condition. Indeed, it is probably the sequence or section where the sense of alienation is clearly evoked that tells one that a film or book is intended to be about the modern condition. I think the word 'assumed' is appropriate here, since although there are many important studies of hysteria, anorexia or, for example, alienation within working-class consciousness of schooling, they have rarely been set within more general ethnographic accounts. In theoretical debates, and in those that refer to post-modernism even more than those that refer to modernism, the sense is that we either live in a constant state of alienation or, if we don't, it is merely evidence for how well we have been duped by the agents of oppression. Quite commonly, consumerism is portrayed as a kind of all-embracing valium, a modern bread and circuses which constitutes the life-world we inhabit to such an extent that we are unable to perceive or fully experience the state of alienation which logically we should be experiencing (e.g. Jameson 1984).

My admittedly very cavalier reading and even more cavalier borrowing from Hegel leads to a rather different conclusion. Alienation is an element in the process of objectification itself, not a necessary implication of the particular modern condition in the world. Within modernity, a large section of society may experience bureaucracies in a Kafkaesque state of uncomprehending passivity, but it is quite possible for bureaucracy to be viewed as the benign arm of egalitarian politics preventing oppressive and hierarchising forces from erupting, as would be the case in much of Scandinavia in the 1960s and 1970s (Fagerberg *et al.* 1990). Similarly cultural dissonance may be experienced as rootless anxiety, but as this ethnography will demonstrate it is quite possible for a group of people, who focus their sense of identity upon strategies of fashion and style, to use these same elements of the modern as their main instrument of identity construction. Mass consumption itself may serve equally well as an instrument for confronting as the medium for creating the sense of alienation (Miller 1987: 178–217). What matters is rather the instruments and resources which are available to a population attempting to appropriate, through empowerment or identification, the institutions and cultural practices which have been thrown up by historical developments. Alienation is most likely to arise through oppressive disempowerment when a population is unable to appropriate those forces through which they are forced to express themselves (e.g. Miller 1985, 1988 for the example of housing).

If the intention of the above section was to evoke a few relatively consistent characteristic features of the modern condition, then it does not appear to be a success. By this stage the portrayal of modernity has become increasingly muddied by apparently contradictory tendencies. How, for example, are we to reconcile a new rational order and bureaucratisation in which things are increasingly related, to a simultaneous rise of fragmentation and sense of the ephemeral? The position becomes still more confused when we appreciate that many of the 'reactions' to modernity have played so major a role as to have to be included in the characterisation of modernity. What, for example, is romanticism – the constant search for images which transcend and reunify? Is this a reaction to, or an exemplification of, modernity? Similarly the constant search for 'roots', the invention and endless elaboration of history, archaeology, symbols of heritage and the manufacture of a sense of the past which become fundamental to all struggles over identity. This seems counter modern but is also clearly a part of the new temporality described earlier on as the starting point for the advent of modernity. Both contemporary religion and history are clearly modern in being inescapably linked to the sense of a secular and ahistorical alternative sense of the present, but they are nevertheless very different responses from the sense of mere ephemera and timelessness evoked in the avant-garde stylistics of the modernists.

The complexity of this issue as addressed today is deepened by the constant desire for self-reflexive critique within the approach associated with the term post-modernism. From this stance, my entire argument so far is merely naïve. The proper starting point should have been a concern with how we came to decide that there was such a thing as modernity, and why we should wish to become involved in creating the apparent object of our enquiry through the classification of experience in terms of a category which we have ourselves devised and elaborated. We would then move from any attempt to characterise and generalise changes in the world to the problem of the 'discourse' of modernity itself and its oppressive or liberating consequences as a discourse. Rather than following this post-modern route I prefer, however, to speculate that the interest in modernity as a discourse is emergent from actual transformations in the world, which give the term salience and create the anxiety over its encompassment. The key issue then is not which came first, the discourse or the experience of modernity, nor the independent effects of a discourse about 'modernity' itself, (i.e. the issue of reflexivity) which would anyway be mainly an effect upon aesthetic and academic élites. Rather more important may be the question as to how we can observe and understand the consequences of a framework for experience that is clearly and increasingly a significant part of all our lives.

Some of these contradictions are simplified by attempts to construct a periodisation of modernity (e.g. Anderson 1984) or the division of modern and post-modern as two periods. This would allow us, for example, to identify the architecture of Le Corbusier as a universalising embodiment of the promise of rationality, which was then superseded by the post-modern architecture which eschews any such pretensions. This clear division is, however, suspect on historical grounds, since all the periods of the modern have seen both universalising and fragmenting goals. The problem of reconciling these contrary characterisations therefore remains. We seem to be able to isolate out specific features and argue that they are either unprecedented or increasingly global in their present form. But we are then commonly faced with the need to discuss other cultural traits with apparently contradictory features which have developed alongside of or in reaction to them. Many of these supposed characteristics may in any case be no more than a claim to global relevance of some regional trait, as when the modernity of Paris is assumed to be more authentic than that of China.

In general, however, we have not subverted the original description by Hegel via Habermas which concentrates on cause as much as consequence. Modernity may not have consistent attributes, but there remains a consistent underlying problem, one in which a new temporal sense has undermined the conventional grounds for moral life. All of these changes may therefore be seen as both exploring the new possibilities opened up, but also as attempts to replace lost certainties with new goals and beliefs, new criteria by which to live, which may either deny their self-construction or celebrate their artificiality. In that sense these various 'traits' may all be understood as potential consequences of what may be retained as a primary model of the condition of modernity.

An Historical Approach to Characterising Modernity

At this stage I will leave this issue in temporary abeyance in order to attempt a brief excursion through history. As an alternative to any attempt to reconcile these contradictory traits, it may be argued that it is contradiction itself which is one of the paramount conditions of modernity. The particular account of the rise of modernity, I wish to emphasise, is one which concentrates first upon this rise of contradiction, but second on its association with the growth of a more extensive material culture. Once again the concern is to find potential analogies with the situation in contemporary Trinidad, in this case the oil-boom, which today carries so much of the burden of the specific consciousness of being modern in Trinidad. It may well be significant that recent work by historians seems to concentrate on the relationship between these two elements: that is, the place of material culture in facilitating the growth of contradiction. The three historical works I wish to consider have a common starting point – the enormously influential argument by Weber on the relationship between capitalism and Protestantism.

The problem faced by all these authors is that the key quality of Protestantism which was held by Weber to be fundamental in the rise of modern capitalism was one which favoured the accumulation of wealth but not its consumption. Indeed, in its most extreme forms of puritanism we find a staunch asceticism which seems most inimical to the rise of modern consumerism. The simplest solution to this problem is provided by Mukerji (1983) who traces the rapid growth of European material culture from the typical medieval paucity as portrayed by, for example, Braudel (1981), through what she calls the early modern period. Mukerji is one of several historians who now date important shifts in the quantitative increase in material culture and also new forms of consumption to a period prior to the industrial revolution (see also McKendrick *et al.* 1983). Mukerji argues for a general rise of materialism: she states: 'Hedonism and asceticism seem, on the surface, contradictory, but they share one feature: an interest in material accumulation. The pure ascetic rationalist of Weberian theory accumulates capital goods, while the hedonist consumer revels in amassing consumer goods' (1983: 4).

A rather more complex argument for the relationship between asceticism and hedonism is provided by Campbell (1987), who places the romantic movement in the pivotal position by which one was enabled to lead into the other. The spiritual and emotional concerns of the puritan are refracted through the new sense of feeling and sentimentality associated with the romantic movement. They thereby develop into the desire for new sensations, which subsequently becomes the motor force behind modern consumerism, with its promise of ever new sensations, which always, once purchased, disappoint.

Out of this trilogy of historians, the most conclusive evidence is, however, provided by the work of Schama (1987). His book *The Embarrassment of Riches* is grounded in what amounts to an historical ethnography of daily life and popular culture in seventeenth-century Amsterdam, brilliantly excavated from pictorial and other sources. While Mukerji attempts to reconcile the two movements of puritanism and hedonism, and Campbell emphasises the historical transmutation of one into the other, Schama appears to portray the contradiction between them as itself entirely sustainable within the complex realities of this new urban life with its massive material culture. Indeed, it seems that material culture itself plays no small role in sustaining this contradiction. The population of Amsterdam is able to move in so many richly elaborated environments, from the domesticity of their home, the public encounter of urban life through to the tavern, the brothel and the church. Each environment allows for both the elaboration of a cultural goal and also its separation from those which would be inimical to it. Although there are many precedents for dualism and cultural contradiction, this period in Amsterdam sees a particularly acute relationship between the rise of both feasting and fasting. This occurs without the kind of direct confrontation portrayed in Pieter Bruegal the Elder's painting *The Battle between Carnival and Lent*. The moral concerns of Calvinism are clearly present as an ideology in which 'the reduction of worldly state and goods to a condition of humility and contrition was the precondition of redemption' (ibid. 33). But this rests alongside the simultaneous elaboration of an unprecedented opulence for the ordinary people of the town employing an unrivalled market for decorative goods and applied arts (ibid. 304). Not surprisingly, there emerges a profound concern with boundaries, as between inside and outside, which might be elaborated in door frames or in the rituals and metaphors of sweeping, important when 'solemnity was never very far away from farce' (ibid. 371). What emerges also is the extraordinary nature of modern life, articulating new abstract principles of rationality and calculation with the most unlikely manifestations. This is most clearly illustrated by the fortunes won and lost in the mania for tulips in the 1630s.

In Schama's account, these burghers were simultaneously developing their sensibilities of diverse and contradictory goals and moralities. These were becoming both abstracted, in the sense of being factored out in new more consistent forms, but also more diverse in that they attend to disparate bodies of objects and aspects of people's lifestyles. This then creates what Schama calls a moral geography. It is as though moral ambivalence runs, rather like the system of canals, through the everyday life of Amsterdam, lapping at both church and tavern. 'As in many other departments of Dutch culture, opposite impulses were harmoniously reconciled in practice ... Nor did it take any lofty wisdom to see that the world was not torn asunder between abstinence and indulgence. Any fool could see that the *same people* embodied, at different times, in different places, the values appropriate to their impermanent role' (ibid. 371).

Schama's work comes closest to the goal of the present work in that it is essentially an ethnographic portrayal of modernity, in which the appropriation of material culture as mass consumption also plays a central role in objectifying contradiction. If we return to the original problem set out through the representation of Habermas and Hegel, we can see contradiction as a likely candidate for the proper representation of modernity. The core dilemma of modernity lies in the consequences of the new temporality: that is, a distinct sense of present, future and past, which leads to an increasing concern with the knowledge of self-construction of the criteria by which we live. Schama certainly echoes these concerns in seventeenth-century Amsterdam, a people constantly alert to the fragility of their fortune, whose religious beliefs did not detract from their awareness of the human endeavour which determined its existence, and the human debate which considered its rectitude. In this work it is clear that modernity is experienced as a dilemma, one which is best responded to through complementary and contradictory strategies, including a simultaneous concern with the demands of a radical sense of the present and the unthwartable demands of eternity. If the structural element, that of contradiction itself, is focused upon, then there are many affinities with theories of modernity more generally. Not only Marx's attempt to make contradiction the motor of history but also Simmel's rather different use of Hegelian ideas on the contradictory effects of liberation and alienation, or even Tonnies who seems to have seen *Gesellschaft* as conterminous with and not a replacement to *Gemeinschaft*.

One final lesson may be taken from this work into the present project. My usage here of this representation of Dutch culture in the

Golden Age should not detract from the constant sense of the specificity of such an ethnographic portrayal. What emerges from the account and indeed is insisted upon by Schama is also the cultural peculiarities of the Dutch – what he calls the mysteries of their temperament (ibid. 3). Turning this particular population into an exemplification of modernity should not reduce our ability to pinpoint cultural particularity. If at a structural level we identify contradiction as a likely prominent dimension of the experience of modernity, this does not allow us to predict how it may be manifested. In another period or place the focus of contradiction may, for example, be more on opposition between totalising and fragmenting impulses or on individualistic versus communal aspirations.

This last point is central to the conclusion of this section. An attempt to characterise modernity should not fall back into a kind of mechanistic logic of stages and functional responses. To be ethnographically or historically grounded means dealing with all those elements of contingency and variability characteristic of humanity which make the social sciences such a fascinating field of enquiry. The point of arguing that there are certain shifts which have expanded to such an extent that it is meaningful to talk of them as global, is not to suggest that there has been some kind of world homogenisation. Indeed, a proposition sustained throughout the text which follows is that modernity has left us with as strong a tendency towards heterogeneity in culture as ever. It is useful, however, to argue for elements of commensurability, and against the extreme relativism common in anthropological enquiries, in order to make this case-study, from its inception, a contribution towards comparative enquiry.

This chapter is therefore not intended as some kind of blueprint for an investigation of contemporary Trinidad. Indeed, the intention of an ethnography juxtaposed to an account of modernity is as much to challenge the suppositions and generalisations made in these debates as to illustrate them. Clearly some relevance is asserted, otherwise the effect would be merely one of relativistic critique, which should remain only one of the various advantages of using anthropological accounts. The ethnography which follows is written up in such a manner as to suggest that there is indeed a foundational contradiction evident in contemporary Trinidad which is directly analogous to that rupture in temporal consciousness discussed by Habermas. Furthermore, the following chapters include a considerable amount of material on matters such as freedom, transience and individualism which do relate back to the traits which may be argued to derive from this condition of modernity. But the particular configurations of these as they appear in an ethnography are quite unprecedented and do not correspond to any prior characterisation of modernity. Indeed, one of the main points that is asserted throughout this book is that while a consideration of modernity helps account for the ethnographic findings, modernity is not a homogenising process as often thought.

Trinidadians have responded through many acts of creative appropriation and transformation to those circumstances which are comparable to European historical events. The result often challenges the generalisations made about topics such as freedom and individualism by producing quite distinctive forms and consequences not necessarily anticipated in theoretical debates. Furthermore, the main grounds for arguing that Trinidad is indeed a relevant case-study for this particular characterisation will be one that neither Hegel nor Habermas would have considered of particular importance. As will be made clear in the conclusion to this book (though illustrated through material presented in earlier chapters), it is with the arrival of mass consumption that the extent to which Trinidad is clearly dependent upon both imported goods and images becomes clear. It is at this point that Trinidadians have most clearly to face up to the need for alternative criteria by which to judge themselves than those which can be said to derive from unreflective custom. In short, the advantages of an ethnographic approach to modernity are intended to be derived from a two-way process. Both descriptive ethnography and theoretical debates on modernity may be challenged by and also interpreted in relation to each other.

Notes

1. The use of this term is derived from Bourdieu (1977). A discussion of its limitations with respect to the present ethnography may be found later in this book.

2. The attempt within a paragraph to explain what is meant here by the term objectification is inevitably cryptic. There exists a much more sustained development of this term in Miller 1987: 19–82. This resulted in a rather particular view of its potential use in relation to modernity, only partially overlapping with the use of the term by other theorists or more colloquially. Similarly it is this earlier account which defines the manner by which terms such as 'alienation' are shifted from the more traditional 'Marxist' usage towards a more 'Hegelian' sense of the inevitability of that tendency towards both self-alienation and reification within human culture.

Chapter 3

Christmas, Carnival and Temporal Consciousness

In a study of Christmas and Carnival on St Vincent, Abrahams (1983: 98–108), following the example of Geertz, argues that such festivals should be seen: 'neither as an aesthetic alternative to life nor as a direct reflection of reality, but as a stylized rendering of some of the central expressive and moral concerns of the group' (ibid. 98–99). Following his analysis of speech-making and song, Abrahams goes on to suggest that Christmas may be related to those values which Wilson (1973: 215–36) termed 'respectability'. These assert religious observance, family continuity and the centrality of the home, order and tradition. A contrast is then made with Carnival which is the time of 'rudeness', that is, of licentious and disorderly activities. The implication of this analysis is that St Vincentian culture incorporates two opposed sets of normative values whose ideals are expressed with particular clarity in the form of festivals. Although there will be a number of differences in my assessment of what is being expressed, in the main my interpretation of the materials presented in this chapter will follow along similar lines. A detailed description of Christmas and then of an aspect of Carnival will be used to explore the possibility that in Trinidad also there are two central, but opposed, expressive and moral concerns which achieve particular clarity in festivals.

It will be argued below that historically there was much less of a clear-cut division in the expressive connotations of these festivals. Recent years have seen an acceleration of this opposition between them, though there is still some leakage. At the heart of the distinction between the festivals lies two forms of temporal consciousness. Carnival will be seen to objectify the very idea of an event and the sense by which transience expresses an ideal of freedom. Christmas, on the other hand, acts to transcend the vicissitudes of the present for an image of an unchanging line of descent. The contrast is pivoted upon the concept of 'bacchanal' introduced in the descriptive section of Chapter 1. The implication of this representation of Carnival and Christmas is that Trinidadian culture is based upon contradiction, in this case between the sense of 'transient' time and 'transcendent' time.

Christmas

A description of the festival of Christmas also provides an obvious starting point for a study of the impact of mass consumption in Trinidad, in as much as Christmas has become recognised as the key festival of consumerism, the climax of yearly expenditure, which often dominates the annual budget. The relationship between Christmas and commerce has become a world-wide phenomenon, but in Trinidad this relationship takes on a very specific character with implications for the particular nature of Trinidadian consumerism.[1]

When Trinidadians present themselves to the outside world, it is Carnival which is given pride of place, since Trinidad sees itself, alongside Rio, as the exemplar of contemporary Carnival. In the annual rhythm of Trinidadian life, however, it is clear that Christmas is viewed with a comparable degree of affection. Christmas is also the culmination of a crescendo of preparations that suggest its considerable importance. Trinidadians often present Carnival as the festival of national unity when 'all ah we is one' but, in practice, Carnival contains a powerful divisive element: a significant proportion of Trinidadians have no desire to take part in any of its associated activities and consider it immoral. By contrast, it is Christmas that acts most clearly to unify virtually the entire gamut of this heterogeneous society. The only exceptions would be a few of the more fundamentalist churches who treat Christmas as a secular abomination. In general, Hindus and Moslems celebrate Christmas with an intensity which is undifferentiated from that of Christians, though Hindus increasingly justify their participation by treating it as a continuity with the Hindu festival of Divali.

It is Divali that signals the beginning of the season of festivals in the Trinidadian calendar, while Christmas, in turn, marks the beginning of preparations for Carnival. These festivals are not merely special occasions which intrude upon ordinary life. The use of the term 'reality' by Abrahams in the above quotation is rather misleading as it implies that ordinary life is somehow bracketed off from such celebrations. In Trinidad, at least, Christmas and Carnival, together with their associated preparations, dominate a period of several months, and the saving up of resources for Christmas, in particular, may begin almost as soon as the last festive season has finished. Christmas and Carnival occupy a central place in the lives of many Trinidadians, such that the rest of the year could almost be viewed as the necessary rest, or breathing space, before the country gears itself up for the next festive season.

Decorating the House

The period prior to Christmas is marked by three closely related activities: shopping, cooking and cleaning the house. House interiors in Trinidad are almost invariably immaculate throughout the year. Despite this, in the fortnight before Christmas, when walking along the street, one invariably finds piles of furniture outside the house, for example, in the front porch, as the interior is swept, dusted and 'cobwebbed'. Not every household repaints every year, but if the householders are intending to repaint the house at all that year, then this is the period in which they will do it. Ideally, the entire inside and outside is repainted, more usually the rooms with most wear and tear such as the kitchen and porch area. Householders stand proud and conspicuous with paintbrush in hand if visitors arrive during the period. Paint retailers note minor increases in their sales marking the festivals of Eid, Divali and the season for new houses, but thanks to Christmas, December sales amount to two to three times those of other months.

A similar situation exists with regard to furniture. For most of the year the Chaguanas car upholsterers work only on vehicles, but in some cases they completely cease this work from the start of November in order to deal with domestic reupholstering. One upholsterer noted that he would like to follow this pattern, but in practice, people only decided to make this expenditure at the last moment. He is then flooded with requests in late December to re-upholster suites of furniture which he cannot possibly finish in time for Christmas. Furniture retailers were among the most assertive about it being hardly worth their while opening shop for the rest of the year, since the bulk of their sales take place specifically for Christmas. Typically, householders who were asked, as part of one of my surveys, about the origins of their house furnishings, noted that, for example, the dining suite, a tablecloth, a sink drainer, some table mats and a set of plates were purchased the previous Christmas, the couch set and some orna-ments, the Christmas before that, until there was hardly an item which was not associated with Christmas shopping.

Although Trinidadians are aware of the stress on gift-giving as the key form of Christmas expenditure in other countries such as the United States, both wholesalers and retailers in gift items con-firmed that the giving of gifts is a small element of expenditure compared to spending on new items for one's own home. Toys purchased for children are an exception here. One major importer noted that December accounts for 80 per cent of annual toy sales. For the gift shops, it is glassware, artificial flowers and items used for furnishing and interior decoration which are the main focus of December sales. Gifts are given between close relatives and are exchanged by older school children and close friends, but these are generally small items. Gifts are not only conceived of as objects purchased for others; the concept also encompasses often rather more expensive items which many people purchase for themselves. Christmas may be the occasion for finally purchasing that dress or those trainers which had been coveted for some time. It is the house, however, rather than the person which is the main recipient of Christmas shopping. The major expenditures, often planned for a considerable period, and aided by hire-pur-chase schemes, are on items such as upholstered couch sets or dining suites. Ideally, the housewife puts money aside week after week during the rest of the year, in order to save for the special expenditures of Christmas, or alternatively uses the 'sou sou' for the purpose of Christmas saving.

Estimates of costs come from a survey[2] of forty households (ten from each fieldwork area). This was carried out in 1988 and there are some problems in generalising from that year.[3] For those who attempted to estimate their total expenditure on items relating specifically to the celebration of Christmas, an average of $289 TT[4] (N=29) was spent on drinks, $554 TT (N=32) was spent on food-stuffs and $320 TT (N=23) was spent on gifts. It is more difficult to estimate expenditure on household items, since much of this is done at other times and then brought out for Christmas, but immediate recollection of expenditure on items such as paint, cur-tains and new outfits gave a figure of $840 TT (N=25), although this is certainly lower than actual expenditure. Overall expendi-ture in the four areas is associated with differences in household monthly income with Ford averaging $1,225 TT, Newtown $1,473 TT, St Pauls $2,313 TT and The Meadows $3,226 TT.

The preparations for Christmas become a focal point of discus-sion as well as activity. A typical seasonal radio phone-in consist-ed of the interviewer telephoning housewives to discuss with them the measures they were taking for that year's Christmas and any special tips about painting and cooking that might be passed on to the listeners. Each housewife would report on which rooms were being repainted and which Christmas foods were being prepared for that year. The newspapers develop a crescen-do of emphasis on the special nature of Christmas with a focus on these same domestic activities. In one of his numerous pieces on Christmas, dialect poet Paul Keens-Douglas (1975: 53–64) takes the perspective of an old-time domestic:

Lord Miss Julie, dis Christmas go' kill me,
Ah don't know why dem people feel
Dey must put up new curtain an' cushion cover
Every Lord living Chrismus ...
De woman cleanin' house since November
Like she married to Fadder Chrismus.

One element in the decoration of the house interior are items such as holly, Santa Claus and paper festoons, in white, scarlet and green, which belong to an international range of Christmas symbols. Twenty households from the survey had Christmas trees (almost all artificial), mainly in the living room or porch areas. Several of the others noted that there were no children in the home to warrant a tree that year. Christmas cards are dis-played, depending upon income, since the average Ford house-hold had sent or received less than one card per household, while in the Meadows this rose to fifteen per household.

There was a desire, expressed mainly by élite groups, to localise Christmas and provide Trinidadian equivalents to imports. The media was constantly asserting the value of developing a truly Trinidadian Christmas. A few households did promote local symbols, such as the poinsettia plant, which flowers at this season and which could provide a local source of red symbolism. One instance was found of an artificial poinsettia (a plant now colonising northern countries at Christmas) being used as a replacement symbol to the conifer tree, but this was in The Meadows where the occupant had obtained a degree in Canada. Similarly, there were many radio items suggesting local replacements for the apples and grapes, whose importation had been banned that year. A newspaper headline advised 'Pawpaw, cashew and melon rinds for Christmas fruit cake'. But when I asked during the survey if people had tried or considered trying such a strategy, the result was almost entirely negative and the relevant media items were disparaged as typical 'chupidness' (stupidity).

Such Christmas decorations are in the main much less important (indeed in many cases tokenistic) compared to the work done on the ordinary furnishings of the house, which will not be put away after Christmas, including the replacement of worn items or the unpacking of new ones. Most labour expended in the period leading up to Christmas is devoted to having the home interior looking immaculate. The work is dominated by the female members of the household, but this is a time of year when men are also expected to take their domestic responsibilities seriously, and many men who at other times are free to escape domestic chores and slip away to drink with their friends (Andy Capp is a long-long-running cartoon in the Trinidadian press) are at this time of year strongly reminded of their domestic duties, particularly with regard to house-painting and chair revarnishing.

The climax to these domestic preparations is Christmas Eve. It is then that the presentation of the house interior becomes most clearly ritualised, in the sense of being framed off, from its mundane equivalent. The normative ideal is that the family stay up late into the night, completing their house-cleaning and decoration as well as their baking. Almost all households who participated in Christmas did stay up. In St Pauls among the Indian population who tend to retire early in daily life, this might be only until around 11:00 p.m. but in the three other areas the majority stayed up till after midnight and a quarter of these till 3:00 a.m. or later.

In this, as in many other activities, 1988 was seen by participants as very low key, and there were many stories of Christmases where couples had stayed up the whole night, often inviting neighbours in to 'lime' with lively accompanying music. In Newtown and Ford in particular, the beating of bottles with spoons to the sound of the newly released calypsos accompanies the tidying and decorating. This is the time when any new items, such as towels or a new stereo system, should be unpacked and brought out for use.

There is also a clear closing ritual to these activities, which is the hanging out of the curtains. Of all the elements of home decoration, it is curtains which are most closely associated with Christmas. Again, retailers confirmed this tendency, in this case arguing that December sales amount to around eight times a normal month. In the survey, eighteen households noted that, despite the recession, they had purchased at least one new curtain that Christmas. A further thirteen had used the occasion to change to a different set of curtains from their stock, while most of the remainder had merely washed and replaced their curtains. The oil-boom may have transformed a tradition of changing curtains to one of buying new ones. Given the number of households who managed to be in the middle of hanging curtains as I visited their homes on Christmas evening, the activity is clearly extended in time for as long as possible. Once the new curtains are up, this is commonly felt to be both the climax, and the end, of the task of preparing one's home.

Overall the intensity of this work establishes that it is in many ways the home itself, the physical environment for 'inside' life, which is the object of Christmas celebrations. For several weeks, most of the household members are feverishly engaged in experiencing the physicality of their home in a manner which changes their relationship to it. In England, by contrast, where 'spring cleaning' is a far less extensive activity, it is probably only when moving home that such a comprehensive attempt to restore all components of the home interior is made, thereby bringing back into focus the minutiae of furnishing which otherwise so readily become the taken-for-granted background to domestic life.

In Trinidad, the Christmas decorations are clearly secondary to the focus upon ensuring the presentability of all aspects of the home itself, whether towels have worn thin, the flooring is inadequate, some paint has been chipped away and so forth. As, however, in the notion of the 'domestic', the physical environment is inseparable from the social values to which it is host, and the implications of this house decoration may be extended by examining, in turn, the use of food and the pattern of visiting.

Food and Drink

When the concept of 'Trini' Christmas is elaborated, as in the songs which are released especially for the period, food and drink are the focus of celebration. The most popular Christmas song for 1988, which was called 'Trini Christmas', told of taking a man from the nearby island of Margarita and giving him *punch a crem*, sorrel,[5] ham and ginger beer, etc. until he admitted that 'Trini Christmas is the best'. In the weeks before Christmas, housewives prepare a formidable array of food and drink, which are associated specifically with the Christmas season. These drinks include those purchased and those made at home. In the former category, householders buy 'sweet drink' such as cocacola, beer by the case, and bottles of rum. In the oil-boom, this last had been replaced by considerable quantities of whisky, but by 1988 whisky was confined to The Meadows. The special purchase of sweet drinks and rum was often referred to nostalgically when talking about Christmas during one's childhood. In the survey, thirty households purchased rum, twenty-five beer and nine whisky. All but one purchased at least some sweet drinks, and in nine cases, this included the relatively expensive Peardrax which is viewed as the most appropriate sweet drink for celebrations (sometimes explicitly as a champagne substitute). The quantity of drinks purchased is obviously dependent upon wealth. In Ford there were households who marked Christmas with the purchase of two litres of sweet drink, and who would be unable to buy such drinks at other times of the year. By contrast, there were households who purchased half a dozen cases of sweet drink and many bottles of rum but where it was the whisky which connoted the special seasonal expenditure, although many may have hoped that the more expensive items, such as whisky, would last well beyond Christmas.

In the survey, the production of homemade drinks is dominated by sorrel, which many householders grow in their yard. Thirty households made their own sorrel that year, while twenty-four made homemade ginger beer. Often mentioned as special for Christmas is a drink made with the strong puncheon rum, condensed milk and eggs called *punch a crem*, made by eight households that year, while four produced homemade wine (popular among Rasta) and two made a rum punch. These drinks are especially significant since, apart from wine and rum punch, it is rare for any of them to be made at any other time.

Christmas is generally regarded as a meat-eating festival. In the Christmas survey no household was found that had not prepared meat, despite the degree of vegetarianism claimed by many Indian families during the main survey. Most popular was chicken with thirty-six households, then pork with twenty, and ham with fifteen, followed by duck, beef, goat and turkey. In nearly half the households at least three different kinds of meat had been prepared. The most common accompaniments were rice, salad, pigeon peas with rice and, most popular of all, macaroni pie in twenty-nine cases. Chinese foods such as fried rice and Indian foods such as *dhalpuri* were also common preparations. Christmas is also associated with baking and twenty-six households had made 'black' cake,[6] twenty-eight had baked some other kind of cake such as sponge, and nineteen had made a sweet bread.[7] In other years, households would invariably purchase at least a token amount of apples and grapes.

Out of these foods it is important to distinguish those, such as pigeon peas and stewed chicken, which are a repetition of everyday fare, from those which, as with sorrel, ginger beer and *punch a crem*, among the drinks, are symbolic of Christmas. Among the foods, special significance is attached to the preparation of ham and of a meat pasty called a *pastelle*. In fact *pastelles* were only made by eight households, though others make these in quantity and sell or give them to their neighbours. There is a similar attachment to the making of 'black cake'. These (together with apples and grapes) are the items which are constantly referred to as making for a 'proper' Christmas.

The significance of items such as *pastelles* is that they are associated with the Spanish traditions of Trinidad (and especially with those regions which have been settled by immigrants from Venezuela). As such, they are related to another key symbol of Christmas which is the *parang* music. This consists of small groups of musicians with instruments such as the cuatro and the box bass, who with accompanying singers perform traditional

Christmas songs in Spanish. Traditionally these were men (and some women) travelling from house to house on Christmas evening, and the term *parang* is said to derive from the Spanish *parranda*, a term for carousel groups (Taylor 1977). In 1988 *parang* had become more closely associated with the competitive playing of more established groups, culminating in a grand competition, although only three households had actually been to see *parang*, and this was at the local mall. The singers often cannot understand the content of their songs and *parang* is not played at any other time of the year, but for this period it briefly dominates the radio. Within the household Christmas music is more likely to be based around homemade instruments such as bottle and spoon or Afro metal spiked comb, brushed against cheese-grater. These are used to accompany the newly launched calypso/soca tunes, also being played on the radio at this time. Nevertheless, *parang* music has a distinct edge as symbolically evocative, especially of some past period when it was itself more common.

Social Activities

This sense of an older established Trinidad, with a more powerful feeling of community and social sharing, is re-established in the pattern of social interaction which characterises contemporary Christmas celebrations. Both the preparations of food or drink and the cleaning out of the house are intended to serve two purposes. In the first instance they provide the setting for the meal of Christmas day which is increasingly viewed as an intensely private celebration for the immediate family. This meal takes the best of the prepared edibles, including the expensive items such as apples, grapes and meats, and utilises the home at its most pristine. The family is the clear focal point of Christmas activities. A feature in the *Express* on 20 December 1988 asked twenty celebrities for a few sentences to express their feelings about Christmas. Of these sixteen mentioned the family, ten the food, six the gifts, five religious activities and four its special nature for children. In general they stress the ideal of relaxing for the day within the home and family environment. This extended luncheon is intended as a quiet interlude between the feverish preparations and the beginning of intensive house visiting. In a country where loudspeakers in cars, houses and shops provide a continual backdrop to daily life, Christmas morning is probably the quietest time of the year.

Boxing day represents the beginning of a period when people may be expected to drop in without invitation or through formal arrangement (though for some this begins on Christmas afternoon). Such visiting is most intensive up to Old Year's Night[8] but in practice 'Christmas' visiting continues for three weeks and more. The survey took place in the middle of this visiting period so it does not reveal the total pattern. But at the time the question was asked, most households had already both visited relatives and had been visited by them. This had so far involved an average of nearly six households of relatives in the Indian case and just over three in the case of non-Indians. With respect to unrelated neighbours and friends (taking just those people they had been visited by) the average was four and a half households for Indians and just under four households for others. Such visiting varies from the perfunctory, by neighbours who feel they are merely following an established obligation, to the use of Christmas for family and friends to reestablish connections which had been in danger of becoming lost. In all cases, the visitor is expected to partake in the special foods which have been prepared and, at the very least, have a piece of cake and an accompanying drink. The food, and more particularly the drink, which accumulates through these successive visits help contribute to a general expansive, festive and immensely hospitable conviviality for this season.

In addition to the visiting by relations, friends and neighbours, Christmas seems to be the only time of the year when it is expected to recognise one's work context through inviting colleagues back home. Many Trinidadians compartmentalise their occupation-related friends and activities and prefer to sustain a considerable distance between work and residence. Even where males lime or party with work colleagues, they clearly prefer to do so in the company of women other than their 'inside' woman (wife or common-law partner) who would represent home life. During Christmas, however, it is common for work colleagues to visit, sometimes through relatively formal arrangements, based upon successive visits as a group to their respective homes. This generally takes place quite late in the season, after relatives have completed their Christmas visiting.

Christmas is recognised at work itself by pre-Christmas parties which expanded greatly during the oil-boom. This probably followed global normative patterns established by multinational companies, though Christmas also vied with 'crop-over' time for traditional festivities in the local sugar plantations. Around a third of those in Newtown, The Meadows and St Pauls had attended such parties. Similar parties may also be held at schools, government institutions, residential areas and churches, though in Ford the only parties attended were local house or children's parties.

Men at Christmas

Most of the activities which have been described as specific to Christmas, the intensive preparations of food, drink and the house refurbishing, are associated with the labour of women. The ambiguous place of men in contemporary Christmas was illustrated for me by the events on one Christmas Eve. I had been visiting households to witness the crescendo of activities by which house interiors (which had seemed already to have been rendered immaculate by weeks of labour) were, once again, being completely rearranged and reordered for this final bout of cleaning, an activity punctuated by drinking and dancing, or beating bottle and spoon when one of the most favoured of the new calypsos was played on the radio. In one of the houses the man decided to use my presence as an excuse for leaving the remainder of this work to his wife, in order to take me out liming. Men generally are fond of finding excuses to escape from domestic chores, but this individual was particularly chuffed at having found a route to extricate himself from these irksome duties.

Ironically, after picking up a liming partner, we then drove to the house of his deputy (mistress). The status of the deputy will be discussed below, but at least one variant of this institution consists of a husband with an outgoing and sophisticated wife, who establishes a second home with a woman who is more domesticated and 'devoted' than his wife. Indeed, compared to his own home, which was relatively sparsely furnished, the home of the deputy was a virtual shrine to the paraphernalia of domesticity. The living-room contained plush (long-haired) carpet and upholstery, 'space-savers' (equivalent to the English 'what-not') crammed full of glazed ornaments such as eagles, stallions, lions and swans, large brass plates with scenes of merchants at taverns, stuffed animals, dozens of china plates with homilies such as the Lord's prayer, a statue of Jesus in an enclosed glass case, among many other religious items, along with cascades of artificial flowers.

Having arrived, the men immediately set to work on all those activities which they had claimed they were escaping from, in particular, the ritual of unpacking objects, which had been purchased at different times during the year, but then saved to be brought out for Christmas Eve. In this case this included a new fan and a new stereo system. After this they became involved in putting up the new curtains.

There is a sense, then, in which the pure male project of freedom from the domestic world cannot be realised at Christmas. Paul Keens-Douglas (1979: 45–54) has a short play, to this effect, written for the media at Christmas. Called *Ah Pan for Christmas* it argues the non-viability of the lifestyle of the hard steelbandsman (who might be seen as the quintessence of 'transience', for which, see below) at this time of year. It begins with the lines: 'Fargo was in ah bad mood. It was Christmas Eve, an' he hated Christmas Eve. Because dat was de one time ah year he used to feel like nobody eh like he. Because Fargo didn't have no family to like he.' The play continues with a mysterious figure telling Fargo to find some family where he could visit, and ends with him being welcomed into the home of a distant aunt.

Once the home is prepared, however, men are expected to play their part as the recipients of the prepared hospitality. Traditionally this becomes the quintessential lime in which a male visits another at his home, they drink for a while and then both leave to visit a third. The result is a snowballing of increasing numbers of men drinking their way through successive homes. On each occasion they may well play music, ideally *parang* (mainly in certain rural areas), in practice often bottle and spoon. This has become a much-loved Trinidadian tradition, but in 1988 it seemed to have severely declined as a spontaneous activity. It was mainly practised in The Meadows where, in at least two areas, groups of men conducted this pattern of house-visiting, but this had been planned for weeks beforehand and was clearly a deliberate recreation of tradition.

One of the effects (or causes) of this decline in specifically male-orientated activity is that women have begun to take a more active part in the visiting of other people's homes and in taking on the role of guest, rather than merely host. They are then able to admire and compare the Christmas preparations of other women, but also to take some respite from a situation where traditionally they carried out most of the work, but had access to relatively little of the leisure activities.

The Church

As in many other countries, the religious side of Christmas is muted. Of the seventeen Christian households in the survey for Ford and Newtown only two had been to church during the Christmas period, both on Christmas day. Some of the Indian Christians from The Meadows had been to midnight mass and a few households contained individuals who participated in the church choir or singing carols, but carol singing is far less conspicuous than *parang* on the media. Midnight mass may well have declined in the face of the rituals of housework and many people seemed to see Old Year's Night as a more important church service than those associated with Christmas. Church leaders will present Christmas messages to the people but these are more often read in the media than heard in church.

There is, however, a general consensual feeling that the values which are being expressed through Christmas celebration are congenial with the teachings of the church, and the church is much involved in the season of preparations. One section of The Meadows is attempting to re-establish the time-honoured tradition of the crèche, and in 1988 this was set up in one of the open spaces, together with a tree and lights. On the evening of its consecration, there was singing by groups from the local churches alongside parang players made up from local residents and their relatives. Once again, it is the shopping malls which take over some of these functions, as they almost invariably have established a crèche, consecrated with formal blessings, and they also sponsor carol groups to entertain shoppers.

Indians at Christmas and Divali

In many respects contemporary Christmas has become the most significant festival for non-Christians in Trinidad but its significance may have distinctive qualities, especially for Hindus. It is a significance that tends to be denied by Hindus, many of whom would dispute the account I present here, while others are increasingly using the festival of Divali as a cover for their involvement in Christmas-centred activities. Officially the state has in recent years been promoting a triad of festivals, Divali for Hindus and Eid for Muslims to balance Christmas. In practice, however, there are important differences, not the least of which is that Divali and Eid remain important religious festivals in the sense that certain religious rituals and duties are central to them. Given the relatively small percentage of Muslims and the fact that their festival does not form part of the winter season, the celebration of Eid does not seem to impinge upon the meaning of Christmas. Divali, by contrast, which comes only a short time before Christmas and, in the Chaguanas area, involves the majority of the population, is of central significance in defining how Hindus relate to Christmas.

A survey was conducted of twenty-five households at Divali, ten each from The Meadows and St Pauls and five from Ford. In terms of religious activities, eight households had visited a temple during this period, almost all had conducted at least a rudimentary Lakshmi *puja* (prayers to the goddess to whom the festival is dedicated) and four had included additional *puja*, five had used an official priest and therefore put up a *jhandi* (flag) to mark the occasion, and all households also offered *deyas* (lighted oil lamps) to the souls of the dead. Five had also been to the more elaborate prayer meetings, known as Ramayana *Yagna*, during this period. With respect to other activities, all but two had visited the *Divali Nagar* (see below); nine had visited on more than two occasions. Apart from those who lit only five deyas because of a recent death in the family, most households lit between sixty and 300 *deyas* and would have spent around $50 TT, including the oil.

Second only to the religious element is the association of this festival with purely Indian values and traditions. One demonstrable element of this is the homogeneity of foods regarded as particular to Indians. Out of the twenty-five households the following foods were prepared by at least ten: *barfee, chana aloo, chataigne, dhal, dhalpuri, kachowree, karhee, khurma, kuchila, ladoo, phoolowree, pomseetay,* pumpkin, rice, *saheena,* sweet rice. The development of *Divali Nagar*, a fair held in the parking lot of a

Chaguanas mall, has become the major festival of Indian culture for the whole of Trinidad. It incorporates stalls which promote religious, cultural and commercial organisations and celebrate events such as the arrival of the first Indians to Trinidad and the resurgence of their music and cultural pursuits.

In recent years Divali has come to be seen as the appropriate occasion for a number of activities that are in effect crossing over from Christmas celebrations. For example, there is the promotion of gifts to children at Divali, and the emergence of a tradition that items for the home should be purchased for Divali. Some households asserted that this was their practice, although others acknowledged their preference for Christmas as the appropriate occasion. Most, however, were prepared to accept Divali as the beginning of that period of home preparation which culminates in Christmas. Four households purchased new curtains for Divali, while all the others changed their curtains. It is considered auspicious to wear new clothing and nine households claimed that at least the children had done so. This was also a popular time to buy new wares for the kitchen or to use new towels.

In conversation Hindus claim that such practices are now concentrated upon Divali rather than Christmas. This is, however, consistently denied by retail outlets. Shopkeepers note a common pattern, with sales to Hindu Indians increasing at Divali compared to other periods, but this being a minor increase compared to that associated with Christmas. The exception was a shop which specialised in lights and light fitments where sales were dominated by Divali, which is the festival of lights. Most households, however, would change curtains at Divali as well as at Christmas.

The focus of Divali celebrations is both the home and simultaneously the public sphere. Most of contemporary Hinduism is home-centred, and both the ordinary *puja* and the occasional Ramayana *yag* are held within one's own home. Compared to Christian attendance at church, Hindu attendance at public temples is much more sporadic, given the overall degree of religious observance. On Divali, however, although the lighting of *deyas* may start within the home, the emphasis of the festival is in the *deyas* that are displayed outside one's own home. These, in turn, blend into the increasing interest in public displays of *deyas* on open spaces by the community at large. In many village communities the sides of whole streets are ablaze, while in others a public space, such as a sports field, is festooned with elaborate sculptures in bamboo representing temples or *Om* signs, which are then covered in deyas to light up in the shape represented.

Divali shares with Christmas an expectation of visiting, though the survey suggests that this custom is less well-established than at Christmas. Most households had been visited by family members but usually only one or two. For some this has become an occasion for feeding one's Creole friends and neighbours. Indeed two households noted over thirty such visitors. However, nine households had only one or no visitors in this category, while others, with more visitors, received only other Hindu Indians. The custom that is more usually established is the distribution of *prasad* to neighbours and others. Prasad is food which has been previously offered to the deity, and, in practice, is a sweet wheaten mixture with added dried fruits. Commonly the children carry small bags of *prasad* around the neighbourhood. Estimates suggested an average of thirty bags were given out per household, only two of the twenty-five Hindu households claiming not to have participated in this.

The events surrounding Divali form the background to the Hindu involvement in Christmas. Earlier accounts, such as by Klass (1961), make clear that the Hindu involvement in Christmas preceded the contemporary advocacy of Divali as the core symbolic festival for Indian Trinidadians. Just as there is a degree of synthesis, with Divali being promoted to take over some of the elements of Christmas celebration, so there is also an emerging set of distinctions between the two festivals. Where Divali is accentuated as the festival of religious Hinduism and the internally bounded category of Indian identity, Christmas is increasingly celebrated as a festival of indulgence and of an expansive identification with wider elements of being Trinidadian.

The contrast between the two festivals emerges most clearly from three elements: eating meat, drinking alcohol and spending money. The practice of abstinence is central to the experience of religiosity for Trinidadian Hindus and is associated with the performance of all religious duties. It takes the specific form of refraining from meat, alcohol and sexual activities, although informants suggested that while all these are claimed, the last is only attended to by the most orthodox. The abstinence associated with Divali is of particular importance; all the households surveyed claimed to have observed it for periods ranging from a day to a month, with the most common claim being for two weeks. By contrast, at Christmas, all the Hindu families in the survey had eaten at least one form of meat. Strict vegetarians such as *pundits* would not eat meat, even at Christmas, but it seemed to be the case that some families who were mainly vegetarian saw Christmas as the one occasion upon which they would eat meat. Furthermore, families who normally eat meat but tend to see pork or ham as forbidden foods (which, surprisingly, is nearly as often the case with Hindus and Christians as it is with Muslim Indians) may well have these meats at Christmas.

The same shift occurs in relation to alcohol. The most orthodox will not drink at Christmas, but many who are teetotal for the rest of the year see Christmas as the one occasion on which they will take a drink. A number of households stated that it was only around Christmas that they would allow alcohol in the house. This was illustrated by the stories of people who had given up drinking, especially in relation to a drink problem, but where Christmas drinking had precipitated a relapse back into heavy drinking. Perhaps the most striking of the three shifts is, however, in relation to spending. One of the central elements of Indian self-differentiation from non-Indians derives from the sense of their thrift and opposition to extravagance, except as applied to appropriate occasions, such as weddings. For Christmas, however, the retailers see Indians as out-spending their African neighbours in providing for their home at Christmas, and several housewives seemed to feel that this comparative extravagance was a kind of sanctioned licence.

Many Indians saw a conviviality associated with Christmas celebration and visiting as a relaxation from the ordinary relative solemnity. Such terms have to be understood comparatively. Even the highly religious and self-consciously traditional Indian household would seem anything but solemn compared to the average secular North or Central European household, but there is a certain gravity by comparison with the more secularised elements of Trinidadian society. Christmas is spoken about as a time of release and indulgence. For all the joy and excitement associated with lighting up at Divali, this does not implicate a sense of release or freedom. In addition, precisely because Divali is bound up with that aspect of identity subsumed in being Indian, the festivities of Christmas are used to express the more general sense of being Trinidadian (for which see the analysis of 'Spanish' ethnicity below.

It is possible that for some of the more strictly orthodox Hindus, who would in no manner participate in the celebration of Carnival, Christmas is being used to express a more muted sense of inversion and licence which makes it their equivalent to Carnival. There is an irony here, since to the extent that this is the case, it means that the same set of practices are being interpreted in almost diametrically opposed ways depending upon the perspective of the participants. What is seen as the most extreme example of constraint by those who associate themselves with true Carnival is seen as a model for comparative licence by those who live in a comparatively constraining environment for the rest of the year.

Christmas Values

The Centripetal Aesthetic

Why should it be the home rather than the person which is the recipient of most of the shopping associated with Christmas? The term 'domestic' is rarely used in Trinidad, but there is considerable employment of the dichotomy between 'inside' and 'outside'. For example, an 'outside' woman is a synonym for a mistress ('deputy'), as opposed to a legal or common-law wife. The focus of the 'inside' world is the home and it is a term which has much in common with the concept of domestic, in so far as it includes social and aesthetic as well as spatial considerations.

The aesthetics of the living-room interior will be discussed in more detail in a subsequent chapter, but, in summary, the major characteristics include an emphasis on covering over and enclosing forms, deep upholstery and pile carpets, and a cramming in of ornaments and artificial flowers together with many religious and secular homilies asserting domestic virtues and pictures of family activities such as weddings. The Christmas emphasis on the restoration of such decorations and furnishings as well as adding to their stock, provides by Christmas Eve the immaculate setting for what is ideally the key annual ritual of family reaffirmation as a moral and expressive order.

In the first instance this ritual is one of consolidation. It culminates in the Christmas meal which is seen as exclusive to the family proper, who receive the gift of the perfectly tidy and clean house and the choicest of the prepared foods and drinks.

Enclosed by the new, or newly cleaned curtains, the family strives towards a sense of quiet solidity. The meal is usually a heavy one and individuals may sleep afterwards. Later in the day, however, there is a marked change in orientation and it is as though the home and family, once secured, become the focal point of a process of progressive incorporation, through which the domestic becomes not merely an enclosed space but a kind of centripetal force striving to incorporate as much of the outside world as possible into itself.

This process is first evident in the pattern of post-Christmas visiting. First the wider family is expected to come and be the recipients of hospitality, with an insistence on guests partaking of the prepared food and drink. Although there are no formal phases, there is a sense that the incorporation of family is then followed by that of neighbours and friends. Finally, as noted above, it is groups, such as work colleagues which, during the rest of the year, have been relatively excluded from this sense of incorporation, who are then drawn in and included in this process.

As Abrahams argues for St Vincent, Christmas is a stylised expression of moral values, rather than merely a reflection of them. If Christmas is taken in isolation, then only a single and consistent field of values appear to be expressed. At Christmas time, everybody has family and a home they can turn to which is the source of their identity. Even though for much of the year there is a powerful dichotomy at work in which many women and most men make great efforts to avoid too much association with the 'inside' world of the home, all this is ignored during a period where, as it were, the whole nation pays homage to the centrality of the home and family and to the sense of being Trinidadian. The ideal may not last for long, and intra-family quarrels, fuelled by the availability of alcohol, may erupt even before Christmas lunch is finished (an event which may cause acute embarrassment). Other counter-tendencies which would undermine the consistency of this ideal will be noted at the conclusion of this chapter, but this should not detract from the clarity with which a model of society is constructed and proclaimed by this festival.

Nostalgia

This centripetal effect is by no means limited simply to the hospitality provided by the home. It is also extended to other aspects of identity formation, including temporality and ethnicity. One of the most commonly expressed sentiments about Christmas is that ideally it should be as it has always been. Indeed, Christmas becomes the focal point for a sentimental and nostalgic view of the past centred upon the celebration of Christmas itself.

In the case of Carnival, although there is a standard structure, everyone is waiting to see how this year's Carnival will be special, will be an event, based around the new styles, costumes, music and so forth which surround it. For Christmas, by contrast, there is a strong sense of the normative. Ideally, Christmas should be unchanging and there is disappointment when it does not live up to or conform to those expectations. The newspapers are full of articles which tell of Christmas past. Typically, a journalist from a rural or low-income background will tell how his or her family made out when he or she was a child, emphasising all the work that was done by hand and the 'warm' atmosphere. For example, Angela Pidduck recalls (*Express* 19 December 1990) how: 'My grandmother pulled out the old hand sewing-machine, she cut the curtains and morris chair cushion covers, we the children (boys and girls) took turns turning the handle ... But there was warmth, sharing and love, not only amongst ourselves at 94 Picton Street, but in the neighbourhood. We shared *pastelles* and *ponche de creme* after midnight mass at home.' Every year there are many such articles in the newspapers. As in this example the family is usually represented in terms of longevity and descent, the grandparents juxtaposed with the children, a sense of continuity with tradition being handed down through the generations. The very concept of family in the context of Christmas has a powerful temporal component, which should be borne in mind in reading Chapter 4 (below) where the family will be studied more as a strategic objectification in relation to the pressures of modernity, than, as is normally the case, a category within kinship studies.

The concept of an unchanging Christmas is complemented by the use of key symbolic tokens, such as ham, apples and grapes. In talking about the past, a shopkeeper's daughter claims that the traditional start of the Christmas season was marked by her father, who would boil up a ham in a 'pitch oil' (kerosene) tin. Everybody in the area, even those on a very low income, would feel it essential to buy at least a token amount of ham, such as an ounce. The involvement of these items is taken as making for a specifically 'Trinidadian' Christmas. This is especially brought out by the reaction to the reimportation of apples and grapes in 1990. As an observer noted, it was not merely the crowds who collected to welcome the first container load of these fruits after the government ban was lifted, but the frenzy with which people would go and buy a whole tray of apples as soon as they were available. There can be few countries in the world whose families are as strongly integrated with international circuits as Trinidad. Most people have some family abroad, and, as the same observer noted, many of those with the money to buy these trays of fruit had probably had apples or grapes in Canada or the United States within the last few months. This did not, however, lessen the excitement with which they responded to their presence in Trinidad. Indeed, so much fruit was imported in subsequent weeks as to massively oversupply the country, and for a short time Trinidad probably became the cheapest country in the world in which to buy apples! Unlike the journalist who was concerned with the dependence upon imported symbols, for the majority of people these fruits are defined anew by their context, they become essential for this process of nostalgia in which all true Trinidadian Christmases include the symbolic tokens of their past celebration.

Being Spanish

The process by which a centripetal aesthetic, including both a spatial, social and temporal element, creates an image of constant unity is further accentuated by reference to what is generally regarded as the most divisive of all social dimensions in Trinidad: ethnicity. Christmas, as already noted has an ethnicity all to itself, based upon the concept of 'Spanish'. This is most powerfully evoked by the music of *parang* and the various foods such as *pastelles* and *arepas* which are recognised as Spanish in origin.

If one asks formally who are the Spanish in Trinidad, then there are a number of possible answers (Winer and Aguilar 1991), depending upon whether one lays stress upon the original colonists who ruled the country, before the transference of sovereignty to the British, but who were never a significant demographic presence, or the Venezuelan élite mentioned by Braithwaite (1975: 74–5), or the migrating peons, also from Venezuela, who formed quite homogeneous villages of the kind depicted by Naipaul (1958) in *The Suffrage of Elvira*. All these definitions, however, would fail to evoke the actual meaning of the term Spanish as used colloquially in contemporary Trinidad. First, the term Spanish in its reference to the original colonists also incorporates the Carib and Arawak precolonial populations. Although when precision is required, an individual, particularly from élite groups, may lay claim to a partial Amerindian ancestry, for most Trinidadians it is the term Spanish which is employed simply to signify an element of Amerindian blood as part of a generic sense of roots which go beyond slavery and indentured labour.

Similarly the term Spanish has become, in rural areas, synonymous with their concept 'mixed'. Thus a person whose actual ancestry includes a mixture of Indian, Chinese, French and African might have been transmuted through the category 'mixed' into a sense of being 'kind of' Spanish. The importance of the term lies precisely in its vague aura of an alternative ancestry which is specifically not pure African, Indian or White. There are few clear claims to pure precolonial ancestry but in many ways this has become intermixed with Spanish and the term Spanish now evokes both the general sense of mixed ancestry but also of ancient or original inhabitation. Similarly, Hindus feel no discomfort in associating themselves with the elevation of 'Spanish' elements as a grounding for all Trinidadians and thereby a factor neutralising any Black-Indian animosity. Indeed, many Indians who would be affronted at the idea of a mixed African ancestry seemed comfortable with the idea their family contained some 'Spanish' blood.

It is at Christmas time that many Trinidadians manage to locate amongst their ancestry at least an element of Spanish. This provides them with a sense that they have a kind of natural affiliation with the associated music and food, but it also has deeper consequences. To have an ethnicity which evokes a sense of Trinidad beyond the images of rupture such as slavery and indentured labour is to evoke a generic objectification of the land itself. This is also suggested by a figure in the rituals performed by Hindu Trinidadians. The propitiation of a spirit termed the Dih seems to have arisen as a link between the present occupants of a house or land and its original owner (see Klass 1961: 176–8; Vertovec 1992: 113, 215). The image of the Dih is also found especially at lower-'caste' Madrassi-style temples, for example at Kali Mai temples, though the worship has a much wider following in the home. A curious feature of Dih worship is that the figure represented appears to have Spanish looks and is seen as representing the ancestral lands of Trinidad (this point and the general significance of the Dih was pointed out to me by W. Guinea). When one worships the Dih, one worships the property upon which one's house is based. The worship is of a syncretic variety involving typically ex-African aspects such as the use of rum and cigarettes. The main distinction made is whether one sacrifices a fowl-cock to the Dih. For many Hindus, who otherwise have nothing to do with animal sacrifice, this is the one point at which such sacrifice is carried out. The Dih then represents the integration of Trinidadian land, as existing before the indentureship, within the wider Hindu cosmology, and indicates a strategy which was probably vital to the significance which property has come to have to this community.

Through these various associations the concept of Spanish ethnicity seems to evoke a generalised sense of the traditions of the land, and is probably the one strategy which enables Trinidadians who are usually characterised (not least by themselves) as comparatively 'rootless', to conceive of their current practices as having a derivation from a general and ideally unchanging line of descent. It is noticeable that this evolution of 'Spanish' has received neither official sanction nor encouragement, but appears to represent the spontaneous dynamics of popular culture.

Christmas and Commerce

As in many other countries, Christmas in Trinidad is associated with a peak of commercial activity and a virtual frenzy of shopping in the final days before Christmas. On these grounds it is here, as elsewhere, commonly condemned by the local media as a festival of materialism, and complaints are made about the financial drain which results from the flow of imported goods. In practice, most people are more concerned that they do not have the financial resources to celebrate it properly.

In examining the details of expenditure associated with Christmas, however, it was found that while a certain proportion of this is specific to the festival, the bulk of purchases are related to the refurbishment of the home. Most of these items represent actual requirements, such as the repair of upholstery or the purchase of a new dining-room suite, which, if not seen to at Christmas would have had to be undertaken at some other time in the year. Furthermore, because of the rituals of Christmas Eve, many items bought at other times are then stored to be brought out at Christmas. In effect, the desire seems to be to associate as much of one's annual purchases as possible with the festival. The result seems to be less a celebration of materialism than a sacralisation of shopping, such that functional materialism is encompassed by a ritual activity which acts to associate these goods with a set of positive values in relation to family and religion (see Miller 1993 for the details of this argument).

Christmas: Concluding Points

It will be argued throughout this book that the values which are most clearly expressed at Christmas are crucial to understanding the dynamics of Trinidadian culture. Indeed, they will be given a specific label, that of 'transcendence', to designate them as a relatively consistent ideology which, although never as fully explicated as during this festival, nevertheless maintains a presence throughout the year as a model for social and moral life. The term 'transcendence' is used because these images are always held as polarised against an alternative set of values expressed most fully at Carnival, and this contrast is one of opposed senses of temporality. At Christmas the image is of constancy and ancestry. It ignores the actual heterogeneous origins to celebrate a mythic time of romantic tradition, when everyone was poor but happy. The mechanism of continuity is the family, and at Christmas one pays homage to a 'way of life' of the family in whose values one is brought up. The family is assumed to be readily identifiable, to have clear lines of descent continuity, and to manifest itself through its relationship to the home and to its material possessions, whose renewal is the core ritual of Christmas. In this ideology there is a stable core which has the capacity to integrate the 'wilder' world of men, of the outside and of the street. With family as the superordinate term, a generalised sense of relationship and unity can be extended through neighbourhood and friendship to almost anyone. The actual complex articulation between Trinidad and other countries is entirely ignored. For the purposes of Christmas there is an unambiguous entity which is Trinidad with recognisable traditions and symbols that make 'Trini Christmas the best'. Even if subsequent chapters reveal that we cannot defend a concept of an integral and integrated Trinidadian 'culture', and that actual family life often bears no relation to that assumed here, this does not detract from the evident viability of an ideology which proclaims that there is such a culture and familial model. Government bans on importations and journalists' diatribes against imports do not seem to have rendered apples and grapes one iota less 'Trinidadian', and, if this is so, it is because the annual enactment of Christmas is neither reflecting, nor mystifying, some wider 'reality': rather it is constituting a viable ideology of what being Trinidadian is all about.

Christmas has been used as an initial introduction to the ethnographic sections of this work, partly because it pre-empts and summarises the major concern with mass consumption which is the subject of Chapter 4. The festival also provides a clear example of the process of objectification (as the term is used in Miller 1987). It transforms the world of commodities, as alienable and potentially alienating into their very negation, the key symbols of the inalienable. It does so by making the processes by which goods are appropriated themselves creative of sociality. In the first place it is the family itself which is constituted anew each year, but this is done through an orientation to the 'inside' in which, as in the related concept of the domestic, it is hard to distinguish between the attention given to possessions and to property on the one hand and to the family on the other, what is created is an integral dynamic which makes each the instrument for constructing value in the other. Furthermore, this same process has been used to construct categories of identity which go well beyond the family, not the least of which is Trinidad itself. Finally, this particular strategy of objectification is one which seems to echo many comparable regional cases where a sense of transcendent roots seems to have been created as a specific bulwark against what is regarded as the ephemeral nature of modernity.

Carnival

There could hardly be a stronger contrast between the lack of academic discussion of Christmas and the voluminous literature devoted to the history and meaning of Carnival (Brereton 1975; Hill 1972; Pearse 1988 (1956); Stewart 1986). In a sense this is quite appropriate, as the inwards-facing festival of Christmas draws its curtains round, and merely seeks to repeat itself, while the extrovert style of Carnival invites attention and thrives on commentary about its latest developments. For this reason, adequate descriptions of Carnival, are, unlike Christmas, available elsewhere, and only a short summary is provided here of those features which are generally understood as being expressed in Carnival revelry. The discussion will then concentrate on one particular feature, the dance form known as 'wining', paying as much attention to the pre-Carnival season as to Carnival itself.

The discrepancy of academic attention to the two major festivals in Trinidad is reflected world-wide. This is found in the virtual absence of social science research devoted to the rituals of Christmas, compared to a substantial literature devoted to Carnival. This latter implicates a set of established attributes to the category Carnival in general, which provides the backdrop to the interpretation of any particular Carnival. Most Carnivals are pre-Lenten and sanctioned by religion. The main revellers are from the lower classes. There are competitions with a totemic element, music, dance, feasting, processions through the streets, the use of masks and anonymity, explicit social critique and a general tension between order and disorder. The best known analysis is Bakhtin's (1968) reading of Rabelais' representation of medieval European Carnival, which emphasises the centrality of inversion and laughter in the population's conception of the mystical terror of God. Both Bakhtin and Le Roy Ladurie (1981) writing about sixteenth-century France, also emphasise the element of social critique. Others such as Da Matta (1977) writing about Brazil emphasise structural inversion, and still others such as Eco (1984), writing, also on Brazil take the opposite view of Carnival as mere catharsis which benefits the dominant group. Finally, some recent analyses such as Cohen (1982) on London's Notting Hill Carnival note the dynamic tension between aesthetic and political themes.

The bulk of the writing on Trinidad's Carnival is concerned with its long-term historical development; the periods when it provided a key objectification of lower-class culture, with ironic and mocking perspectives on both colonial and middle-class life; the times also when it has successively incorporated groups which had earlier on opposed it, including the middle-class (Powrie 1988). Stewart (1986) provides the most complete summary of the more recent history of Carnival and its contemporary structure, focusing upon the political context, as Carnival is increasingly appropriated as a symbol of national culture.

Much of the literature on Trinidad's Carnival stresses the development of key characters such as Dragons, Midnight Robbers, Jabjabs, Pierrots, Sailors and so forth (Crowley 1956; Hill 1985). Whether as individuals or bands, these had their own costumes, choreography and elaborated speeches, and were justly famed. This literature was, however, of very little relevance to the Carnival which I observed in 1988. Then there were no Jabjabs or Midnight Robbers except as deliberate recreations of tradition. Carnival 1988 did, however, incorporate a sequence of events established over a considerable period. There was 'Dimanche Gras', the name given to the evening which sees the finals of the Carnival King, Queen and Calypso Monarch competitions. This was followed by 'Jouvay'[9] morning during which mud-splattered bands with titles such as 'Barbarians' or 'Kids in Hell' with their ironic and critical commentaries emerged into the dawn. Finally, there was the so-called 'pretty mas' when bands, sometimes thousands strong, in uniforms by competing designers, danced and 'jumped up', crossing the main stages in competition and otherwise thronging the streets. Carnival still retains something of its sanctioned position in the Christian calendar, as illustrated by the newspaper advert 'the Friends of the Dominican Fathers will be holding a Carnival jump up on ...'

As with Christmas, Carnival is a seasonal festival, with a structure and many elements which could be described as secular ritual. In this case, however, the emphasis is upon this particular year's Carnival as a major event. The relationship between structure and event may be illustrated most clearly through one of the activities closely associated with Carnival: calypso, which in its contemporary form is usually called soca music (for a comprehensive history of which see Rohlehr 1990). Calypsos themselves are seasonal. Each calypsonian launches his or her new calypsos in the period immediately following (although these days this is spilling over to the period before) Christmas. There then follows a period of intensive playing of soca. All the 'maxi-taxis', which had spent much of the year playing 'rap', 'dub' and imported sounds, suddenly shift to almost continual soca. Indeed, one of the most popular protests by calypsonians is about the apparent refusal to play their music outside that specified period. The playing of soca sounds diminishes rapidly after Carnival, and it is often remarked that calypsos should not be played during Lent but may be returned to after Easter, though this is not strictly adhered to today, if it ever was.

Before I came to Trinidad I had heard of only two calypso singers, the Mighty Sparrow, probably the best-known living master of the genre, and David Rudder, the most prominent of the new soca stars. In the first (1987–8) carnival period I observed, Sparrow's calypsos were simply never played on radio, his tent attracted small audiences, indeed I was not altogether sure if he was still alive. Interpreting this in the manner of the trajectory of singers in Britain, I concluded that to all intents and purposes his career was finished. The star that year on the media and the streets was David Rudder, and there were many complaints that the radio seemed to play almost continual repeats of his two main new songs 'Bacchanal Woman' and 'Panama'. In the following year, particularly during the earlier period, just after Christmas, the position was reversed; Sparrow's calypso 'Congo Man' was the most widely played at all the local parties and fêtes I attended, while Rudder could barely raise applause from the audience.

In Trinidad, although there are some expectations based on the past, singers cannot expect careers with clear trajectories; rather, each year is a new event in which one starts almost from scratch. Success only comes in as much as that year's calypsos and performance appears to warrant it. There were many similar cases of a major calypso from a singer who had hardly featured in competitions for more than a decade. This effect is countered by the tendency for an individual at the peak of her or his career towards consistently fine productions, and there were half a dozen figures such as Shadow, the Black Stalin, Gypsy and Baron for whom this expectation was usually realised, but it guaranteed no more than an initial hearing.

The same emphasis on the event can be traced through the use of costume for playing mas at Carnival. Today most such costumes are purchased from designers and are organised into a sequence of groups, each in identically dressed costume, who together make up the theme of that particular designer's band. At the end of the Carnival the costume is discarded. Although the tradition of self-made costume has markedly declined, it has always been the case that, even where an individual is intending to wear the identical costume, such as a Midnight Robber or a Sailor, every year the costume would be discarded and a new one constructed for the following year.

Both calypso and costumes contend in one of the most ubiquitous features of Carnival which is competitions. The list of competitions associated with Carnival is prodigious. The *Dimanche Gras* show consists of nothing more than the finals of several of these, including the Calypso King usually based on the more serious, for example, politically inclined, calypsos. This is complemented by the equally prestigious 'road march'. The criteria for road march are its suitability for dance, fête and jump up; the decision is made on the basis of how many bands choose to play this tune during the time when they pass the judges' stands. The procession of bands is also in the form of a competition. Perhaps the most competitive of all the associated events is Panorama, which is based on the steelbands who often pick a tune from the calypsos of that year as the basis for their presentation. In the past, the steelbands have had a reputation for rivalry which spilt over from the musical competition into violent conflict. Given the association between the steelband and a particular area where the panyard is situated, this has had something of the character of 'gang' warfare. Contemporary Panorama is a somewhat quieter affair and is one of the two annual competitions, the other being based on their performances from the classical repertoire.

As with most Carnivals there is an element of masking and anonymity associated with taking part. This takes two rather different forms. Traditionally male Carnival included the option of playing a highly individualised role as, for example, a Midnight Robber, with one's own particular speech and mannerisms, which can be related back to the general sense of style as performance practised by many men and women at other times of the year. This form of individualism has tended to be replaced, however, by an individualism created by anonymity, in which one forms part of a larger band wearing identical costumes, but within which there is the freedom to play mas with an abandon which would otherwise not be sanctioned. In part this reflects the shift from the dominance of males to that of females in playing mas. The crowd then becomes itself a kind of mask, within which the individual may be encouraged to emerge, as by the common expression 'play yuhself'.

Ideally the exuberance of the event will allow the participants to 'break out' and play with a degree of abandon and 'wildness' which contributes to the general sense of disorder which is affectionately termed 'bacchanal'. In its opposition to the constraints and order of other times of the year, this period may be referred to as the season for 'bacchanal', where the encouragement is constantly to 'free up'.

The orientation of Carnival is clearly to the street and to display, as participants are literally exposing themselves in the streets over two days. Beyond this there are many motifs which relate to a sense of the inside coming out into the open, or dark coming out into light. Indeed, this is the theme of that part of Carnival which today is often seen as the most profound experience for the participants. This is the 'inversion' period of *Jouvay*, where bands dressed in mud and ashes or old clothes assemble before the dawn to reveal themselves in the first light as the 'truth'. These include the 'ole mas' bands with their satiric exposures of the pretensions of established order. A major attraction of this part of Carnival is that it integrates steelband, for which many of the participants have a tremendous affection; also it does not require any expensive costume, and is therefore available to lower-income groups whose associations are more informal and less planned (although there are larger Jouvay bands which are on a par with pretty mas). A final attraction is that the formation of *Jouvay* bands can be much more *ad hoc* and spontaneous than is possible with pretty mas.

The portrayal of *Jouvay* masqueraders as Barbarians or as Primitives seems to echo the Bakhtinian interpretation of Carnival as more generally tending towards the exposure of hidden truths about one's own gross materiality against the façade of cultural control, as in the Rabelesian image of the grand fart that allows the grossness of life to explode out of its hidden depths. A favourite target in 1988 was the television evangelist Jimmy Swaggert who had recently been revealed to harbour inner carnality. There is a positive moral connotation here of 'truth' or revelation of that which has been suppressed or repressed. This ideal spills over into the connotations of the term Bacchanal itself which is partly synonymous with 'scandal', but at Carnival time this becomes a positive force which promotes the revelation of a deeper truth which has been circumscribed by an unnatural order, and the spirit of bacchanal is therefore celebrated in many of the calypsos.

These are a few of many values whose relationship to Carnival is well-established, and which represent a clear distinction from, if not opposition to, Christmas. In this case it is the outside and the street which is celebrated, an orientation towards display which could be termed centrifugal. This may take the form of an extremely individualistic and competitive style, but increasingly, as will be illustrated below, women are seeking literally to lose themselves in the dance. Where Christmas closes itself in with curtains, Carnival is concerned with revelation; where Christmas looks for a transcendent temporality, Carnival celebrates the spontaneous and the event.

All these themes may be examined in more depth through a consideration of one particular dance form know as 'wining' which is strongly associated with Carnival. One reason for doing so, is that, although wining is found and is prominent in all Trinidad Carnivals, it was the 1988 Carnival at which wining became the focus of a heated and sustained debate within Trinidad. It seemed likely that this debate might help in our understanding of the latest transformations in the meaning of Carnival. In particular, it might throw light on the most evident change over the last two decades which is the new dominance of female participants, found in current estimates of eight or nine females to every male present.

Wining

'Wining' is a dance movement based on gyrations of the hips and waist, which may be performed by individuals, or upon another person, or in a line of dancers. Wining is not exclusively associated with Carnival. Related dance movements are recorded during the period of slavery, as in this 1806 account from nearby Barbados: 'Making the head and limbs fixed points, they writhe and turn the body on its own axis, slowly advancing towards each other or retreating to the outer parts of the ring. Their approaches ... are highly indecent ... but of this they seem to be wholly unconscious' (Handler and Frisbie 1972: 30). Dance movements based around pelvic gyrations are also well-known in Latin America, including the Bahia region of Brazil, also largely populated by ex-African emancipated slaves. Within Trinidad wining is also associated with the 'cuss-outs' or cursing that can occur especially in low-income groups, for example, among cohabiting couples. In Ford minor cuss-outs were a daily occurrences. Occasionally these erupt into long confrontations with possible fighting but mainly verbal abuse.[10] Cuss-outs may collect audiences who, if the verbal debate is – as one person put it – 'sweet enough, wine with the sweetness of it', sometimes, as in party wining, lifting skirts above their heads to facilitate the action. But this variety of wining has become rare today. Wining at cuss-outs may be related to excitement but not necessarily to eroticism. Similarly at a party, a casual bumping side to side or a light rubbing of genitals to bottom will take place between brother and sister or between parent and child. There is a continuous gradation between this and the clearly erotic character of most wining at parties. Wining can be encountered at a wide array of fêtes, parties and other occasions for dance, although it is most evident in response to calypso or soca music, which are associated more particularly with the Carnival season.

Most of my evidence for the centrality of wining to the 1988 Carnival comes from conversations and observations, but the newspapers certainly came to the same conclusions, and saw this as intensely problematic. The establishment *Guardian* suggested (22 February 1988) that: 'this year's celebration, particularly Carnival Tuesday's presentation has been noted as the most vulgar and immoral display ever witnessed on the Savannah stage. Women, particularly, no sooner spotted cameramen than they began their lewd dance, which brought the bile up from most men's stomachs rather than lure them into pronouncements of the charms of the opposite sex'. Later it commented (3 April) that: 'let us not forget that many of the TV viewers were small children and the scandalous and lewd cavorting of these women, many of whom took the pains to simulate the sex act in full view of their audience (and some of whom no doubt schoolteachers who would become models of decorum when they appeared before their classes on Ash Wednesday morning) tells us a good deal about their everyday morals and character'.

Several letters and articles in the papers claimed that wining encouraged rape and that feminists should oppose it. The more salacious weekly papers, such as *The Bomb*, were full of comment and even more full of photos. *The Bomb* noted (26 February) that: 'this is how this Carnival turned out to be – bossy sexy and *wassy*[11] by the women in rut ... when it comes to wining and simulating sex on stage, women have no inhibitions. They would lie on their backs, roll on their bellies and pump.' The band 'Savage' was described as: 'a bevy of meaty belles who appeared to have spent some months in the gym toning and re-shaping their love muscles'.

Apart from comments such as those cited above, the newspapers had few clear ideas about to what lay behind the rise of wining at Carnival, though one publication summarised the current debate (Baptiste (ed.) 1988). Some of the more intellectual commentary, for example, by the novelist Lovelace or the journalist Pires, claimed that Carnival wining was non-erotic, mainly on the grounds that it was performed by women on air rather than on men (Baptiste (ed.) 1988: 47–54), although as the newspaper extracts will have made clear this is rather a minority view. Much more common among male conversation was the idea that Carnival has revealed an enormous growth in 'zammees' (lesbians), an idea met by my own female informants with incredulity. The weeklies concurred with the dailies in seeing Carnival wining as an affront rather than as an invitation to men in general.

Obscenity is one of the oldest accusations to be made against the Trinidadian Carnival and the *pissenlit* ('wet the bed') of the nineteenth century, with their rags of menstrual blood, caused as much of a stir in their time as modern wining, and women were also central to the construction of this 'Jamette[12] Carnival'. Wining, then, is related to a tradition of Carnival, but the specific form it takes and the response to the 1988 Carnival may be interpreted in relation to certain recent shifts in the wider context of sexuality and gender relations, and through this to the very possibility of sociality for a section of Trinidadian society (Miller 1991).

The newspapers tended to concentrate on the upper-class women in costume, who were most evident to the television cameras and who are not associated with wining outside of Carnival itself. Most of my informants on wining, however, came from low-income areas, such as Ford and parts of St Pauls, and although very keen on wining they could not afford costumes and therefore had to jump up on the periphery or at Carnival in towns other than the capital. The analysis which follows is based upon these low-income women, who are numerically at least as important. In particular, it focuses on those women whose orientation is to the outside and to transience, who are often generalised locally by the term 'bacchanal', and who wine at fêtes throughout the year. It is a commonplace within Trinidad that Carnival itself is dedicated to these 'bacchanal' values.

It is quite possible that the conclusions to be drawn here would also apply, in some measure, to the middle- and upper-class women, mainly from the capital Port of Spain, referred to by the newspapers. For such women, Carnival represents a temporary association with the expression of values, which at other times they would hold in abeyance or oppose. The coverage of my fieldwork did not extend to this group, however, and therefore I cannot confirm the relevance of my interpretation to them. Another qualifying remark applies to the history of wining. The implications drawn here are taken from the events of the 1988 Carnival. If one listens to the content of the calypsos of David Rudder, the emphasis is on the exuberant wining in which men are involved and it is implied in the lyrics that the activities associated with fêtes, parties and Carnival may be associated with a culture of emancipation and resistance in which men play a dominant part, although Rudder distances himself from the misogyny of early calypsos by his sympathetic incorporation of women into these aims and values. Wining as a dance movement has undoubtedly been appropriated within a number of expressive traditions, and both dance and music have a deal of autonomy as a genre which has developed over a considerable period with their own significance.

Calypsos in recent years have, however, been increasingly acknowledging the importance of unrestrained female wining. Indeed, the calypso form has itself increasingly bifurcated into a dualism closely reminiscent of Abrahams' 'rude' and 'serious' forms of West Indian oral arts. At one end of the spectrum is a genre of hard-hitting political calypso, lampooning current governments and politicians, some with extremely serious intent, backed up by various genres of praise songs to, for example, the nation, the elderly or the woman who brought up the calypsonian. In these calypsos the serious topics of the fallibility of the current government, or ethnic rivalry, take precedence and they may play a conspicuous role as highly controversial interventions in such debates, as was the case in 1988 when of the two winning calypsos, one called for a general election and the other was titled 'Corruption in Common Entrance'.[13]

Such calypsos are, however, matched by those competing for Road March, which tend to be those played at parties and fêtes.

These are devoted to less serious topics: the most popular contemporary topic is 'free up', and men being embarrassed by the energy and moral abandon of women's dance. The 1988 Road March winner was typical in being about a woman who evades the police and all others as she bursts into a fête without a ticket to dance. There is a vast array of calypsos with titles such as 'shaking it', 'feeling the feeling', 'doing dat ting', all of which adds to the chagrin of those who feel calypso ought to be more confrontational and political, a debate which may parallel the current critique of 'slackness' and 'dancehall' in Jamaica.

The Culture of Fêtes

In examining the place of wining at fêtes, the ethnographic evidence is drawn from a particular group of lower-class women, for whom fêting was of profound significance. Such women would not expect to have any regular employment; their income comes from occasional jobs such as shop assistants or domestic labour, to a lesser extent from illegal activities including trading in drugs and pickpocketing, but mostly from their relationships with men. Fêtes and parties are the activities which dominate their lives. This is, above all, what they want money for. While in other places people may go to parties in order to form relationships, for these women it is quite clear and explicit that they form relationships in order to have the resources to go to fêtes: 'yuh need someone(s) husband for that'.

Of considerable importance is finding the right fête: it is a source of much disappointment and displeasure to end up in a fête that is not a success. A key element is that a fête should be crowded and people should 'get on': that is, the dance should develop its more exaggerated forms of wining and grinding. There are many different kinds of party in Trinidad. Perhaps the most important are the paid fêtes, especially in the period between Christmas and Carnival. These usually have live groups and calypsonians who are associated with that group, as well as well-known DJ's. There are certain large open areas in Port of Spain such as Soca Village which can contain several thousand revellers. Somewhat smaller are block parties (blockos), where a particular section of a residential area is sealed off, in order to provide the venue for a paid fête. There are also house parties, which are generally by invitation, and the hosts will provide the alcohol and usually something to eat, such as a *pelau* (typically rice, chicken and pigeon peas). Paid fêtes are advertised in the newspapers but the most important channel of communication is the radio, and people will often exchange news on which fêtes have been announced and which they would like to attend.

As noted by Freilich (1960: 102), for the very different context of males in rural Trinidad in the 1950s, the very definition of friendship seems to be those with whom one fêtes. There is a loose association between friendship and kinship. Out of the large pool of relatives, such as siblings, half-siblings, cousins and so forth, there may be several who are regular companions at fêtes but who are thereby on a par with companions who have no kin ties. For the women of Ford, money to fête is often a problem and they may be sitting at home resigned to watching television, when a companion turns up with enough money for a few tickets, and the atmosphere is radically transformed. At this point there is considerable attention paid to the selection of clothes and women may try out several possibilities before they are satisfied, although the ideal is always to wear something new. Money is also needed for transport, though for these women the journey may be free, if, through 'sweet-talking' the taxi driver and vague hints of meeting again, he can be persuaded not to charge.

Although the period December through to March is the key fêting season, when many people who would not party at other times of the year will come to fêtes, these women belong to that section of the population for whom this represents only a slight increase in an orientation to fêting which lasts throughout the year. At other times they would look to clubs, and to house parties and the more occasional paid fête. In Chaguanas the shopping malls host fêtes on a weekly basis. At such times it is a DJ rather than live music which dominates and there is usually a preponderance of males. Couples form one component of the participants at fêtes, but they are usually in a minority compared to those who have come to find partners at the fête. Men are more likely to arrive singly or with a friend, while women tend to come in groups of three, four or more. Quite common is a larger group of around seven women with one associated male for 'protection'.

At fêtes outside the Carnival season, the music is predominantly Jamaican and North American rap and dub and reggae. The main form of dancing might be called 'display' dancing by men and incorporates American 'breakdance', or Jamaican 'rough wine' forms in which men break into fancy routines, either as individuals to impress their peers, or as a small group, often calling 'watch mi' to gain attention and 'just now' to retain attention from those around. The selection of tracks is generally conventional, since it is important the music becomes well-established, as many people will join in at some section where a favoured phrase or 'rude' bit comes up. After perhaps six or seven of such tracks, the DJ then plays two or three slow dances, in which couples pair off and, often with closed eyes, move dreamily together. Some wining may take place but this is muted. In the months between Christmas and Carnival, however, calypso and soca music tend to take over and wining between men and women is more predominant.

Either wining or what is termed the 'hugging up' of the slow dance may develop into a further activity known as 'grinding'. This usually entails couples retreating to the edge of the dance floor and with one partner supported by the wall, they rub genitals and gyrate more systematically. This may involve only a few couples, though I have attended fêtes at which no one was left on the dance floor, as they were all distributed in grinding around the walls. Grinding, even for long periods, does not necessarily indicate a sexual relationship between the couple, unlike kissing which is done in dark corners or preferably away from the dance hall and is seen as much more indicative of sexual intent. In general in Trinidad, genital contact gives less cause for attention than oral contact (the exception being among upper-class people who have received education abroad).

Wining itself only really becomes dominant in the fêtes held in the weeks leading up to Carnival, and on the streets during Carnival itself. At these fêtes, where the slow dances give way to an exclusive emphasis upon soca music, the men may gyrate against the bottoms of the women in front, both may be enclosed within a line, or couples may gyrate front to front. In recent years bands, as well as calypsonians, launch new soca records, though each band will also play the most popular tunes that are emerging at that part of the season, even if they were first brought out by another band. As one moves still closer to Carnival, wining starts to transform from women and men wining on each other, to women wining alone or with each other as found in Carnival itself.

For the women at a fête, it is quite possible to dance either on one's own or, more commonly, in the company of two or three other women throughout the evening, the only exception being at fêtes with slow dancing in which case all dancing is in couples. At a soca fête it is quite acceptable for a male to select a female he does not know and start to wine on her. She may decide to acquiesce or simply move away. It is the very rare and usually very drunk male who would try and continue to wine on a reluctant female, in which case, if she has companions, they will intervene. Such wining may last only for the current song, or may develop into a partnership which lasts the evening. The major criterion is the style of dancing itself. A woman is looking for a partner who she feels comfortable dancing with and who will move to the music, change speed and degrees of intensity in harmony with her desires. If the couple feel comfortable they may evolve into grinding front to front. Quite commonly the partnership will be one of several that are engaged in and then broken off during the course of the evening.

The dance calypsos constantly refer to states of dance. Phrases such as 'jump up', 'misbehave', 'getting on bad' or just 'get on', 'feeling the feeling', 'wine down the place', 'bump and grind' punctuate almost all such songs, and the singer will exhort the crowd that 'we all come here to get on bad'. The very success of the music is seen in terms of the degree to which it leads the crowd into precisely such activities. In a sense, dancing to soca can move through two stages, though there are no clear boundaries. A poor party will have people dancing but not really wining. A better party will have most of the participants wining but then has to move towards other features of the dance in order to really 'get on'. Essentially these relate to the sexual connotations of the dance. Even in its more demure forms it can begin a kind of erotic autostimulation. In a soca fête men tend to wine upon the bottom of the woman in front. As the mood of the dancing develops, some women start to bend their bodies forward until their hair is almost touching the ground. At this point they are clearly simulating sexual intercourse. Generally, the sense of heightened excitement carries through to those dancing nearby who may then give cries of encouragement. If a woman dances in this way she will certainly be considered to have 'misbehaved' and to generally have had a good fête. There may, however, be a competitive element to this. It was remarked that even where a woman was not particularly proficient at sex she would dance this way in front of her female companions just to suggest that she is well able to satisfy her man. In such cases the dance is influenced by a more general sense of rivalry and intra-female competition. Although they are less clear, there are several other dance movements, such as the couple wining down low into a squatting position, which provide a similar sense of 'getting on'. Many women who go to fêtes will rarely, if ever, dance in this way, though for the particular group of low-income women concerned here, at least one or two could be expected to dance in this manner at every fête.

Any further relationship between the two persons dancing together is by no means established by this activity. In many (probably most) cases the woman pairs off with a man who provides the right form of complementary dancing, but does not talk to him (something which is anyway quite difficult given the volume of the music). Even when the couple have remained together throughout the evening and developed into hours of grinding, once the fête ends (for example, when her companions signal to her that they are ready to go), she may leave the dance floor with merely a token wave, sometimes without ever knowing who the male was. Men may or may not be content with this, and one of the most popular calypsos for 1991 was called 'Teaser' and included the lines:

we dance all night until we wet,
but when I ask you for your number,
you give me a negative answer,
you ain't nothing but a teaser,
a dirty, dirty, dirty teaser.

This is not the case when the two come as a couple to the dance, and equally a relationship may well develop. Also men are more likely to dance on a female they know from other fêtes or friendships. It is also very common for people to form a small group of, for example, three males and three females. In this case, during the course of the evening each male will dance with each female, and they may well leave together, but the relationship is one of a group rather than of specific partnerships. In this context kin, including siblings, are commonly partners for ordinary wining. Men may well come to fête with similar sentiments to the women, but in general they are more likely to desire to pick up a partner and to be seen by other men to do so.

Wining at fêtes may, however, be viewed in terms of relationships, and quarrels frequently arise following local neighbourhood fêtes as males accuse their female partners of going over the limit in their wining with other men. What constitutes acceptable wining is a common theme of discussion among women. Carnival does, however, assume a certain licence, and women generally feel they can go further at Carnival time, with less risk of being beaten, though the degree of licence may vary from highly restricted housewives simply being allowed to participate, to women who habitually wine agreeing to fewer constraints about whom they 'free up' with.

For this particular group of women, the nature of their relationship with men was often problematic. Quite often they were mortified at the idea of having to take their current partner to a fête. When they came as a couple they would quite often pair off and grind with them for much of the evening, but they were unable to fully participate in the wilder 'free up' of the more general dancing; indeed, they often apologised later to their companions for their relatively restrained behaviour at that particular fête since they felt that they had in turn made it more difficult for their friends to 'get on'. The problem, remained, however, that the money which allowed them to attend the fête often came from their current partner, and they would feel under some obligation to accompany them to wherever the male decided was the place for them to go that evening. However, many men would feel even more restricted were their partner to insist upon accompanying them to a fête, following them around as an unwanted 'tail'[14] to quote a 1989 calypso by Bally.

There is, however, another aspect to the reticence of these women, which derives from the commonly observed relationship between the dance and the state of gender relations. On many occasions a woman whose partner had offended them, for example, by going off to Tobago with, they suspected, another woman, declared beforehand that she would really 'misbehave' that night. This was usually a self-fulfilling prophecy and the 'worst' dancing was often by those who were clearly feeling some antipathy to a man or to men in general. This was not, however, intended as promiscuity: the women had no intention of finding an alternative partner (unless the relationship had actually ended). Although they would use one, or several men, to dance with vigorously they had essentially no interest at all in who those men might be. This was a clear pattern in the pre-Carnival fêtes, but it becomes particularly important in understanding the implication of wining at Carnival itself.

The clue to the interpretation of wining at Carnival may lie in the most common interpretation made by men, which is that it is lesbianism gone rife, and there were plenty of pictures in the newspapers showing women rubbing their genitals against another female with one leg lifted high into the air. For those women among my informants whose lifestyles would be associated with transience this interpretation was received with complete incomprehension. Such women certainly enjoyed wining at fêtes and almost every other occasion, and they saw Carnival as of central importance to their lives. In response to my questioning they continually stressed that to understand them one would have to see them at Carnival. Since I was not to see them (I got to know them after the 1988 Carnival), they insisted on holding some 'women only' parties in which they could 'get on bad', or 'free up', outside the presence of other men, in order to show me what it was like. While dancing they continually parodied the manner in which males respond to their assumed sexual indiscretions. For example, one might roughly pull a friend from her wining partner with feigned anger.

All of this is taken a stage further in what becomes the almost exclusive female activity of wining at Carnival. What is then enacted is essentially a sexuality which does not require men; it is not lesbianism but autosexuality. The women in Carnival, as they become involved in the dance, are not tremendously interested in who or what they are wining upon, they will wine on men, they will wine on each other, most often on no one at all, but the object of wining is in most cases really themselves. It is an expression of a free sexuality which has no object but itself, and most especially it is a sexuality not dependent upon men (see Miller 1991 for an elaboration of this point). Stewart (1986) relates the decline of male participation in Carnival to a loss of authenticity, echoing the male view that these masses of women who buy their designer costumes and dance 'pretty mas' with beer in hand, mingling with tourists, is a fall from the 'true' Carnival of jabjab and dragon. What he takes as the end to certain oppositional Carnival themes may, however, turn out to be simultaneously a beginning for new themes as the meaning of the dance shifts from political emancipation to gender emancipation.

This autosexuality is only a moment of Carnival inversion, and Carnival ends traditionally with a return to 'normal' sexual relations. It is often seen as a period when old relationships are ended and new ones are begun, since at the end of Carnival there is a high expectation of finding a more lasting sexual partner. Demographic statistics suggest a very slight baby boom nine months after Carnival, but anecdotes about November 'carnival babies' suggest a much larger one. An alternative route towards a sexuality which is no longer constitutive of cross-gender exchange is to form a transient relationship with an outsider such as a tourist who has come to view Carnival and this is a common and sometimes explicitly declared strategy for such women (as also, for slightly different reasons, many men).

It was evident from the newspaper coverage that wining is seen more as a threat than as an invitation by men, who are otherwise not reticent in responding to the sexually alluring. Most of the letters of complaint in the press were written by men. When an article in the *Express* (20 February) says of the Carnival women that: 'In fact so secure are they that they seem to spend much of the time taunting men who fail to perform', it is precisely echoing one of the most common conflicts within the home. Increasingly, it is the tourists who attempt to join in as a response to the jump up activity.

This sense of threat became evident to me as an observer, not at Carnival 1988 but some weeks before the 1989 Carnival at the Chaguanas shopping mall. I had attended several fêtes at this site to dance for five or six hours with a group of friends, and was looking forward to what was billed as the first soca fête of the new season, which meant that the mainstream Jamaican and North American music was going to be displaced by the new soca calypso tunes which are launched just after Christmas. But when the soca started to play most of the male youths simply stood still, while a minority of women really let go and danced with an abandon that I had only occasionally seen previously. The men came back in only when the DJs included some of the more familiar rap and dub sounds. The men seemed unable to respond to what was always represented as the true Trinidadian sound.

While the dance is individualising it is also rhythmic, constantly invoked by music which is an ubiquitous presence in Trinidad.

Among the flimsy housing of the squatting community it was often remarked that neighbouring women could be seen dancing energetically by themselves in the daytime. Music is certainly the form which acts during Carnival as mediator between the structured ritual in which the crowds are engaged and the atomistic individualism of the participants. The dancers often describe themselves as merely surrendering to the imperative which arises 'naturally' from the powerful beat of the extremely loud music. Rhythm acts here not to express the relationship between the members of the group but to provide a level of abstraction at which each individual may become attached without involving any such relations and through which finally they may transcend themselves.

Carnival Values

Using this extended example comprising one element of the repertoire of Carnival activities, the values which are expressed may be more clearly demarcated. In the culture of fêtes can be discerned a clear attitude to cross-gender relationships. The desire is to retain control over such relationships such that they remain an expression of one's own voluntaristic agency. If wining is seen as a stylised expression of wider social relations, then the implication is that both partners wish to see their relationship as something they choose to enter into and then remove themselves from, reducing to a minimum any sense of obligation which would constrain the larger project of maintaining a sense of freedom of action. The relationship is reciprocal, an exchange, in which each facilitates the desires of the other, but with a caution about anything that would lead to their individuality becoming subsumed by the relationship. Relationships in general seem kept to a minimum: people often dancing with a person they hardly speak to and do not know. There is a continual reference to the event itself, each of which is taken independently as an opportunity for style and for certain kinds of experience.

At Carnival itself this general trend in social relations is taken a stage further to a state where the individual may literally 'lose' themselves in the dance. The concept of a centrifugal aesthetic which is opposed to the centripetal force of Christmas is found to be not merely an orientation to display and the street, but a process which literally empties out the self. The very excitement and loudness of Carnival is opposed to the exceptional quiet of Christmas day, just as the disorder of bacchanal is opposed to the months of ordering one's home. The treatment of family members in the dance tends to accentuate the manner in which they can be accommodated in the same category as friends and companions: relationships which are constituted not by given ties but merely by one's fêting together. The emphasis is on an expressive and often competitive individualism, reconstituted by each event. In so far as they express ideals about social relations, then, the two festivals are literally poles apart.

If the home becomes the central idiom through which the values associated with Christmas are expressed, then sexuality seems to inhabit a place of equal prominence in Carnival; it is through sexuality that transience, freedom and disorder are marked and experienced. There is an exploitation of sexual relations as mere events which do not of themselves require much more than simple mutual acquiesence but are purely voluntaristic, remaining under the control of the participants and free of accretive consequences. In these festivals the two idioms are merely kept apart, but in the next chapter it will be found that there is an immensely important direct relationship of opposition between property and sexuality which may be traced through many other sectors of Trinidadian society.

It would be much more common to express the values of individualistic freedom through an examination of the world of men, since it is men who most commonly articulate these as positive values and exhort each other in them. In this case, however, a group of women may be observed to explicate these values in their practices quite as fully, and to challenge thereby any attempt to reduce the opposition between these values to gender itself as is commonly done through the elaboration of concepts such as domesticity (Wilson 1973). Furthermore, given the transformation of Carnival, there is some evidence that women in general are now taking the possibilities of freedom to a more absolute extreme than men, at least on this particular occasion (Miller 1991).

The Relationship between Carnival and Christmas

What is manifestly clear is that neither Christmas nor Carnival could stand on its own as an expression of 'Trinidadian' values.

As argued at the beginning of this chapter, the evidence suggests that there have arisen two diametrically opposed representations of values and cultural projects. They occupy, however, too powerful a place in Trinidadian life to be thought of as stylised renderings of a reality which lies elsewhere. In the succeeding chapters the same dichotomy will be traced through the organisation of kinship and in the appropriation of mass consumption, but it would make equal sense to see these other domains as everyday and mundane objectifications, as merely the preparation for their 'true' enactment in festivals, as it would to portray festivals as merely achieving some autonomy and clarity in their expression as against the more compromised and pragmatic worlds of the everyday.

The largely synchronic description which has been provided of the relationship between the festivals of Christmas and Carnival, seems to lend itself to an analysis in the tradition of formalised anthropological structuralism. In the following section it will be argued that the opposition between Christmas and Carnival only fully manifests itself at a particular and recent historical period, but this should not detract from the clarity of distinctions which can be located in the current forms of celebration. Christmas is recognised as the 'official' start of the Carnival season. It is as though Christmas fires a starter's pistol which launches the calypsos which have until Carnival time to compete for the public's affection and win road march. There is also a kind of mid-point between the two where the values expressed by each come into direct juxtaposition: that is the celebration of what in Trinidad is termed Old Year's Night, the existence of which provides, perhaps, the strongest evidence for the emergence of a clear structural relation between Christmas and Carnival.

The significance of Old Year's Night lies in its two major attributes. It is simultaneously quite clearly the most important church service of the whole year, and also the most important party of the whole year. Although midnight mass on Christmas eve has an important formal place in the Church calender, and is attended by religious Christians, most people excuse themselves on the grounds that they are simply too busy with Christmas preparations. Although acknowledgment is given to the religious origins of the festival, for example, in the *crèche* at the local shopping malls and an address by the Archbishop reported in the newspaper, actual religious involvement is quite muted.

By contrast, although it has only minimal religious sanction, the midnight mass held on Old Year's Night is of considerable importance, and for a proportion of Trinidadian Christians it is the only annual service they attend. The service is often intense and has an aura which many people regard as quite 'special'. Many services, for example, among Baptist congregations, may last four or five hours, ending at one o'clock or two o'clock in the morning. The atmosphere thus created may be extended and the more 'transcendent' of families may use New Year's Day as a kind of second Christmas. They prepare the home for a large meal in which the extended family partakes, and which may continue until late in the day.

There is, however, another side to Old Year's Night which is that while Carnival is the most important season for party and fête, within the pre-Carnival season it is this night which provides what is clearly acknowledged as the single most important party or fête of the year. A common topic of conversation while sitting around on Christmas day, and certainly in subsequent days, is the choice of Old Year's Night party. The radio is listened to that much more intently as the primary source of information on fêtes. The clubs in Port of Spain and in the shopping malls have their most exclusive and expensive 'do' on this night, but there are also countless 'house parties'. As with the church service, if one goes to parties at all, one will go on this occasion.

This is the evening which divides Trinidad symbolically into three sections. Those families who could be labelled as of exclusive transcendent orientation would go to church and feel it quite inappropriate to then go on to a party. Those individuals who could be labelled as of exclusive transient orientation would go to party and have no interest in going to church. But by far the largest section, who live through the contradictions expressed in holding both of these orientations, go first to a church service and then straight on to a party. This categorisation mainly works for Christians (though many non-Christians will attend church on Old Year's Night), but everyone in Trinidad is affected by the atmosphere and aura which surrounds Old Year's Night, an evening which, with its benign refusal to acknowledge contradictions, seems to be as important to the contemporary sense of being Trinidad as either Christmas or Carnival.

Christmas may still contain certain aspects of the sense of bacchanal which otherwise has been fixed on to Carnival and should have left it entirely cleansed of such associations. The most common acknowledgement of this comes in the embarrassed stories about the effects of alcohol leading to intra-family quarrels over the Christmas table. While the tradition of male groups drinking their way around several houses, ideally singing *parang*, has virtually disappeared, giving way to the modern 'quiet' Christmas, there is some element of an alternative male-centred and more disruptive celebration which may attempt to assert itself on occasion.

More generally in popular culture there is a tendency to find a niche for injecting some 'spice' into Christmas. The most conspicuous example of this in recent years has been the emergence, particularly in 1990, of 'soca parang', that is calypsonians launching a calypso with a *parang* rhythm and lyrics concerned with Christmas, specifically for that season.[15] There was considerable debate over the appropriateness of these. The *Express* of 22 December 1990 is particularly instructive. The most popular soca *parang* tune 'Anita' had been launched by Scrunter, following his success with 'I want a Piece ah Pork for my Christmas' the previous year. A typical section is as follows:

It is a time for sharing, and everybody getting someting, that's the reason why I ask yuh, I confuse of what to give yuh.
You have TV, I gave you fridge, I gave you land, You have man, You have radio, You have stereo, I gave you ring, anyting. I want my breakfast in my bed boy,[16] me no want no ham and eggs boy, give me black pudding[17] instead boy, Christmas pudding in my bed. Ay Anita.

In the *Express* of 22 December there were three separate references to this song. The first was a full-page interview with Scrunter fronted by a picture of the singer trying to look as innocent as possible. In this article Scrunter noted that 'Anita' was being played around twenty-five times a day on the radio, but proclaims 'I don't know how to talk ... people take everything I say as double meaning' and goes on to ask 'what else resemble pork/black pudding beside pork/black pudding?'. His grounds for this complaint was evident a few pages away in an interview with the Archbishop of Trinidad who warns: 'Christmas is not Anita in bed with black pudding. It is a time of cheer, but a special cheer. Christmas is about Christ.' In the same issue, the debate section written by Kelvin Baldeosingh and situated next to the editorial is entitled 'Celebrating Life'. It attacks an editorial in its rival paper the *Guardian* which had stated that: 'the rise of *parang* soca at this time could only mean a further thrust in the materialisation of our society and a widening disregard or contempt for its spiritual values and underpinning'. The *Express* journalist, by contrast, defends this new form of celebrating Christmas and even argued: 'The fact that Anita has been given everything frees her from materialism'!

If Christmas is continually under threat from the eruption of bacchanal values which are then monitored and debated, an exactly symmetrical problem occurs with Carnival. This issue has been the subject of a paper by Stewart (1986) who focuses on the interference in Carnival by the state. He argues that by promoting Carnival as official national culture and attempting to direct it and control it through state authorities such as the Carnival Development Committee, Carnival has lost its authenticity, and many Trinidadians have felt it is constrained from expressing the spirit of spontaneity and bacchanal. Indeed, Stewart makes the point that this is only the most recent of a long series of attempts to control Carnival and promote its more 'serious' qualities over the last century and more.

There is, however, a problem in talking of a loss of authenticity in Carnival, since in some ways it is precisely the attempt by spokespersons to make claims to authenticity which may detract from the ability of Carnival to continue to undermine and represent disorder. Something of this may be found in the internal dualism which has arisen between the 'serious' political calypsos, and the 'rude' dance soca, which refuses to pay proper obeisance even to the history of calypso.

History

The analysis which precedes is based largely on synchronic material, but the dynamism of both festivals should be clear. Carnival seems to change its implications almost each decade, facing about to address different aspects of Trinidadian society, now emancipation, now class, now gender. Other festivals have been equally dynamic. Divali has shifted from being a relatively low-key, private celebration, to become promoted as of national significance, while Hosay has been correspondingly demoted (for reasons which closely parallel similar developments in Fiji, see Kelly

1988). In examining historical records, however, the festival that has undergone the most profound change may well be Christmas.

In the earlier sources it seems clear that almost all the elements which are today associated with Carnival arose originally in Trinidad, and indeed in the Caribbean more generally, under the auspices of Christmas. Dirks (1987), under the title of *The Black Saturnalia*, has compiled considerable evidence for the immense importance of Christmas during the period of slavery. On the one hand this was the season when the slaves received their clothing and other new provisions, and was, from the first, associated with special foods, liberal drinking and feasting. At the same time this was also the period of bacchanal, the beginnings of masquerade, an invocation of egalitarian relations between slave and master (ix–xi, 1–8), and by far the most common season for the eruption of slave revolts. Indeed, Dirks suggests that, as with later Carnival, this is the festival in which a certain kind of truth is provided with its stylised rendering, one which normally remains hidden.

The centrality of Christmas to the emergence of local culture is certainly clear in contemporary accounts, which also refer to Christmas (as opposed to Lent) as the proper time for Carnival activities (Abrahams and Szwed (eds) 1983: 226–79). Detailed descriptions are also available for Trinidad as by Carmichael (1969 originally 1833). She provides considerable information on Christmas festivities, but also some detail on topics such as the emergence of display in house interiors, and the importance of clothing and especially the newness of fashions associated with Christmas (ibid. 129–31, 147). For a much later period there are recollections of elements of early twentieth-century Christmas in oral accounts from elderly people in the Chaguanas area today. Several such informants noted that at that time it was Christmas rather than Carnival which was more likely to be associated with fighting and exceptional heavy drinking. Their accounts often differ markedly from the stress on domestic calm which is found in the nostalgic newspaper accounts.

It seems, then, that the strong dichotomy in the relationship between these two festivals, which has been drawn in this chapter from contemporary and synchronic evidence, was not necessarily so marked a feature in previous times. Indeed, the historical evidence implies that many of the elements which make up this dualism have their roots largely in a single cultural event, that is Christmas. It is relatively recently that Christmas has sloughed off many of the attributes which would have associated it with a sense of bacchanal and disorder. Similarly, these same elderly informants often stress in their references to Carnival its customary and traditional features, which had developed over a considerable time period. There are nostalgic reminiscences of the particular masquerades that would reappear every year. There is again some discrepancy between these accounts and the contemporary focus on the event and the originality of dress.

As was noted above, there are still counterpoised tendencies to 'spice up' Christmas and to sediment Carnival, but historically there is a longer-term movement towards duality. This historical sequence will not be pursued for the present. In subsequent chapters it will be provided with a larger context in terms of other movements towards a greater dualism which appear to have been associated with the rise of affluence and have been concretised particularly with the oil-boom. The same historical trajectory may be evident in domains such as kinship and most particularly in the appropriation of the possibilities of mass consumption. The theme will be returned to, however, since it may provide important evidence for the assertion that the dynamics of Trinidadian society are relevant to an understanding of the fundamental nature of modernity.

The two sets of values expressed in these two festivals will be referred to throughout the rest of this book by the terms 'transient' and 'transcendent'. This is intended to imply that there exists a distinction hinging upon the moral and experiential consequences of two intrinsically related forms of temporal consciousness. On the one hand there is a celebration of an ephemeral present that in its absolute form appears to deny all possibilities of sociality, through an exhilarating sense of freedom within the maelstrom. Opposed to this is Christmas, the time for constructing a sense of roots and tradition, also associated with planning for the future and family descent. Christmas provides a sense of continuity which is constructed as almost pure incorporative sociality in systematic opposition to the perceived dangers of transience.

It is this characterisation which relates the analysis of these two festivals directly to that which in Habermas' account of Hegel is rendered as the foundational condition for the experience of modernity. What these festivals imply is a consciousness of temporality that is radically ruptured from any given sense of customary morality. Rather, we find two diametrically opposed senses as might well have emerged from the kind of contradictions which were analysed in the previous chapter. In the first place, we have a sense of custom and tradition, but not as given. Rather, we see tremendous efforts put into its systematic cultivation in direct refusal of the transience with which it coexists. Nostalgia is the self-consciousness of tradition and Christmas is thoroughly nostalgic.

In the analysis of Carnival we find the other side to this new temporality, again a systematic working through of the logic of transience, a festival which creates a sense of event such that popular culture can achieve that which for writers on modernity was previously best captured only by individual poets and dandies. Once again this seems to be a cultivation of the transient in direct consciousness and repudiation of that sense of time which is constructed around Christmas. As might be expected there are both similarities and distinctions from those traits drawn from European forms of modernity. There is no sense of fragmentation associated with Carnival, rather there is the sustained working out of transience as a project.

The potential affinity between these major festivals which dominate a significant period of the Trinidadian year and the more abstract writings about the foundation of modernity is thereby drawn. But festivals themselves are not enough. It remains to be shown that this same radical rupture of temporal consciousness also effects everyday life and more embedded aspects of ordinary social relations, such that modernity is not merely an enactment but the pervasive framework of Trinidadian life. This will be the task of the next chapter.

Notes

1. For additional material on this relationship between Christmas and commerce in Trinidad, and a more elaborate attempt to account for this within a comparative context, see Miller 1993.

2. This survey was originally carried out with Bill Guinea alongside a survey of Divali in relation to research he was conducting on Hindus. I would wish to acknowledge his help in this regard. In the event, I have used only my own survey materials, which related exclusively to the four communities I studied and where I feel more confident in my knowledge of the context.

3. Christmas 1988 was certainly not a typical year, in that it seemed to mark a turning point. This was the year when many people recognised that the recession might not be a tem-

porary phase, prior to an improvement in conditions. As a result, Christmas expenditure was generally regarded by commentators as exceptionally frugal. Furthermore, the government (which *knew* that it had run out of money) signalled in a dramatic fashion that Christmas could not be normal by banning the importation of apples and grapes. The effect was on a par with banning the importation of Christmas trees in those countries where such trees are the norm. As a result the standard Christmas greeting became 'I would like to wish you a HAPPY Christmas but ...'. Thus, although the figures are taken from 1988, the description also rests on the observation of Christmas 1990 which was a more normal Christmas.

4. At all points of the text 'TT' refers to the Trinidad and Tobago dollar. The value of this has changed with devaluations but was worth approximately 0.23 US dollars at the time of fieldwork.

5. Sorrel is a drink made from the red blossoms of a member of the hibiscus family which flowers at this time of year.

6. Black cake is a rich fruit cake made with chopped dried fruits soaked in alcohol (rum or cherry brandy) and is the equivalent of the steamed Christmas pudding made in other countries.

7. Sweet bread is a heavy cake often made with coconut.

8. Old Year's Night is the night of 31 December, New Year's Eve.

9. *Jouvay* is a corruption of the French Jour Ouvert.

10. Lise Winer (personal communication) notes the term 'skin yuh bottom' for the abusive-insultive action of women showing their buttocks to other women within a cuss-out.

11. *Wassy* means uninhibited, wild, carrying-on.

12. The Jamette (or Jamet) Carnival is the term, used by Brereton (1975: 48) and others for the Carnivals of the 1860s and 1870s. They were dominated by an underclass, derived from the Port of Spain slums, which formed anti-establishment bands associated with stickfighting, verbal wit and explicit sexual provocations.

13. Common Entrance is the entrance exam for secondary school in Trinidad. This calypso alleged ethnic bias.

14. The term 'tail' does not have quite as derogatory a connotation as in current North American usage.

15. Lise Winer also notes (personal communication) the recent creation of a 'Christmas Road March' as the hottest pre-Christmas *parang*.

16. The term boy (or man) is sometimes used to address females, as well as males in Trinidad.

17. Black pudding would in this context be widely interpreted as sex with a black woman.

Chapter 4

Household as Cultural Idiom

Introduction

The previous chapter established that the two festivals which dominate Trinidadian life for several months of the year express a core dualism in Trinidadian culture. The values so forcefully expressed by Christmas have been termed 'transcendent': that is, concerned with the longer term, both planning for the future and establishing roots. This may then be contrasted with the set of values termed 'transient' which are expressed most clearly in the event-orientated emphasis of Carnival. If the spatial domain is emphasised, then the contrast would be a 'centripetal' quality of the domestic as against a 'centrifugal' orientation to the streets.

A chapter on festivals, however, can be no more than an introduction to a larger claim about the possibilities of an ethnography of modernity. Festivals, as also rituals, are commonly regarded as themselves a rather abstract form in which the logic of, or contradictions in, cultural practices may be worked out with a clarity which may bear but little upon the more contextualised and often more complex concerns of everyday life. A rather more challenging case would be presented by that area which has dominated previous ethnographic investigations, which is the investigation of social structure.

The anthropology and the work of anthropologists in this region poses, in turn, its own problems for the intentions and orientations of the present work. Because of the specific traditions of the discipline, there is a tendency for anthropological studies to focus in upon social structure on the grounds that this is usually seen as the foundation for the organisation of other domains of culture, such that if there is an element of reductionism this is the area to which other domains are most likely to be reduced. Indeed, given the traditional divisions between anthropology and sociology, it may be inferred that anthropologists tend to identify their object of studies with situations in which kinship seems to be the dominant idiom for social life.

Certainly, any review of anthropolological studies of this region would quickly reveal the dominance of work on kinship over all other areas of concern. Given the high level of sophistication and complexity of studies by scholars such as M.G. Smith and R.T. Smith, it would be evident that the anthropologists are well aware of a potential parochialism in such studies and have endeavoured, in various ways, to open up the study of kinship to a consideration of the wider context. In the first part of this chapter I shall briefly review some of the studies of West Indian kinship in order to demonstrate how they have shifted from documenting a specific regional tradition under the title of 'West Indian kinship' towards a set of wider issues in which kinship may be of concern more because it acts as idiom in relation to other domains, and less in order to pose it simply as a specific form within comparative studies of kinship.

This survey will thereby establish the foundation for my own intentions in dealing with the topic. While much of the material in this chapter will deal with the forms, and more particularly the tensions, in household definition, I do not wish to imply any privileging of this area of social life as in some sense a dominant idiom. Rather, the point I am hoping to establish is that even this aspect of social relations is thoroughly permeated by the same dualism which was viewed more abstractly in the previous chapter. The lines of articulation are already suggested in the description of festivals where it became clear that property has a particular significance to the values expressed in transcendence, while sexuality was prominent as an expressive medium for transient values. The dualism which is thereby established will also clearly resonate with others such as the public versus the private which have been used in general discussions of the development of modernity (Sennett 1977).

Writings on West Indian Kinship

Until recently much of the anthropological writing on the Caribbean has centred around the nature of a specific regional tradition termed 'West Indian' kinship, particularly associated with groups of African origin, which has tended to be characterised by its tension with those norms promulgated by both the church and colonial governments. Such writings have tended to focus upon categories such as 'female-headed household' or 'matrifocality' which have been seen as characteristic of ex-slave populations of the Caribbean. The work which is often regarded as establishing the importance of these features was the study by R.T. Smith of the Negro family in British Guiana (1956). Using ideas from Fortes, for example on the developmental cycle of domestic groups, Smith argued for a particular sequence of household forms, with late entry into co-residential unions and relatively limited male domestic authority. This original portrait of the matrifocal family was not founded upon either a conception of the female-headed households nor marital instability (Smith 1973: 125). Both of these, however, became associated features in the subsequent literature.

Smith's own work has developed markedly over the subsequent thirty years. A constant concern has been the relationship between kinship and class, but increasingly attention has focused on the importance of understanding the local 'folk' categories of kinship (Alexander 1984). New techniques, such as the longer interview or oral traditions, have also been used to broaden and deepen the context for kinship study. Throughout, Smith and his students have endeavoured to demonstrate that the discrepancy from imported expectations of nuclear or extended family forms does not imply an absence of a clear alternative concept of family with its own normative expectations. Most recently, their work on genealogies has emphasised the considerable number of relatives who come under the folk domain of kinship.

The original desire to provide a characterisation of the specific forms of kinship, but with a sense of their dynamism rather than merely a set of static categories, was also behind a series of highly systematic studies of comparative household and family structure by M. G. Smith. Through a comparison of five sample areas, Smith argued that: 'it is clear that the mating organization governs the form of the domestic system and provides the central principle of the family structure' (1962: 219). More specifically he argued that the three main forms of mating – visiting, consensual and legal – tend to form a developmental and stable sequence in rural areas, but simply coexist in an unstable pattern in urban areas (1962: 207–8).

Overall the emphasis of these and later studies has been on lower-class black families (though Smith 1988 provides a more serious consideration of the middle class (see also Braithwaite 1975: 87–117). When generalising these findings, writers often accentuate those features which are seen as resistant to legal or orthodox religious ideologies, such as:

(1) The early entry of women into childbirth but late entry into legal marriage.

(2) The common existence of relationships such as visiting where the male is not resident, or common-law where the male is resident but the relationship is not formally sanctioned.

(3) the considerable scope for sexual relations outside any formally sanctioned unit.

While much of the earlier work emphasised male marginality emergent from historical conditions, Wilson (1973) provided a distinct contribution by focusing more on what males actually do as peer groups, providing a vivid description of the viability and attraction of this male-centred sociality. If Wilson helped to give substance to the male world, a number of feminist social scientists have in recent years concentrated on exploring the female role and perspective on these relations. In the main, however, the work of Barrow (1986a, 1986b 1988) and Massiah (1983, 1986 (ed.), 1988) has suggested not the strong West Indian woman as mistress of her own fate and dominant over important social domains, but rather women strong in adverse conditions coping with difficult subsistence strategies under conditions of limited support (Senior 1991: 82–102).

The generalities uncovered by this extensive pan-Caribbean work are most clearly represented in Trinidad by studies of 'lower-class' Afro-Caribbean families, (Rodman 1971 though see Harrison 1975 for a dissenting view). Rodman suggests seven characteristics of kinship as observed in his study:

(1) Husbands and fathers are often marginal members of the nuclear family.
(2) Marital-shifting takes place frequently. During their lifetime, most people will be involved in several different marital relationships.
(3) 'Friending' (visiting) takes place more often than living together, and living together more often than marriage. In other words, the

more responsibilities a marital relationship involves, the less often it takes place.

(4) There is a casual attitude between spouses.

(5) The rate of illegitimate births among this group is high.

(6) Child-shifting takes place frequently. It is usually the mother's mother or mother's sister who takes over the care of the child when the mother cannot.

(7) There is no strong feeling that the biological mother must bring up her own children.

(Rodman 1971: 171)

Overall Rodman describes a kinship system, which is less geared to structural norms, role expectations or given obligations and more to the actualisation of a particular relationship at a particular time determined by contextual circumstances. This would be true not only for the establishment of mating and childcare but also more generally for the determination of whom one is interacting with or asking for favours or advice on a day-to-day basis. In such an ethnography one is dealing less with a normative household than with a 'household in effect'. These generalisations are generally supported by other accounts which focus specifically on lower-class African populations (see relevant sections of Braithwaite 1975: 120–44, and Freilich (1960, 1968) for Trinidad, and the summary by Senior (1991) for the Caribbean more generally). Recent accounts have, however, challenged this assumption that these attributes are specific to lower-class life (Smith 1988; Young 1990).

This interpretation of kinship as embodying an opposition to externally given norms is in a way confirmed by the recent research by R.T. Smith (1988), though that may not have been his intention. Smith demonstrates that if in forming relationships people tend to avoid structure and normative forms, this is certainly not through lack of knowledge of where structure could be derived from, i.e. the extensive relationships within which one might see oneself as constituted by the facts of genealogical derivation, since there is a tremendous investment in genealogical knowledge. This need not be paradoxical, however, if one argues that the desire is to be fully briefed as to the possibilities of such connections, but then to feel a voluntaristic sense of choice as to which ones are actually utilised at a given time.

Smith studied genealogy, and the literature generally tries to retain these findings as observations on kinship specifically, but I suspect that (at least for Trinidad) a very similar situation would be found with regard to non-kin, which transforms kinship into simply another expression of a more general tendency in social relations. In Trinidad, individuals are well aware of a large range of potential non-kin contacts. These may be derived from people one was at school with, people in the neighbourhood or networks established through mechanisms such as *whe whe, sou sou*, the church and so forth. But friendship in action often appears unstructured in the sense of being dominated by one-to-one relations determined pragmatically. In general, writings which at one stage emphasised the development of local norms in opposition to cultural stereotypes which refused to acknowledge norms in the black diaspora family, are now moving towards an emphasis on the flexibility of relationships and the extent to which they are defined dyadically.

This tendency in kinship studies is exemplified by Gonzales (1984), another anthropologist who has changed her ideas as a result of long-term investigations. In comparing surveys in 1957 and 1975 she found that family forms had not been as responsive to economic change as anticipated and therefore queries her earlier emphasis on poverty as a causative factor.[1] She is also led to question her earlier attempts to construct clear family typologies. She now argues that households overlap and fluctuate in membership, that people flow between affinal and consanguineal arrangements in a manner which does not suggest a firm commitment to either one of these. She concludes that 'the individual, rather than the nuclear family becomes the basic unit or building block' and that as for matrifocality 'women have become central, perhaps by default' (1984: 8) which echoes the findings of feminist social scientists on men's refusal to undertake domestic responsibilities.

There are problems in applying any general characterisation of 'West Indian' kinship to Trinidad. First, there are other examples of kinship analysis applied to Afro-Caribbean populations which emphasise corporate groups and a descent orientation (Besson and Momsen 1987). Indeed the pioneering study of kinship in Jamaica by Clarke (1957) although segmenting by class, does suggest a powerful counter tendency towards a normative nuclear domestic family with cognatic descent, associated with inalienable family land and home ownership.

Second, within Trinidad, Africans represent only 40 per cent of the population. They include a substantial middle class and there is an expectation of a move away from this stress on voluntarism towards the establishment of more formal relationships with age. This means that the pool of people who might actually be expected to conform to the patterns described by Rodman (1971) are a relatively small part of the population overall. Few authors have examined other elements in African kinship, but both Braithwaite (1975) and Macdonald (1986) have focused attention on the particular importance of the African middle class in recent Trinidadian history.

In practice, the main alternative traditions in kinship studies have emerged from studies of other ethnic groups, especially the extensive work on (East) Indian families. Such studies suggest that Indian kinship in Trinidad has been extraordinarily dynamic. Most arrived only two or three generations previously, largely as individuals rather than family units, with a high preponderance of males, but relating to familial systems which require genealogical depth. This leads for Klass (1961) to the rapid reconstruction of such 'traditions' as described in his ethnography of Amity in the 1950s. Others have argued subsequently that this was actually a syncretic amalgamation of various regional elements and local innovations (Vertovec 1992: 86–126). Recently, Klass has compared his original ethnography with the work of Nevadomsky (1982, 1983) in the same village and his own return to Amity in 1985. By comparing the three accounts he is able to indicate the considerable changes which have taken place over thirty-five years. Indeed, the recent ethnography suggests that most of the institutions of kinship, from the use of Hindi terminology to the arranged marriage, which make up the substance of his 1950s account have virtually disappeared since (Klass 1991: 45–68).

Despite this considerable dynamism in actual kinship practices among the Indian community, there remains an ideology about family which is pervasive and resilient against these transformations. What seems to matter to the community is less how one defines a 'joint' family (Macdonald and Macdonald 1973; Nevadomsky 1982, 1983; Schwartz 1965), than the reification of the concept 'family' itself which has become central to the distinctive ethnicity of being Indian. This ideology of family is invested in a sense of long time depth, of clear continuities from South Asia and of enshrined and established 'traditions'. Within this ideology there is the desire that the individual is properly subsumed within this larger enterprise, that there is considerable financial interdependence with salaries given over in the large part to the family, and with powerful claims by close kin over possessions held by individual family members. The sense of being family is expressed in the use of family networks in business and patronage, in creating exchanges between rural produce and urban skills, and in providing an idiom for a particular kind of sociality which can be transposed to non-family members, or even the ethnic group itself, as a kind of superordinate family. In short, many Indian Trinidadians think of themselves as that segment of the population whose primary orientation is to their family.

There are still elements which appear to indicate continuity with South Asian origins, though today these are largely truncated forms. For example, rather than true virilocality it has become customary for newly married couples to spend at least a token period of time within the household of the husband's parents. There may also be constraints on sons in the presence of their fathers, and women in the presence of men. Such practices may, however, be evolving from unexplicit forms of 'habitus' and sentiment, into increasingly explicated duties with respect to the self-conscious preservation of tradition and difference – symbols of being Indian.

For this reason, such features of the contemporary family are best considered within the larger context of Trinidadian culture, where the Indian family may have become the objectification of the 'transcendent' family more generally, and in turn has responded by attempting to embody the ideals and values for which it is seen as the traditional repository. In the next section it will be argued that this can be most easily discerned through the construction of transcendence through the experience of property and inheritance, which then become the imperative behind most other elements of family life.

Despite the fact that an ideology which equates a powerful concept of family with one ethnic group is used to objectify a powerful set of values within Trinidadian culture, this may not impinge very much on the remaining practices of that group. From the level of more general surveys of Trinidadian family life, the ethnic distinction appears to be rapidly diminishing.[2] Formerly Indians were being entered into arranged or semi-arranged marriages at an early age: 'But, there has been a dramatic change in the mating patterns; for among younger women it is now the non-Indians who enter their first union at an earlier age. Moreover, more women of both ethnic groups are now entering a visiting union as their initial relationship; and young women, particularly the better educated ones, are increasingly tending to remain in a visiting union rather than shift to a more stable relationship as was formally the common practice' (Abdullah 1988: 461). This would suggest that the ideology of the Indian family as the bastion of certain Trinidadian values has arisen during the same period when actual ethnic distinctions in familial practice have drastically reduced. This discrepancy should be borne in mind when considering the evidence for kinship and household in the four communities which will be considered below.

Both the brief survey of kinship studies and, more particularly, the treatment of the history of the Indian family suggest the incorporation of social structure within a more general description of the imperatives of moral and cultural order. The subsequent section will attempt to flesh out this reflection on Indian traditions in order to construct a more general view of transcendence as a mode of social organisation, and will then apply the same procedure to the material on 'West Indian' kinship which is thereby transformed into a general account of transience as a mode of social organisation.

Property and Transcendence

To associate the family with the house is hardly novel. In many regions from Greece (Du Boulay 1974) to Colombia (Gudeman and Rivera 1990: 39–53) studies demonstrate an intense devotion to the continuity of the 'house' in a manner which would make it foolish to attempt to disaggregate the physical elements of property and the social relations of family. In many regions the terms for house and descent group are identical or closely related.

This is not the case in Trinidad, where the English terminologies, which have become universal today, in most (though not all) cases tend to assume a more discrete set of social units. Nevertheless, there is abundant evidence to suggest that among certain sections of the population it is the sense of property which dominates kinship. This means that we have to eschew the narrow legalistic sense of the terms 'property' and 'possessions', and try and evoke a much deeper emotive sense – the high sentimentality of the long-held possession, or the sense of identity virtually riveted on to a piece of land.

A local adage states that the first thing a Trinidadian does on obtaining a house is to 'renovate' it. Considerable supportive evidence for this contention has already been noted from The Meadows and Newtown. Partly this represents a process of consumption which takes the property from its origins in the market or the state and constructs it as expressive (compare Miller 1988), but in Trinidad this is also part of that centripetal aesthetic found in the activities associated with Christmas, where the sense of family and household is created through the process of building and filling up a home.

Beyond renovation is the attraction of the construction of one's own home, which has again become elaborated within ethnic self-definition. An examination of the records held by the company which constructed and still owns the land at The Meadows revealed that nearly all those who bought plots of land rather than houses were Indian.[3] As Africans use wealth to demonstrate their escape from economic conditions where they were forced to build their own houses, Indians are developing a sentimental attachment to their own participation in building. Even where building skills were limited, people could be eloquent about the part they had played in the design of the house and the directions given to the builders. 'As a child the first thing the parent will tell you when you are working is to try and save some money to build your own home.' This counsel is internalised as a young Indian male asserted: 'When you turn your own key, you change from being a boy into a man, you are controlling everything.'

In a study of a commercial store during the period 1977–85 (Mohammed 1987) it was found that the owner was buying at least one piece of land per year. This evidence could certainly be repeated for many other Indian families. There are many reasons given for the constant purchase of land. First, there are plots of land for the children to occupy and build their houses upon when the time should come, for which reason some of the wealthier Chaguanas families had bought several plots of land in The Meadows. Second, there is the idea that some land will be used for building residential communities and will thereby vastly increase its value. Third, there is the general desire to invest in land for agricultural purposes. In practice, with the recession, some land is certainly coming back into agriculture, but that is

usually purchased on more pragmatic grounds according to precise requirements, and the kind of intermittent land purchase that
is of concern here seems to be little attuned to the actual requirements of agriculture, and is subsequently of fitful use at best. Of
greater importance is that, as Klass notes for Amity, 'To an
Indian, a man who sells land, and thus deprives his children, is
beneath contempt' (1961: 244). Conversely, to add to one's stock
of land had, by the time of the oil-boom, become a primary component of self-esteem.

Several cases were found of orthodox Hindus establishing
shrines on the land which their grandparents were first granted,
or first purchased, after they left indentured labour. For many
families the tradition, until recently, has been that notwithstanding the official legal system, selling land to non-family members
is forbidden. This meant in many cases decisions about the land
were not vested in the senior title holder but shared throughout
the male membership of that family. Ideally, only land added to
the original family stock could be traded. This ideal appears,
however, to be another casualty of the rapid changes and reorien-
tations of the last decade for Indians in Trinidad. A more general
association with the land may be affirmed in the Dih worship
referred to in the previous chapter.

By the late 1980s the relationship to land presented above was
becoming outdated. The oil-boom may well have brought about
the climax of this desire to establish a relationship through land,
with massive purchasing of additional plots of land, but at the
same time it indicated that the future lay elsewhere. The new generation of Indians, in particular, repudiated much of this concern,
associating agriculture with the 'backwardness' of their parents,
and became orientated towards much more mobile instruments of
business and the professions as forms of family enhancement.
This does not mean, however, that the underlying project of transcendence was diminished: rather that its forms of objectification
are dynamic.

Perhaps the most interesting transference of these values is
found in the attitude to educational qualifications, which seems
to retain many familiar elements but in a form which allows for
the increasing individualisation of family members more appropriate to the 1980s. Seen as part of the investment in one's children, the desire is expressed to see the 'filling up' of the corporate
family body with qualifications, and making the children literally

'substantial'. One of the main consequences of recession was a rapid growth in unemployment and the realisation that job security in all sectors was increasingly ephemeral. I found it therefore surprising, if not shocking, that several of my acquaintances in The Meadows and Newtown were proposing to leave secure employment in order to gain further educational qualifications, when most of those concerned already had an abundance of such qualifications, which had often not proved as effective as once hoped in securing well-paid employment.

The decision seemed to be based on the belief that the constancy of the core lies in its solidity and breadth as against the ephemeral nature of transience. In a period which seemed generally to be leading towards instability and event-led dynamics, the response was often to try and firm up the protection against the influence of such forces. Both persons and families were constantly described in terms of their educational achievements, as in meeting 'So and so BA', or the religious ceremonies for a family who had gained seven degrees for the seven children, or the display of these qualifications as part of the living-room decoration set against mother's day and wedding paraphernalia. For example, a mother talking about the risks of her children coming under bad influences stressed that with their background and education they were preserved from such things. Education also fits well with the sense of planning and the core temporal consciousness which defines transcendence. It is viewed as an intangible accretion to the body of the group or individual which, once achieved, cannot be lost or spent. As a result, an area such as The Meadows is awash with university degrees, and contains a dozen kindergartens for children from two and a half years up, with a strong academic content from the very beginning.

Inheritance

The issue of inheritance among Indian Trinidadians is much confused by three competing influences. First, there is that which is perceived as traditional Indian custom; second, there is Trinidad state law; and third, there are forces which are perceived as emanating from modernisation and change. Traditional Indian custom as constructed in Trinidad is for unilineal male inheritance. Ideally, property should be held jointly by the sons, but, if it is to be divided, there is a tendency to favour the eldest and the youngest sons. Dowry is minimal, but daughters may receive gifts during their life, especially jewellery, which then becomes regarded as their share of the patrimony. The owner of a gift shop noted, however, that even in early childhood the better-quality gifts are given to sons rather than daughters. Married daughters are generally viewed as gaining land through their husbands, and there may be more concern to make allowances for unmarried daughters.

To the extent to which such values are maintained, it is important to try and retain one of the sons of the family within the house of the parents. Of the two dominant styles of architecture in Trinidad, that regarded as the 'Indian' style comprises a house built on stilts (though this style is by no means restricted to Indians). Initially the section below the house may be used for commercial activities or as a yard, but there is commonly the expectation that walls will later be built around this area and then converted into a full-sized home for the son and his family. Alternatively, one or all of the sons are provided for with plots of land in the immediate vicinity for building their own homes. Many such family colonies can be found in the areas outside Chaguanas although they are more difficult to construct within the constraints of urban land and housing. In recent years it has become more common for the youngest, rather than the eldest male, to have pressure put upon him to remain with the parents, since the other sons have left the home, and parents become increasingly concerned that at least one son should remain for their old age.

There has emerged a further contradiction between two opposing criteria for establishing the basis of inheritance. On the one hand, there is this ideology which dictates preferential concern for sons and the male line, as symbolising the continuity of the family, which is the overarching project of transcendence. On the other hand, there is increasing concern with an opposing, more pragmatic, sense of reciprocity which says that rewards should be given to whomsoever 'minds' (looks after), the parents in their old age. This, however, is much more often the daughter, who may remain single for that reason. It is assumed today that even where sons wish to help, they will be deflected by the concerns of the daughter-in-law who will lead the son 'astray' into concern for the affinal family, and will at best neglect or at worst abuse their own parents. Typically, parents will imply that 'who mind me will get' but then fail to act upon these sentiments and leave their property to their sons anyway.

The reason behind this discrepancy between declared intention and actual practice is complex. To justify inheritance on the grounds of such a pragmatic morality of reciprocity is more closely associated with transient values. For a family committed to transcendence and the sense of lineal continuity, this is difficult to embrace. Furthermore, there may be ethnic connotations to the relevant behaviour. The effect of this reciprocity would be to move from a patrilineal descent to what would become matrilineal. This move may be partly blocked because of the sense that the latter is an 'African' form. Ironically, given the increasing use of ethnic-based ideology of this kind, Africans in turn may come to regard their own traditions of descent continuity and patrilineality as though they were emulatory of Indian custom.

Another problem over inheritance arises from the discrepancy between all such normative expectations and values and a legal system which largely ignores any such concerns on the grounds of imposing equal division between all recipients and, in particular, recognises females as equal to males in their rights to parental property. It is the law which prevents the establishment of inalienable family land, as a lawyer noted: 'Previously they would say this land is going from ancestor to ancestor and that can't move but that is all gone away, you can't do that, it is illegal to do that, but people still want to do it.' Similarly, clients want to impose conditions such as marrying within the faith. Historically, the Indian community has been estranged from state family law because of the late recognition of Hindu marriage as legal,[4] and the subsequent treatment of inheritance as though it were based on illegitimacy. The community is also seen as intensely litigious, especially with respect to property.

These various conflicts between tradition and modern egalitarianism, between familial and legal perspectives and between principles of reciprocity and descent come together to constitute the environment to the extremely fraught and often violent events that surround many disputes over inheritance. It would be far too simple to see such disputes as merely based on control over important resources, even though this is often a major factor. A striking feature of property disputes is that the land concerned is often of marginal potential utility. Most of those concerned lived in Chaguanas and limed in the capital, while the land held by the family might be in the inland 'bush' and, apart from some old cocoa trees, have little of economic benefit. Even those interested in reinvigorating agriculture, given the recession and expensive nature of imports, were more interested in investing in new, more appropriate land than plots that happened to be theirs by descent. Thanks to the oil-boom it was often the case that each brother had already achieved his own house and a reasonable standard of living in association with it. Yet the same family which had seemed so indivisible and where identity was largely subsumed by the corporate unit could erupt into disputes which could lead to the wounding and killing of cousins and, in extreme cases, siblings and parents. This view would not be shared by many Indians who insist that disputes are over the material benefits rather than a sense of family descent, but several of the cases I actually encountered suggested that the protagonists were attempting thereby to justify as simple interest, more deeply sentimental imperatives.

One lawyer noted that the main reason people make wills was not to include people in, but to exclude them from inheritance. To disinherit is the most effective way to remove an individual from membership of the family and this action seems to be a common response to a disapproved marriage, for example. Parents may give away all, or a substantial amount, of their land before death. There are, however, many local stories paralleling the lessons of *King Lear* or Zola's *La Terre*, which expose the dangers of such action leading to aged parents being turned out of their homes by ungrateful children. Hindu Pundits would warn parents against trying to secure their care by signing over their property while still alive. There remains, however, a discrepancy between a law which views property as subject to individual will, and a tradition which insists upon family-based principles of ownership, such that the children may assert moral rights over property and dispute their father's sole control. For example, on the death of their mother, they may insist upon some security of inheritance (against the occasion of their father's remarriage), especially if there is land which comes to them specifically through the maternal line. On occasion, children's rights may be expressed through the threat of violence against their father, as one taxi-driver noted: 'And if ah doh give he the house, he go burn it, an he eh (isn't) making joke, the young people eh (haven't) got no respect for their elders.' It was equally common, however, for husbands to will land to their sons but not to their wives, especially where she was not the mother of the children concerned. In such cases the woman could find herself, on her husband's death, unexpectedly removed from what she had taken to be her own home.

Even more common, and perhaps more surprising, is that many Indians who might have been expected to do so, in fact make no will or provision for what should take place after their death. In decades past, wills may have seemed a new or a foreign thing, and there is also the feeling that this act, or even to talk about one's death, can tempt fate. However, many who are no longer beset by such constraints are still reluctant to make a will, precisely because of its impending divisive nature and their sense of the unresolvable contradictions between reciprocity and duty. As one put it, they would die without such provision and then 'let the battle commence'. Elderly males often feel that this is the issue upon which their lives are being judged. Ideally they must pass on all they have themselves inherited and preferably should have added to the family assets.

In most cases the landholder dies leaving lawyers to work on letters of administration which pertain in the absence of a will. Officially the land should then be distributed equally, but in many cases the daughters withdraw from their share rather than be involved in disputes with their brothers. Parents, in leaving their home to their children jointly, may hope that this protects its inalienable status since they assume the children will have difficulty coming to the kind of agreement that would make selling the home possible. In practice, the policy may work rather too well as the home is unoccupiable and neglected, losing both value and interest. In other cases, a child may have continued to live at home or have minded the parents and there will be an amicable agreement as to their subsequent rights.

Even if there is no dispute at this stage, by the next generation, where cousins feel less tied by bonds than siblings, households living in close proximity are commonly involved in boundary disputes. Sometimes in St Pauls it seemed as though there was no border between two houses which was not subject to such a dispute and almost no family which did not claim to have been the subject of some underhand disinheritance in the previous generation, leaving a legacy of family factionalism and cousins no longer on speaking terms. Indeed, the story that one's ancestors would have inherited considerable land but for the dishonesty of their relatives is virtually a *leitmotif* in oral histories. Accusations were commonly made of lawyers or surveyors having been bribed to secure the desired settlement. One result was that there were far more disputes in areas such as St Pauls, where land was surveyed and registered, than in Ford where there exists no formal rights to land by any of the occupiers, and boundaries result from *ad hoc* resolution and mere consensual practice.

A nurse at a local health centre remarked that when people came in with chops (wounds from a cutlass) it always seemed that Africans had been chopped by strangers and Indians by their own family. A barmaid noted the extent to which her Indian customers regale her with constant tales of intended revenge on family members. Such remarks reveal the extent to which the above account now forms part of an ethnic ideology of the Indian family, polarised against the now stereotypical African family based in urban and lower-class transient values. Most of my evidence for inheritance disputes derives from the Indian community, so that I am not able to comment on (or challenge) these as stereotypes through comparison with African families.

If my ethnography does not provide an alternative scenario, there are plenty of alternative sources of evidence which would, including earlier reports based in Trinidad or by a comparison within the Caribbean more generally where these 'Indian' constructions of their relationship to property find strong parallels in the African community. Several ethnographers have noted the centrality of having a home to the institution of marriage among Africans (Herskovits 1947: 84). For nearby Barbados, Greenfield (1966: 83) quotes a man as saying: 'A man ain a man till he can call the house he live in my own, and it ain't matter how small it be once you can call it a house.' Elsewhere in the Caribbean, there are many examples of dissolute youth turning to respectability upon the inheritance of house or land (Kuper 1976: 82–3). As such authors point out, the house is seen as having precedence over marriage, in so far as claims to be married were hardly taken seriously unless a home could be provided. Indeed, this linkage is often blamed for the low rate of marriage, as people feel they cannot marry without the appropriate environment.

There is another group of writings on the Caribbean, recently summarised by Besson and Momsen (eds) 1987 which would argue the same point, but with respect to land rather than the house. This literature provides abundant examples of the key symbolic significance of land as representing descent rather than as merely an economic resource. There are equivalent instances of establishing ancestral shrines, of physically coherent family compounds, of a strong sense of the inalienability of family land, and some hint of inheritance disputes (Clarke 1957; Rubenstein 1987: 77–9; Wilson 1973), all of which find echoes within African traditions established in Trinidad. Indeed, in so far as ethnicity is referred to in this literature, it is with exactly the opposite assumption that all of these would be distinctive features of the Afro-Caribbean tradition which opposes them to the more pragmatic and economically orientated concerns of the Indians as portrayed by Smith and Despres for Guyana (Hanley 1987: 184–9).

Within Trinidad this polarisation also makes it difficult to deal with the traditions of the African middle classes, who had, for rather different reasons, already invested substantially in the symbolism of educational qualifications and until very recently clearly dominated most middle-class professions and educational institutions. According to lawyers among other informants, property disputes are also of considerable importance in such families. It is therefore important to maintain the distinction between the emergence of an ethnically based ideology which uses ethnicity to objectify the sense of dualism, and assumptions about actual differences in behaviour between the ethnic groups – a point which will be returned to in Chapter 5.

These stereotypes lead to an expectation that transcendence will be found largely amongst the Indian, the middle class and the female domain. This may be valid as a generalising tendency but some of the best illustrations of these ideals were also recorded from impoverished African males in Ford. Here they are most likely to be closely associated with the avoidance of unnecessary social contacts which might promote bacchanal and by the centrality of religion to the maintenance of domestic respectability as illustrated by the following two quotations from Ford: 'If a person is a family man and he is having a problem and let us say he wants to ease the tension, a little liming will not solve the problem ... if you stay home and meditate and a little prayer with your family things will change.' A woman from the same area notes: 'Me and my brother we does walk the road straight, Good morning, Good evening, right,[5] right and that is it.'

Overall then it seems more reasonable to regard transcendence as an increasingly syncretic tradition of attachment to property and renovation which in practice may be encompassed by sections of all ethnic groups in Trinidad. Thus ethnicity is increasingly irrelevant to Christmas where such values are most clearly promulgated. Indeed, out of the four communities the most intensive spate of renovations was found in the solidly African community of Newtown. Many of the families who moved there were concerned that this shift in their property status should be associated with marriage, sometimes delaying either their move or their marriage in order to effect this. The degree to which this linkage between property and marriage remains a contemporary concern is evident in that out of the twenty-four married couples, seven managed to achieve this exact simultaneity. Both Indian and African families seemed more likely to stress this concern for land to be ideally inalienable and ancestral, when their own family background was from rural areas.

Although inheritance disputes have been discussed here exclusively in terms of those families more orientated towards transcendent values, they may also represent a dilemma even for those less concerned with the long term. This may be illustrated through the fictional character of Tanti Merle, invented by the dialect poet Paul Keens-Douglas. As the author puts it:

Now Tanti Merle have two acre ah land up in Curepe
All it good for is buryin' people,
So I don't want she land.
But she always puttin' me in de will,
An' takin' me out de will,
Puttin' me in de will,
An' takin' me out de will,
Ah go in an' out ah dat will so much,
Ah catch ah draft.
(Keens-Douglas 1979: 91–2)

Tanti Merle will be referred to several times in this work, since she epitomises the African woman with pretensions to transcendence, but who is constantly the instrument for a collapse back into the values of transience through bacchanal. With respect to inheritance she uses the strategy of manipulating her will, but, in this case, rather too quickly, responding to every event in a manner which reveals her roots in transience.

Transcendence as Household Form in Four Communities

Although most clearly emergent in the evidence from inheritance disputes, transcendent values are also implicated in other elements of household formation, particularly in communities such as The Meadows which are constructed in their image. The identification of transcendence can be problematic, however, as is indicated by the case of the 'joint' family. Of the four communities, St Pauls provides the clearest example of an Indian rural community and, in relation to household form, a tendency to larger extended families. Six of the forty houses have nine or more members, the largest being twenty-four. These are composed, in the main, of parents with married sons and their families. Although it is much less acceptable for married males to move in with their in-laws, the imperative to save for one's own house rather than pay rent clearly outweighs any stigma and there are several instances of matrilocality which seems to be increasing with the recession.

Table 4.1 Average household size (of 40 households per area)

	MALES	FEMALES	TOTAL ADULTS	CHILDREN	TOTAL	AVERAGE HOUSEHOLD SIZE
PLACE						
NT	32	48	80	78	158	3.95
FO	46	55	101	125	226	5.65
SP	66	67	133	127	260	6.5
ME	38	45	83	97	180	4.5

KEY
NT = Newtown, FO = Ford, SP = St Pauls, ME = The Meadows

On closer inspection however, these populous houses may not be good examples of the 'joint' family in Trinidad. Although living within the same property, it is common for that property to be divided either physically or conceptually into quite discrete units, and the element composed of, for example, son-daughter-in-law-their children, will cook separately, have their own television and in general have very little to do with the other families present. In more extreme cases it was found that the intra-households units were not on speaking terms with each other, often the result of a dispute about some aspect of collective expenditure such as the phone bill. In many cases, each unit within the house has complete financial autonomy, although there may be a formal agreement as to who is responsible for collective expenditures such as the electricity bill or the mortgage. In a sense, then, the survey covers fifty-four rather than forty families in St Pauls. Given that the dominant rural pattern has become for married sons to build their own houses in the grounds of the parental house, but as independent units, it seems that the St Pauls pattern is essentially an artefact of greater constraints on land and is merely a collection of separate households architecturally combined. Indeed, it is often where there are separate houses and thereby less conflict within the larger family unit that there is found more genuine sharing of resources between the various houses in what is conceptually a compound, even if the houses are not actually contiguous.

If we accept this 'compound' system of nuclear families linked into a superordinate descent group, then there would be little to distinguish it from a commonly found pattern in African families in the area, for example in Ford, where again several households of one family often operate as a close kindred, for example, five brothers working as masons together with their wives often cooperating in cooking. Similarly, there has been a decline in the number of Indian married couples who live with their relatives after marriage, and, given that this is a not uncommon occurrence among the other ethnic components, again suggests convergence in normative patterns of household formation.[6]

Table 4.2 Marital and other relationships

	A	B	C	D	E
NT	21	6	8	0	5
I	1	0	1	0	0
A	14	4	6	0	4
M	6	2	1	0	1
FO	8	15	7	1	9
I	3	2	4	0	4
A	4	8	2	1	3
M	1	5	1	0	2

Table 4.2 Marital and other relationships (*continuted*)

	A	B	C	D	E
ME	31	1	4	0	4
I	16	1	0	0	2
A	8	0	3	0	2
M	7	0	1	0	0
SP	17	4	2	0	17
I	13	3	2	0	16
A	3	1	0	0	1
M	1	0	0	0	0

TOTALS BY ETHNIC GROUP

	A	B	C	D	E
I	33	6	7	1	22
A	29	13	11	0	10
M	15	7	3	0	3
	77	26	21	1	35

TOTAL   160

Table 4.3 Marital and other relationships (with extended households disaggregated)

	A	B	C	D	TOTAL
NT	24	6	12	0	42
I	1	0	1	0	
A	17	4	9	0	
M	6	2	2	0	
FO	11	21	10	1	43
I	5	6	5	0	
A	4	9	4	1	
M	2	6	1	0	
ME	35	1	6	0	42
I	19˙	1	0	0	
A	9	0	5	0	
M	7	0	1	0	
SP	42	6	5	1	54
A	4	1	0	0	
I	37	5	5	1	
M	1	0	0	0	

TOTALS BY ETHNIC GROUP

I	62	12	11	1
A	34	14	18	1
M	16	8	4	0
	112	34	33	2
TOTAL	181			

KEY:
ROWS
NT = Newtown, FO = Ford, SP = St Pauls, ME = The Meadows
I = Indian, A = African, M = Mixed or Other

COLUMNS
A= Married (with or without children)
B= Common law (with or without children)
C= Female adult only (with or without children)
D= Male adult only (with or without children)
E= Extended

Notes to Table 4.2 and 4.3

The table of household forms is provided in two versions. In Table 4.2 there are five basic categories: those based on legal marriage, those based on common-law, those without a male adult, those without a female adult and extended families. In Table 4.3 the category of extended has been disaggregated, where (see main text) these comprise separate households with distinct boundaries which can be thereby categorised separately. The results should only be used as a rough guide. The categories themselves are sometimes problematic: for example, there are no visiting units, because this concept was experienced as inappropriate in describing contemporary life by informants, even though the practice it describes may continue.

There was evidence that the replies to such survey questions are often inaccurate, and, as will be evident in the text, such formal descriptors do little justice to the actual complexity of both residential and mating arrangements and to the centrality of informal mating in some communities.

The survey findings with regard to marriage and mating suggest that class may be at least as important as ethnicity in determining formal arrangements. Table 4.2 reveals only a single case of common-law relations in The Meadows, a settlement within which arrangements such as common law may face considerable animosity and be blamed for crime, incest and general social breakdown. In comparison with the other three areas there is an overwhelming sense of privacy, and there is much greater involvement of men within the domestic sphere, which men may see as their responsibility.

The evidence from St Pauls illustrates the problem of an over-emphasis on ethnicity. With one exception, all the cases of common-law or female-headed households are Indian, even though these are a minority of ten as against thirty-seven households based on legal marriage. This confirms the evidence from Ford that there is increasing empathy among Indians for the refusal of formal marriage, with a growing proportion of families corresponding to the more transient forms associated with the African population. In Ford only a minority of Indian families are in legal marriage, and this is true for the larger joint families as well as for nuclear families. To take one case, the senior adults have been in a common-law relationship for fourteen years, the female having previously been in a 'fix-up' (arranged marriage). They have six children living with them and another living elsewhere. Of those living at home, one son is together with a common-law wife and two children, one daughter has two children and another daughter has one child, but neither of them are married. As such the household combines an attribute usually associated with Indians: that is, the joint family household, together with mating arrangements often regarded as distinctly non-Indian.

It is certainly too simplistic to equate common-law with transient. Some of these households reflect a long-standing tradition within this community for first marriages to fall apart early on as a result of parental pressures, but partners then co-residing with new companions without going through a formal divorce with their original spouse. Second, while Ford and The Meadows attract a homogeneity of household form by their nature, and Newtown is a transitional artefact, St Pauls retains the heterogeneity of the Indian community within itself and includes tight domestic groups with males orientated towards the household interior as well as limers. Once again it is dominant ideologies, as found in The Meadows, which attempt to construct a consistent moral interpretation of mating arrangements. In practice there are a wide variety of complex factors which underlie the diversity found in more heterogeneous communities.

The transcendent family should ideally be structurally based around a series of set categories and their expected relationships.

Relationships such as gender should form complementary symbolic systems and individualism should be minimised. However, given the antipathy of modern life towards such formal structures, these have been rendered implicit rather than explicit. Thus structure has to reconstruct itself without the simple appeal to tradition. As noted above, the traditions of South Asian family structure have been replaced by a general ideology of the close family. Specific role relations have also been reduced to a general sense of the proper position of at least parent-child, marital, sibling and generalised cousin relations. The older precision of Hindi kinship terminology is replaced by a set of generalising English terms and a general sense of the 'appropriate' forms of behaviour. The result is once again much closer than hitherto to the stress on the importance of 'aunties' and 'uncles' in the African family.

Superficially, then, this would result in the unstructured ego-centred family of 'complex' systems, often associated with 'Westernised' societies. In this context, where I would argue transcendence is becoming established precisely as a bulwark against the sense of the ephemeral in Westernised modernity, the result is very different. In practice, for an individual defined as within the family circle there is an intensity of affective relationships that is often quite overwhelming. This is also true for friends and visitors that have been incorporated conceptually (and which I experienced in the form of hospitality). There is considerable diversity in individual households, but there is also a clear normative form upon which this account is based. There is a continual emphasis on the subjection of individual desire and interest to the wider group, with particular emphasis on the subjugation of female interest. But for the males also, wages should always be directed in the first instance to the long-term welfare of the family. In such a context a purchase by one family member is considered by all, decisions as to the educational or employment possibilities of an individual are expected to relate to the enhancement of the family as a whole. Finances, in particular, are still often viewed as largely integral, with the household as the major unit of consumption. Thrift within the family is often the background to conspicuous expenditure with respect to contexts in which the family faces the outer world. This is particularly the case for life-cycle and religious events, such as a Ramayana *Yag* for Hindu families or giving monies to the church, starting with a tithe, for some Christian families.

Internal relations of the family are still often defined by the pattern of exclusive or shared use of possessions. Requests for the use of possessions by close relatives should only be refused with exceptionally good reason. Equally, there is an assumed sense of reciprocity. Relatives, while visiting, will often request the best fruit appearing on the tree, the fattest fish caught with considerable effort, but such requests are usually acceded to, indeed, they are commonly pre-empted as gifts. Some Indians add an element of hypergamy to this relationship where husbands are particularly demanding from affinal relations. Similarly, within the joint families (which again is not defined by contiguous residence), there is considerable permissible borrowing of possessions: a sibling might complain to a parent if refused the loan of items such as shirts or shoes. Many items ranging from cosmetics to soaps may be purchased as family rather than individual property, with a general informal sense that each member with resources should be looking out for what needs replenishment.

Such practices also allow for emergent relationships to be recognised, for example, as courting becomes serious the potential in-marrying individual may be the recipient of gifts from both siblings and parents of the prospective partner. This may then transform into regular gift-giving to sister and brother-in-laws. A woman whose courtship was not approved found this reflected in the fact that her siblings refused to borrow items which her fiancé had given her. Within these values family dominates over friendship, especially given the tradition of larger families where the existence of literally dozens of cousins may leave little time for other relationships. This is often enhanced by the common practice of younger family members going to spend their holidays, or stay while taking courses, with their more distant relations.

A characteristic of transcendence is that attitude to categorisation where there is a preference for clear groups with strong boundaries and a dislike of ambiguity which makes them exemplary of the approach to categories discussed by Douglas in *Purity and Danger* (1966). The same process by which the family homogenises within a bounded category is found in the complementary strategy: that is, the forms of exclusion. This has already been noted in the case of inheritance disputes but may also occur around other intra-family conflicts such as the choice of marriage partners. For some of the Indian families living in Ford the very cause of their settlement in that district has been some family conflict which forced them out of their natal area. A number of these households noted that the remainder of their family had cut them off completely. They were never visited, since relatives claimed they could not find their way there. In more extreme cases they simply became non-persons: their family members would not acknowledge them if they passed on the street and clearly they had formally ceased to exist. This particularly caused bitterness when the Ford household felt that the sole cause was a discrepancy in fortune. That is to say, where several siblings had achieved a high educational and occupational standard, they might start to exclude a single sibling who had failed in these areas and who therefore became literally an anomaly, contradicting the new self-conception of family, and was thereby removed from the category. This was more likely to occur if that sibling was not living at the parental home. This is not to suggest a lack of generosity. Rather it is to document the extreme difference between the treatment of households still regarded as part of the larger family, where impoverished members may successfully make considerable demands on the more affluent, as against the complete disregard of those not categorised as family members.

A similar if more dramatic break may be engendered by a misalliance. In this case the fission was often between parents and a daughter who by making a match which was not approved was rendered a non-family member. The cases observed divided equally between those where a reconciliation was made after the birth of the first child, and those where it seemed highly unlikely that a reconciliation would ever occur. While in transience the response to a rift is the externally expressive form of a major and public cussing-out, without lasting grudges, within transcendence a quarrel almost always involved a long period of non-communication. During the survey many such families could give at least one current instance of two members of their family who were not on speaking terms; most commonly this would involve cousins in dispute over land. In most cases the fission is pronounced since the degree of intensity of previous relations, for example the mother and daughter who had seemed inseparable at all times, is then matched by the complete absence of any communication between the estranged units of the family, as in the mother who literally never sees her grandchildren. The sense of a complete break may be evoked from the other side by the gesture or actuality of suicide. The numbers of younger Indian

women (and some males) who attempt suicide by drinking agricultural poisons, currently gramoxone and previously paraquat,
is such that there are periodic fears in the media of some kind of
spreading 'epidemic'. In practice, most of these are the occasion
by which the individual woman attempts to express anger at the
familial body which is refusing her desires which are usually formulated in terms of romantic (and tragic) love. Many families
who have permitted misalliances admit that this was because
they took the threat of suicide very seriously.

The issue of estrangement resulting from a disapproved marriage leads to the more general question of endogamy. Most studies of Trinidadian society have contrasted the inclusive tendencies
of the African population to treat all other groups as potential
marriage partners with the strict endogamy of the ex-Indian population. Even as recently as Clarke's (1986) study of San Fernando,
there was good evidence for the continuation of at least a tendency to respect the general hierarchy represented by caste, though in
a much weaker form than earlier in the century, when such divisions had been reconstructing themselves out of the rupture represented by the original migration. To represent Indian endogamy
as a clear 'tradition' now in retreat is historically misleading. In
the period after settlement, partly as a result of an extreme gender
imbalance, women seem to have been much freer in their choice
and form of relationships, a tradition which was only disestab-
lished by a spate of murders and violence against Indian women
in the late nineteenth century (Trotman 1986: 170–6).

Today two groups are still regarded as having at least a degree
of separate identity: those who claim Brahminical status, a group
which may well have grown steadily over the last century, and
those associated with the Madrassi population who, at the time of
Klass' 1961 ethnography, still appeared to have something of the
status of untouchability associated with them. Although I have
no figures, general conversation suggested that the social mobility of the period of the oil-boom may have put paid to almost all
the remnants of the caste-based endogamy that Clarke observed.
Even more striking was the degree of inter-religious marriage
among the Indian population. Such marriages can still be fraught
with continual disputes over the holding of the wedding service
with elaborate compromises resulting, such as one religion evident at the service, another at the family reception and so forth.
Although these certainly made people uncomfortable there was a

recognition that such inter-religious marriages were now extremely common and a more fatalistic attitude of resignation seemed the conventional response. Even the most fundamentalist Christian families seemed to find their children marrying into Islamic and Hindu families.

Whenever this topic of the breakdown of religious endogamy was discussed it was in a contrastive mode which confirmed the endogamy of ethnicity even as it relaxed the endogamy of religion. I would strongly dispute the findings of a recent survey (Ryan 1988: 226) which argued that the Indian community is becoming much more open to inter-ethnic marriage with only fifty-three per cent in 1976 and thirty-one per cent in 1987 objecting to marriage to Africans. I suspect this is largely an artefact of the sensitivity of the community in response to accusations of racism and knowing the now-appropriate answer to a formal survey. When it comes to their deeply held feelings and beliefs, the overwhelming majority of the Indian community is not only opposed to such marriages but maintains a strong sense of revulsion with regard to them.

One result of the passionate concern over ethnic endogamy among Indians is the problematic role of the *Dougla*. There is a sense in which mixed-race persons divide conceptually into two groups, the *Dougla* who is specifically the result of sexual relations between an African and Indian, as against all other mixed ethnicities with terms such as 'red' '*callaloo*' or 'Spanish'. The *Dougla* has a notoriously difficult time, given the ambiguous nature of their ethnic double identity which is the subject of various calypsos and other comments. Evidence from my survey as well as from Clarke (1986) suggests that, on the whole, they are orientated towards the African inclusive community rather than the Indian exclusive community.

To conclude, the family understood within the framework of transcendence has several marked characteristics. It is best viewed as a kind of centripetal process which strives to draw its members into the fullest identity with the family as a descent project and to subsume individual and present interests within collective and long-term concerns. It tries to construct inclusive but also exclusive categories with clear boundaries and a dislike of ambiguity. This may contribute to the radical and sometimes violent breaks which lead to complete disassociation, especially around inheritance disputes through which the family identity

must be restructured. Family forms do not necessarily correspond well with residential units. Nevertheless, property itself
provides the most powerful objectification of transcendence as
the material culture of descent, though there is increasing concern to reconcile the individual nature of educational qualifications within the moral imperatives of transcendence.

V. S. Naipaul and Transcendence

I had intended to characterise each project in turn, with a more
extended ethnographic portrait. For several reasons, however, I
have instead turned to examples from Trinidadian literature. The
first reason is that I found I was unable to give the kind of detailed
portrait of an individual, which would have been required, while
retaining the anonymity of informants which I had guaranteed
during fieldwork. I also feel that, while such a portrait, together
with a series of direct 'choice' quotations, gives a sense of authenticity to this kind of ethnographic account, and makes the interpretation appear to spring from the subjectivities of Trinidadians,
this is in a sense misleading. In this book I am elucidating a dualism based on an analytical reading of the ethnographic material,
and rather than attempting a 'post-modern' image of the immediacy of experience, I would rather continue to point out the necessarily artificial nature of this academic exercise. I certainly came
across individuals who objectified each of the two tendencies, but
they are atypical of Trinidadians. Most people embody better the
tension between them. It is in literature where one finds the
strongest characterisation of these traits, tied in, as might be anticipated, with ethnicity. This is because in literature there is a parallel with the present work in the desire to communicate in a more
generalised fashion key concerns within the culture of the
authors. Although in both the cases I am using here, the authors
are much too sophisticated to remove the sense of contradictory
tensions from their characters, they nevertheless provide a clarity
of representation which accords with my own intentions of finding apt illustration rather than typical individual subjectivities.

Some of the characteristics of transcendent values and the centrality of property within them, as already established prior to the
oil boom, may therefore be summarised with reference to V. S.
Naipaul's (1961, but set in the 1930s) felicitously named novel *A*

House for Mr Biswas. A central motif in this book is the relationship between Mr Biswas and several houses, culminating in the one he owns. There is considerable detail lavished on the little items of house interior and the almost physical emotions of desire and of disgust which these inspire. The alienation created from a sense of non-ownership: 'he had lived in many houses. And how easy it was to think of those houses without him!' (ibid: 131), and also the final sense of ownership are particularly strongly evinced. The novel plots every new possession from the hatrack that 'they had acquired, not because they possessed hats, but because it was a piece of furniture all but the very poor had' (ibid: 187) through to the heavy red curtains reflected on a polished floor (ibid: 10).

The place of property as the culmination of the life-project is clearly presented as the basis for constructing a family succession. The prologue ends with these sentiments: 'But bigger than them all was this house, his house. How terrible it would have been, at this time, to be without it: to have died among the Tulsis ... to have left Shamas and the children among them in one room; to have lived without even attempting to lay claim to one's portion of the earth; to have lived and died as one had been born, unnecessary and unaccommodated' (ibid: 14). Interestingly, the point that the title is virtually synonymous with 'A Family for Mr Biswas' could be duplicated almost exactly for the relationship between property and family among those Africans who were described by Herskovits (1947) and would have been contemporary with Biswas. It would be hard to imagine a more eloquent characterisation of the centrality of property to a fundamental sense of ontology than is found in this novel.

The central section of the book is set in a still-extant house in Chaguanas ('Arawak' in the novel), and consists of the desperate and largely pathetic attempts of Biswas to escape from being totally submerged in the extended family of that house, to which he is recruited for no individual quality, but simply as a member of the Brahmin caste, suitable as a spouse for a daughter of the household. The search to escape from a subsumption in someone else's descent group means challenging the powerful centripetal force objectified in the house of his affines, and permeated through principles of religion, family order and domesticity. Indeed, although the term centripetal has been used here as an analytical term, when viewed through Biswas this becomes a more experiential sense of a force emergent from the construction of both house and household which firmly holds the individual in place. Indeed, one of the most poignant failures to exert individuality is through an attempt to give a doll's house to his daughter, which is then destroyed under pressure from the other occupants. It may be noted that although the novel is set in an orthodox Hindu environment, Christmas is the only festival upon which the novel directs specific attention (ibid: 212–15).

Typically for this developmental cycle, this struggle for freedom in youth becomes replaced later on in the book by the desire to found just such a new dynastic succession based in a property which Biswas himself owns. There is some sense of change, however, in so far as for the next generation, the concern becomes an investment in their education, and this resource starts to replace land as the basis of family security and continuity.

The tragic-comic element of the novel is furthered by granting the protagonists some knowledge of their own limitations. For Biswas these are cruelly exposed: even the final house is a ramshackled affair, jerry-built for a quick profit, full of faked and insubstantial elements, 'hollow bricks that rested on no foundation' (ibid: 574). Interestingly, Biswas is able to appropriate the property as his own despite its faults: 'What could not be hidden, by bookcase, glass cabinet or curtains?' (ibid: 580). Biswas' desires and achievements are characterised by Naipaul as not merely modest but profoundly pathetic. However, for most ordinary people in Trinidad, with little pretensions to art, the achievement of such small-scale 'petty bourgeois' goals, given their roots in extraordinary oppression and alienation, need not be so derisorily dismissed and are clearly maintained in contemporary Chaguanas.

Although the character Biswas is based upon Naipaul's own father, Naipaul as a novelist (and son) clearly distances himself from any such limited attempts to construct one's own ancestry and future. Nevertheless, there are striking parallels between Naipaul's own life and the dilemmas of transcendence. In his writings on Trinidad, Naipaul harshly repudiates any sense of roots claimed by his natal country, as a place without the foundations upon which culture might be constructed, condemned only to borrow from outside (1962, 1967), a portrayal which has offended many Trinidadians. But the very stridency of this condemnation may reveal the sensitivity of the issue, and Naipaul's more recent work finds him inescapably bound to this same search for roots. In *The Enigma of Arrival* (1987) Naipaul identifies himself with this search, but utilising an alternative aspect of Trinidadian identity based upon British colonial education. Naipaul locates himself virtually in the shadow of the prehistoric monument of Stonehenge, in southern Britain, perhaps the quintessence of any concretisation of such British 'roots'. 'Here was an unchanging world – so it would have seemed to the stranger. So it seemed to me when I first became aware of it: the country life, the slow movement of time, the dead life, the private life, the life lived in houses closed to one another' (ibid: 34). Naipaul envies the image of people at one with their own setting, their seasons and landscape (ibid: 33). Here, at last, may have appeared the perfect fulfilment of transcendent values, a time that transcends the event, an interior free from externality and with no taint of bacchanal. In the course of this book Naipaul has to confront the lived experience of the people who inhabit the area and comes, with some difficulty, to see this history as life, that is to view it positively as activity and event and not mere decay (ibid: 87). Indeed, the line from the failure of Biswas to the disillusionment of the son with the possibilities of Stonehenge seems remarkably straight. There is some clue in his latest book on India that Naipaul (1990) is coming round to a view of authenticity as self-constructed rather than based in origins, perhaps as he has shifted from aesthetic to more ethnographic/documentary goals, but he has yet to come full circle and apply this conclusion to Trinidad.

As with Biswas, though on a much grander scale, *The Enigma of Arrival* presents the same tragic environment of a character (in this case the author) who is coming to the self-knowledge of the impossibility of his own life-project, given the creolised nature of his identity torn between India, Trinidad and Britain and accentuated by his restless travels. Naipaul himself becomes the quintessence of a typical Trinidadian tragedy, the transcendent man without property, but with the self-knowledge that makes Naipaul, like Conrad, a keen observer of contradictions of modernity. Meanwhile, life certainly seems to imitate art as his own work as a writer seems destined to evolve into a pseudo-descent group as suggested by the positive response to the republication of his father's (Seepersad's) writings, the reputation of his late brother Shiva Naipaul as a writer and the laudatory comments Naipaul has written for the novels of his nephew, Neil

Bissoondath. Writing has thereby become the 'property' of this transcendent descent group.

Sexuality and Transience

Transient Families

The consideration of an opposing imperative within kinship, generated from the same set of values as 'transience', is complicated by a general resistance to the idea of a kinship system which either lacks, or is opposed to, structure and continuity. One of the major influences on this topic has come from developments in the study of the African American family, and in particular the debate which took place over the publication of the 1965 Moynihan report, which implied that lack of structure in such families was a pathological condition, understandable, given the historical conditions of slavery, but nevertheless responsible for a variety of contemporary ills including continued poverty and therefore in need of transformation. In response, there been considerable historical research, especially in the United States, concerned to deny the representation of the family that Moynihan assumed (Gutman 1976; for the Caribbean see Bush 1990) and also a proper academic refusal to allow any social system to be stigmatised because it does not conform to a particular normative type.

The second point of resistance to the concept of the unstructured family has been social anthropological concern to treat West Indian kinship within the general domain of 'Kinship Studies' and the sense that this requires the identification of clear normative systems which can be characterised in traditional and comparative studies. For this reason categories such as matrifocality, which within the context of the metropolitan West represent distinct norms, but norms nonetheless have been stressed. It may be, however, that by the 1990s, the points against Moynihan will have been accepted, at least by academics, while the established approaches in anthropological studies of kinship may be insufficiently sensitive to the specifics of the local situation. These changes permit a return to the direct consideration of a possible opposition to structure as the defining feature of a kinship system, without this being seen as either pathological or an inability to achieve what kinship ought to be.

A third problem with this approach is the sensitive nature of sexuality as an issue, since it provides the focal point of a common derogatory stereotype based on the racist conception of essential 'black' nature. The centrality of sexuality to the formation of racist categories has been most forcefully explored by Fanon (1986) drawing upon the earlier attempt by Sartre to confront the centrality of money to anti-Semitic racism. Fanon's study, particularly of the sexual practices of West Indians as they arrived in Europe, identified racism as the key factor in the internalisation of sex itself as paradigmatic to identity construction among the contemporary black populations. I would argue that this is one element among several, another being the potential of sex as an activity for the objectification of freedom (see Miller 1991 for details).

Trinidad may well provide a suitable site for an investigation of these elements of kinship precisely because they cannot be held as typical of or typifying Trinidadian society. It is clear that there is more than one tendency working its way through kinship practice in Trinidad and although a local equivalent of 'West Indian Kinship' certainly exists, it does so in relation to strong and conflicting cultural values. Furthermore, given the wealth, education and sophistication of this island (Macdonald 1986), the maintenance of this form of kinship over more than a century, and (as Gonzalez 1984; Smith 1978, and others have noted for the Caribbean more generally, see above) its comparative refusal to acknowledge, through transformation, some massive changes in economic and class position, suggests that there are imperatives that sustain its continuation which are regarded as positive by those involved and have proved viable in the long-term.

As noted earlier, the focus upon lack of structure rather than norms *per se* can appear to be merely a local version of the 'modern' tendency towards ego-centred and complex kinship systems, as, for example, in the United States. But what will be argued for Trinidad is rather the coexistence in direct antipathy of two models, one of which is highly structured and subsuming of individualism. Within Trinidad this is increasingly identified with Indians by repute, but elsewhere in the Caribbean it is viewed as an alternative tradition of descent-focused and highly structured family traditions.

The term unstructured needs a more precise definition here by opposition. In transcendence there is a core group of intensive sociality and a peripheral kindred with distinct but dissimilar expectations of reciprocity, along with very specific qualities engendered by the sibling relation or being a grandparent. What is striking in the kind of environment being considered here, however, is the ability of individuals not to respond to such a sense of obligation. The pool of kindred may be extensive, but within that the preference is for the construction of kin reciprocity as a voluntaristic and dyadic practice. For example, out of various siblings, the potential of a relationship with some may be ignored, while others remain regular companions. What is resisted is structure as obligation, as something done even when it is not desired by the participants, i.e. something which constrains individualistic freedom. The sense of obligation leads to the feeling that one is being put upon, or in local parlance the 'pressure' which almost automatically creates a corresponding sense of resistance. It is this which leads to the commonly observed disparity between social parent and biological parent (see below), or where two distantly related kin may take on a powerful patronage relationship with a strong sense of reciprocity, but only for a particular period.

In most of Western Europe there is a clear ideology which asserts an historical shift from the subsumption of individuals within family expectations towards a 'modern' family, increasingly denuded of such structure or obligations, although this idea of a 'traditional' family may be more a projection backwards than a historical legacy. The Trinidadian situation is rather different, in so far as the transcendent with their powerful and, if anything, growing sense of religion and family obligation, and the transient with their ability to refuse sibling and parental obligation with no sense of guilt, both appear as more extreme ends of this spectrum of structure and anti-structure and are developed in self-conscious opposition to each other. The implication of this dualism is that the fluidity and voluntarism in relationships is not simply the result of poverty or 'adaptive responses' (as suggested by Barrow 1988: 162–7; or Sacks 1974 for Afro-American families), but represents a more positive expression of certain key concepts, such as freedom (see Smith 1978: 353–7 for the rejection of any simple linkage between economics and kinship).

What is here termed the transient tendency in kinship cannot be seen as simply constructing itself in some isolated arena of lower-class life. The pressures towards legal marriage and the nuclear family are that much greater since those hegemonic groups which cherish these forms are well aware that they are having to suppress and overcome a long-term alternative. The pervasive propaganda from the media, the church and the state all assert links between the lack of legal marriage and phenomena such as crime, lack of protection for children and poverty. This local pressure is intensified by the development of a global discourse which either explicitly expounds the positive moral values of, for example, having a resident father or implicitly enshrines these norms in, for example, the conventional television sit-com (for example the Cosby Show). There are also resource-based pressures such as the reluctance to provide mortgages to unmarried couples which in part may explain why they are virtually absent in a settlement such as The Meadows. Finally, this pressure is reflected in the attitude of couples who are legally married and who tend to emphasise the disparity between their status and common-law relationships.

Table 4.4 Average period of stable relationships

	YEARS MARRIED	TOTAL CASES	YEARS COMMON LAW	TOTAL CASES
NT	8	22	8	1
FO	11	10	10	14
SP	15	18	10	4
ME	19	31	20	1

KEY:
NT = Newtown, FO = Ford, SP = St Pauls, ME = The Meadows

Note
Many households did not provide the relevant information and since the rate of response was almost certainly biased towards those who were in long-term relationships the result suggests a picture of greater stability than is the case.

Despite such pressures towards a church and legally sanctioned marriage, which have been present at least since emancipation, the practice of common-law is strongly affirmed by both its historical longevity and its contemporary stability. Table 4.4 suggests the stability of the relationship is hardly less than that of legal marriage, although its stability does not reflect a monogamous mating pattern; this also would be true of legal marriage (as also noted by M. G. Smith 1962: 255). To consider this further, however, the pattern of family and household form in the four communities will, as in the previous section, be considered in relation to an idiom, in this case that of sexuality.

Sexuality and Gender Relations

The centrality of sexuality to sociality among what has in the past been defined as the lower-class black population of Trinidad has been expressed in very explicit terms by previous ethnographers. Based on fieldwork in the 1950s Freilich developed his concept of the 'sex-fame game' with males 'begging' and 'sweet-talking' women into granting sexual favours (1960: 78–90, 1968; see Yelvington, forthcoming, for a more recent example based on an ethnography of a factory). Although subsumed under a concern for kinship and, in particular, mating patterns, an even more prominent role is given to sexual relations in Rodman's (1971) discussion of such a community, and he is the most explicit in associating this with a value system which he terms the 'Circumstance-Oriented Man' (ibid: 159–75). Bell (1970) sees the explicit acknowledgement of the centrality of sexual relations as one of the key distinctions between Indian and Negro perceptions of marriage. In perhaps the most extreme case Lieber sums up his experience of street life in Port of Spain by suggesting that 'most of the men I knew regarded women as sexual objects and little more' (1981: 108).

These ethnographic characterisations clearly tend to exaggerate if they are taken as full social descriptions. Within transient-orientated communities are also found stable, affective relationships with emotive and involved fatherhood and the culture of romance. What can be extracted from these accounts, however, is the extent to which cross-gender relations may be dominated by sexual relations.

In Trinidad, as compared to the metropolitan countries often visited by Trinidadians, the public attitude to the display of sexuality, for example, in pornography, is relatively prurient, although this is being challenged by the weekly papers. There is, however, a fulsome discourse about the sexual act itself. In conversation with both men and women there is a common reference to sexual performance and, in particular, to discussion of the number of orgasms or 'rounds' (or 'breaks') before a man would be unable to continue. The term 'sex-fame game' continued to be appropriate: 'The men here go for a lot of fame, so they can tell their friends, I was with this one's wife. They don't mind spending the money.' The centrality of sex was often claimed in terms such as 'everything come back to sex, it doh matter what yuh do everything come back to that, its true thing' or more succinctly the common phrase 'sex is it'.

Men are expected to build up their strength, or even go into training (i.e. workouts), in order to prolong their sexual performance. Doctors jokingly complained of men over seventy who had sired many children coming in for treatment for being sexually weak. Sexual relations are constantly alluded to wherever cross-gender associations can be observed. In a cuss-out between a couple the most common public accusations screamed at volume across the yard is first that he is not providing funds, second that he is sleeping around but third that he is not sexually satisfying his partner. In one example, a woman complained loudly and publicly that her man is panting after one round, but later on when the couple are reconciled she is seen conspicuously going to a local store to buy seamoss, a favourite enhancer of male potency. This is also a common theme in calypso which stress that this is the main way in which a man can fail a woman. By contrast it was not common for a woman to be seen as either frigid or unable to 'perform' adequately. In summary, the discourse of gender strongly suggests that the main gift that a man presents to a woman is his own body.

For both sexes it is important that sexual activity is regular, providing release and 'cooling'. Without such release, women, in particular, are said to suffer headaches, backaches or even madness. A common anecdote is of the priest who went mad by eating too many peanuts (viewed as sexually enhancing) while remaining celibate. A case in point was the reaction to a confession by American television evangelist Jimmy Swaggart, who admitted going to watch a prostitute and therefore had to resign his ministry and cancel his impending visit to Trinidad. The popular response was that such activity was essential and in no sense demeaning or contradictory to his mission, and his visit might well have been the more successful had it been allowed to continue as a result of this confession. This attitude to sexual performance need not be aggressive or outside the context of affection. For example, an elderly and clearly very affectionate couple were

engaged in sexual banter, where he complains that the programmes coming on television these days are so stimulating that
he will hurt his wife, to which she replied that sex for them is
really only 'a long time thing' (a thing of the past).

Although most writers think of the 'sex-fame game' as only a
male imperative, in Ford at least both sexes participate: 'If he
could make plenty rounds he is considered a macho man and
also good because the lady involved will go and tell her friends
that the man is good in bed, so when you catch yourself he has
about six or seven women and women will go for that, even if
they doh get money. A lot of girls now, they like the men who are
sexy. If it have a man down there and he just dress right all the
women will run after him and each of them keep fighting for that
one particular man, even if they doh get money from him, that is
their man, so he is like a sweetman, even married women in their
house does the same thing.' The best evidence for sexuality is the
babies the women make for the men, such as the twenty-two-year
old male who begged his girlfriend for a baby on the grounds
that he was the only one in the office who didn't have one.

The observations at the level of community are readily confirmed in two other areas, commerce and the media. One of the
most conspicuous aspects of advertising in Trinidad is the
emphasis on a product's ability to enhance sexual performance
even where these products (for example ginger wine or vitamin
supplements) are sold elsewhere on entirely different grounds.
Television advertising is full of women in leotards exchanging
knowing winks with men who have been working pneumatic
drills or training in the gym, with slogans such as 'healthy lift day
and NIGHT'.

These and a multitude of pharmacy products such as vitamins
and tonics with endless 'enhancing' properties act in effect as
commercial substitutes for a previously existing and equally
diverse set of 'bush' and other natural products such as seamoss
and oysters. Sexual power is more generally commoditised
through the concept of protein. The effects of education on the
importance of protein in the diet is transformed into a concern
with protein as essential for sexual adequacy. For example, a
female advertising executive remarked scornfully that her male
colleagues were wasting their time going out at lunch for
seamoss, since laboratory tests had now shown that seamoss only
contained six per cent protein. For a similar reason peanuts are

sold at a street corner under the cry 'bullets for your gun'. Taking such 'enhancing' substances is often interpreted as a sign. For example, a wife finding ginseng in the home might well suspect her husband of having an affair, as many males are assumed to require such assistance mainly when conducting several relationships at once.

The clearest public expression of these concerns comes in the weekly newspapers such as *The Bomb, The Blast, The Heat* and *The Punch* replete with 'girlie' photos and articles which look for a sexual explanation to a wide variety of events. Most violence reported in the weeklies is assumed to derive from 'horning'[7] and sexual indiscretion. The classic case, which occurred on a number of occasions during the fieldwork year, was the story of the male who himself was accomplished in his extra-marital affairs and renowned among his male peers for his sexual activities, most especially a man in uniform, such as a policeman. The individual discovers that his own wife or partner has been horning him and reacts either through suicide or murder together with suicide. The usual comment is about the men 'who give horn but can't take horn'. Considerable space is devoted to the issue of sexual potency, for example under the headline 'I can cure impotence' a journalist writes: 'In these days of the sexually potent, macho image, men who experience the slightest drop in feelings rush frantically to drugstores and bush medicine specialists willing to try anything for sexual lift' (*Blast* 1 June 1988). The general expectation of horning may be used to promote itself. For example, a man will attempt to persuade a married woman with the remark that 'look how yuh husband doing ... you come and friend with me'.

This stress on sexuality is justified by the degree to which sexual relations may become synonymous with gender relations. Several instances were found of a reluctance to allow women to work because it was assumed that they would have to sleep with their boss as a condition of their employment (see Lowenthal 1972: 110 for the Caribbean more generally). The very ordinariness of these expectations comes over best in conversations about other subjects. For example, a woman was attempting to explain to me the meaning of the term 'merchandising' which consists of sales representatives filling up the shelves of supermarkets with their products and then promoting them. During the conversation she surveyed all the major supermarkets in the country with respect to a particular product range. In every case where one brand seemed to have gained greater shelf space than commercial considerations might have warranted, the cause given (in an entirely matter-of-fact manner) was a sexual relationship between the relevant merchandiser and the store manager. Similarly a woman trying to give an objective and reflective description of a hospital in which she had worked for many years, estimated that of the men fifty per cent have 'outside' (i.e. additional) sexual relationships at any one time, ten per cent have several at once and only ten per cent never have such relationships. The point here is not the actual extent of such relations; an equally 'objective' survey of the women would produce an assumption of much greater fidelity and would certainly not be compatible with these figures. What is evident, however, is the consensual belief about the importance of sexuality as constituting the key component of everyday social interaction, the stuff of paramount concern and conversation. In effect, observations about social relations are constantly being considered best explained by suppositions about sexual relations.

It is an environment where cross-gender relations are otherwise kept to a minimum or surrounded by mutual apprehension and antagonism, which then renders sexuality an act of exchange which constitutes the core of a non-accretive sociality. Throughout Trinidad, women are regarded as the sex responsible for the maintenance of those 'inside' values expressed so clearly during Christmas, but in addition to this there is an axiom first, that a woman must have a man in association almost at any cost to herself, and second, that it is always easy for a man to find a woman but hard for a woman to keep a man. The justifications given are various. Women may claim that without a man there will be a grave security risk, and that she will not be protected if neighbours want to steal from her or abuse her. Most commonly women reiterate the ideology about the problem of finding and keeping men, which is sometimes associated with a (mythical[8]) idea of a massive imbalance between the sexes resulting from male emigration from Trinidad. For example, one woman explained it as 'most Trinidadian women feel they have to have a man around in order to feel good or enjoy themselves ... they feel they have to or it's a disgrace'.

This makes the expressions often found in the academic literature about the 'female-headed household' or 'strong independent black woman' somewhat misleading. The latter phrase, in particular, seems to assume a degree of autonomy in self-definition which is not found except among the Port of Spain élites. The vast majority of women who have autonomous control over households do so because they have failed to achieve their actual desire for a man to take a much larger role in household responsibilities and concerns. Such women may certainly be seen as strong in terms of coping with adversity and making ends meet under extremely difficult conditions, but for most women in Ford or Newtown independence and autonomy are the symbols of pressure and exploitation. As fieldwork by the *Women in the Caribbean* Project (Massiah (ed.) 1986; Senior 1991: 82–102) is starting to reveal, there is a strong association between such independence or autonomy with poverty and depression.

If men are viewed as hard to get then there is pressure to keep the one in association. Husbands will often hint to wives that if she should fail to please he knows of another woman who would be only too happy. For example, a woman in The Meadows with ten years of stable marriage refused to go on an educational course abroad for fear of finding herself displaced. The main use of *Obeah*[9] in these communities is by women trying to keep or 'fix' a man. Having a man in association does not necessarily mean that he is resident but that a woman is recognised as being at least formally 'minded' by him. The external appearance of this relationship should come from the money he gives her or the services, such as clearing the yard, that he offers her. His obligations may go no further, and among those orientated to the transient mode it is generally expected that women alone will take responsibility for decisions pertaining to children, and although he may 'do market' (go shopping) in many cases there are few cross-gender activities. A typical joke during a wedding speech in Newtown noted that the wife would make the 'little' decisions such as how to spend their money and the children's future, while the husband would make the 'big' decisions, such as who would win the next election.

Women are often seen as ambivalent in relation to these values, but there are a minority of women, especially younger women, who not only enter into these elements of transience with the same commitment as men but also refuse to assume responsibility for those domains which men would project on to them. Such women may use heavy irony and conspicuous disregard for convention, in order to emphasise that they do not see themselves as concerned with the 'inside'. As such they pay as little attention to cooking or to the house as a site for elaborate decoration, and tend to leave childcare to older relatives such as their own mothers or aunts. These women are in no sense anomalous, because the normative model presented here is not an objective structure, it is rather a commitment to certain values which may be entirely rejected by some.

On the street gender relations are most evident in the calling out after women who pass by a male lime. This is very much a constant of everyday life. Women estimated that while shopping or walking they could expect verbal assaults around six to ten times an hour. These follow a fairly set pattern, as described in a letter of complaint to a newspaper: 'On the roads, I am Psst'd at by many males ranging from ages eight to 50. If I ignore them, I am then addressed as Dahlin, or nice Thing or whatever suits their fancy. I am given a complete run down on every part of my body, including my most private parts. At the supermarkets and banks I am addressed (by guards customers and so on) to the effect: Mornin' sweets: or "sis" or "sexy" or some other suggestive and derogatory term. I am constantly invited to "go up by de beach" to engage in sexual activity by men whose wives, I am certain, are at home attending to household chores and material responsibilities' (*Guardian* 11/3/88). The 'rule' of the encounter is that the female must acknowledge the 'greeting', if not then she is considered haughty (or 'social') and much more abusive comments follow behind her. On the other hand an acknowledgment by the woman can lead to an expectation of conversation or even liaison, so that the accomplished female will respond often with a stock reply of her own, but keep walking, or make the reply distance-creating unless she wishes to make contact through the encounter. These encounters are important if only because their frequency makes them a constant feature of daily life

It is while liming that men generally construct their consensual view as to the fundamental nature of women which they use to oppose to themselves as a group.[10] Generally women are seen as duplicitous tricksters, out to fleece a man of his hard-earned money and resources and to tie him down. Women are seen as the culvert through which men are drawn from their freedom and world of male sociality into the artificial world of the transcendent sphere. From this will follow all the other forms of institutionalisation, being bound to an occupation, ensconced in little hierarchies and the emergence of an anti-social pride and disdain for one's fellow men. Equally, women at home are seen as constantly looking for opportunities to have affairs and to horn (cuckold) their men. There is a clear dilemma between conversation about men's sexual prowess and conquests especially of other men's wives or partners and the implications this may have for one's own 'inside' woman. The fear of 'horning' is especially strong if the man has limited income: 'now as long as the man stop working the woman pick up herself and look for work, sometimes she find another man and tell you she is working, but she does fuck out so everybody still eats around the dining table and you have a big smile but half the time you eating the next fella sweat ... she could get a drop down Chaguanas, when he reach Chaguanas he say let's go Felicity, she gone in the bed with him he drop her back Chaguanas and hand her a 5 dollar or 20 dollar as the case may be, when they come back they done do their mischief and their nastiness outside, they come back to you like the Lady of Fatima.'

Women in turn are essentially symmetrical in their opinions of males as a group and are at least as derogatory. Males are seen as lazy, greedy, irresponsible and dishonest, with little thought for the future and only putting on their 'sweet talk' to make fools out of one. Most of all they fail in the expected reciprocity of providing support as in these three complaints:-'You meet a fella and at that time they will bring down the moon and stars for you and when they done they can't give you anything so you have to try and get rid of the man and get involved with someone who could help you.' 'If a man wants to stay, he should give towards the house and the food, that is what they supposed to do but they don't.' 'It seems that with the recession the men have stopped minding their women and children and are looking for other women who don't have any children.'

Obviously many of these statements about the other sex in general are based around stereotypes which are by no means a reflection of actual social relations which here as everywhere contain tremendous diversity. When talking about their present partner both genders could be lyrical in their praise. Or as here when talking about an ex-partner: 'my first set of children, their father from Tobago and he lives across there, and they went for August holidays, and he gives them all money, he don't treat the older ones (i.e. his) different, I think he spoils every one of them, he loves children'. There arises therefore a problem of distinguish-ing the often aggressive feelings about the other sex held in gen-eral with the strongly positive feelings felt about one's particular partner of the moment. This disjuncture was particularly promi-nent with women who were more likely to have a romantic vision of their present partner. Thus the image of males as an actual class of people was tinged by this vision of the exceptional male who accorded entirely with the canons which were increas-ingly constructed around imported photomontage romantic comics such as *Kiss* and *Darling* or stock romantic novelettes such as the Mills and Boon series. This provides an alternative image. Among women most expressive of transient values, however, it was more likely to find consistent scepticism even with regard to the present partner, and in any conversation with regard to men in general the key themes of their duplicity, meanness and nar-rowness were paramount.

Calypso Comments

This generalised antagonism existing between the two sexes when each is considered in the abstract is a constant feature of one of the best-regarded expressive forms in Trinidad: that is, the calypso lyric. The calypso has a very particular place in Trinidadian society and expressions drawn from them are in con-stant use in daily conversation. Some such as 'no money no love' become part of general folk wisdom; most, such as 'woman is boss' or 'wet meh down' are in the repertoire only for the particu-lar Carnival season in which they are sung. Equally important is the generally held contention that the calypso has a privileged access to certain fundamental truths about Trinidadian society. A constant refrain to the ethnographer is that they should look to the calypso for general statements about the 'true' nature of Trinidadian society.

Work by Austin (1976), Elder (1969), Rohlehr (1988, 1990) and Warner (1982) all note the essentially misogynistic character of calypso, but also as Rohlehr says of the lyrics of Sparrow, the most influential of living calypsonians (1970: 90): 'Males and females are the exploiters of the human jungle; each uses every device to outsmart the other.' Sparrow first came to prominence in 1956 with the calypso 'Jean and Dinah' which took on the post-war theme of how the Yankees were gone and the local men would take back the streets and exact revenge upon the women who had spurned them. He sang:

things bad is to hear them cry.
Not a sailor in town, the night clubs dry.
Only West Indians like me or you,
going to get a drink or two.
Since we have things back in control,
ah seeking revenge with me heart and soul.

In 1988–9 the idea of a gender war emerged in a more explicit but playful competition between two popular calypsos. In 1988 Denyse Plummer, representing the still rare female calypsonian, was tremendously successful with the calypso 'Woman is Boss', arguing for the increasing power of women in recent times. She rallied her audience with a developing crescendo including the call 'raise your hand if you is boss' and almost invariably she provoked considerable and enthusiastic response from the women in the audience. In 1989 one of the early hits of the season was by Swallow with a song entitled 'The Man with the Pepper Sauce is Boss'; the starting point of the song was directly addressed to Denyse Plummer's 'misunderstanding' and has various choruses pointing to the centrality of male sexual prowess for women. Denyse Plummer's 1989 entry was interestingly about the magnificence of the champion West Indian man. Most recently several female calypsonians have been advocating a series of feminist complaints and solutions, for example in 1990 one of them complained in song that if a woman talks to men she is accused of affairs, if to women she is accused of gossiping and if to herself then she is mad!

These themes are clearly in fun, and, for the earlier period, Rohlehr warns against taking calypsos as though they were social descriptions (1988: 305). Nevertheless, they are consistent with the more general conversational representations which each sex, in the privacy of its own company, makes of the other. It has already been noted that none of this prevents individual relationships from achieving strong affectivity and constancy, especially when other factors such as parenting are taken into account. The overall effect of these gender ideologies is often to reduce gender relations in transience to a basic exchange relationship based

around sexuality. It is this which suggested the particular interpretation of wining as an expression of autosexuality and thereby
a repudiation of cross-gender sociality (Miller 1991).

Transience and Household Form in Four Communities

The clearest expression of transient values established as household
form is found in Ford, the community which also demonstrates the
greatest resistance to the pressures towards legal marriage. Of the
seven nuclear families based on marriage, four had at least one
child before the current marriage. Although this feature is commonly found in wider Caribbean studies, one of the most common
categories used to describe households in the West Indies, that of
the 'female-headed household', seemed particularly misleading for
Ford. One could make a distinction, for example, between the fifteen households with a male present in a common-law relationship
and the seven households without a male present, but two examples may serve to illustrate why this is distinctly problematic. On
the one hand there are deputy relations (see below) where the
female lives on her own or with children and is maintained by a
male who is married elsewhere. But that male may well spend
more time here in Ford than with his marital partner, and, while
acknowledging his legal wife for formal occasions, invests most of
his emotional and expressive life through the deputy relationship,
which may well have continued for six or ten years. By contrast,
there are males who are recorded as in common-law relationships
domiciled within Ford who spend the vast majority of their time
liming and are not seen at 'home' for days or even weeks on end,
and provide only minimal financial support for the home.
Nevertheless, the female of the house prefers at least formally to
present herself as within a stable relationship with a male present.

The lack of correspondence between these various levels of
description is not just a problem for the analyst; they are well
known to the people of the area and the resultant sense of 'confusion' in social relations is part of the positive self-characterisation
of this area as the place of 'bacchanal'. The inhabitants of Ford
thereby celebrate precisely the discrepancy between their household patterns and what they are well aware are the officially
sanctioned orders of other areas.

The clearest expression of this distinction is the difference between the representation of formal relationships and the quite different pattern which emerges from the general beliefs held by members of the community about who is actually having a sexual relationship with whom at any given time. Obviously, fieldwork does not provide direct evidence for such relationships, only for what might be called consensual gossip. This is difficult to evaluate but it is relatively easy to affirm relationships mentioned in gossip because of the flimsy nature of houses constructed from car-part boxes, the general unemployment which leaves a large constant resident population and the extent to which many people stay up at nights. Not only are movements around the settlement evident, but intimate conversations within the home can often be overheard. Furthermore, although some took pains to be discreet in the carrying out of sexual liaisons, others of both sexes were clearly making little attempt to hide them.

There is some evidence for a degree of community 'endogamy' of mating, if gossip is accepted. The results of just one conversation on this subject breaks down as follows. Household A with five members (siblings) is referred to as participating in eight recent relationships of which six are from within the community. Household B with one member is noted as involved in five relationships, all from within the community. The two households become continually related. One member of household A is associated with two relationships. The first is with a female from household C whose common-law husband is one of the four related to household B. The second is with a female who subsequently had a relationship with his sister's husband. This same sister's husband is cited at another point as involved with the sister of one of the other men involved with household B. In addition, another of those involved with household B is the uncle of a woman cited as involved in a relationship with a member of household A.

Almost all the above cases were independently mentioned during the course of conversations with others living in the area, without being directly solicited. Most such relationships are sequential although this is not the case with Household B. Attitudes to this degree of intra-community sexual activity vary. One informant noted that after she had slept with a male within the community, other men organized a fairly public betting network as to who would be the next, as a result of which she determined from then on to switch to a practice of excluding members of her own neighbourhood. In several cases, members of households would be associated with a number of relationships during which time their common-law or marital relationship would be constant. Indeed, gossip did not suggest that the existence of a long-term common-law or marital partner diminished the frequency of outside sexual relationships as against those who had no such formal attachment. This again demonstrates the partial picture presented by a reliance on the kind of formal survey data about formal relationships used in much of the kinship research in the Caribbean.

Ford recognises that it draws to itself the households which do not conform to dominant values. There is also the correspondence between the transience of lifestyle and the transience of housing which can be put up relatively cheaply and quickly compared to other areas. As noted in Chapter 1, an effect of the rise of distinct housing areas is that they tend to crystallise in relation to particular kinds of cultural and social project without the mixing between quite diverse groups which may have been evident in earlier semi-urban settlements. Ford is not homogeneous, however, as there are also many households whose values are centred on transcendence but have been forced into Ford by financial destitution.

One consequence of the transient ideal is that the ambiguity and fluidity of relationships do not have the factional consequences which are commonly recorded in ethnographies of 'peasant' villages. The circumstances in which relationships end are often extremely antagonistic, since it is most commonly the result of the discovery that one of the partners is engaged in a further relationship. Furthermore, the official partners may react violently to being 'horned', resulting in both cuss-outs between women and the use of cutlasses between men. In the main, however, once a relationship finishes, the events are not allowed to intrude into the generally very friendly atmosphere which exists in communities such as Ford, in comparison to the others studied. The same group of people will work together in organising charity events for the children, in sports, self-help of a formal or informal kind, and cooperation coexists with often clear competition. While anger is commonly confronted, resentment or bitterness seems quite rare in the community. The local dialect is particularly rich in a terminology which condemns those who fail to accept transience or bear grudges. Such people 'give yuh horrors', they 'eh easy'. These terms can be ambiguous when they imply respect for the man who is 'hard', but there comes a point in which pure condemnation comes into play for an unforgiving character, in which case the common appellation is that they are 'miserable', and would tend to 'get on ignorant' (that is quickly reacting in an angry, threatening, violent manner).

Transience also provides the framework for parenting in this area. In Ford and Newtown parenting is essentially gender-divided. Males provide money and services but the decisions within transient households over matters such as the child's education are made almost entirely by females. A constant concern is with paternity, partly because paternity is always the subject of at least discussion, if not dispute, and many children are assigned through gossip to other males within the same community than the current partner. The transience of relationships makes father-ing also complicated by the fact that most children in this com-munity are not those of the current male partner. Most women did not see men as capable of acting equally to their own and to previous children, and this was one of the principal causes behind having children minded by grandparents, aunts and other relatives, to protect them from inequalities of treatment and beyond that a fear of incest, though there were many exceptions.

Among households with a particular reliance on transient val-ues the assumption that biological parents will in fact take on active parenting is weakest, and here it is most likely to extend to mothers as well as fathers (as elsewhere in the Caribbean e.g. Price 1988: 123; more generally see Senior 1991: 8–24). The practice closely articulates with the lifecycle element of the same polarity, such that as women age they often move from transience to tran-scendence. By the time they have their first grandchildren, women are often much more inclined towards active parenting and to set-tling into the values of home and religion. The result is that women, in effect, reconstruct parenting such that those who wish to engage in this social activity do so at the time in which this desire is strongest, with the older generation taking the children from the biological mothers of the younger generation, again replacing an obligatory relationship with a voluntary one. This practice is often condemned by international canons of normative nuclear families as detrimental to the child. But those involved argue that it may actually work to the child's advantage (compare Goody and Groothues 1977: on grounds for fostering). Although not usually put in quite this way, there is a sense that the grand-mother is given or wrests the grandchild from the mother because she is both more willing and more able to provide what is seen as the appropriate context for bringing up an infant than a reluctant, irreligious and youthful biological mother.

The Deputy

In Trinidad there exists a well-established expectation that marital relations are often coexistent with at least the partial maintenance by the male of a mistress based in a separate residence. This additional person is termed the 'deputy' and requires detailed consideration since she assumes an importance in many Trinidadians' conception of their society far greater than might seem warranted by the actual numbers of households involved. The prominence of this institution in general conversation was often reminiscent of the French farce of the period of Feydeau. A typical calypso-tent joke tells of two men who dive into the bushes as two females approach. As they re-emerge one explains to the other, 'I had to hide, that was my wife and my deputy' to which the other replies, 'well for me it was the same thing'. Not only jokes and gossip but serious discussion about the domestic situation of individuals often revolve around this issue.

Evidence for the actual number or nature of deputy relations was hard to determine for an outside observer, though to a degree this would also be true for most Trinidadians. There is a general assumption that most men have deputies, despite the demographic impossibility of such a claim in a population with roughly equal gender proportions. Demography is, however, ignored in conversational accounts, which assume its ubiquity: 'it's a sort of prestige thing with the Trinidadian male, you have a wife, you must have an outside woman, the deputy is essential, it is too common because fathers – ok a son growing up in a home and seeing that and he too would do the same thing when he gets older. The guys in (armed) services do that because it's expected of them, you are working for a salary and if your friend see that you are just giving it to your wife, first thing they are going to say is that you are a mama-man, you eh no kind of man, when work done you are running home.' Most deputies are assumed to be younger single women: 'you see the other woman don't have the children bawling and making noise, they eh coming home to meet no wife looking the way I do, I mean the outside woman have all the time to curl up her hair, have long nails because you are doing nothing around the house period, that is what our men like, but get sick who is the first person they running to – the wife.' It seems likely that the deputy phenomenon had become particularly pervasive during the oil-boom when men who suddenly found themselves with large amounts of money were able to maintain several households at the expense of poorer men, but that with the recession this had markedly declined as was noted: 'well right now they are in what we call monkeypants, they are wondering which tree to climb on, and in most cases they up with the wife and become more subtle'. It was hinted that many households in Ford had originated in this way but relationships had since either stabilised or been abandoned.

The term deputy covers a variety of stereotypical situations. One of the firmest beliefs was that all men in uniform such as soldiers, police and coastguards had to establish deputies almost as a mark of their profession ('all of them men with buttons want to have plenty ladies'). They were required to spend considerable time away from their marital home and therefore could use this as an excuse to establish a separate household. Indian males with religious and dutiful wives were also expected to have deputies who could accompany them to fêtes and similar occasions for which their wives would be unwilling or unsuitable companions. There was also some suggestion of the opposite phenomenon (although I was only able to clearly document a single instance), where a man from Newtown, whose own wife was relatively easygoing and not inclined to remain within the domestic sphere, in addition kept a deputy who seemed to represent transcendent values. In this case both partners were African but it was suggested by some that it was more common for wealthier African males to seek to find an Indian deputy who would represent the faithful, reliable and subservient domestic female which was 'missing' in their marital life. Anecdotally this phenomenon was particularly pronounced in the area around Pt Lisas (in the south-west section of Central Trinidad) where Africans with high incomes were living in an area surrounded by rural Indian villages.

One deputy relationship which had been established for over a decade involved a male who had married his wife after getting her pregnant while young and established the deputy through initially not revealing his marriage until the relationship was already well-developed. By 1988, however, the relationship was generally known about and accepted. The deputy would strive to wear fancy clothes and look good when accompanying her man to fêtes and on limes, he would bring his workmates to her house since they would not feel comfortable in the atmosphere of religiosity in his marital home. The deputy checks that his clothes look good, and is increasingly involved in his family life to the extent that on Mother's Day she buys presents on his behalf that his wife's children can give to their mother; she will also make the cakes used in his family celebrations. Although some of his wife's family refuse to welcome or acknowledge her, others have accepted her role in relation to both him and his children. She receives a regular income, but recognises the problems he is having in maintaining two homes with the recession and is anxious both to earn as much as she is able independently and also to refuse his more extravagant gestures of fancy clothes and other items. In this, as in other cases, the wife faced with this situation had intensified her religious devotions and took solace in conspicuous respectability and religiosity.

Having a deputy tends to enhance rather than threaten a man's reputation, though men who are in high positions are expected to be discreet. Women in service jobs such as clerks or nurses may be less reticent in talking about their 'by the way' relationships with men in senior positions such as managers or doctors. In Newtown, discussions over corruption in the allocation of houses generally assumed that a percentage of the single women would represent second households established by prominent men in the public service.

The implications of deputy relations are complex. In one case it became clear that the wife had become increasingly restricted, for example, being prevented from taking outside employment in case she should come to hear about the deputy. Although deputies are often seen as young women with high-spending lifestyles, in practice, especially for Indians, the deputy relations could emerge as more like a second household with parallel anxieties about levels of commitment. Deputies are often expected to be more faithful, given the ease with which they can be thrown out of their house, and the newspapers featured several spectacular murders of deputies who had 'horned' their men, during the year. As in French farce there are constant stories about the anomalies of this system, about half-naked individuals escaping from windows, or vindictive deputies eager to supplant the wife and leaving underwear where the wife will find it.

Lovelace and Transience

The role of sexuality within the values of transience may be sum-marised with reference to another fictional character, that of Aldryck, the protagonist in the book *The Dragon Can't Dance* by Earl Lovelace (1981), a novel which like *A House for Mr Biswas* seems to have become accepted very quickly as a 'classic' in Trinidad. Lovelace is one of those who wish to oppose the gener-al interpretation of wining in terms of sexuality, and in his other books and articles (e.g. 1988) he has demonstrated his consider-able concern with the major issues of Trinidadian history and society, including the evocation of African traditional roots and the political role of high culture. Nevertheless, in his fiction and in this novel, in particular, Lovelace provides a sympathetic and exceedingly insightful account of the key characteristics of tran-sience, which is generally taken by local readers to ring true. The quintessence of transience is:

> Aldryck Prospect, an aristocrat in this tradition, not knowing where his next meal was coming from, would get up at midday from sleep, yawn, stretch, then start to think of where he might get something to eat, his brain working in the same smooth unhurried nonchalance with which he moved his feet, a slow, cruising crawl which he quick-ened only at Carnival. (ibid: 11)

The centrality of transience to this novel is evident from the core motif, referred to in the book's title. Aldryck performs every year in Carnival as Dragon. Despite this continuity, what might otherwise be seen as tradition, the novel is at pains to emphasise that the Dragon costume has to be remade each year, and that this is symbolic of the way in which Carnival escapes from being insti-tutionalised as ritual. Rather, each is a new event, its dominant characteristics unpredictable from the year which preceded it.

In the first half of the novel Lovelace establishes many of the parameters of transient culture, the difficulty in constructing communality within an intensely competitive context, giving rise to a strong individualism celebrated as colourful 'characters'. In the portrayal of female figures Lovelace notes the centrality of sexuality, both in competitive relations between females and in constructing relations across genders. The key figure here is the sexually alluring Sylvia:

to him she was the most dangerous female person on the Hill, for she possessed, he suspected, the ability not only to capture him in passion but to enslave him in caring, to bring into his world those ideas of love and home and children that he had spent his whole life avoiding. (ibid: 31)

In their first encounter, Aldryck puts forward the ideal of gender relations as essentially sexual encounters without accretive consequences, where the women don't stay more than a night. This is opposed to the image of love associated with property (ibid: 32). The key symbol in the initiation of exchange is the purchase of a Carnival costume for Sylvia, but it is clothing, in general, that will be the gift she received for her sexuality, clothing which is constantly referred to in the central competitive rivalry between the women of the Hill (ibid: 29).

The image of exchange is explicit in this novel:

She knew then, already, with that instinctive knowing refined by seventeen years on this Hill, that between this man, the rent collector, and her mother, a woman with seven children and no man either, she was the gift arranged even before she knew it, even without the encouragement and connivance of her mother. She was the sacrifice. (ibid: 25)

A constant motif is Aldryck's temptation but resistance: 'but to make even that offer now was to contradict the very guts and fibre of his own living: Aldryck was a dragon. He was a hustler' (ibid: 44).

T'aint the costume alone. She's a woman with all those things in her, those woman wantings ... I use to say to myself, Aldryck, you living the life ... no wife, no child, no boss, no job. You could get up any hour of the day you want to, cuss who you want' (ibid: 101); 'in a way it was better it was Guy [the rent collector], who could give her a little money and buy her some clothes'. (ibid: 31)

The threat to Aldryck is that he would not longer be able to keep things on the surface, and once having an 'inside' he would lose his freedom: 'All his life he managed in such ways to disconnect himself from things which he couldn't escape and which threatened to define him in a way which he didn't want to be defined, and go on untouched, untouched by things that should have touched him, hurt him, burned him' (ibid: 131). He is nevertheless hurt at Sylvia's explicit rejection of him at Carnival on the grounds that she now has her man: 'He really wanted to laugh, to make some gesture of uncaring, of superiority' (ibid: 128).

The representation of gender relations remains close to that presented in the calypso and very similar to the anthropological conflict between male 'reputation' and female 'respectability' presented by Wilson (1973). The tragic element of this novel is the portrayal of an evident corollary of transience, its apolitical nature. In such a novel relationships are constantly viewed as forms of objectification which make manifest larger cultural values and projects, and beyond that their contradictions. Lovelace, as evident in his other writings, would wish to associate with radical political action, but has to confront the problem that politics of all kinds is, like religion, a mark of transcendence, a subsumption of identity in specific projects which have to be sustained. In pure transience politics can only be an event. In the second half of the novel, Aldryck combines with several other characters on the Hill who are dissatisfied with injustice and the encroachment of commerce upon the authenticity of their environment. They commandeer a jeep and call themselves the 'People's Liberation Army', but can do no more. Aldryck: 'began to hope that the police would try to stop them. That would save them. But, they were not to be rescued by the police' (ibid: 180). As their lawyer puts it: 'The authorities trusted these men to fail, that is why they made no move to stop them. They trusted that they would be unable to make of their frustration anything better than a Dragon dance, a threatening gesture' (ibid: 183).

Lovelace was undoubtedly influenced in his composition of this novel by the Black Power revolt of 1970, though focusing upon a much smaller scale and personalised fictive case. Certainly political commentators have suggested that this was a revolt which was much clearer about what it was opposing than about what it was hoping to construct. A possibly better exemplification of the central theme of the book came with the events of 1990, with the attempted coup associated with the Jamaat Al Muslimeen led by Abu Bakr. Once again this coup consisted mainly of a rhetorical form, the seizure of the parliament with its enclosed politicians and of the TV buildings. The leaders seemed to understand their role as negation, and their action was welcomed by many in so far as it opposed the government, but the leaders seemed to have very little idea of what they could or should do once the gesture/dragon dance had been accomplished.

The other notable feature of this coup was the response of much of the population. The 'classic' description of this came from the journalist who noted that Abu Bakr asked the people to rise up and help him, but instead they rose up and helped themselves. In my talking to those directly or indirectly involved in the extensive looting, the evidence suggests that few of them either predicted the coup or supported the specific group, although they would have been happy enough to see the then government thereby overthrown. What then appeared most striking was the extreme rapidity with which the looting spread to encompass a considerable proportion of the country's retail trade, extending well east of the capital. Many commentators interpreted this as demonstrating the planned nature of the looting, but there is no clear evidence to support this. By contrast, I believe the looting suggests the considerable importance of spontaneity, that value so positively ascribed to in transience. This is best portrayed by Lieber (1981; see also Eriksen 1990) in his book on street liming in Port of Spain, which describes the endless hours spent walking around looking for some action. But when action is there, the liming population is experienced in exploiting the possibilities offered with alacrity. Indeed this mixture of 'entrepreneurial' ability to exploit the potential of the event, and networks which spread information about the event, are often hailed as the positive side of Trinidadian transience.

Transience comes across in Lovelace's book as an objectification of freedom, the imperative which makes sexuality in and of itself the best, the 'safest' medium for cross-gender relations, allowing for the retention of the key qualities of voluntarism and individualism. It is therefore precisely these values which are so forcefully repudiated by those households which have migrated from Laventille (the setting for the novel, fictionalised as 'the Hill') to Newtown (in Chaguanas) and are trying to create as much distance as possible from transient values. In the survey of the four communities a question was asked as to where would be the worst place to have to live in Trinidad. By far the most common choice was Laventille with twenty-eight households, the next most common being the run-down Beetham estate along the East-West Corridor chosen by twelve. It was also noticeable that the community which most disliked the idea of living in Laventille was Newtown where fifteen gave this response. It is Newtown that has by far the largest number of migrants from the

Port of Spain area, indeed eight of them mentioned being born in Laventille or nearby Belmont. Lovelace is by no means the only Trinidadian to focus on Laventille as the quintessence of certain Trinidadian values: this district is frequently mentioned by calypsonians such as David Rudder as the site of the 'soul' or 'heart' of steelband, or of Carnival if not Trinidad itself. The extremes in attitude to Laventille is again suggestive of the importance of dualism within cultural values.

The Mutual Antipathy of Sexuality and Property

The problem which Lovelace highlights is that it is the same sexuality which, within the idiom of wining, is an expression of individuality and transience, which in another form threatens to become the vehicle which seduces men out of transience into its very opposite. Lovelace has at least three specific moments when the threat to transience of sexuality, as inculcating a desire for property, is made explicit. The most sustained is the opposition between Sylvia as the temptation of property and Aldryck who claims: 'You see me here, I is thirty-one years old ... I ain't own house or car or radio or racehorse or store. I don't own one thing in this fucking place' (1981: 110). The danger to this state represented by entering into an exchange relationship with Sylvia is that she is the kind of woman who will transform exchange as a mode of transience into possessions as the foundation of transcendence, a prophecy clearly fulfilled when Aldryck returns from prison to see Sylvia in her new home: 'He had seen the radio and TV and stereo and the chairs and the knick-knacks, and the framed pictures of cut-outs from magazines, and prints of a couple of local scenes, and there was a picture of *Bless this House* over the door' (1981: 198).

A similar theme operates in the condemnation of a calypsonian who becomes successful and leaves the Hill for a residential area similar to The Meadows, and also in the tension surrounding the presence of an Indian who appears at one moment to threaten the egalitarian competitiveness of the neighbourhood through his purchase of a bicycle. By contrast, Naipaul treats the threat of sexuality to property by ignoring the subject. It is virtually absent in the detailed discussion of the relationship between Biswas and his wife, who seem embarrassed by intimacy (1961:

147). Where sexuality is referred to, it tends to be in association with Negros, either in terms of their sexual exploits (ibid: 488), or as the mistress of an Indian (ibid: 59).

For the transient, the key symbol of relationships apart from the sexual act itself is the giving of money. It is commonly expected that relationships between parents and children will, as early as possible, take a monetary form, with the children providing funds for the services with which the household provides them. A sexual relationship is usually established and acknowledged through the regular transference of money or services (such as repairing the house or yard) from males to females. This permits a monitoring of the relationship by the women involved. 'You can tell that a man care for a woman by the things they do for you.' For many women who are extremely sceptical of their sweet-talking males' actual intentions towards them, the constant marking through this exchange is an important resource in establishing their value. They recognise that this is not a constant and they note any falling off in the males' provision as a likely sign that their partner is weakening in his commitment. As in most elements of transience the exchange relates to externalities, and the sense of 'no money no love' is quite literal. Love has to be seen as external form for it to exist, the love is actually then in the money as exchange. Externality is also important, for one of the most common uses made of the money received is to buy new clothes. This is also seen as a reciprocal return of the gift, since clothes make the woman look stylish and this rebounds to the credit of the partner they accompany to events such as fêtes.

Because of the dominant ideology of competition by women over men, women may also be the bearers of gifts: 'Wives spend more than husbands now, she knows she has to buy something expensive for he to stop with she in the house.' This was especially the case when women had more money during the oil-boom. A woman reminiscing about her time as a stewardess on the national airline noted: 'They used to buy clothes for their boyfriends, and then quarrel about it, because when they leave the girl they would complain that "he left with my clothes, with the shirt I bought for him".'

From the vantage of transcendence, the nature of sexuality as exchange has been constantly denigrated as virtual prostitution. The implication of 'no money no love' is an anathema to hegemonic moralities imported from abroad where these two are more generally defined in opposition. The view is supported by the general Western ambivalence about money, which defines the authenticity of relationships such as parenting and courtship by the absence of an expectation of monetary exchange. But, for those involved, it is precisely this exchange which demonstrates that this is not merely prostitution or a one-night stand, but rather a relationship with both constancy and value. A barmaid noted that it is the receipt of money that makes a woman feel human, that she is not being merely used as a 'convenience'. A better parallel than prostitution would have been with institutions such as brideprice or dowry. Where there exists cohabitation without institutionalised marriage, then the relationship has to be constantly reaffirmed as a sequence of events. In this sense the exchange of money might be taken as the kind of continual brideprice, a dyadic exchange which is also the sign of the existence of a relationship. Within transience money is not opposed to value but is the measure of it.

The relationship to children is also more likely in transience to be seen positively in monetary terms as a form of exchange. The expectations parents have of children are quite often posed in terms of the child's financial contribution once they have reached the relevant age, and as with cross-gender exchange the explicit monetary element has no negative connotation as being opposed to affectivity. It is possible that this view of money as having positive moral connotations has affinities with more traditional African views of the relationship between money and human values (M. Rowlands is currently working on this theme: personal communication), but, as with so many elements of transient kinship, it conforms to various negative images held in the hegemonic morality to which it is opposed.

In this context there is not surprisingly a close symbolic interconnection between sex and money, in which sex seems to provide the dominant idiom for the experience of money. Both should be spent out regularly, because both also contain a threat to become the medium of possession and thereby of property. As one person put it: 'I used to feel when I was working and got my pay check, I has so many things to do with it, used to be a worry on my brain, I had to get rid of it very fast, when I got rid of it my brain will feel eased. Money, I wouldn't like too much of money because I would have to think of too many things at one time, money is really too much pressure, it gets to me sometimes, once you buy and enjoy what you buy, that is release.' The symbolic connection to sex as release from pressure may have experiential consequences in the sense that the pleasure derived from spending may evoke something of the release associated with sexuality.

Similarly, a woman in Ford who had worked some years for a multinational company and retired from it in the middle of the oil-boom had received a very substantial sum upon leaving. She and her daughter told, half wistfully, but half in celebration, of the speed with which the money was dispensed with, to leave them in the present wooden construction as squatters: 'They gave me a lump sum after twenty years, I got twenty-nine thousand dollars and we ate and we drank the best, we drank Harvey's [sherry] like water, that was just four years ago and it finished, you just live the joy of this is mine and you spend and spend and when it start to finish you think, but then it's too late ... I think keeping money is like a pressure on you, it is not that you are throwing it away but you are just spending it, comes like a burden so it is better to end it. The Indians are different it will be there for years and it just won't bother them.'

In no sense should this be seen as some desire for poverty. Few groups could be said to have less ascetic tendencies. Rather the preference is for money to flow through, as it were, regularly and be spent out regularly more on analogy with sexuality. It should be a process. The issue is politically sensitive since a refusal to desire wealth as property may lead to poverty being seen as one's own fault. The opposition here is clearly with the transcendent where the emphasis is on storage and accretion.

The derogatory stereotypes also work in the other direction. When the transcendent (often generalised in ethnic terms as the Indians) are condemned for their wealth, this implies more than a class conflict with those who deny resources. It also suggests that these people have stored internally a substance which should have remained on the surface. This is both their mistake and consequently their downfall. Their thrift and retention is the likely cause of their bad character and unhappiness, evident in their tendency to become 'social' (meaning anti-social), that is to lose their ability for sociality.

The symbolic opposition between property and sexuality may also have problematic consequences for transcendence. This is illustrated by a conversation with a doctor who was attempting to confront the problem of obesity in married Indian women which had emerged as a serious health hazard during the oil-boom. As far as many husbands were concerned the doctor was being rather too successful. As the doctor put it: 'You see by losing weight you create problems too, the woman feels much better, she eh treated like a footrag again (anymore), but the menfolk have more pressure on them. They are happier with them overweight, when nobody gave them a second look, this was the best situation for them because in any case they have a deputy outside. She will wash, take care of the kids, keep the house clean, that's great, this is how they see their wives, one to take care of the home and one to go out with, to lime with.'

Although some wives may acquiesce in this placement of themselves, many do not, and part of the frisson expressed in the concept of 'bacchanal' is the sense of a discrepancy between the ideological projection of the asexual (most commonly Indian) wife and her actual sexuality.[11] This arose in diverse circumstances: the owner of a videoshop expresses shock at the number of matronly figures wearing traditional 'orhnees' (head scarves) who ask surreptitiously for a 'blue' film. There is also the well-known lascivious dancing that takes place during the women's night before a Hindu wedding, and the increasing syncretism between this and the act of wining. Such wining may now involve large matronly figures, during highly public competitions featuring 'chutney', Indian soca and other syncretic musical forms. One of the hit calypsos of 1988 was entitled 'Nanee Wine', the title being a pun on the word Nanee which can mean either an Indian grandmother or a vagina. Within the home, the denial of this sexuality may well be associated with the commonly asserted problem of alcoholism among Indian housewives.

Several doctors complained about how much of their time was taken up dealing with male impotence. They noted how often it was the wives who would push their husbands into seeing the doctor about this complaint, and assumed that this was because the wives might feel this condition was proof of their husbands' extramarital affairs, unless a physiological cause could be found. Doctors I spoke to felt that the root cause was always physiological, with the emphasis being placed on the incidence of diabetes, but several examples provided by the doctors suggests an alternative explanation. In at least some cases it was evident that the male concerned was having normal sexual relations with one or more outside women at the same time as complaining of impotence with his wife.

In one extreme example, a doctor found that a patient who was being treated for long-term impotence had been murdered in revenge for an adulterous affair he was conducting at the workplace. If the impotence is not physiological, it may well be caused by the male's difficulty in responding to an active sexuality at home which he has been at some pains to deny as inappropriate. These males may have responded to dualism by projecting two ideal and opposed concepts of the female, one wholly domestic and asexual, the other wholly outside and lascivious, rendering them unable to deal with an ambiguous sexuality within the domestic realm.

The question of impotence came up more often with respect to the Indian community, but the same tension clearly plays a problematic role within the African community based on the same fundamental opposition between sexuality and property. The norm which establishes property as the proper vehicle for descent is constantly espoused by the church. The battle waged continually by the church is against a family pattern which permits sexual relations and child-rearing outside the sanctioned context of marriage and the home. To an extent the state colludes with this, for example, in its constant encouragement for the African population to establish home-ownership as against rented accommodation as the basis for a stable family. In the tradition of the notorious Moynihan report of the United States, the dominant ideology sees the actuality of family life as a mixture of sin and social pathology. This discourse and the relationships it establishes are too powerful to be disregarded and their effect is clear in the dynamics of kinship. At one level the church has been extremely successful at establishing its own values, asserting the sense of the domestic and its proper setting in religiously sanctioned marriage and a home. But ironically the response from the population to this success has been, if anything, to increase unsanctioned unions until this proper setting has been achieved. Thus marriage and religious observance should only take place within the 'appropriate' setting of one's own property and both are delayed until one can afford one's own home. One of the most commonly observed features of West Indian kinship may then reflect an acceptance of church teaching but with an effect which completely negates the intention of the church in spreading this teaching.

This does imply, however, that for many Africans as much as for the Indians, the sense of property and the control over sexuality are regarded as an inextricable relation. The same acceptance of the necessary connection between these elements is evident in families, most commonly in Ford, who not only reject the family structure, and in some cases, the legitimacy of owned property, but have virtually abandoned any pretence of going to church except when using Baptist or Shango elements most commonly as a 'pragmatic' solution to specific problems.

This dualism not only works within groups defined by ethnicity, but may be crucial in influencing the relationship between them. For some of the Indian families from St Pauls or The Meadows, the antagonism between sexuality and property may be emerging as a constant tension between the basic principles of descent and affinal relations. Property, as has been constantly noted, is more a process than a thing. Too often, in anthropological writings about descent, the emphasis is upon a juridical and structural formation, which fails to acknowledge the experiential importance of property and descent as constructing a sense of temporality and life-project. The process of descent creates an orientation towards familial integrity and inalienability. For Indians especially this is often conceptualised in terms of a male line. Even in less dualistic contexts, patrilineality is often expressed through mechanisms which separate out the daughter who is destined to be the procreator for another line. She is not provided with 'real' property but with dowry or movable items which are detachable from the sense of descent-property continuity.

Given the pervasive dualism of contemporary Trinidadian society, certain features of this act of separation become accentuated. The daughter is individualised for an act of exchange to become the sexual partner within another family. These two attributes, individualism and sexuality, have to be acknowledged in order for this social fission to take place. Conceptually, however, the process virtually inverts a logic which associates Indian women with asexuality and subsumed individuality, and projects individualism and sexuality as the transient features which are the essential character of the African. In a sense, then, the separation of the daughter requires her to be at least temporarily aligned with a norm usually viewed as 'African'. There is therefore considerable concern over the formation of relationships by females, making this a cause of intra-family trauma and strife second only to inheritance disputes.

Clearly this is only a particular manifestation of a more general contradiction between the principles which underlie descent and affinal relations, or between blood and marriage, which in other societies may manifest itself in alternative idioms. In some African contexts this takes the form of witchcraft accusations against affines and in South Asia in forms of hypergamy and extreme asymmetry between the families of husband and wife. It emerges in Trinidadian ethnicity in the constant refrain about potential sexual relations between Negro males and Indian daughters. Any suspicion of such a liaison could quickly turn neighbourly relations sour and such couples are usually ostracised. The question of Indian males' marriage to African females was rarely discussed, although this asymmetry was often justified by the near ubiquitous statements (by elder Indians) that African women held little attraction for Indian males (something not supported by general observation) but that Indian women were almost irresistible for Negro males.

The point at issue here is that much of the fear felt by Indians of the individual black male is actually a projection on to ethnicity of a contradiction emergent out of kinship. The colonial projection of sexuality incarnate upon the black man, as analysed by Fanon (1986), is taken a stage further in this context, since the idiom of sexuality is immediately resonant with the threat to the ultimate project of descent continuity, which may apply equally to the homogenised sense of family, and to a homogenised sense of being Indian. Thus the ruination of one's daughter through seduction by Negro sexuality is a fear that totalises the whole project of transcendence for those Indians committed to these values. This is why this fear arises as an obsessive motif in daily conversation, especially when drinking, and seems to lie close to the surface of consciousness constantly waiting for release as explicit accusation.

If anti-black racism may be understood in relation to the threat to property located in individualised sexuality, there is a certain symmetry in African anti-Indian sentiment. Africans tend to racism against the collectivity of Indians, and often assert that they cannot be racist since whatever their general feelings about Indians they will often befriend an individual who is seen as detached from the stereotypes associated with that group. It is, however, the Indian community as a whole which tends to be seen as oppressive, and especially the Indian community characterised as controlling commerce and wealth and property. That is, Indians as a collectivity come to objectify the threat of property to transience as freedom among Africans.

To conclude, these are generalised characterisations, and there are many practices and tendencies which neither fit them well nor are subsumed well within them. The degree to which they are seen in ethnic terms serves badly both the Creole middle class and the individualising young Indian male. A chapter which attempts to explore dualism tends also to concentrate on the two polarities. It would be quite wrong to try and divide all households or even all individuals into transient or transcendent in orientation. Nevertheless, an exploration of dualism clarifies a great deal more than it obfuscates. In particular, the larger opposition between property and sexuality can assert itself as the core of ethnic consciousness and antagonism, and also as the central axis around which two competing forms of kinship and household are related. By this means dualism may help to account for a considerable amount of ordinary practices, and for the taken-for-granted legitimation of these practices.

The imperative behind the generalisation and theorising of these observations lies in the return to the comparative project of this book. The intention of this chapter was to demonstrate that the radical rupture of temporal consciousness discussed in theoretical terms in Chapter 2 and in the form of festivals in Chapter 3 may also be found, if with much less clarity, within the everyday social relations of contemporary Trinidad. Again the 'traits' of modern life to be found in Trinidad are often specific; there is a concern with freedom which is at least as important in this context as in the debates on modernity derived from European historical experience, but there are other elements such as the relationship to possessions which are not usually accredited with the same importance elsewhere.

The importance of this juxtaposition is not merely to suggest affinities between the general writings on modernity and the actual experiences of Trinidadians but, as will be argued in Chapters 6 and 7, it may be that these forms of kinship, property and ethnic relations are in part to be accounted for precisely as attempts to objectify the sense of being modern and the contradictions which emerge from that condition which the theoretical debates have engaged with but are rarely systematically explored within the practices of everyday life.

Notes

1. Though it should be noted that poverty, and more specifically marginalisation, is still the most favoured explanation of these patterns in Caribbean studies including the newer

feminist perspectives, see Senior (1991: 9–18) on the key example of child-shifting as 'flexible' kinship.

2. The clearest evidence for this comes from a mating and fertility survey (Harewood 1984). This reveals that while East-Indian women had formally formed early married unions, the divergence has decreased during the oil-boom. For example, for the age cohort now 45–49, the figures for when they were aged 20–25 were 64.1 per cent married and 13 per cent visiting or common-law. For the age cohort now 20–25 the figures are 22.5 per cent married and 24.3 per cent visiting or common-law (all these figures are for first union type). On general the proportion of marriage rises with educational level. The oil-boom period also sees an increase in the number of visiting relations by non-Indians in the 20–29 cohort. Overall that group showed for current union status 25.6 per cent married, 15.6 per cent common-law and 31.1 per cent visiting. By the 30–39 cohort the majority (50.9 per cent) are married.

3. Since by no means all East-Indians have names which signify their ethnicity, it is not possible to accurately quantify the results of this investigation.

4. The state recognised Hindu marriage in 1945, Muslim marriage in 1936.

5. 'Right' in this context is an informal greeting.

6. During the survey married couples were asked if they had lived for a period of time with relatives before settling on their own. Twenty-two Indian couples affirmed that they had done so, but so did twelve African and seven Mixed couples.

7. 'Horning', a much-used term in Trinidad, indicates adultery or sexual relationships outside a supposedly exclusive relationship.

8. Abdullah notes (1988: 442) the near numerical parity between males and females in the 15–64 age group, with a sex ratio of 998.

9. *Obeah* is a set of beliefs and acts, mainly derived from West Africa systems of magic and witchcraft, though with some syncretic influence from similar South Asian ideas. Those wishing to use the associated powers will consult an expert Obeahman or Obeahwoman.

10. The major exception to this generic category of women is the concept of mothers who are viewed quite differently, and provide the main alternative model of female behaviour.

11. This active sexuality is certainly recognised in traditional images of the South Asian female as embodied in the principle of female Shakti energy.

Chapter 5

Mass Consumption

Modernity is by no means synonymous with mass consumption, but the relationship between a sudden change in the availability and variety of new goods and the consciousness of being modern is a familiar one in human history, which the effect of trade on the Athenians of the fifth century BC would serve to exemplify as fully as more recent cases. What has been less remarked upon, however, is that the specific nature of mass consumption as material culture may have consequences for the manner by which modernity is experienced. This was briefly suggested in Chapter 2 during a discussion of the work of Schama on seventeenth-century Amsterdam. It is this same question as to the particular forms taken by modernity and the consequences of the media of objectification which underpins the interpretation of contemporary consumption in Trinidad which follows.

Although the effects of the oil-boom on Trinidad were dramatic, it would be misleading to represent the country as unfamiliar with mass consumption before that period. Many Trinidadians had, for a long period, enjoyed a high standard of living relative to that of other Caribbean countries, in large measure because of the oil industry which has dominated the economy for most of this century. By 1930 the value of oil exports already exceeded sugar and cocoa combined (Alleyne 1988: 19). Perhaps the primary precursor to the oil-boom in its social impact, however, had been the Second World War and the associated construction of American air- and sea-base facilities. For the people of the Chaguanas area this had been a period of dramatic change in economic consciousness. The extreme differential in both wages and treatment between the oppressive British colonial regime of sugar production and the relatively liberal American military had a lasting impact, which in turn was firmly associated with the sense of wealth and excitement, and the possibilities of broader worlds (though see de Boissiere 1956 for the negative impact of these same events). In many ways the development of political independence was also accelerated by this experience, which established a sense that history could arrive in dramatic epochs in which new wealth signalled many new possibilities.

Further developments after the war had accentuated this impression of mass consumption. First, there was the increased level of contact and remittances between Trinidadians and émigrés in the United States, Canada and Britain, facilitated by the shift from sea to air transport. Second, there were developments of media technology which brought consumption images into the living-rooms of even those who did not travel abroad.

Nevertheless, up until the oil-boom Trinidad was unambiguously within the category of a developing country and for all these 'preparations' the islanders still seem to have experienced the oil-boom as something on a par with a tropical storm, which, with hindsight, passed over the country leaving an astonishing trail of detritus in its wake. The oil price sped upwards in 1973 and the impact was felt within two or three years among the general population of a country which had seen income disparities diminish since independence (Henry 1988). In Chaguanas it was the manual labourers for the council who saw their wages grow exponentially, as much as the store keepers who found banks begging to lend them money to expand.

The oil-boom, which for consumers centred on the period from 1976–83, is now a period of legends – of those who flew to Paris for their wines and oysters and to Miami for the spare parts for their new cars. There was the bacchanal over obtaining new cars through patronage and bribery, associated with a second-hand market in which cars seemed to increase in value over time. This was the period when a lime could take in a few small islands, and when parties and whisky seemed in unlimited supply. There was also the ratcheting up of expectations of educational qualifications, of established infrastructure, the massive government sector and employment programmes. Not everyone in Trinidad had an oil-boom, and while those in The Meadows continue to assume international links established in this period, for those in other communities the effect was more likely to be a first and last tour around the other Caribbean islands. In general, however, because of both the small size of the country and the political agenda which followed the 1970 black power revolt, the dividends were more widely distributed than in most oil-boom states. Even Ford has abundant oil-boom anecdotes.

To understand the effects of such an experience is a more problematic exercise. There is probably only one consensual theory which pervades academic and official discourse and is most easily found in media reportage. This is the theme of affluence as the loss of authenticity. There are many symptoms of this retribution of wealth. There is the decline in the knowledge of traditional folklore, attached to agricultural labour, medical diagnosis and treatment, the supernatural, and traditional folktales, as well as traditional foods and customs. Then there is the dissolving of family and community life as siblings travel, have independent lifestyles and reject older moralities. There is an associated loss of specificity as the country is flooded with international brand names and a culture of mass consumption indistinguishable from Indonesia or Alaska. Naipaul's (1967) title *The Mimic Men* describes the trajectory which leads to a deadening of sensation as culture empties into a blasé acceptance of wealth, a slavish adoption of all new imported fashions, in turn tied to a new economic dependence and an end to hopes for self-sufficiency when, as happened here, local production of food is devastated, to be replaced by a taste for and demand for imported cuisines.[1] There is also a consensus about government employment projects devastating the 'work ethic' and of industrial white elephants.

Although the local version of this neo-global rhetoric dominates official and media representations it is not the dominant image found in popular sentiment and cultural response. For many people, especially those with a background in poverty, there are few qualms about celebrating the impact of wealth, and the main regret with regard to the oil-boom is that it has gone. For the Indian younger generation able to opt out of following their parents into the cane-fields, and instead gaining degrees in foreign universities, or even for those in Ford who are faced now with a biting recession, it was more than just a relief from oppressive constraints. For many it was a period of excitement, of fulfilling themselves in the cultivation of style and new freedoms. It was often seen as the time when cultural projects which had already been formulated could now actually be accomplished.

The issues posed by oil-boom and recession and especially those of dependency and power will be discussed in the subsequent volume to this one. Here I shall concentrate on the evidence for considerable continuity found in ideals already objectified in other domains such as kinship, which were then refined or extended through mass consumption. Indeed, it will be argued that mass consumption enabled dualism to emerge with a clarity which then in turn makes more evident what was still somewhat obscured when it was expressed largely through kinship (compare Sahlins 1988; Thomas 1991: 83–124). This perspective demands a radical break with more traditional views of these topics. Typically within the social sciences we look for images of sociality in kinship, while mass consumption becomes the instrument for its dissolving away. Here I wish to argue that the two idioms of kinship and mass consumption collude, as it were, in the development of this dualist rendition of the possibilities of sociality and freedom. There are, of course, many differences between these two media of objectification. Perhaps most important is the ability of mass consumption to ameliorate many negative consequences of contradiction. It may have been that the main desire for many of those using consumption forms was to make dualism not only envisageable but increasingly unproblematic. It is a strategy which helps articulate the specific developments in Trinidad with wider issues surrounding the social experience of modernity.

In order to illustrate this argument, consumption will first be considered as the clear fulfilment of the expression of transcendence and subsequently of transience. Once this has been established, consumption forms will then be investigated in order to study the dynamics of these cultural fields. This leads to the argument presented in this volume's conclusion that, contrary to the dominant discourse on the effects of mass consumption, it is precisely through consumption that the specificity of Trinidadian culture is constructed and in the main preserved.

Mass Consumption as Transcendence

The key arena for the construction of the image of transcendence will be evident enough from the previous analysis of Christmas and property. These have established the imperative for a centripetal project of interiorisation, of drawing things into a core which is substantial and transcends mere events. Thanks to the resources of the oil-boom, many households in Trinidad were able to construct a consensual image of this core which may be illustrated through an investigation of what is probably its most important site – the living- room. The following analysis of the living-room is based upon some 800 photographic slides taken of 128 living-rooms, together with survey and participatory data on the households of the four adjacent communities (for the survey details presented according to ethnicity and income see Table 5.1, below). What emerges from the material is very different from the class-based antagonisms of taste found by Bourdieu (1984) for France. Rather there is a single ideal, with multiple forms of realisation, a kind of polythetic but normative category. From this may be discerned a gradation away from this norm arising through either a lack of resources or a lack of desire to fully constitute this particular ideal type.

Table 5.1 Household furnishing in relation to ethnicity and income

| | Ethnicity | | | Income | | | | |
	AFRICAN	MIXED	INDIAN	A	B	C	D	E
TOTAL IN SURVEY	54	23	51	25	40	38	18	7
Maroon upholstery	20	10	30	14	19	17	8	2
Brown upholstery	31	10	14	7	16	18	8	6
Maroon coordinates	18	5	21	6	16	17	4	1
Buffet	16	10	30	10	19	18	6	3
Space-saver	30	8	20	6	14	20	13	5
Doll/animal Stuffed/boxed	16	5	23	7	17	13	5	2
Religious icons	13	8	36	10	19	17	6	5
Homily	36	13	28	10	31	19	11	6
Several artificial flowers	25	14	39	15	24	26	7	6

KEY: Declared household income per month in TT dollars.

A= Less 1,000 B= 1,000–2,500 C= 2,500–5,000 D= 5,000–8,000 E= Over 8,000
Notes:
1 Of the 160 households surveyed there were 128 where photography was permitted and the results sufficiently clear to be used.
2 Being based on photographs, the material does not provide a comprehensive picture of the living room. Many of the features tabulated do not appear in the section covered by the photographs. For this reason the table underestimates conformity to a 'normative' model. There is no reason, however, to consider the figures biased with respect to ethnicity or income, the variables the table is used to illustrate.

In each category of furnishing there are two or three varieties which dominate the selection and which together construct this polythetic ideal. With regard to flooring, the most conformist form is a high-pile carpet locally termed 'plush', followed by terrazzo and then wooden planking. As in many other areas of furnishing the ideal to be conformed to is by no means a traditional form. The dominant furniture consists of thick foam-based chairs covered in artificial velvet, arranged in sets of one or often two couches, plus armchairs often comprising upholstered seating for eight or more people. Sometimes there is an extended single couch turning a corner which will seat six by itself, sometimes separate two- and three-seater couches with associated armchairs. The arms are either upholstered or there is a standard square cushion which can be used either for the seat bottom or the back and which are laid against a frame of dark brown to black veneered wood emulating French polish. The fake velvet easily dominates the materials employed to cover such furnishing, but some leatherette is used. The dining-table has a similar veneer, as often do the dining-chairs which have ornate spindle backs and upholstered seats and sometimes also backs. Advertisements speak of 'padded high backed chairs in fine Belgian fabrics'.

The furnishings are in the main maroon.[2] The main alternative to this is a range of gold to brown shades. Only three cases were found of upholstered furniture that did not include one or other of these colours. The maroon of the upholstery may be picked up in curtains, carpets, coverings for tables, artificial flowers such as roses and countless other decorations. Less commonly the brown-gold may also be generalised through designs such as gold to brown leaf or plant designs on a beige background found in upholstery, curtains, cushions and tablecloths.

The dining-table is covered by a white 'lace' (often in fact plastic) cloth with a central mat on which is a vase or bowl and artificial flower arrangement. Artificial flowers are extremely common, often set into elaborate arrangements with perhaps half a dozen examples within the living-room. This may be merely a few paper or plastic roses or carnations protruding from a thin-necked vase, but often includes extensive arrangements established as wedding-style displays on pedestals to become a dominant decorative form. When individuals claim flower arrangement as a hobby it is these artificial flowers which are being referred to. Such displays may be supplemented or replaced by house plants in a variety of ceramic containers or hanging from macramé and other holders. While many house plants are found within the living-room the most elaborate displays are usually found in the front gallery.

In the centre of the room will be a coffee-table with a set of 'lace' coverings. These covers are normally white, although maroon and more rarely yellow are found. On this is placed a centrepiece such as a vase of artificial flowers or a bowl of ceramic fruit. More rarely are found food or cocktail trolleys to hold drinks and ice.

The kitchen is often attached to the living-room, in which case it is commonly separated by a row of kitchen cupboards, above which (but separated by wooden spindle supports) is found a row of glass cabinets. This is called a buffet and will be filled with china and glassware; it may also have internal lining of white or maroon plush. Where this arrangement is not found there is a smaller floor-based glass cabinet (buffet), often with drawers on either side, placed against one of the walls of the living-room.

A key piece of furniture is some wooden shelving linked by spindle legs in two or three layers, called a 'space-saver' (equivalent to the English 'what-not'). This is somewhat of a misnomer since apart from holding stereos (with associated records and tapes) and televisions and videos, the main function is to hold an array of ornaments, which can be very abundant. The most common decorative ornament is a swan, but one also finds cats, dogs, chickens, peacocks, eagles, stallions and dolls, etc. Examples of swans were found in glass, brass, wood, plastic, concrete, inflatable plastic and ceramic. There may also be sports trophies: still more common are one or more sets of encyclopedias, but not novels.

Somewhere in the room will be stuffed toys or animals, such as teddy bears, dogs and rabbits. As confirmed by a questionnaire, administered by a market research company, these are for decoration rather than children's play and commonly appear with the cushions on the sofas. This is consistent with the general lack of toys in the living-room area. The presence of toys in a few examples in The Meadows tends to imply considerable contact with lifestyles outside Trinidad. Retail outlets note a desire to match the colours of furnishing with these objects and a gift shop contained many examples of maroon stuffed animals. Also to be found are a pink-fleshed female doll clothed in an elaborate round costume made from triangles of artificial silk. These may be purchased or homemade and versions may be used as a spare toilet-roll cover. Occasionally there will be an aquarium placed against the wall, but a fishbowl or birdcage may also be present.

Net curtains are found on all windows and doorways. These may be plain white or maroon but are often panelled with patterned and coloured sections such as of brown or maroon flowers, and may be supplemented by full curtains, or framed in what a retail outlet terms 'American antique red rich satin' with ruching in the most elaborate cases. Lighting from the ceiling will be of four or six Edwardian-style glass shades emerging from a gilt candelabra, with a full chandelier in some cases. Ceiling fans are also found sometimes with elaborate wood and gilt decoration.

Wall decorations will be dominated by a machine-made tapestry with a religious theme such as The Last Supper or a mosque, or a secular scene such as puppies or toddlers. Machine-made reproduction oil paintings with gilt frames will almost always be of scenes of coniferous forest glens with deer and a background of snow-capped mountains. Prints with a West Indian theme would very rarely be found in the normative living-room. Equally common are plates with decorative edges and brown ceramic plaques. Both typically contain homilies, the most common being 'God grant me the sincerity to change the things which can be changed, humility to accept the things which can't be changed and wisdom to know the difference', but also common are 'Have you tried prayer', 'God bless this house', the Lord's Prayer, etc. Such homilies will also commonly be found in non-Christian households. Of the secular comments, most common are jokes about gender relations such as 'Men have only two faults, everything they do and everything they say', or 'I am boss in this house'. After the ceramics the next most common decorations are in wood (both three-dimensional sculptures and plaques), for example of horses and eagles. Clocks are ubiquitous, sometimes set in elaborate gilt columns. Other features may be certificates such as educational qualifications or long-service awards, often set above the front door. Brass plates with Portuguese/Dutch-style merchants with beer or sailing ships are found. Mother's Day paraphernalia such as certificates of best mother or homilies on mothering are very common, sometimes including a photo of the person concerned. Equally important are calendars especially for Hindu homes, where pictures with a religious theme will be incorporated, but there may also be commercially sponsored calenders and more rarely one with a theme coming from local culture such as the great calypsonians.

In low-income homes, wall decoration may rely more on cuttings from colour magazines, where tanned European or American models are found, or local models from the more salacious weekly newspapers. In such homes particular ornament styles such as a plastic red rose set in a glass dome are common. In general the source of the decorations is not an issue; where commercial items are not available self-production will be used. For example, a person from St Paul's who felt that a wall area needed a picture, painted a local scene, but did not thereby consider himself a 'painter'. In another house an artisan had turned his hand to producing some brass engravings for the wall; again, however, no preference is given to either commerce or self-production as the better source of the object. Although when questioned about their 'favourite' object in the home, the most common response was an object received as a gift or a token of achievement.

Icons in the form of pictures of deities appear with some abundance in Hindu homes or as pictures of Jesus in Christian homes especially over the front door, above windows and other openings, sometimes with coloured lights overlaying them. Jesus seems to be dominant over all other representations, and Mary is rare even in Catholic homes in the Chaguanas area.

Family photographs are common and are dominated either by wedding pictures, usually of the couple who own the property, old or deceased relations, or young children. Souvenir pictures and plates are also found, by far the most common being of Toronto. Black felt pennants with painted designs of Trinidad and Tobago or other West Indian islands are also an occasional display. Strings of greeting cards, for example from birthdays, may be found on the walls or on space-savers.

A feature of the normative-type living-room is for things to be covered over; this includes 'throws', that is a sheet or piece of cloth thrown over the couches and armchairs and removed to reveal the upholstery only on special occasions, if at all. As an alternative, the upholstery may be covered by clear plastic so that one doesn't sit on the actual surface. 'Lace' covers are found over the head-position on couches and armchairs, also over tables, shelves, loudspeaker tops, videos and indeed any exposed surface. A notable feature of some living-rooms is items such as dolls or stuffed animals which are displayed within their original plastic wrappings, or dolls kept in their original boxes. In the bathroom an ubiquitous item is the five-piece set of cloth covers, with the cistern and the spare toilet roll commonly covered.

The above is a brief summary which can obviously be elaborated. As house furnishing these arrangements are rarely commented upon. The analysis of Christmas, however, suggests several themes which are being expressed here. First, there is transcendence expressed in a desire for things lasting or being preserved. This is evident in the preference for artificial things such as artificial flowers. These in turn are associated with things being covered over, ranging from the 'throws' on the upholstered furniture to the abundant lace covers. The declared intention with regard to the items which remain inside their plastic bags and boxes while supposedly on display is that they are being 'cherished' and will supposedly be brought out at appropriate occasions such as Divali and Christmas. In practice this may occur, but equally they may simply be left in their packaging awaiting some vague future event. Overall the material appears to imply a desire to transcend the present and is associated with memories of the past and preserving for the future.

Second, there are a large number of generally cheap ornaments with conventional themes such as swans and domestic animals. Although the furniture itself may be expensive, the general effect is not a display of conspicuous wealth since the bulk of ornamentation and decoration within this normative style is not usually of an expensive variety. It is rather conformity to a type, such that most houses have examples of the basic range of ornaments and furnishings.

As a third characteristic this filling up of the interior space with abundant ornamentation can be set alongside the 'plush' carpets[3] and the abundant upholstery to create the general sense of interiorisation, an enclosing and incorporative aesthetic based on creating and filling a space with a series of layers; the same process which can be observed in action during Christmas. Following from the conventional nature of these objects is the idea of specific categories kept in their places. This is accentuated by the practice of keeping things layered or separated. Drinks, for example, would be served on coasters which are then set on trays.

Explicit symbolism is dominated by pictures related to religion, whether Christian, Muslim or Hindu, though the last-mentioned will usually have Christian pictures included. This religious theme is juxtaposed with scenes of family, especially weddings and Mother's Day paraphernalia. A subsidiary theme is education represented either by encyclopedias or certificates. Other achievements such as competitive sports may also be prominent. Cementing the links between such themes are the scattered homilies with their general sense of an expressive morality.

In those living-rooms which either fail or do not seem to desire to exemplify this normative type this will be most evident in the relative scarcity of ornamentation and wall decorations. There may also be less upholstery, fewer religious and other such themes, fewer lace coverings and so forth. In such homes one finds a prominence accorded to the ubiquitous television and stereo which is in part a result of the lack of other features. As opposed to this lack of definitional items, there are a few cases which exhibit a tendency to what might be called 'modern' forms of glass and tubular metal furniture. In The Meadows this may be associated with a more restrained aesthetic cultivated from international journals of interior decoration, which are found in such homes. Upholstery may be covered in chinoiserie and there may be a few items such as prints or graphic-design elements set on the walls rather than an accumulation of objects and wall motifs. Living-rooms may also contain many individual or unusual features; for example in one case there is a bar within with a large Guinness sign. Another home (not part of the survey) incorporates a disco to encourage the children to entertain at home rather than going out all the time. None of these, however, seem to amount to a clear alternative aesthetic in opposition to the normative form.

The mere existence of this normative type and its pervasive influence suggests that the typical sociological parameters which were being searched for, such as class and ethnicity, did not emerge from the material culture analysis as distinctive aesthetics (although religion may be indicated). Prior to the oil-boom many of these same items would have been restricted to a relatively clearly demarcated local bourgeoisie, but today they have become the expectation of mass consumption. The survey (Table 5.1, above) suggests that Indians tend towards maroon upholstery, religious icons and buffets and Africans tend to brown/gold upholstery, homilies and space-savers, but all items are well represented in all ethnic groups, and it is doubtful that a Trinidadian (contrary to their own expectations) would be able to identify ethnicity from the evidence of living-room decoration alone.

Ethnicity can be represented in specific symbols. Non-Christian religious imagery is automatically representative of Indians (or Rastas), and occasionally there are objects from India although these are rare. Specific evocation of Africa appears to be limited to two small groups. On the one hand, there are a few houses in The Meadows and Newtown with African-style prints or textiles, associated invariably with élite groups within the public service sector. The second influence has come from Rastafarianism which is found only in Ford and is associated with low-income groups. Rastafarians may produce a homogeneity of style based around the colour combination of green, gold and red but also specific artefacts related to Haile Salassie, Bob Marley and other associated symbols such as lions. In other respects the impression gained is that while a few Rastafarians eschew this investment in living-room decoration characterised as the normative type, most Rastafarians appear to conform to normative principles and the values of transcendence as expressed in the home. Typically the emphasis on heavy, dark veneer and upholstered furniture is associated with artificial flower arrangements in red, green and gold and other explicit Rasta symbolism.

The origins of the dominant symbols and forms are rarely obvious or simple. The swan, which is the most common house ornament, is also the vehicle of Lakshmi the Hindu goddess of wealth and as such is an appropriate symbol within the domestic environment, but is not so commonly used by Indians in India as a separate symbol. The cock on the other hand is often used as a protective device, for example, on the outside of the home in some West African traditions. The positioning of some swans by Africans outside the front door appears then to suggest that in a sense the swan has become a substitute cock. The swan may also be understood as a commonly used British symbol of the homeland which has been incorporated by the colonised. In discussion it carried connotations of peacefulness and grace but also majesty. The use of maroon may be related to the auspiciousness of red for Hindu Indians but has strong colonial linkages in West Africa as it does for South Asia. For example, a shopkeeper stated: 'Maroon is a colour which is red but not red, but it is more Englishanese, North Americanese, Europeanese, I have never been there [England] but I believe they use a lot of this reddish off-reddish in their upholstery.' Such examples suggest that an item comes into prominence when syncretic tendencies reinforce the significance it already assumes for any one group. A similar point could be argued for the now general practice of taking off one's shoes before entering a carpeted house, or the use of verbal and visual imagery in positions which seem to guard the 'orifices' of the house.

Colonial or post-colonial emulation seems to be implicated in the wall pictures with their coniferous forest glens. In general there is also an association between degrees of ornamentation and degrees of religiosity. This means that groups such as Pentecostals who tend to a more pervasive religious fervour than most Catholics will also tend to have an abundant array of ornaments, both religious and secular, quite unlike the more puritan aesthetic of such Protestants elsewhere.

Ford is difficult to compare to the other areas, because in many cases poverty means an almost complete lack of basic furniture and accoutrements. In the very worst cases this amounts to bare walls and a few possessions in cardboard boxes. However, where materials are present, the impression gained is of emulation of the normative image, using, where available, elements such as maroon upholstery, homily plates and religious imagery. The upholstery is often very worn or even reduced to plain foam without any covering, but clearly reveals an identity of taste, if a difference in the ability to realise its related aspirations.

The materials found in the living-room are, at least in their abundance and their mainly imported origins, the results of the oil-boom. Yet in many respects they negate many of the expectations that would be raised by most debates about the oil-boom. Such discussions continually stress the exotic and expensive objects that were available, the status competition and materialism. There was a marked discrepancy between the actual contents of homes and the expectations raised by such conversations. The degree of convention that is found in the houses is certainly not a reflection of the lack of availability of diverse goods in the shops in Trinidad, which during the oil-boom were well stocked with international products. In very many cases wealthy households, who visit New York and Miami, nevertheless show a preference for an accumulation of obviously cheap but conventional ornaments and other furnishing paraphernalia. The living-rooms display an otherwise unstated preference for quantity over quality, a desire to include representative items of a conventional category rather than status symbols *per se*. Wealth does emerge as an ability to better exemplify the ideals and in the quality of certain goods such as the basic furniture, but this is subservient within the normative form, and where wealth appears as the primary vehicle for display, as in some houses in The Meadows, these appear as a contravention of the normative order.

This evidence based on the actual content of living-rooms contradicts the statements of householders who, when talking about interior decoration, tend to assume a concern largely with status hierarchies. By contrast the evidence is quite compatible with the accounts given in conversations with local Chaguanas shopkeepers, who may be exasperated when the known wealthier customers are uninterested in the more costly items but want the cheapest example of a given category, while it is often the less wealthy customers who look to the more obviously expensive ornaments.[4] One put this in ethnic terms: 'Indian people are traditionally not big spenders, in terms of quality, maybe because of lack of exposure or sophistication, they have traditionally been buyers of very poor quality stuff at low prices, so you find that in Chaguanas a lot of stuff is made in Korea and Taiwan.' Another focused on the ubiquity of maroon and the irony that this is often defended by customers as being 'bright', a term which in Trinidad has connotations of being modern and up-to-date: 'Trinidadians have a funny mentality, now they feel they must have maroon in their house whereas I don't think so because if I had my way and the funds to do it, you will find every room have a different colour. Their mind is sort of one track mind, what the neighbour have they want, in that way it leave you, the tradesman supplier, on a sort of one-colour basis. You making chairs, they will come, first thing, look give me something maroon, it bright – but I can't see what in it that is bright.'

The survey of living-room interiors may be assessed in relation to the activities surrounding Christmas, which make clear that the home interior has a particular niche within Trinidadian cultural construction. The homogenisation of this space was found in Chapter 2 to be established in opposition to the expressive symbolism associated with the exterior and the event. It is at Christmas that the use of the 'inside' as transcending ethnic and other distinctions to create a homogenised image of 'rooted'

Trinidad becomes clear. The purchase of most of these items may be directly associated with Christmas time itself, during which period they are used to construct an ideal of intensive sociality and a friendly unintimidating environment for the conduct of social relations. This ideal is generally accepted. Although men may strive to avoid an association with what they see as a kind of entrapment, they nevertheless give respect to the centrality of interiorisation as a means of constructing something valuable and lasting, a project to which they entrust their children.

As Bourdieu argued through his concept of habitus (1977), the sense of order established through such normative taxonomies of minutiae tends to be repeated in other cultural domains, and it is this tendency to form homologies which makes practices which might have been dismissed as trivial, in effect, ideal locations for the objectification of fundamental moral principles. On occasion the imperative towards a certain ordering principle may emerge as a highly valued skill. In Trinidad the interest and significance accorded to cake decoration provides a further example of the concern for enclosure and covering found in the living-room. Several housewives were found to subscribe to specialist magazines and to import cake-icing equipment from the United States and Australia. There are abundant advertisements for courses in cake decoration in the media, including television. The local course available in Newtown involved sixteen sessions of four hours each. A woman from The Meadows was considering going on a course in Michigan (USA) on the advanced icing of orchids and other flowers. This highly elaborate decorative art with its constant overlayering and elaborated rosettes and fluted shapes, so resonant in dress and furnishing, but with the additional sense of an enclosing practice which then hardens and preserves for the purpose of family-focused presentations, seems remarkably apt for the objectification of transcendence. The same housewives may once have been concerned to create their own preserves, pickles, chocolate and other non-perishable foodstuffs, skills which certainly grew from the necessities of a background in rural poverty but which are now replaced by a skill which better corresponds to the suburban context and is viewed as in itself a sign of being modern. As the survey of furnishing makes clear, a desire to objectify transcendence is in no sense antagonistic to the desire to objectify the modern.

This interpretation of cake decoration is reinforced by evidence for its negation in the explicit sexuality which surrounds the ceremony of 'sticking the cake'. There are a number of variants of this ceremony but in all cases a male and female is required, one holding the knife and the other another implement, either a second knife or a fork. Even a young male child on his birthday should have a female counterpart, with perhaps pink and blue ribbons tied to their respective cutlery. Immediately the cake is cut the older couple should engage in an extended and preferably passionate kiss, almost the only occasion when kissing is evident in public. At this moment the symbol of transcendence is revealed as in practice quite ephemeral.

Terms such as habitus and objectification allow us to refuse the desire (derived especially from our own gendered ideologies), to disregard such activities. Instead, cake decoration may be viewed as the transformation of a general imperative towards interiorisation into an aesthetic and a skill. This skill is of considerable significance because of its particular ability to express a larger ontological desire. The physicality and beauty of enclosure and of elaboration is important to this. Just as an ethnography set in a non-industrial context can locate the re-enactment of basic cosmological principles in an activity such as weaving baskets (Guss 1989), so also an activity such as cake decoration which tends to be derided as trivial by ideologies set against the feminine bourgeois, can instead be re-established as an attempt to totalise experience, in this case as an activity through which people come to know and appreciate their own sense of transcendence, the project of preservation and covering to which they dedicate their lives (compare Parker 1984 on embroidery). There are many other examples where the resources of the oil-boom have allowed for a considerable expansion in the aesthetic representation of such ideals, and as such they have emerged with a greater clarity and can be that much more easily elucidated.[5]

When transcendence is viewed from the condemnatory stance of the transient, emphasis is placed on the perceived hypocrisy, the exclusivity, the lack of privacy and a kind of claustrophobic sense of being incorporated into a project in which individuality is constantly diminished. From within transcendence, however, emphasis is placed on the tremendous generosity, the degree of mutual and unhesitating support, the strong sense of achieved and accretive identity, the embodiment of a morality, divinely or traditionally ordained and the unselfish commitment to longer-term and wider concerns often going beyond the family to ethnic group, church or nation. The living-room, seen as a static entity in this chapter and as a dynamic process in the analysis of Christmas, demonstrates that mass consumption, so far from being inimical to these values, may become the very instrument through which they are fully objectified. As the next section will demonstrate, this may be achieved with still greater effect through the use of contrast and opposition.

Style

In the investigation of the living-room, it was found that there was only one normative and no oppositional model. This implies that although there are Trindadians who either have little interest in living up to this norm, or simply prefer not to be identified with any domestic array, the majority of the island's population make some attempt towards transcendence in this context. When it comes to the objectification of transience the same becomes true of clothing. Clothing as style appears as a highly personalised and self-controlled expression of aesthetic ability, a search for the particular combination of otherwise unassociated parts which can be combined to create the maximum effect. Here originality is a major criterion of success as is the fit to the wearer. Thus the bearing of the person, the way they move, walk, turn, talk and act as though in natural unity with their clothes is vital to the success of the presentation.

These ideals are well-expressed in fashion shows which are an ubiquitous feature of modern Trinidadian life and are found at all income levels. The people of The Meadows might go to the show of a well-known Port of Spain designer hosted by the Lions or Rotary club, or at a major hotel in the capital, but they also might meet people from St Pauls or Newtown at a fashion show hosted at one of the shopping malls. Fashion shows are also held for small fund-raising ventures in Ford and at many schools or church bazaars. For wealthier audiences the models may perform as rather cold or austere mannequins; as such they are essentially vehicles for demonstrating expensive items for sale. This is, however, the less common form of modelling which is reserved for the more exclusive designer shows. In most fashion shows, and in all those associated with low-income groups, the clothes are displayed in a very different mode which emphasises a unity between the form of dress and the physicality of the body which displays them. Movements are based on an exaggerated self-confidence and a strong eroticism, with striding, bouncy, or dance-like displays. In local parlance there should be something 'hot' about the clothing and something 'hot' about the performance. For fashion shows at bazaars, schools and in Ford or similar communities, the models are not professional but local people and the clothes are either purchases of or made by the wearer or even borrowed. At these local events there is no attempt to sell the clothing and the whole ethos of the show is outside the commercial arena. The origin of the clothing is often of no concern to the audience nor is any intrinsic quality such as monetary value. The clothing is really an adjunct to the performance itself, to the way the persons move on the stage, and the frame for the performance is established by the models being friends, relatives or schoolmates of the audience.

The concept of style which emerges from such shows and the people to whom the term is applied comprises three main elements: competition, individualism and transience. Men create a highly competitive sartorial display for occasions such as fêtes and house parties. Here the key elements are shoes such as designer trainers, jeans and a wide variety of hats. Although using items derived from fashion, the intention is to give them a highly individualising treatment which makes the wearer stand out from his peers. Clothing becomes one aspect of a larger activity which is constantly refered to as 'making style'. Out of this group a certain portion attempt to carry through such conspicuous dressing into their everyday appearance. It is they who elicit remarks such as: 'Men are very fashion conscious, very trendy too, we still call them saga boys, sometimes we call them youth men, dudes.' These males combine sartorial originality with ways of walking and talking that create a style which is generally regarded as never letting up from a self-conscious display mode. A common term for such behaviour which originated from sports but is now applied much more widely is 'gallerying'.

Individualism emerges through a necessary fit between the clothes and the wearer. The person attempts to develop a sequence of sartorial forms which are seen as expressive of them and their character. The clothing is complemented by selections of belts, costume jewellery, shoes and a wide variety of hair forms and styles. Although these may refer to current general trends such as 'ragamuffin' style or tie-die, they are also idiosyncratic juxtapositions of elements in ways that make this wearer conspicuous and able as against the competition. The sartorial achievement is easily incorporated into a general sense of easy accomplishment at a variety of arts, ranging from music to witty speech. Individuals soon find out about the impression they have made, as clothing, in particular, elicits frequent comment. A young woman noted that: 'The guys just stand in a row and look at girls, they would say so many things, they would comment on this, or a slit in the skirt, hairstyles everything'; in turn: 'If the boys come out in something we don't like we tell them and most likely you won't see them in that again.'

This personalised element of dress makes it a domain of struggle for those engaged in different interpretations of, for example, femininity. A recently divorced woman discussed the tensions of her marriage in terms of conflicts, where her husband had wanted her to change from jeans to dresses, from long hair to short, from skirts with slits in to figure-hugging 'tights' cut off at the ankles. Both are constructing a notion of the modern woman, but with very different perceptions of that emergent category. People of a more transcendent orientation often do not think of themselves as conservative; on the contrary, they may take pride in their sense of being up with fashion and adopting a 'modern' look, but this has to be a consensual version and is not the self-construction of the individual which is the key imperative for style.

The third element of style is its transience; the stylist may take from the major fashion shifts in Trinidad but only as the vanguard. Hand-painted shirts are fine when they have yet to be acknowledged as the dominant fashion, but at that point the forms are given over to be incorporated into more conventional forms, such as young teenager fashion, while the stylist moves on always to something new. Stylists clearly aim to possess a new outfit for every new occasion. Clothing is purchased for a specific event, and only on second wearing is designated as part of a general repertoire for daily wear. At the most 'they would wear it twice but not on close occasions, they feel people would see that they wear it before'. This trend is helped by the seasonal nature of occasions, as consumers buy a new outfit for carnival or Christmas, or a new swimsuit for going to the beach during the long Easter weekend.

Originality is easier to accomplish when the item is hand-made by a seamstress or tailor. Even where items are purchased ready-made, they can be altered through hand-painting, adding buckles, buttons and other accessories. The exceptions are imported clothes which can be both ready-made and unique. The oil-boom encouraged imported elements when 'everybody and their tantie went to the Big Apple and returned with designer or imitation designer things'. Local production also meant that ideas from soap-operas or other influential television shows such as *Miami Vice* can be appropriated that much more quickly. The seamstress is a common figure in every part of Chaguanas. It is one of the ideal forms of work for the still often severely restricted Indian woman, since it can be carried out at home and since nearly all women were brought up with some knowledge of the sewing machine. It is also a possible profession in areas such as The Meadows and Newtown where the house deeds do not permit more conspicuous commercial activities. Both seamstresses and their clients talked of the extreme demands of the oil-boom period when clients were expected to have a new outfit made for every event to which they were invited. Two new outfits a week was often quoted as common for women in work.

For the stylist the source of the originality is, in a sense, irrelevant. The item may be expensive or it may be cheap, it may be fashionable or something that was around a long time before. For the stylist it is not the cost, the place from which the article comes or its place in the fashion cycle which determines the meaning of the clothing, but the process of consumption. Ultimately it is the overall look the individual achieves at a given event. The stylist is primarily concerned with external appearance, in contrast to the dress code associated with transcendence which is focused upon layering. This may range from dressing children in elaborate flounces to the insistence that proper dressing requires stockings, and is clearly related to the emphasis on layering in the living-room. My evidence is slight, but there was a suggestion that some of the more domestic 'quiet' young women focus their attention on high-quality and exotic lingerie, wearing and sometimes collecting the kind of imported 'exotic' or 'sexy' underwear which would not have been associated with such women. But this remains the clothing of the interior, seen mainly by themselves.

This portrayal of style is of an ideal constructed from conversations with stylists and their suppliers such as seamstresses, but, in practice, this ideal was increasingly difficult to achieve. Tailors and seamstresses who work with a particular group such as a male liming set or females in a neighbourhood relate that the common request following a particular fête or event in town is for a copy to be made quickly of someone else's pants or dress which had been a major success (the two are unlikely to clash since the assumption will be that the style leader will have moved on to something else). Ideally these individuals would not resort to such copying but in practice style is often based upon competitive display among a few peers and it is originality and expressive ability with respect to this small group that is paramount.

The demand for new clothes by women is often linked to the presence of a current relationship (or marriage), since the money that males are expected to provide to the females they are with may be the source of any new clothing. This competitive dressing among women is also related by them back to competition over men. Some women, for example deputies, see their concern for dressing as part of the exchange relationship they have with the man or men who provide them with their income. In this there is a degree of gender symmetry, since the concept of saga-boy relates back to a period when the gender roles were reversed. During the Second World War, when one of the main sources of income was from American soldiers via prostitution, men dressed competitively as saga-boys and depended for their income upon the women who admired them and for whom they in a sense displayed; a role which today would be termed a 'sweet-man'. It would be wrong, however, to reduce style down to a competition for resources, since this would not account for the willingness of each sex to support the other. Although evidence of new outfits may be taken by the community as indicating that a relationship is taking place, and although clothes often form part of gift exchanges between the sexes, the evidence from seamstresses and informants suggests that the demand for new outfits is equally strong for the single working woman, so that it is the financial resources rather than the relationship itself that seems to be the key to the level of purchase.

This may be taken further. The need for clothes was continually being linked to the workplace, with individuals going to Caracas to purchase a new wardrobe of clothes on hearing they had obtained work. Although the office party is particularly the occasion for tight-fitting dresses with sequins and frills to the bottom and bare back and shoulders, the daily work place is also an arena of intensive sartorial display and competition. Where there is a standard uniform, small variations and alterations are still discernible that allow room for this element of transient display; the 'girl working at a bank would make sure she has good leather shoes, leather handbag and the wallet in her handbag would be Gucci or Pierre Cardin'. The implication seemed to be that it was the workplace itself that demanded the continually changing new clothing rather than a relationship with a male. 'They are so dressed up for work that when they go out they don't look any different since they always have their finery, they are dressing to compete with other women, they want to be the first one in a new style.'

In the survey questionnaires, one of the enquiries made was about shoes. From the responses it emerged that some families which appeared to be hard hit by recession, which had very little in the way of material items in their houses and which generally appeared to be struggling, still included individuals with a dozen or twenty pairs of shoes. (This was despite the narrow definition of the terms 'shoe' used by informants which appears to exclude sandals, so that even silver closed female footwear may not be counted as a shoe because it is flat.) One commented: 'I love shoes, I mean I cannot afford them the way I like them, but if I could have afforded it, I would buy every possible shoe colour there is, people have a lot of shoes is because they doh like to be seen in the same shoes twice.' Even in recession shoes remain a priority, and there is little relation between the wealth of a community and the frequency of buying shoes.[6] Shoes are indicative of style since the notion of the shoe matching the outfit is central to the taste criteria applied to style; many shoppers would feel it was incumbent upon them to purchase new shoes for every new display outfit. Shoes, however, differ from some other clothing items because they are not directed across gender lines. 'The men are looking at your outward appearance, they will look at mini skirts, especially a tight blouse or low cut, shoes is the furthest thing from their mind.' It is often remarked, however, that shoes are the first thing another woman will look at. It may well be that competition was increasingly focusing upon shoes as the recession intensified rivalries between women. Men also use shoes for intra-gender competition, as with expensive designer trainers. Newspapers often reported gangs which stopped youths on the street to relieve them of their trainers.[7] This suggests a strong degree of autonomy of intra-sex sartorial competition and that it is not merely a competition over access to the other sex.

The transience of clothing is not just an oil-boom aberration, although it may have been taken to extremes at that period. Freilich, conducting an ethnography in the 1950s in a small village with neither water nor electricity, noted the comparative high expenditure on clothing among creoles and records how: 'The wife of one of the peasants said every new function needs new clothes. I wouldn't wear the same dress to two functions in the same district' (1960: 74). Although today people associate the extreme consumption of clothing with the oil-boom, for example, a tailor noted: 'like in '82 men used to order five pants one time and by next month they come and they want four more', but it is clear that in effect this was merely the realisation of a desire which goes back much further in time. In recession it is once again becoming clear that the imperative to purchase new clothing is not based on having money to spend: 'Some people go out even if they don't have money. You won't imagine some of the best dressed people on the street and they don't have any money. They have the clothes there so they dress up and go out into the street.'

Freilich associates this behaviour exclusively with one ethnic group but this distinction was much less clear by 1988. Most elements which contribute to the stylistic use of clothing and accessories would themselves act to diminish ethnic distinction. This was particularly evident in the case of hair care which along with shoes and jewellery provides a major item of expenditure. Although Indians are restricted in being unable to attempt some of the elaborate hairstyles which are possible for those of African origin such as cane row braiding, a tight mass of gleaming 'jeri curls' or some of the interweaving of purchased artificial hair, on the whole, as several people remarked, hair seemed to be the part of the body in the vanguard of a striving for inter-ethnic unity. This was reflected in the abundance of forms by which curly hair could be straightened or 'relaxed' into a variety of hairstyles and the equal number of methods for curling and perming straight hair.

There is some tendency for African hair to be related to wider dichotomies: the same people relaxed their hair for a christening as braid their hair for carnival. Hairdressers emphasised the effects of the current recession in contrast to the extreme investments in hairstyling which had characterised boom-time behaviour. Occasionally individuals might be associated with particular hairstyles as was the case for the best-known male calypsonian living in Chaguanas whose jeri curls were part of his established look, a highly cultivated and glossy style set off by his gold jewellery and shiny apparel. A similar situation occurred with hats where a few individuals fixed their identity with respect to their constant appearance in, for example, a particular old felt hat or new style broad-brimmed 'American'-style hat. More often hat-wearing was diverse and unpredictable, with teenagers competing for designer hats with specific logos and appropriately high costs.

Through this creative juxtaposition of clothing, accessories, hair and body look, contextualised in forms of movement and speech, a sense of style is constructed. It differentiates itself from that fashion which merely follows convention through a number of derogatory characterisations. Two of the most common terms used are *mooksy* and *cosquel*. *Mooksy* is a general term for things which look old-fashioned and has related connotations of rural or poor backgrounds. *Mooksy* then is the unsophisticated back-woods look which has yet even to acknowledge its own demise or indicates the inability of the person to enter into competitive display. There is not surprisingly a resistance to such depreca-tion.

The other pejorative term cosquel is a term for something overdone or juxtapositions which fail; it is a vulgarity that indi-cates an attempt to style but a failure of taste. The wrong colours have been placed against each other, or an effect has been over-done and thus its possibilities lost. 'You will say she is *cosquel* because the clothes she is wearing not matching, is not only older people who dresses *cosquel*, anybody, and is not Indians alone dress like that, it is not a question of race, those people just want to be noticed so they are not aware of style, they don't know how to put everything together and then they have the behaviour to go with it.' There are also some more general taste parameters, for example, too exclusive concern with matching colours shows wealth in that this can be an expensive project but also a certain lack of taste, since, as a retailers put it: 'some who would know better, will contrast'. Terms of approval often use reverse slang, as the well-dressed are flattered by being told that they are look-ing 'sick', 'bad' or 'cork'.

Both the terms *mooksy* and *cosquel* as also the general opposi-tion between style and normative fashion may be used with ethnic connotations. The Indian will be viewed as tending to both *mooksy* and *cosquel*, while the African carries the vanguard of style and its artistry. As with many such dichotomies, it should be stressed that actual patterns imply only a loose articulation, since many Indians would be among the most accomplished stylists, while there are many Africans who are clearly most comfortable with shiny conventional materials, adopting fashions only when they have clearly passed into general approval.

The key to style as transience lies in the more general refusal to take things inside, to interiorise their effects. Indeed, one of the most common expressions heard in response to any misfortune from a passing insult to the break-up of a relationship, is 'doh take it on'. Littlewood (1985: 277–8) provides a clear instance of this in his analysis of a depressive condition known as *tabanca*. This is a kind of moping sickness, leading to solitary contemplation and even suicide, but as Littlewood notes it is also something of a standard joke. The reason for this is that *tabanca* represents a failing in the maintenance of the values of transience. A man in his relationship with women is expected to retain his phlegmatic cool: relationships are something he can take or leave. If, however, he starts to become more deeply involved, if he allows this relationship to become internalised as something in which he has invested himself, then he stands in danger of considerable loss if the relationship should fail. When this woman leaves him or when she commits adultery his failure to keep the relationship on the surface becomes evident, and *tabanca* follows.

Austin, in her work on Kingston, Jamaica, has a similar point to make with the emphasis on the implications of property. She notes that it is after a man has bought the furniture in the house that his partner's infidelity would make a complete fool out of him (1983: 231). The weekly press in Trinidad contain many stories which exploit this theme, the hard 'bad-john' who has fallen in love. Women, by contrast, use this as evidence for their toughness and resilience. In women's wining, described in Chapter 2, the search for pure freedom goes beyond even this, to become the celebration of those who 'doh take it on' who invest in no social relations and are thereby at least for an instant self-sufficient, using autosexuality to defy ontology (Miller 1991).

Underlying this gender distinction may well be the impact of liming, which is central to male life in Trinidad. Perhaps the most important verbal ritual associated with liming is *picong* or giving 'fatigue'. This is based on a mixture of insult and boasting. One of the attributes of fatigue is to ensure full group participation in events. For example, on a river lime, the individual who did not strip down and bathe would leave himself open to becoming the major recipient of the developing rounds of insults. The individual characteristics of the limer would then be picked upon, an older male might be asked: 'when you alive yet you could cook?' or about whether the remaining hair is really his. An inappropriate piece of clothing, an accident or mistake might be thrown back at the guilty party many times in a variety of forms with appellations such as 'mother-arse'. Ethnicity is a major component of picong in inter-racial limes with jibes about supposed coolie and nigger traits, though with the Chinese as the most popular butt of jokes. Such *picong* almost always remains good-humoured, though even with the extreme facility developed through practice, over several hours and many drinks it may become more repetitive with less concern given to the nuances and let-outs which ensure that it remains 'framed' within the canons of accepted humour.

The activity of fatigue and *picong* is one variant of a larger concern with humour and wit. There are two main anthropological approaches to this difficult domain: one which stresses the profundity and insights and immediacy of humour, the other which looks to its place in the displacement and diffusing of conflict. Trinidadian humour tends more towards the latter, but is not encompassed by such an approach. Most Trinidadians would certainly assert humour and wit as central to their self-definition and would see it as contributing to their sense of cool, and their ability not to take things on, as well as their sense of style. The person without a sense of humour would be in danger of being seen as 'ignorant' and prone to violence. Humour also helps to keep things on the surface; its keeps conversations focused on delivery and style rather than content and message, and in this sense is a good complement to clothing.

The verbal repartee of the lime consists of witty and barbed invective in which friends tear into each other such that the lime becomes a kind of training-ground in which one is steeled against taking in the abuse which can be received in life. At the same time the lime provides for men a sociality based on the establishment of peer groups which ameliorate competition and may serve to weaken some of the individualism characteristic of these values.

To the extent that women have no institution equivalent to liming in which they subsume their individuality, this may account for the evidence that it is they rather than the men who take the project of transience to its greatest extreme (Miller 1991). This may also be the reason why women are associated with an environment of more unremitting competition and friendships which while briefly intense have a sense of fragility based around the prospect of a cuss-out or equally intense disagreement.

The concern with fashion seen from this perspective can be directly articulated with the preferences expressed in kinship and in the formation of relationships. With the latter, reciprocity becomes a key factor as the basis upon which dyadic relations can form without denying the principle of transience. The relationship is largely constituted by exchange, which is an active process that has to be constantly reaffirmed by the participants. The environment is both individualistic and competitive. Men may compete not only over the women they have been associated with but also over the children these women bear them. As Wilson notes in the estimation of his peers: 'Virility is far more than sexual potency' (Wilson 1973: 150). Such competition reinforces the individualism and indeed for many women virtual atomism that they may feel has become their lot. These strategies help to prevent interiorisation, which is linked in turn to the general refusal of institutionalisation. Both kinship and clothing then become modes of freedom.

Transience as kinship starts with individuals as the fundamental units and the way in which they cautiously construct transient relationships avoiding the sense that they are doing so merely in order to fulfil normative obligations. Where, as in the work situation, the placement of the individual in a context lacks both spontaneity and forces institutionalisation, the implications are resisted through several strategies (Yelvington, forthcoming). One of these is simply to reduce work to a minor aspect of life, such that it is leisure which is considered to be the true and proper arena where real life takes place, while work is a mere interlude. This is precisely the inversion of the relationship between producer and production which was so paramount in nineteenth-century Europe that Marx could treat it as the natural condition of mankind.

Transience is clearly deeply concerned with a sense of temporality, but it is not a cognitive attribute. It certainly does not mean that people in transience are, for example, somehow less patient or unable to perceive time in a particular way. There is no intended return to Levy-Bruhl or that anthropology which attempted to locate different cognitive abilities in distinct populations. I assume that all Trinidadians are equally capable of the same kinds of temporal perception and order, so that when a woman accuses her husband of an inability to plan, her anger is expressed at what she sees as his obstinacy, not a literal disability. Her husband will not have the slightest difficulty in attending a five-day cricket match and finding it immensely exciting, almost too brief. This is a feat which astonishes, for example, visiting Americans who would see this as quite apt for the British but hardly befitting the stereotype of the West Indian. There is no reason why the appreciation of this event cannot be shared by those associated with transience and those such as C. L. R. James who would be associated in most respects with transcendence: after all, much of the time we may be talking about the same people.

Similarly an organisation can be built up, if with considerable difficulty, in sports or music. A steelband can form and persons put in many days of practice in order to give a performance of Bach or Wagner, but with a feeling that this is within their own control, it is a voluntary organisation in competition with others. As researchers on such topics have shown (Mandle and Mandle 1988; S. Stuemphle personal communication on fieldwork among steelbands) this environment can produce complex organisations and institutions run on a voluntary basis but highly sensitive to any attempt to impose control or threaten the self-conscious voluntarism of the participants. Furthermore, such collectivities are often undermined by stylistic individualism emerging as exhibitionism which is, for example, seen as the curse of Trinidadian basketball (Mandle and Mandle 1988: 12).

This network of ideals which makes up transience helps us to understand the link between a number of prominent motifs in Lovelace's *The Dragon Can't Dance* which has previously been introduced as an illustration of the values of transience. First, there is the assertion that consumption should not lead to accumulation, but itself be an element of the temporality of transience: 'but nobody here look at things as if things is everything. If you had more money, you buy more food; and if is a holiday, you buy drinks for your friends, and everybody sit down and drink it out, and if tomorrow you ain't have none, you know everybody done had a good time' (ibid: 103).

It is consumption, and most especially the purchase of clothing as reciprocity, which establishes relationships especially across gender: 'With Guy keeping her now, she had shoes and new dresses, and every Friday evening she went into the city to have her hair straightened' (ibid: 137). This clothing is central to the project of externality but may become problematic as when the calypsonian Philo, embarrassed by success: 'decorated himself in gaudy shirts and broad-brimmed hats with long colourful feathers stuck in them, as if he wanted to hide himself, to make himself appear so *cosquel* that any fool would know that he had to be found elsewhere, apart from the costume, within it' (ibid: 155).

This concern with the relationship between the surface of the person and the nature of self is central to the motif of masking which is evoked by the title of the book and by Carnival itself. This self is created by its display: 'he wanted nothing but to live, to be, to be somebody for people to recognise, so when they see him they would say: "that is Fisheye!" and give him his space' (ibid: 59). The book ends in the tragic consequences of transience as a medium for radical action, but beyond this to the contradictions of transience as the construction of being: 'So many things we coulda do, and all we wanted was to attract attention! How come everything we do we have to be appealing to somebody else? Always somebody to tell us if this right or wrong, if it good or bad ... Is like we ain't have no self. I mean, we have a self but the self we have is for somebody else. Is like even when we acting we ain't the actor' (ibid: 188). Under such conditions a political revolt could be no more than playing mas.

Dualism

In the previous sections it has been argued that the two habiti that are the basic ordering and moral principles which dominate much of Trinidadian life and which had been developed in large part before the oil-boom, may have been extended, clarified and in a sense completed using the resources provided by the oil-boom and the elaboration of mass consumption which followed upon this. The underlying dualism which holds that these two exist in explicit opposition to each other has also been illustrated by the well-established contrast between the life of the home and the street discussed by Abrahams and others. In contrast to the transient emptying of the self, is the traditional Indian motif of the millionaire whose shabby external appearance never gives away what he is really worth. Many Trinidadians are well aware of the different implications of an emphasis on one or another material culture domain, contrasting the juxtaposition of home decoration and concern for the future with the event-based concern of clothing, as in the following quotation from a woman chatting to a friend in a gift shop: 'I like to dress the house, not so interested in clothes, I like to cook, I dohn like every week to buy new dress, new shoes, new lipstick like so, I ehn interested in that, I am interested in nice house and well kept, that is the beauty. I spend all my money on ornament, glass ware, all them things, furniture and ting, then they come and admire your house and they say, yes this girl have ambition.'

Mass consumption most forcibly impresses itself as fashions which break like waves over the shores of Trinidad or occasionally arise internally. Women's clothing fashions during the year's fieldwork included a type of treated denim material called acid wash, the use of very broad belts sometimes eight inches wide, or of a particular belt buckle in the shape of a butterfly. Slightly longer-term fashions included tie-die cottons and handpainted dresses or T-shirts. Retailers told of vast stocks of acid wash sold out within days, but the sheer initial success of the style then involved it within a new set of relationships in which it became accepted as the year's key symbol of being up-to-date. Such fashions seemed to speed up during the oil-boom as a host of new consumer forms such as drive-in movies, amusement arcades, snooker, microwaves and food processors came and went, generally leaving little trace. The continuous demand for newness, a refusal to replace with the same as last year's form was also noted by retailers in goods such as paints and curtains.

These examples may illustrate the distinction between being a stylist and simply being in fashion. Stylists are desperately concerned to be the first, at least within their own peer group, to wear the latest fashion. But once such a fashion has come to prominence it changes its nature dramatically. It is then the sense of transcendence which takes over and insists that everybody should have a representative sample of what has now become a conventional form. The result can be seen from the survey in which acid wash becomes virtually ubiquitous, at which point it becomes the inverse of both transience and individualism. Thus following fashion, as opposed to initiating fashion, can be a sign of conformity. Indeed, as Simmel (1957) notes in one of the most profound analyses of the phenomena of fashion, this tension between a potential individualising and socially normativising role is the central contradiction intrinsic to modern fashion as an act of consumption. Here also lies the complexity of interpreting fashion since it can be both an agreement to conform and a struggle for a symbol of transience and disconformity; indeed, the same object can work in both ways depending upon what point in its trajectory as fashion it is located and analysed.

The result of innovatory fashions being exposed to two quite contrastive tendencies emerges in the surveys conducted by marketing research. While retailers tend to gloss the dualistic distinctions in terms of ethnic group or age, e.g., it is the Indians or the young who do this or that, marketing researchers provided a similar set of distinctions most clearly in terms of regions. Trinidad is divided in the perception of many market researchers into two kinds of area, one roughly based in Port of Spain and its extension through the East-West Corridor and the other in central and south Trinidad. This latter region is often seen as highly conservative in marketing terms and tends to an elision of two kinds of category: brand name and product group. Thus for people in those areas toothpaste is always [brand A], detergent is always [brand B], a beer is always [brand C] and so forth. There is a relatively small market share given to the other competing brands for that product and relatively little incentive to try out new or imported products. However, when these areas do change they change massively and fairly swiftly. Marketing people talked in awe of how a region appeared to shift overnight from solid allegiance to one brand of beer or soft drink to its competitor; from thenceforth it was the replacement brand which took over as the synonym for the product itself as customers would say give me a 'brand name' rather than the actual brand name of a specific product.

This pattern is seen as quite contrastive with town-consumption tendencies. Here the key concern is with innovation, new products and most especially products introduced from outside Trinidad, which are looked for and picked up with alacrity. Indeed, it is often said that the key to each year's innovation is an emergent trend based on what is termed 'town talk' which focuses especially on the period leading up to Carnival which is seen as a kind of speeding up of the possibilities of change, where the ideas of the previous year are finally laid to rest to make way for a new set of ideas and tendencies. This yearly cycle is also found in retailing, where the common request is for what's new this year (which does impose some structure on fashion as flux). In general, there is much less dominance by a single brand and market share is more equitably held. The rare but massive shift which seems close to the kind of cusp model developed in catastrophe theory is replaced here by the more usual lenticular curve familiar from studies of the acceptance of innovation and diffusion (Clarke 1968: 199-210).

This distinction between urban and rural consumption patterns may also be relevant to the larger interpretation of the ethnographic material. Several workers in marketing expressed frustration with their attempts to understand the marketing data coming out of Chaguanas. The lack of a clear pattern may reflect Chaguanas' currently transitional status, still distinctly rural when compared to Port of Spain, but closer to the urban pattern than the rest of central and south Trinidad. If this is the case it may in part account for the particular clarity with which dualism emerges from fieldwork at this site.

A marked dualism was certainly noted by shop assistants in terms of shopping strategy. On the one hand there is the shopper whose aim is to purchase an object which represents a conventional category. She wants a 'gold' earring. It is immediately clear that it matters little which particular gold earring is chosen, the main concern is likely to be price, and the cheapest item which fits the requisite category of a gold-coloured earring is purchased. The other type of shopper, who probably has less disposable income, wants jewellery to match an outfit, but has few preconceptions about what would work until she has tried a wide range of possibilities; the final outcome may be cheap or it may be expensive, its attraction may come from its fashion element or an unusual juxtaposition of a conventional form. Once determined, however, the shopper must have that particular piece whatever the cost or any other problems involved.

When asked for her definition of bad taste, one informant noted the practice of having the best side of the curtains facing outwards on to the street. In practice most modern curtains have no inferior side, but where they do the tendency is for it to face inwards. The alternative of 'dressing' the street was seen either as façade covering up the problems of recession or, as for this informant, an indication of loose morals. Indians note how their religious icons used to be displayed outside on the porch/gallery. Interiorisation is understood historically as a reaction to theft, which may, in part, be the case, but also seems to relate to a wider dualism. The Meadows houses with their 'layers' of interiorisation from outside grass verge, through gates, guard dogs, porches, burglar-proofing and so forth, certainly add to the effect of barriers which may or may not be crossed. Generalised as ethnicity, Indians are seen as keeping interior lights on, while Africans are seen as watching television in the dark and projecting outwards from the house or car in the form of loud music. Indians would be expected only to project loud music on to the street for public occasions such as weddings or a *pooja*. A paint retailer also saw Indians as buying more paint for inside work, Africans more for outside work.

A similar division is be found with respect to the impact of a recent fashion in sports. This is the move from group sports towards a concentration on the individual, a shift in which Trinidad has followed international changes. Gyms, for example, are constantly featured in local television advertisements. Within this fashion, however, a division may be discerned. One group tends to relate most closely to the fashion for jogging and the concept of keeping fit. This relates to an emphasis on internal health within the body and its effects are not necessarily evident to the observer of the person unless they catch them jogging or doing marathons. In contrast there has been a simultaneous growth in the interest in body-building, with associated magazines and high profiles for body-building competitions in the media. In this case the emphasis is on the externality of the body as a vehicle for display, and the competitions themselves consist of the striking of a variety of poses which flex and display the body form.

Many such examples can be found which suggest that a particular material domain should best be regarded as split in consumption strategies into two opposing tendencies rather than simply as expressing homology with one habitus. For example, there are alternative clothing styles which embody the values of transcendence. Women's clothing at lifecycle ceremonies is often dominated by a few basic elements which are constantly repeated in combination among the various dresses. Preferences may be for silver, gold, metallic greens, blues and reds, and shiny or slinky black, pearl and white. There is considerable use of layer-

ing and ruching in dress and skirt patterns, always complemented by stockings and high-heeled shoes. Stockings appear to be
one of the key emblems of a more formal dress, which carries
over to work situations. The garment industry statistics confirm
that despite tropical conditions stockings continue to be the normal female apparel. Shoes must also be appropriate, the tendency
being to wear closed-in forms for church and open-toes for
leisure. These elements are then recombined as permutations.
Indeed, the dresses themselves often appear as patchworks of
elements with a silver lozenge set within a pearly white layered
bodice for example. Among the older generation, in particular,
these are associated with wide-brimmed hats of similar shiny
materials.

Just as there is transcendence in clothes so also there is transience in living-rooms. Here, however, it is more a case of refusing to become involved in this domain. Leiber in his book on
street liming in Port of Spain precisely illustrates this logic, since
many of his informants clearly preferred to have as little association with any interior living-space as possible, merely having a
token and transient place to store their prized possessions such as
their stereo while trying to keep their distance from any particular place and any particular domestic context.

The Dynamics of Culture: The Car

The construction of value through its objectification in material
culture is a dynamic process, and it not only exhibits such values
with clarity through repetitive, though in this case pluralist,
structural homology but also enables individuals and groups to
weave complex trajectories through these domains in a manner
that can profoundly alter their lives. Two examples will be given
here in some detail to illustrate the role played by mass consumption in shifting allegiances and identity. In the first example
the car will be shown to be a vehicle not only for transporting
people spatially but also conceptually from one set of values to
another. In the second example the consumption of a soap opera
will be used to illustrate the use made of the tension between
transience and transcendence.

In many respects the car contributes to the expression of dualism and can be seen to embody certain values in opposition to

other domains, but when the car is considered in terms of the populations which use it, then its dynamic contribution may be appreciated. Although the car only came in reach of most people as a possession with the oil-boom, it now dominates the Trinidadian self-image. In the 'Spot the Trini'[8] competition, the car was far and away the most common context for the entries – whether it was people who throw away empty chicken and chips boxes out of their car window, or have the wrong change for the taxi driver, it was in the car as public space that you recognised the true 'Trini'. In contemporary Trinidad the car is probably the artefact which outweighs even clothing in its ability to incorporate and express the concept of the individual. Three elements of the relationship between persons and vehicles seem conspicuous: the first is the tendency to use cars as a shorthand labelling for persons, the second lies in the antipathy to other modes of travel and the third lies in the physical transformation of the cars.

From early on in fieldwork I became used to having persons described through their cars. Individuals were to be located not through their house number but the car in front of the house, friends were recognised as having gone fishing through the number plates of the car parked near a river. A person is introduced as the only seamstress in the area who drives a Jaguar. Weekly newspapers will often refer to a car in a vague manner so as to provide innuendo without actually naming anyone: 'Would you believe there is a ring of homosexual taxi-drivers operating in Penal? The leader has a nickname which resembles that of a popular large local fruit, and he drives a taxi which is neither too dark or too light' (*The Bomb*, 21 December 1990); or will talk of an AIDS victim 'whose husband drives a Mazda'. Retailers routinely decide their expectations of a particular customer entering their shop on the basis of their car, and so I would be told that a Laurel driver bought this but a Cressida driver would not buy that. The identification of persons by their associated cars is then not the exception but the norm of daily social discourse. Drivers also frequently maintain total discretion over window, door and other controls. They can then respond to or ignore requests as they choose, often to passengers' disgruntlement.

The situation in Trinidad is not quite as extreme as that recorded by Manning (1974) for Bermuda. He reports that number plates may come to designate individuals to the extent that a party may be announced as being hosted by a person simply des-

ignated as a number plate, or the number plate noted on an obit-
uary notice to help people recognise who it is that has died. What,
however, would also be true for Trinidad is that: 'The recognition
of number plates is also a means of gathering the kind of information that is eventually disseminated in the gossip network
characteristic of West Indian societies' (ibid: 126). A Trinidadian
who was trying to deny reports that he had a deputy claimed that
it was simply that a similar-looking man had a number plate
which differed in only one digit from his own.

The same form of identity carries through into relationships. A
very common term addressed to young women is that of 'gasbrains'. A friend defined 'gasbrains' as 'girls who choose their
man from the body of the car, while often ignoring possible defi-
ciencies in the body of the driver'. Street wisdom certainly insists
that women will not look at men who don't have cars, and this is
repeated even in Ford by women whose men have not been able
to afford a car for some years. Many car parts and actions have
common sexual connotations (though these may not be standard-
ised), for example, oiling the chassis, park inside, headlights,
beams, blowing the horn, tailpiece, red lights etc. These innuen-
dos are sometimes taken up in calypso ('Drive it' by Crazy, 'Bus
Driver' by Poser, 'Taxi Driver' by Small Island Pride).[9] A car may
be seen as a wife or deputy: 'a car is so expensive, it's more than a
luxury, it like a second wife so they take care of it' or a deputy in
turn can be referred to as a 'spare tyre'.

The second feature is an unwillingness to walk, once in possession of a car. A queue of cars may form in front of the school
gates as each waits to park directly in front of the entrance rather
than walk the few yards from a more convenient parking place.
At a children's playground in San Fernando the parents
inevitably park the cars at the edge and remain inside while the
children are sent out to play. A common entry in the 'Spot the
Trini' competition described how two cars in opposing traffic
streams stop in the middle of the road for a conversation and
when the cars behind sound their horn they respond with a hand
gesture meaning 'fly over the top if you can'. Workers are said to
drive 200 yards from home to work. People seem quite unwilling
to leave their car, as one commented: 'Someone should invent a
house into which you could drive your car, people would buy
this and probably sleep in the car too.' One of the main sources of
crime during the year came from persons in cars who would

force other cars off the road and rob them, especially after following them from the airport. While in some societies cars are seen as
relatively private space, in Trinidad cars are treated as forms of
individualisation which are displayed in public. Indeed, the
point often made (especially by men) was that people see the
results of one's aestheticisation of the car but may not see the
money and time spent on the house. Apart from the frequent con-
versing between cars, people often see themselves as being
looked at and appraised in the ubiquitous traffic jams. Ironically
for this symbol of movement, much of the time spent within cars
is almost static.

This activity was compounded by an often extreme concern
for car care. Anecdotes were common about neighbours who
wash the car at least once a day, twice if it has rained, and with
particular attention paid to the area within the treads of the tyres.
A Hindu pundit might typically in a sermon call for people to
pay the same degree of attention to their spiritual life as they do
to their car care. There is an assumed gender differentiation, as
where an informant described the contrasting relationship with
the car held by her brother and sister. The brother not only had
made a wide range of changes to the car, as described below but
was obsessive about anyone scratching the paintwork and clearly
froze in tension should anyone slam the door. On the other hand,
the sister was cavalier about the car and clearly saw it as the
brother's role to fix up anything that might go wrong. Similarly,
it is often remarked that when men have money their first priority is the car while women might look to the home.

This degree of concern with the car has been rather accentuated by the oil-boom. Before the oil-boom cars were relatively
scarce in Chaguanas and people talk of playing cricket in the
streets, a far cry from today when the one-way system has done
little to prevent traffic jams. Cars had been around for decades,
and people talked of the days of Austins and Westminsters, but
most of these would have been taxis. Display was then centred
more on bicycles; girls were supposed to be impressed with the
lights attached to the wheel-mounted generators. With the oil-
boom cars were clearly a priority expenditure for the new
incomes, but the government imposed restrictions upon the
importation of cars since it was developing local assembly plants
in conjunction with Japanese firms (indeed, Trinidad had the first
such plant in the Caribbean). Since demand easily outstripped

supply the primary mode by which privilege or patronage could be demonstrated was early access to a car which could anyway be immediately resold at a profit. Imports are still restricted and a spectacular car purchase can still make the news. For example, the *Sunday Punch* (24 July 1988) reported on the twenty-three-year-old whose parents had bought him a million-dollar (TT) Lamborghini, for his birthday, sub-titled with the quote 'I don't like to gallery says lucky youth'.

Cars are certainly prestige items. For example, Royal and Super Saloon models were continually identified as suitable for bribes (as with the case of the local Chaguanas magistrate who was jailed for this offence during the year), or a conspicuously extravagant payment to a Hindu pundit for services rendered, or as the anomalous vehicle for a mere drain cleaner who worked in The Meadows and thereby affronted its inhabitants. This particular competition was again muted by the recession. A typical history came in a discussion with a self-confessed 'car freak' who detailed how in the oil-boom he had moved swiftly from expensive to more expensive cars with larger engines, until the recession, 'after which good sense prevailed' and he settled for a modest car. Instead he would now add an extra item: 'and be happy with that little fantasy that I am driving a nice car. So you spend 100 dollars on a steering wheel and you feel a million dollars instead of spending a million dollars and making yourself poor.'

The car, then, is as well-established as a vehicle for expressive identity, as it is a vehicle for transport. However, once the consumption of the car is examined in more detail the basic dualism described as the transient and transcendent soon reappears. As often with industrial goods, expressive consumption is most clearly established in the transformation of the commodity by the consumers (compare Hebdige 1988: 77–115). An area of Chaguanas which was the focus of the general expansion of the town eastwards over the last few decades is Montrose. If all commercial outlets of the main street and streets just behind are counted the importance of the car becomes evident. Out of 176 establishments thirty-eight are solely concerned with cars such as car electrics, garages, car parts, as compared to twelve bars and rum shops, thirteen cooked food outlets, eleven groceries and parlours and six insurance offices. Among the car-related stores, there are three establishments which stand out as being of an altogether different size (although one has moved slightly north of this area). The three owners are thought of as extremely wealthy and own much of the property around their stores. They rent this out to other retailers and in addition own many properties in The Meadows. These three stores are devoted to upholstery. Around the Christmas season this is domestic upholstery, and some have a sideline in marine upholstery, but otherwise upholstery here means car upholstery. Although these three stores dominate the trade there are many more smaller car upholsterers in the Chaguanas area. Given the general lack of industry, this suggests that car upholstery has become the single leading commercial concern of the town.

With the deepening recession car upholstery increasingly referred mainly to repairs of private cars, the furnishing of taxis and the small coaches termed 'maxi taxis'. Upholsterers estimated that whereas only ten per cent of business today consists of new cars having their upholstery changed, in the oil-boom this was between sixty per cent and eighty per cent of business. These newly purchased cars were stripped out and replaced with fancy styled upholstery. One upholsterer noted the three most common designs as fake tiger skin, fake snake skin and a black leatherette streaked bluish and silver, marketed under the title of 'New York by Night'. The upholstery did not just extend to the car seats. The sides of doors could be covered in long pile plush materials, residential carpet applied to the floor, the ceiling and also the inside of the trunk (boot). The dashboard could be upholstered, cushions added, and the whole complemented by a variety of paraphernalia such as perfumes, religious icons and stickers (the latter especially in taxis). Cars could also be feminised, for example, with heart-shaped satin cushions with projecting pink frills and central flower designs.

There has, however, been a rapid decline in such activity in recent years, not only because of the recession leading people to buy removable and cheaper car-seat covers, but also because the rise in car thefts is leading to rapid changes in attitudes to car aesthetics. A journalist reported on how he was removing some of the accretions of his new second-hand car (*Express* 20 October 1988):

> The tiger-skin covers came off on day one, as did the red plastic steering wheel cover; as did the little duckie. The white JPS emblems made it to day two, but no further; nor did the 'I love my Mazda' sticker. Presently slated for retirement are: the dashboard heart that lights up in red with the words 'love caressing'; the pair of little green bordello

cabin lights; the red hyphen lights above the front number plate; the fog lights inscribed Denji; and at least one of the three antennae. None of this will however, I fear, quell my newfound paranoia, that somebody's already out to steal my Mazda.

While the upholsterers are essentially concerned with car interiors, in the same high street are found other shops which are devoted essentially to the car exteriors. One shop, for example, which advertises itself as customising cars, in effect concentrates on just two operations: the tinting of window glass and the adding of stripes to the exterior. Both these are extremely common practices. The tinting is often of a very deep kind beyond that allowed by the government, and sufficient to ensure the anonymity of the driver and, more to the point, the driver's companion. Another shop concentrates on wheel hubs, a key fashion item that at the time was shifting from metallic to white. Also common have been extra-wide wheels, despite the effect these have on dirtying the exterior and the subsequent need for still more frequent cleaning of the car. A final exterior change was to add a bonnet scoop, though this was not as common as the other features.

The existence of distinct shops concentrating on car interiors and car exteriors respectively appeared to suggest that the two activities might appeal to different groups of people. That is, those who focus upon re-upholstery were often not those who would focus upon tinting and stripes. The distinction is not total; the car with fake tiger skin and a pink plush interior may also go for flashing lights on the exterior, but here the inside seems as it were to have spilled over to the external surface. In general, retailers sensed a difference between the advocate of a 'cool' look emanating from stripes and tinting and the 'flash' look embodied in some of the more outrageous upholstery.

Commonly these different orientations to interiors and exteriors tend to be associated stereotypically with the ethnic contrast. Conversation described the stereotype of the: 'Indian with gold on his fingers and hair greased back who wants crushed velvet upholstery but can only afford short pile acrylic but spends ages brushing it the right way' or of another who: 'buys a Super Saloon for a taxi with the finest upholstery covered with blue tinted transparent plastic, his logic being that one day he will sell it looking like new ... but people don't want it used as taxi'. In contrast there is the image of the black dude, with his deputy, projecting loud music from a car with tinted glass and stripes. There is no complete dualism; there are plenty of Trinidadians who simply like adding things to the inside, outside or any place where there is room, but a tendency to dualism is nevertheless apparent.

Women do become involved in such changes but much less readily than men, and retailers saw women as merely carrying out a task and far less likely to exhibit the passions of identification which were evident for many males. The most poignant recession vignette illustrating this relationship in 1988 was the two households in Ford in which parents complained to me of sons who were still cleaning and spending money on decorating cars which were in need of such major repairs that they were clearly destined never again to go out on the road.

Any discussion of cars has to confront the rather loose distinction between private cars and taxis. Public transport in Trinidad is divided into three almost equally important forms: buses, which are very inexpensive and work on fixed routes; maxi taxis, which are more expensive but more flexible in picking up and putting down passengers; and taxis, which are the most expensive but also the most flexible although even they also work essentially on fixed routes and have to be paid extra to deviate from these. Any private car owner can be a taxi driver if they pay to have their car registered with an H number plate, and although a taxi has slightly less prestige than a private car, many people do this and thereby obtain spare income. The situation becomes somewhat more confused by an activity termed 'pulling bull', whereby drivers whose cars are not registered as taxis nevertheless use their cars for taxi work, using a hand gesture to tell potential passengers of their role. These are usually termed PH: a combination of the P for private licence and H for taxi licence found on car number plates. Approximately a third of all pickups made in Chaguanas during fieldwork came from such private cars. Cynical critics of the boom years assert that this was the primary occupation of many government workers during that time, who, having signed on for work, would then come out and 'pull bull' for most of the day.

The extensive use of upholstery and also covering it over with clear plastic implies a linkage with the upholstery of home furnishing. Indeed, upholstery is generally evocative of interiorisation. The other upholstery industry along the same street is found in the funeral parlours, where coffins and the more expensive and luxurious caskets are almost invariably lined in deep recessed upholstery. The car also evokes the living-room through the use of maroon elements and the use of plastic-covered seats to suggest a general sense of transcendence.

These linkages help provide a lead into an explanation for the sheer importance of the car in contemporary Trinidad, and its place in objectification. The car expresses something of a contradiction, a replication of the aesthetic of the interior which then has the potential for protecting the values of transcendence by maintaining them in the 'outside' world. Equally, the car provides an ideal objectification of individualism and mobility, to be used in opposition to any association with the home. In so far as the majority of people in this part of central Trinidad are of East Indian origin and a proportionally higher percentage of men tend to own cars, the male Indians are the dominant car-owning group and the majority of customers for the shops in Montrose. As a group they appeared to be using the car as a key element in resolving a clear tension expressed by many of them. Although largely positively avowing their own ethnicity, there is a clear emulation of the sense of freedom which is associated with the lifestyle of African males, in particular the supposed more active sexuality of the latter and their lack of familial constraints.

The younger Indian males constantly asserted their desire for greater freedom as an individualised independence. This was clearly associated with their desperate desire to obtain a car. Once they owned a car there arose at first an equally strong anxiety created by the tension between a desire for exclusive control and use of the car and the traditional claims of friends and relatives to use one's possessions. Much of the fanaticism of car care seemed aggressively aimed at those who might wish to make use of the car. The anxiety is also clear in the common recapitulation of the stereotypical trajectory of car ownership which is usually told as typical of African men but seemed also the experience of many Indian men. This is the story of the individual who persuades his parents to buy him a car, claiming that he will use the car for taxi work and thereby pay back the expenses involved, but soon after obtaining the car lends it to some friends who go out drinking and 'bounce' (crash) the new car.

The actual ownership of a car often brings to actuality many of the fantasies of those who strive for them. This was helped by the oil-boom itself which meant that car ownership was coincidental with an era of new possibilities for many people. For such men liming has become almost inextricably linked with driving. It is the means by which they do indeed escape the scrutiny of their families, it is often a major element in successful seduction and the fulfilment of sexual fantasy and it is a form of property which can be individualised. The car is a substantial possession which gives its owners the experience of that which was understood to be incompatible with substance. This does not necessarily mean that the driver abandons one set of values for another; the aim is rather to use dualism instrumentally to have both the security of the domestic and the excitement of the outside. Some of the men concerned can be seen to be shifting into what is locally seen as creolisation, eschewing all those values aspired to by their parents. Others see this as a period of youthful bacchanal before returning to sobriety. Most, however, seem to be desirous and increasingly capable of a longer-term commitment to both goals, retaining a deputy and a lifestyle outside the home entirely inconsistent with the values they continue to insist the home should express. More than any other item of mass consumption the car has become that classic instrument of modernity: the means of enabling contradiction without anxiety.

Bacchanal and Soap Opera

The second example of the effect of mass consumption will be taken from one of the most important agencies through which consumption practices have spread: that is, television. The example is chosen because it illustrates another facet of the dynamism of dualism: the changing objectification of its internal relationship. This relationship is expressed in the term 'bacchanal', which is central to Trinidadian self-conception. Indeed, if one asks a Trinidadian to summarise their country in one word, the likelihood is the response will be 'bacchanal'. The term has a specific meaning in Trinidad which is distinct from its traditional usage in the European tradition, although the two come together in the use of the term as a description of the prevailing atmosphere of Carnival. Bacchanal at Carnival can refer to the general level of excitement and disorder, as well as the expressive sexuality, but its more specifically Trinidadian meaning is brought out by what many people take as the core ritual of Carnival which is *Jouvert* morning. That is, the emergence into light of things which normally inhabit the dark (see Chapter 3).

In Trinidad *Jouvert* is directed against the pretensions of various establishment forms, revealing their hollow or false nature. A favourite target in 1988 was the television evangelist Jimmy Swaggart who had recently been revealed to harbour inner carnality (by visiting prostitutes while preaching against fornication). The calypsos of 1988 indicate that the first synonym for this term bacchanal is clearly 'scandal'. David Rudder sang 'Bacchanal woman, sweet scandal where she walks', while Carl and Carol Jacobs sang, 'We people like scandal. We people like bacchanal'. In the 1988 Carnival queen competition there was an entry with the title of 'Bacchanal Woman'; the costume consisted of a voluminous pink/scarlet dress with exaggerated breast and buttocks, but above this was a headpiece, a spreading fan of layers like a peacock's tail emblazoned with a series of open eyes.

The second clear connotation of the term bacchanal is confusion or disorder. The two are linked by the term '*commess*'. *Commess* may be translated as extreme confusion, but it normally carries the connotation of confusion which results from scandal. Indeed, it seems that the Trinidadian language has retained a set of terms from earlier French *patois* (among other sources) for constructing a network of concepts which are perhaps better nuanced than their English equivalents. My work as an anthropologist in uncovering or listening in to gossip rendered me a '*maco*', or '*macocious*', potentially instrumental in spreading news or *mauvay-lang* (*mauvaise-langue*) which again leads to *commess* and to bacchanal.

This very particular use of the term bacchanal is closely related to the way in which transient values seek to undermine the claims of transcendence. It is scandal and exposure to light which constantly demonstrates that the pretensions of establishment figures and institutions are nothing but façades, underneath which lies a hollowness, not the substance which is claimed. Whether through the prim schoolteacher's sexual indiscretions or the politician's uncontrollable self-interest, a truth will inevitably emerge as to the reality of a world whose claims beyond transience are false. There is then, for many Trinidadians, a moral value in this idea of exposure. Scandal and confusion have highly ambiguous moral overtones, at once undermining patiently constructed systems of order and stability but also bringing us closer to the true nature of social being.

In the Introduction, when the four communities were initially described, it was found that the concept of bacchanal was perhaps more important than that of class in understanding the tensions which existed within and between them. Much of this focused upon the effect of gossip and the need for privacy: 'Here the men mixing with the ladies and the ladies mixing with the men and people always come to hear about it in the end, as the old people say what is in the dark must come to light, and that is why I find it should not happen.' This was why the owner of a parlour in Newtown noted, 'I don't encourage chatting in this shop, people would do it, but I always busy, because if they come to gossip is about the neighbour they talkin about and some customer would vex if I hear something about them and didn't tell them anything ... then 'I am not coming here to buy' ... So if you have a lot of gossip you would lose the customers.' Similarly, this factor accounts for the high number of those surveyed who claim they have either never or very rarely been over to their neighbours.

In 1988, the term bacchanal was most commonly illustrated to me by Trinidadians through reference to one of the most powerful exemplars of modern mass consumption: that is, a soap opera. Although the reasons for the astonishing international success of this genre are still much debated, a key component seems to be the narrative structure, which for an hour a day simulates the ongoing character of ordinary life, giving it a realism which is unmatched by other cultural media. Trinidad has been the recipient of many soap operas in the last two decades, mainly imported from the United States and Australia, though with some local productions. None of these, however, achieved the level of success that *The Young and the Restless* was enjoying in 1988.

This was introduced as a lunch-hour soap and was not expected to have the same weight as serials such as *Dynasty* and *Dallas*. Advertising space was consequently cheaper at that period, which is seen as the housewives' slot, although by the end of fieldwork retailers were insisting that the producers target this time slot. The appearance and content of *The Young and the Restless* would, however, be familiar to anyone who had previously encountered other established American soap operas, concentrating on the domestic life and turmoil of wealthy families in a generalised American city. Evidence that the popularity of this soap opera arises from the salience of its content and is not merely the product of well-targeted television comes from the manner by which it has completely overthrown the power of the primetime slot and from the manner in which Trinidadians have refused the logistical constraints and insisted on watching the series, even when conditions should have prevented this.

A local marketing survey carried out early in 1988, before, I suspect, *The Young and the Restless* had peaked, suggested that seventy per cent of those with TV watched the show regularly, slightly more than the news, both of these being well ahead of the third highest rating which was less than thirty per cent. In my own survey of 160 households, out of the 146 who had access to a television all but twenty watched *The Young and the Restless* regularly. There was no evident association with ethnicity, but only five out of seventy-one in the lower-income bracket did not watch this show while fifteen out of seventy-five in the higher-income bracket did not watch. In a separate question where forty-four households mentioned their favourite programmes, thirty-seven gave *The Young and the Restless* as one of these. *The Young and the Restless* became a motif throughout Trinidadian culture, the butt of parody at *Jouvert*, the title of both a gang and a bout of influenza, a pun for advertisements for children's clothes and other goods. The dominance of this TV show over other media was shown by a comparison of readership figures for newspapers in 1988 and then again in 1990.[10] By the latter date, one of the weeklies had hit upon the idea of carrying a resumé of the forthcoming week's content for a number of soap operas, exploiting the fact that these are shown in the USA before they reach Trinidad. As a result it had become the best-selling newspaper in the country, whereas previously it had lagged some distance behind its rivals. There was a general consensus that this new ploy was the operative factor.

One of the most common comments about the show was its relevance to contemporary conditions in Trinidad. Typical would be: 'The same thing you see on the show will happen here; you see the wife blackmailing the husband or the other way around. I was telling my sister-in-law, Liana in the picture, just like some bacchanal woman.' 'It really happening this flirtatious attitude; this one they living together that partner working this partner, and have a date with the next one or in bed with another.'

From this sense of relevance comes also the idea that there are direct lessons to be learnt from the narrative content for moral issues in Trinidad: 'It teach you how husbands could lie and cheat and how a wife could expect certain things and never get it, the women always get the short end of the stick.' 'I believe marriage should be 50–50 not 30–70. The woman have to be strong, she have to believe in her vows no matter what … that make me remember *The Young and the Restless*, Nicky want her marriage to work but Victor is in love with somebody else, but she still holding on.' Or (as in a current story): 'You always to go back to the first person you loved, in my own family my elder sister went with a Moslem boy, and so was married off by parents to a Hindu man, but she left her husband, gone back to the first man and had a child by him.'

The reasons for this programme's success were given by the calypsonian Contender in a highly successful calypso called simply 'The Young and the Restless' launched for 1989. This consisted largely of a summary of the plot but the chorus alternated:

'You talk of *commess*
check *The Young and the Restless*,
commess at its best
check *The Young and the Restless*.
 With the words
They like the bacchanal
they like the confusion.

In most of the conversations in which the show was discussed it was again clear that it was its power to encapsulate the lessons of bacchanal that gave it its local 'realism'. The implications depended upon the values of the speaker. For those in The Meadows who loathe bacchanal it has negative overtones. For them, the government party, which was called the National Alliance for Reconstruction, but which was in practice falling apart into warring factions, was a clear case of bacchanal. The previous government's insistence, through fairly heavy-handed control, in keeping its internal divisions from public view was seen as a much more 'serious' form of rule. In trying to interview people within the very private and protected houses of the middle class, women, in particular, were extremely fearful, sometimes literally terrified, that their husbands would get to know that they had been talking to me (but equally to my female research assistant), about their domestic circumstances. These women are understood as the gender responsible for the domestic world. They not only build it but equally they are seen as the weak link whose revelations or wrong behaviour would lead to its collapse. When, as often happened, an apparently stable and close family is broken asunder into disordered fragments following a dispute over inheritance, the appellation of bacchanal has nothing good about it.

Many of those in Ford, by contrast, would espouse the positive side of bacchanal associated with Carnival and *Jouvert*. They tend to particularly look to scandal as sexual transgression as bringing about the collapse of façade. For this purpose there is a wide range of possible exemplifications from actual 'cuss-outs' and scandals in the neighbourhood, through to the semi-fictional accounts which provide the mainstay of the weekly newspapers which, with titles such as *The Bomb*, *Heat*, *The Punch* and *The Blast*, have developed a bacchanal press which complements the more serious daily press. The weeklies provide a sustained development of ordinary daily rumour and each feeds on the other. For example, an article (Mirror, 22 April 1988) starts: 'The Chaguanas Police have been unable to confirm reports that a man with AIDS was caught squeezing blood from a wound on his hand into the ketchup bottle of a leading fast food outlet.' In all four communities people could name which fast food outlet was implicated, though I have no idea whether the rumour preceded the report or vice versa. By 1988, however, it was the entirely fictive form of *The Young and the Restless*, which dominated inter-household gossip.

Many in Ford identify with their own area as a locus of bacchanal. It is here that gossip flows freely through the walls of houses built from the boxes in which car parts are imported. Bacchanal may lead to confusion, fighting, etc., but it is still a welcome return to a kind of natural state. Friendship in bacchanal is spontaneous, relationships are dyadic and transient without the constraints on freedom imposed by social convention and structure. For some there is not enough bacchanal: 'People in *The Young and the Restless* can't have fun like people in Trinidad. Their sort of fun is boring. There's more bacchanal here than in *The Young and the Restless*. In each soap you can tell what's going to happen, but around here you can't tell.'

A major preoccupation in the soap opera is the manner by which individuals are, as it were, thrown off course or driven to extreme actions by sexual desire. For example, on one storyline, a woman writing a critical biography starts an affair, almost against her will, with the subject of her work. In another, a woman working hard to integrate within the respectable family of her child's father, is seduced from these efforts by a good-looking man recruited for the purpose. Here, as in the Trinidadian ideology of the domestic, it is often the women who assert one morality but find themselves inexorably drawn through sexual attraction into overturning these same principles. One viewer notes: 'Look how she is a *commess* maker, just so some women come to some people house and do the same thing.' According to Cantor and Pingree (1983) *The Young and the Restless* is one of a group which tends to a greater orientation towards sex and social breakdown than the prime-time series; within the field of soap opera, *The Young and the Restless* is situated in the 'liberal' group (ibid: 94). This may account for its relative success as against previous imported soap operas in Trinidad.

Another particular feature of this soap opera in Trinidad which develops the earlier discussion of clothing is the manner by which individuals identify with the fictive characters on the screen. It is rarely the character or personality of the individual which is seen as the point of identification. In the first instance it is almost always the clothing which mediates the act of identification, as in the following quotes:

> I love Lauren, how she dresses and I identify with her.
> I like Nicky the way she dresses; my name is Nicky too, she is a loving person.
> I look mainly at *Dynasty*. I like the way Alexis dresses, she is so sophisticated and I like the way Crystal dresses.
> I like Nicky's and Liana's dress. I always look at Nicky's hair, her braids and bows and stuff. Mrs Chancellor does dress nice.

This identification may often translate into direct copying of clothes, so that seamstresses may conceive of watching the soap operas as part of their job. Although it was a different programme being described, this quote from a seamstress talking about a client illustrates the point: 'When you see that show is about to start, the phone does ring. Gloria yuh watching it ... like every dress she see she say, 'Oh God I want one like that,' and how many yards to buy and I think she was writing on the other end.' The important point about this use of clothing is not that it shows the superficial level at which the programme is absorbed, but quite the opposite. Given the principal exteriorising, centrifugal aesthetic of bacchanal, it shows the centrality of the programme to that aspect of Trinidadian culture.

As in the case of the living-room, the car and clothing, there is both continuity with previous forms of objectification and also subtle changes. Clearly the serial represents a displaced form of gossip. Bacchanal is generally associated with innuendo and is not entirely provenanced, which means that a considerable amount of gossip can take place in which people's actual interests are not involved, as was commented: 'I prefer that, you see it is safer to talk about the celebrities' business than to talk about people's business. You won't get into trouble, nobody will cuss you if you say Chancellor was with this one husband ... but it is just bacchanal ... all them soaps is bacchanal.'

Such comments help account for the particular significance of *The Young and the Restless* at this point in time. Trinidad is an extraordinarily dynamic society. With the oil-boom post-1973 it was catapulted into the world of mass consumption, but with the decline of the oil price, especially in 1986, it has suffered an almost equally precipitous recession. I would argue that bacchanal is more important than wealth *per se* in determining the local equivalent of class. The disdain felt by the suburban for the squatters is based on the uncontrolled *commess* of the latter. Wealth, however, is of considerable importance in allowing groups to struggle towards the respectability of transcendence and its instruments of interiorisation and enclosure.

The oil-boom gave a tremendous impetus to the growth of the middle-class to the extent that they emerged at its peak as dominant both numerically and culturally. With the recession, however, many of the more fragile pretensions of the *nouveau* element within this class are becoming exposed. There is a continual discourse about the financial plight that exists behind the closed doors of the domestic, which is only brought to light by events such as cutting off the phone because of unpaid bills. Even in the suburb there were frequent rumours about how many properties were back in the hands of the banks or deserted by migrants to Canada. The crisis was largely financial but it is very possible that this was instrumental in the displaced crescendo of activity around the concept of exposure based on the more familiar theme of sexuality. Therefore this unprecedented orientation towards an imported soap opera may well have its roots in the near exquisite tension that had built up between transcendence and transience and which is highlighted by the focus upon bacchanal.

Many of the writings on soap opera and serials tend to assume that these provide some reassurance, stability and so forth as part of their power. Much of this viewpoint may stem from the legacy of the mass-culture critique which treated soap operas as a kind of visual valium that stupefies its audience in the interest of some dominant will. In certain cases this may well be the impact, but not in Trinidad. Here, far from patching up a wound, or 'functioning' in the interests of social cohesion, the attraction of the programme is that it forces its point into the key fissure which manifests the basic contradiction of Trinidadian culture, at a time when this is especially sensitive. This is precisely why Trinidadian television cannot produce a programme of this kind. *The Young and the Restless* reinforces bacchanal as the lesson of recession which insists that the domestic and the façade of stability is a flimsy construction which will be blown over in the first storm created by true nature.

Compared to previous objectifications of bacchanal, the soap opera is closer to the everyday activities of those for whom bacchanal is a more constant experience: the world of gossip, scandal and confusion that generates the constant narrative structure of community life. It may thereby comment more directly on the current dynamics of the domestic, while Carnival reflects more on a slower-moving structural dualism within which the domestic is implicated. This is the sense in which Trinidadians echo the more academic commentary on soap opera as a new realism, aware of the linkage to social life as itself open-ended and of narrative form which may be used at a time of such dynamic tension. This sense is compounded by the manner in which *The Young and the Restless*, in particular, colludes with the local sense of truth as exposure and scandal. The soap opera is not just Trinidadian, but, as in a popular local expression 'True True Trini'.[11]

My account of this soap opera, as indeed of fashion, car upholstery, living-room furnishings and other aspects of mass consumption, does not accord with the commonly expressed views of Trinidadians on the effects of the oil-boom. In each case I have stressed continuity between the values being expressed through commodities and cultural projects already established. This is not to imply lack of change, since in many cases the flood of new materials and images radically affects the process of objectification such that Trinidad has been considerably transformed by this experience. But these changes have often been in the form of giving clarity or extension to previous values rather than replacing them or rendering them antiquated. As I will argue in the concluding chapter, the increasing reliance upon arrays of objects and images as documented here, as opposed to categories of person as discussed in the next chapter, is itself a change of considerable importance.

Indeed, it would be ironic to dismiss my interpretation of imported goods simply because it does not accord with the statements of most Trinidadians on the subject. The dismissal of mass commodities as constituting a new superficiality based upon mere mimicry of other regions is itself an imported discourse, as evident in the fact that there is hardly a place on the globe where people do not affirm that this is the prime effect of the rise of mass consumption. I would conclude that on the whole Trinidadians have found it more difficult to appropriate and render specific the discourse about mass consumption than the objects of mass consumption. I suspect such a difference between practice and discourse might also be true of other 'imported' ideologies about, for example, gender and class. Once again, this suggests that material culture and visual imagery may have an important role to play in cultural change which is missed when too great a reliance is placed upon verbal self-representation and legitimation.

It is, however, in relation to this question of imported or emulated culture that Trinidadians most clearly evoke a number of core debates on the nature not only of modernity but also the condition of postmodernity. Indeed, in many ways it is the debates themselves that most clearly demonstrate the original contention that it is the self-consciousness about temporality that underlies the experience of being modern. As Wilk (1990) has convincingly argued for Belize, the goods themselves often becomes the media through which models are constructed of past, present and future states, though in this case it is the state of being Trinidadian that is most commonly at issue. It is in relation to this material rather than that of the previous chapters that we find the sense of fragmentation and degeneration, but also an exhilarating sense of riding the crest of waves of change.

The brief account that was given of Schama's (1987) book *The Embarrassment of Riches* in Chapter 2 can now be reintegrated in relation to contemporary Trinidad. Schama focuses on Amsterdam as one of the first examples of a society wealthy in material culture; he documents how this was used to construct with greater clarity a dualist moral geography, in which two opposed attitudes to the possession of goods were objectified and maintained not as reconciled but as coexisting forms. Schama (and in a rather different way Campbell 1987) has used historical sources to challenge the relationship between Protestantism and capitalism assumed by Weber. Just as in contemporary Trinidadian Protestantism, this wealth in objects seems to act as a stimulus both to an elaboration of what in that case was Calvinism and that to which religious moralities were opposed. The sheer provision of material culture allowed for each to be developed within its own sphere of reference. In this chapter a similar point has been made, but in this case it is less the dispute over lavishness and thrift *per se*, which seems to have become dominant within the prevailing dualism but a sense of normative and unchanging tradition held against the ephemeral possibilities of individualising style. This reflects back rather more directly on a rupture in temporal consciousness that not only pervades the accounts in previous chapters of other aspects of Trinidadian life, but also provided the foundation for a theoretical account of modernity.

Notes

1. The value of food imports nearly tripled between 1974 and 1978, while the production of crops such as citrus collapsed to a tenth of their previous size. By 1980 90 per cent of domestic food consumption was based on imported foods (Auty and Gelb 1986: 1166, 1169). Yelvington (1991) portrays the situation of recession in 1988; see also Rampersad (1988) for a brief overview of the economy during the period since Independence.

2. Maroon here stands for a variety of shades from burgundy to red but clearly of a general type.

3. These 'plush' carpets are woefully maladaptive to the tropical climate. They harbour a flourishing insect life and require constant cleaning, especially as a result of wind-blown ash from the nearby canefields which are regularly burnt prior to harvesting.

4. It seems to be a characteristic of surveys based upon the material culture of home interiors that they contradict the self-representation of these practices in language. Surveys of home interiors in Canada (McCracken 1989), London (Miller 1988) and Tennessee (Forrest 1988) have found constellations of similar nostalgic and enclosing forms which in some cases is poorly articulated in language, though in one case conforms to a local category of 'homeyness'.

5. Another example would be the horror of ambiguity and love of category integrity associated with transcendence. This proved to be the key link between the difficulty in obtaining consumer goods in recession and the extraordinary wave of emigration which occurred, mainly of East-Indians to Canada during 1988. This event will be analysed in the succeeding volume to the present work.

6. During the survey a question was asked as to when the informant had last purchased a pair of shoes. Of those who answered this question the results were as follows:

	NEWTOWN	FORD	THE MEADOWS	ST PAULS
LESS THAN A MONTH	1	4	8	1
MONTH TO 6 MONTHS	14	8	14	20
6 MONTHS TO A YEAR	7	4	16	7
MORE THAN A YEAR	3	1	0	7
TOTAL	25	17	38	35

7. Not surprisingly the more salacious weeklies were especially interested in the manner by which ladies might be relieved of their clothing by gangs. *The Heat* for 27 February 1988 under the title 'Guard your Acid Wash' (the latest fashion item) noted: 'That people are even being dis-robed and robbed of their Acid Wash at gunpoint. This leaves the hapless victim with no alternative, but to return home in their underwear and panties after a fête'.

8. A radio competition in which listeners were asked to write in and say how they would spot a Trini anywhere in the world.

9. Thanks to Lise Winer for pointing these out.

10. I am grateful to both the marketing company which carried out these surveys and the Advertising Agencies Association of Trinidad and Tobago who commissioned the surveys for permission to view and use these surveys.

11. For a more detailed discussion of this example see Miller 1992.

Chapter 6

Origins and Articulations

The previous chapters are written as though there is a clear emergent dualism at the heart of Trinidadian culture. I suspect many readers of this material will have been frustrated by the lack of an equally clear correspondence between the cultural orientation to a set of values and a specific social group which holds these values: that is, the failure to discriminate clearly in terms of categories such as ethnicity, gender or class. Anthropologists in particular might suspect that if and when this were done, the dualism itself would be revealed for an over-objectified analytical dichotomy, and a more subtle and 'experiential' presentation of the ethnography would then be able to emerge. Alternatively, a less synchronic perspective which was more sensitive to the various historical influences which have given rise to the present complexity of Trinidadian culture might be thought essential to clarifying these various strands and accounting for their presence.

The style of the previous chapters may appear obtuse in their refusal to acknowledge the 'significance' of the typical sociological parameters, even where the discussion often uses ethnic generalisations. In reading more generally within Caribbean anthropology it is evident that the major concern of most social scientists is precisely the elucidation of these classic social divisions, such that it is clearly appreciated that underneath any cultural dualism lies the 'real' world of opposed genders, classes or ethnic groups, which can then be satisfactorily understood in terms of their historical genesis and contemporary tensions.

In the case of Trinidad, there is no doubt as to which of these divisions becomes paramount as underscoring almost any opposition which is put forward in discussion. For Trinidadians themselves, to discuss society is to discuss ethnicity, and virtually all the major features of dualism so far identified will be understood as emerging from the character of the main ethnic communities. In the cruder debates this may implicate the supposed innate and essential characteristics of the race. In more self-aware and self-critical discourse this polarisation is noted, but to be explained by historical forces, especially marginalisation. Thus the marginalisation of the Black community in colonialism led to its opposition to hierarchising institutions, while the marginalisation of the Indians by the Africans led to its inward-looking cultural endogamy.

This chapter is intended to respond to such expectations and as such has three main aims. First, to consider the manner by which the distinctions and generalisations so far made might articulate with these same sociological parameters and classifications. Second, to consider these in relation to the available historical information which might provide an explanation for the specificities elucidated; and finally to interpret the results within the context of the comparative literature on the Caribbean.

An attempt to articulate dualism with social differences will provide little comfort to those who wish to see dualism as merely the imposition of an abstraction by the author, working with a genre established by Abrahams, Wilson and others, and owing more to structural anthropology than ethnographic sensitivity. I certainly don't wish to claim dualism is the only way in which one could treat this material, and a book which emphasised other cultural domains such as religion or politics might well prefer to represent cultural generalities and distinctions from an alternative perspective. Nevertheless, it is hoped that the materials in the previous chapters have been sufficient to demonstrate that dualism is at least one of the legitimate forms by which such ethnographic observations might be presented, in so far as there is considerable evidence to suggest it plays a central role in the habitus of most Trinidadians, internalising, and in turn producing, the orders in things.

In attempting to account for dualism in the present chapter it will soon become evident that the problem lies not with the lack of plausible explanations, origins, sources and comparative evidence. Indeed, it is only too easy to provide explanation through these routes. The problem will be rather the very plurality of potential accounts which could encompass many of the observations made. It is this which finally may makes one suspicious of an over-reliance on any one variable or historical sequence. Furthermore, it will be argued that the privileging of any one dimension tends to be an artifact of a kind of social reductionism. Thus if we start from gender we can reduce many other areas of West Indian social practices to gender by demonstrating at least partial homologies or oppositions. But the same is true of class, of ethnicity, of age and other social dimensions.

In general, social groups are better understood as objects in this process rather than subjects. That is to say gender, class and ethnic groups are constantly used as the means of objectifying a sense of order and are inscribed with particular characteristics thereby. We understand some particular attribute such as 'thrift' or 'style' as the natural property of 'males', 'youth' or the 'middle class'. Therefore whenever the anthropologist privileges a social dimension, they tend merely to acquiesce in a process of naturalisation which tends to make these characteristics either essential, or at least historically 'given'. In the concluding chapter I will argue that for this reason analyses based on material objects and images as attempted in Chapter 4 are often preferable to attempts to analyse in terms of social dimensions as in the examples which will be criticised below.

Gender

The best known precursor for an assertion of the centrality of dualism to Caribbean culture is certainly Wilson's (1973) book *Crab Antics*. There are several reasons why the dualism he presented in terms of 'reputation' and 'respectability' has had a considerable influence on later studies. First, he grounds his ethnography in a larger analysis of comparative and historical materials. Second, there is generally credit given to the sensitivity of observation and quality of writing of those, such as Abrahams and Wilson, who have promoted this theme, as against more conventional ethnographies. Third, most of the competing approaches which have stressed the effects of marginalisation or the culture of poverty have been less able to account for the precise relationship between these factors, which are common to so many other areas and regions of the world, and the specific findings of Caribbean studies.

Wilson provides close equivalents for many of the major distinctions which have so far been described here. His concept of reputation is based primarily on observations of male peer groups which seem, as he notes (ibid: 186–7), similar to the Trinidadian concept of the 'lime', and their anti-institutional anti-hierarchical nature is strongly emphasised. There are other elements which, while muted in his account, have been stressed here by using the term transience. Equally, Wilson's portrayal of respectability with its evocation of lives orientated towards the domestic and the church clearly parallels many of the elements here glossed as transcendent.

Gender is central to Wilson's (and Abraham's) account as each sex is unambiguously associated with the polarities of this duality. There is also an historical logic to this argument, derived from what Wilson calls women's preferred status within colonial culture (ibid: 234). Others have seen this as partly a result of women's sexual depredation by the colonisers, and partly the differences between women employed in the domestic realm and men employed in the fields. Olwig (forthcoming) has recently explored this historical link more closely with her work on Nevis, examining in detail the doctrines and practices of the Methodist church and the cult of domesticity associated with it.

From the content of the previous chapters it should be evident that gender in Trinidad could convincingly be portrayed on lines similar to Wilson's representation of gender on Providencia. In Chapters 2 and 3 the association between women and the inside, men and the outside was established, in a manner which clearly evokes Wilson's contrasts. In general, men express individualistic freedom with their own mode of reputation, while women dominate religiosity and the concern with the long term. Other accounts would confirm this picture. Yelvington's (forthcoming) study of gender in a Trinidadian factory notes the employer's view that women are regarded to be more suitable as line workers simply because they are thought more likely to stay. Men, with their ideology of spontaneity and change, do not wish to be identified with any particular work and are apt to change jobs with some frequency. Numerous similar supportive generalisations could be added.

There is also, however, considerable material in the previous chapters which would introduce a cautionary note to this identification. Gender relations are dependent upon their articulation with a more fundamental dualism and by no means dominate it.

Within an orientation to transience, it was found that gender relations were minimal, reduced down as far as possible to specific media such as sexuality and events. Although men may have been numerically preponderant in transience, there is a significant section of women who share these values and excel in living in accordance with them. In Chapter 2 it was argued that it is women, not men, who provide the most extreme exemplification of transience in wining. Although the case for symmetry is not quite so clear, at least in The Meadows, it appears that men provide the most assertive exemplification of the values associated with transcendence. Furthermore, the articulation between gender and dualism is cross-cut by other factors of which the most important is ethnicity, but would also include class and life cycle.

The historical sequence is also not quite as straightforward as is sometimes assumed. It may well be that certain colonial forces favoured the cult of domesticity which linked women with the interior, but there are marked differences between the forms taken by respectability in the Caribbean and that of colonial society. It is not at all clear, for example, why the church should have been able to establish a link between the stable conditions of property ownership and the sanctity of marriage to such an overwhelming extent that there is a consistent refusal to marry until the home is properly established, thereby negating the intention of the churches in the first place. Nor is it clear why transcendence should have established the particular concern with roots and ancestry which seems characteristic. The subsuming of individuality in family, including extended family forms, seems to take ideas of domesticity either to extremes or at least into variants which are not to be located in the domesticity taught by the church and located in British colonial practices.

Most importantly there is the distinction of dualism itself. In the British cult of respectability the middle-class domestic home is a vicarious reflection of the same respectability of the middle-class Victorian male in his work and male peer culture. This is very different from the gender-based opposition portrayed by Wilson. In both Wilson and Olwig's account there is a much less clear trajectory for the development of reputation, which tends to be defined largely by its negation of the domestic, as some kind of anti-colonial resistance. It would be equally plausible, however, to locate reputation in the influences of colonial forces. After all, the culture of mistresses, the sexual liaisons, the leisure activities of colonial males provide as firm a precedent (Smith 1987). As an example, one could point to the powerful French influence on Trinidadian culture, evident in Carnival, calypso and many other arenas. An excursion into French culture at the time when it started to become influential in Trinidad reveals forms of kinship and household far removed from those which are assumed to characterise contemporary European domestic ideology.

In an article on illegitimacy and foundlings in pre-industrial France, Meyer (1980: 249–63) points out the extraordinarily tenu-ous relationship betwen parents and chidren of the time. The eighteenth-century sees a massive rise in the practice of foundlings, that is children effectively abandoned by their par-ents, rising sometimes to around thirty per cent of births in Paris. The extremes of this practice are echoed in a quotation from Rousseau: 'five children resulted from my liaison with the poor girl who lived with me, all of whom were put out as foundlings. I have not even kept a note of their date of birth, so little did I expect to see them again' (ibid: 259). French culture of this period seems to have developed several traits, including an acceptance of illegitimacy, a general distance between biological parenting and actual parenting and a development of complex sexual liaisons, including, by the nineteenth-century a virtual cult of the mistress, all of which have a clear echo in what are taken as the particular characteristics of 'West-Indian kinship' and yet which are rarely linked to the specific culture of what in Trinidad was clearly the most influential section of colonial society (see also Flandrin 1979: 180–4, 203–9). Olwig (forthcoming) has similar ref-erences to pre-industrial English society which again could pro-vide an argument for the influence of colonial precursors to reputation. An alternative means of accounting for the impor-tance of sexuality for the embodiment of a sense of freedom would be the internalisation of sexual essentialism which was projected on to black people by white racism during the period of colonialism and whose effects were most profoundly analysed by Fanon (1986).

If then an argument can reverse Wilson's logic and make repu-tation the legacy of certain key influential features of colonial practice and then colonial racist discourse, it is also possible to complete this inversion by arguing that respectability is the vehi-cle of 'resistance' to colonialism. The material presented by Clarke (1957) in *My Mother who Fathered Me* and the collection edited by Besson and Momsen (1987) seems to indicate a strong desire for property-based descent emergent out of the same historical conditions which also produce the traits of West Indian kinship and the refusal to institutionalisation. Given the conditions of slavery, the difficulties in maintaining family bonding and the treatment of slaves as property themselves, it is just as reasonable to see the female-centered search for respectability in stable descent groups with long-term ambitions for family development and the cultivation of property as the true form of resistance (Bush 1990). Indeed, in Trinidad the history of the post-emancipation period suggests that the key imperative was precisely the creation of this kind of small-holding and property-based rural household. The ideal of a nuclear family and respectability may at this time have been less a continuation of colonial dominance, than the primary form by which groups were able to overturn the oppressive constraints of slavery.

The point is not really to insist on one or other trajectory but merely to demonstrate that there are plausible alternatives to what has tended to become the accepted sequence, (following Wilson 1973: 215–36), of female respectability born of colonialism, and male resistance. These assumptions may have more to do with contemporary political ideologies than actual historical developments.

There is undoubtedly an association between gender and dualism in the Caribbean, but the problem is how to interpret this. Strathern (1988) has attempted, using Melanesian materials, to refuse the essentialism of gender and argue how the specifics of distinction in that region are at some point articulated with male-female categories but at times and places which would not necessarily accord with the assumptions given in the semantics of gender as imported from English or colonial societies. Such an option is not open to the Caribbean where a relativism based on prior differences would fail in the light of the particular history of the region. In the Caribbean, for a century and a half, gender has been worked out in relation to increasingly normative and global concepts of domesticity which have had hegemonic pretensions when applied by the establishment, which, even while it did not practise the prescriptive form itself, nevertheless exhorted the mass of society to move towards such nuclear familial forms. As the material from Trinidad shows, there is a clear consistent model of the domestic which is constantly trum-

peted as morally superior to all other forms of family construction. But Trinidad, and perhaps the Caribbean more widely, has
never been able to contain within itself the compromises, and
what would locally be seen as hypocrisies, of the colonial model
of the domestic, but has pulled apart its contradictions into disparate forms.

If gender and dualism are to be related, then, it is not by pos-
ing gender as the prior basis upon which dualism is then constructed, but by examining how gender itself is fabricated in the
light of an underlying dualist habitus which then creates gender
as systematic opposition in ideology and practice. The grounds
for seeing it this way round are greatly strengthened by the
observation that gender is only one of a series of social distinctions which could otherwise have been argued to be equally good
candidates for the origins of dualism.

Class

Given the particular history of colonialism, any attempt to reconstruct the origins and present tensions of Caribbean societies solely in class terms would be bound to look forced. If, however, the
term class is reconstructed to incorporate elements of other distinctions, most especially ethnicity, which have clearly played a
major role in the construction and experience of inequalities, then
class starts to provide a clear alternative to gender as the fundamental principle upon which dualism is built. The historical evolution of this system seems unproblematic, in so far as a hierarchy
based on the coercive principles of slavery or indentured labour
could easily transmute itself into one in which a consistency of
oppression is maintained through the alternative vehicle of social
class, rendering the descendants of the slave or labourer as simply
low-class with little prospect of gaining either resources or privilege. Most of the major historians of Trinidad, for example
Brereton (1981), present their materials in terms of relatively clear
ethnic/class fractions. This combination of class and ethnicity is
clearly articulated with the evolution of the relations of production, although economic control by the dominant white fraction
has grown in subtlety, especially since independence.

This leads to the portait of Trinidad by Braithwaite (1975) in
the 1950s, at which time social stratification is portrayed as

embodied in a clear colour/class gradation of hierarchy with white at the top and black at the bottom (there is relatively little consideration given by Braithwaite to the Indian population). The situation is seen to reflect a semicaste-like structure with virtual endogamy among the white upper class and coloured middle class respectively, designed to maintain boundaries against those lower down. As in many such hierarchies the differences are internalised as a kind of emotive 'gut' revulsion and fear which keeps contact with those below one to a minimum. As in Henriques' (1953) model of Jamaican society, the emphasis is upon a single goal of emulatory desire embodied ultimately in the physiognomy of the whites.

Certain elements of this portrayal are still valid. Even the casual visitor cannot fail to be struck by the colour-coding in occupations. It is still the case that the institutional employees who deal with the public, such as airline stewardesses or bank clerks, will tend to be of a lighter complexion. Brown is clearly advantaged at the expense of black, although the strict relation to the organisation of production has certainly become a much looser structure of tendencies and spheres of economic influence (see Ryan 1991a). Even with the rise of black political power through the government of the PNM it is possible to retain this basic class structure as long as there is a group of black people who would emulate the same categories and boundaries which they inherited: an accusation which is certainly evident in Trinidadian attacks upon what they call the 'Afro-Saxons'.

Today, however, it is Jamaica, rather than Trinidad, which would provide the best example of a continuity from this 1950s snapshop portrait. If Wilson provides the best exemplar of the argument that dualism is best located in gender, then it is probably Austin (1984) in her recent ethnography of Kingston who presents the clearest articulation between class and dualism. There is considerable evidence in her work for the importance of a dualism represented by the distinction between what she and her informants see as 'outside' and 'inside' worlds. But although she acknowledges the relation of these terms to issues of gender and the construction of domesticity, the main thrust of Austin's (1983) critique of Wilson is that he underplayed the importance of class and ideology. She argues that institutions such as the church and most especially education play a crucial role in the reproduction of hegemony, and by structuring her work in the comparison of two communities, one low- and one middle-class, she makes class the central vehicle through which any cultural dualism is carried. Within this context the actual content of this dualism is highly reminiscent of both Wilson and the descriptions given in the previous chapters of this book. Trinidadians who have visited Jamaica seem to share Austin's perspective: while they would describe their own conflicts in terms of ethnicity, they tend to describe those of Jamaica in terms of class.

Class as a descriptive feature of Trindadian society will be discussed further in the subsequent volume, but it may be noted that the term class, when used as one of a series of sociological categories in describing and analysing a society, may be divided into a 'strict' and a 'loose' definition. In the first case there is the strong category of class which is derived from Marxist theory and which turns upon the relationship to the ownership of productive forces and of property. Trinidad is, however, a long way from the circumstances of either a factory system or a mass peasantry for which such concepts were originally formed and then developed. Indeed, it will be clear from the material presented in Chapter 4, that it would be quite misleading to analyse property relations solely from the perspective of the political economy, since the almost obsessional concern with property within transcendence is often distinguished from the perception of its actual or even potential value as an economic resource. A Weberian or some other and looser treatment of status conceptions and boundary construction might therefore seem more appropriate.

The description of the four housing areas given in the Introduction provides the context for an analysis of contemporary social hierarchy. It was found that the development of more homogenised housing is a key factor in the evolution of contemporary social distinctions in Trinidad. There are wealthy capitalists in Chaguanas, though most would tend to migrate to the capital. More important in a development such as The Meadows would be first, a stratum of senior civil servants and the executives for multinationals or major local corporations and second, a stratum of professionals, especially teachers but also doctors and lawyers.

The importance of social stratification was equally evident at the other extreme in Ford where, for many, the conditions of impoverishment are such that, as one person commented, 'here we doh even have water to make style on each other'. In practice, despite lack of resources, the area exhibits considerable small-scale internal competition. Even a children's party designed to help the impoverished elicited considerable competitive concern for the appearance and behaviour of the children. Since, however, this competitiveness tends to be based on transient criteria and events, it does not amount to the institutionalised forms connoted by the terms class or even status.

It is, however, in Newtown where a sense of class and status conflict seems the central imperative of household relations. Here the homogeneity of the settlement means that most of its inhabitants come to feel that their own status and identity is bound up with that of the area itself. As such, neighbours are both competitors in differential house renovations, but also to be blamed if they fail to keep up the standards of the whole. Many regard their neighbours as appearing 'to have the air' and to 'act social'.

Trinidadians tend to define themselves as a 'who you know' society (Oxaal 1982) and would generally see this as more important than wealth alone in the ascription of power. As such they operate a wide variety of systems of patronage with widely recognised expectations of reciprocal obligation. Many Trinidadians again see the epitome of such systems in Jamaica. Jamaica is understood as operating a system of rival parties with the ability to dispense a wide variety of jobs and services as a product of political office. Similarly, the PNM government in Trinidad was understood to have utilised its patronage potential in the development of village councils, in schemes for the unemployed, housing and other service provisions. This patronage was seen as ethnically biased (an accusation supported by Hintzen, 1989: 90–103).

Nevertheless, there are many who see the system as not as fully established in Trinidad as in Jamaica and dependent upon the actions of political parties over the next few years to repudiate or repeat this process. Historically such systems of ethnically based patronage were well established by the colonial authorities, and it is their system of clubs which still provides a more pervasive model than political patronage for the extension of such networks. In the Chaguanas area, groups such as Rotary and Lions are of considerable importance in gaining prestige, and emulate the white community in Port of Spain which continues to develop clubs whose exclusivity has now to be based on more subtle forms of exclusion than explicit racial grounds.

Although there are then grounds for a class perspective on contemporary Trindadian society, the articulation with dualism is complex. The category of class presents quite different problems from that of gender or ethnicity. These two last dimensions represent categories which most people outside academia commonly resort to in providing foundational causes of cultural distinction. Trinidadians, but also people of many other countries, will grant them essentialist characteristics. It is in the 'nature' of women to be orientated to the home interior, it is an 'African' trait to be only concerned with the present, and so forth. In general, academics, such as anthropologists, tend to use their materials to confront and demolish these presuppositions. Using relativism and other means, they expose such views as racist or sexist, and tend to argue that the perspectives that create these views are ideologically constructed and must be understood in their social and political context.

Almost the exact reverse is the case when it comes to class. Apart from a minority mainly influenced by larger discourses from times spent 'away', the concept of class is not a primary mechanism of identification in Trinidad, and it is unlikely that many Trinidadians would be willing to see ethnicity and gender, for example, as secondary to an underlying set of class relations. By contrast, class, and relations of power more generally, are typically privileged by academic writings as having an ontological status which allows them to be excavated as the hidden, in a sense, essentialist dimension which is therefore fundamental to the appearance of other distinctions. To argue that class should not be privileged in this way is likely to elicit criticism with a strong moral element. It is liable to be castigated as a 'right-wing' position, since for all the weakening of earlier base-superstructural models, the belief that class relations are foundational is still a signifier of affiliation with generalised left-wing positions.

There are many writings on the Caribbean which do see differential access to resources as the key to understanding any generalisations otherwise presented as 'cultural' traits. Thus the particularities of West Indian kinship are linked to male marginalisation as failed bread-winner or migrant labourer. Alternatively the 'Circumstance-Oriented Man' uncovered by Rodman (1971) is explained by him as typical of the culture of poverty among lower-class families. It is also possible to construct an argument which makes class the foundation for an understanding of the dualism of transience and transcendence. There is the closure of transcendence and its storage of wealth, the accruing of possessions and property, its conservatism and its exclusionary stance. All this could be argued to act as the ideology which secured the advantages of the dominant class and establishes boundaries to exclude the dominated. This is close to the argument propounded by Austin (1984) with particular emphasis on the general acceptance of education as providing a secure dimension of hierarchy which becomes accepted as ideology among the dominated class.

Unfortunately for such arguments, these same patterns which have been argued to be an adaptation to poverty seem as well 'adapted' to wealth. Olwig (forthcoming) has recently examined the remittance-based economy of contemporary Nevis and shown how the use of kinship to create linkages may be used to provide the mechanism by which money is channelled back into the country from the new international family that is becoming the norm here and elsewhere in the Caribbean. Gonzalez (1984) and others have found little trace of any changes in the norms of kinship which seem to emanate from the tremendous economic changes which have occured since the Second World War, although this finding would be less true of Trinidad than elsewhere in the Caribbean. Most important of all are the recent studies which show that the assumption that 'West-Indian' kinship is a lower-class phenomena is just that – an assumption. Recent work which includes the middle class within the ethnographic study either rejects the assumed relation to class (Young 1990) or suggests the historical linkage between class and family form to be far more complex than previously appreciated (Smith 1978, 1988)

In Trinidad there is some relationship between the distinction of transience and transcendence and that of wealth. The oil-boom wealth was certainly used by some to construct respectability based on property in a manner not previously open to them, as is evident in Newtown. By contrast, people in Ford sometimes talk of money spent out in the oil-boom in order to retain values which are threatened by wealth as accumulation.

As an ethnographer I found the highly nuanced class relations of British society to be very distinct from the situation I encountered in Trinidad, while the concept of bacchanal would be difficult to apply in the British context. Although the term class is more common in Port of Spain among both those educated abroad and more radicalised groups, locally it is rarely employed. A question about class in the survey found sixty out of 107 households describing themselves as middle-class, but this may be largely an artefact of the term 'middle-class' having the most salience. Very few people had a clear idea of some alternative term, often describing themselves as 'not middle' or using terms such as 'ordinary'. Many more households simply declined to address the question. A term which at first glance may appear to serve in its stead is the term 'social', but once again on closer inspection it may be used to suggest that class is refracted through dualism rather than vice versa. The Trinidadian word 'social' implies that the people so designated refuse to mix and, as noted above, this is certainly a feature of domestic life in wealthier communities such as The Meadows. This, however, is probably a simplification of a more complex concept. There are plenty of individuals in Ford who would be regarded as 'social', and yet do not have either the wealth or respectability which would lead them to aspire to a position above that of their neighbours. Equally, there are households in The Meadows who have fencing for security against robbery but are extremely well-known and outgoing either as limers or in terms of community activities, and would therefore never be described as 'social'. The term is also applied to events and occasions, for example, a woman at a fête or party who feels that people are not joining in and 'freeing up' may leave in disgust at the 'social' nature of the persons there, or a man who refuses a drink during a lime may be regarded as 'social'. The idea of being 'social' is more closely bound up with more specific and localised concepts of gossip, bacchanal and privacy.

The argument against using class as central to self-reference is made by Trinidadians themselves in discussing their ability to undermine the pretensions to class through their self-confidence and wit. The caustic taking people apart in the 'picong' of the lime may well extend to inter-class relations, as in one anecdote where an individual entering a new house may observe, 'what, you got a big chandelier there, boy' and expect to provoke uncontrollable laughter. It is a phlegmatic refusal of deference which is contrasted with what is seen as a more serious and often violent response projected onto Jamaica.

To take another example, Oxaal, who puts much more emphasis upon class relations, assumes that a hotel such as the Hilton would be intimidating to working-class Trinididadians in much the same way as institutions associated with power in Britain alienate those who feel excluded from them (1982: 16). My experience was quite different, in particular, I recall attending a wake in Ford where a conversation was taking place between four individuals, all impoverished and with little prospects of improvement, about the facilities at the Hilton and the relative merits of the various major hotels in Port of Spain. The discussion was extremely casual and had no sense of bravado or of inappropriate context. Part of the information imparted was about those events held at the Hilton which were free, as opposed to those where fees were charged and were therefore of no immediate interest, but this information was given in a factual mode with none of the frisson felt when one is self-consciously exploiting a system intended to deny one.

Many Trinidadians are very concerned with the possibilities of 'freeness', that is events such as fêtes and wakes where a meal or simply fun may be had for nothing. The search for 'freeness' plays a central role in many of the entries to the 'Spot the Trini' competition. Within the transient perspective, success is generally held to have come from luck rather than merit and to be a temporary attribute such that pretension today will soon be met by mockery tomorrow. Transience refuses any criteria which would render people as permanently high or low and insists that bacchanal will reveal the fundamental truth of equality. It is in transcendence, associated with possessions and at least aspiring storage of wealth, where deference is likely to be encountered.

The use of the term class is therefore of very variable analytical utility. It is most appropriate for those (and this would include a reasonable proportion of households in The Meadows) who have been educated abroad (or at University within Trinidad) and think in terms of the global concept of class. Use of the term in its global sense also becomes more relevant the closer one is to Port of Spain. It is also important in that consciousness of a race/class historical oppression which has become an increasing explicit category since the the time of Marcus Garvey and is therefore of greater resonance to some radicalized Blacks than for example, most Indians. But for the majority of the population, while they recognise transient distinctions in status between, for example, 'big-shot' people and the 'little man', there is a marked refusal to internalize class as an institutionalized form with its associated sense of deference and stability. Within transience, in particular, there are many strategies which undermine its pretensions.

This account of class as subjectivity would not, of course, in any way diminish an argument on Marxist lines for the existence of radical inequalities or forms of exploitation, the evidence for which is if anything accentuated by a perspective on four residential areas distinguished by extreme disparities of income and habitation. What does follow from the above account, however, is that the sense and experience of class pressure may be obfuscated rather than comprehended by attempting to lodge it within analytical forms which make class relations the causal foundation for a dualist habitus.

As was the case with gender it is perhaps easier to find class itself being re-constructed according to dualism. I noted above that there was little of interest revealed by the direct answers to the survey question on class. What was of considerable interest was the manner in which people considered the implications of this question. The context for the question is the rapid changes of oil-boom and recession, as a result of which many people, who would not previously have done so, started to think of themselves in terms of a middle-class category.

It is the recession which then splits the population radically. For those orientated towards transcendence, class or status seemed to be something which is achieved slowly through accretive development, and, once achieved, rather like an educational qualification, is internalised as an aspect of personhood and not at all easily lost. External conditions are the foundation for its development, but fluctuations in such conditions do not easily lead to a shift in personal self-classification. Recession, then, does not signify a fall in class position, rather it meant that external conditions were becoming inconsistent with one's achieved status and this was a contradiction which needed to be resolved. For many Indians (but also Chinese and Whites) the major resolution was emigration to North America, the land of 'real cornflakes'[1] where middle-class life was actually envisageable since its accoutrements were available. Where, as in this case, class was established as an aspect of being, then this disjuncture had to be resolved through a change in the external circumstances themselves. Because of the close association of lifestyle and place, Canada became the site where, even if one has less money, at least that money can be translated into goods which are of the requisite quality befitting the kind of person one has become.

The contrasting response was to reflect on the recession as itself symptomatic of a shift in class position. From the perspective of transience, class is a signifier of current status only. In discussing the possible answer to this question, it was suggested that a year or two earlier the response would have been to say middle-class, but, given the fall in the real value of salaries, the rise in prices and so forth, class position has clearly moved downwards. Class here is not internalised as a description of personhood but is a relationship between persons and a rapidly shifting external environment. Class position is to be read off circumstances and must change accordingly. In this case, class itself is transient.

Ethnicity

One of the main reasons gender and class appear less convincing candidates as foundational to cultural dualism in Trinidad than elsewhere in the Caribbean, is that in Trinidad there is an overwhelmingly obvious alternative candidate, that of ethnicity. This is certainly the dimension that is first looked to by most Trinidadians in their explanation for any generalised behavioural trait. I have little doubt that many Trinidadians will regard my refusal to label dualism in ethnic terms as being merely an obfuscation or political contrivance to avoid the accusation of racist or at least stereotypic intent.

In making such an identification the lines of articulation would be relatively straightforward. Structured kin relations, conservatism, an immense concern with property and inheritance, a propensity towards accumulation, brand and shop loyalty, normative furnishing and an antipathy to fêting might all be regarded as the abiding characteristics of the Indian population. By contrast, dyadic kin relations subservient to a pragmatic ethos, and an abiding concern with style and fêting especially in relation to Carnival, would be seen by many as characteristics of the African population. In terms of the specific temporal implications of the terms transience and transcendence, the Indian community is often characterised in relation to tradition and the long term, while the African community is viewed as orientated towards the short term (LaGuerre 1988). Such stereotypes are by no means restricted to the opposed community. An African taxi driver will 'apologise' how 'we people can't keep money' quite as often as an Indian will insist that 'we people must learn how to "free up".' Such stereotypes have for long been the source of strongly derogatory sentiments as noted by Klass for Indians (1961: 244) and Trotman for the African calypso (1989).

In a recent innovative and sensitive analysis of the development of similar ethnic stereotypes in Guyana, Williams (1991) argues for the importance of colonial policy and discourse. She notes (ibid: 127–54) how the images of ethnic groups were transformed in Guyana to facilitate the needs of the colonisers. As in Trinidad, Africans are rendered as lazy when planters want to argue for the importation of a new workforce to replace them. These stereotypes then become internalised by the ethnic groups themselves to become the competitive arguments about relative contribution to the nation. The impact of this hegemonic meta-discourse thereby continues to constrain the self-image of people dominated by the sense of shame, despite formal political indepedence. Many of Williams' arguments and characterisations seem to fit earlier developments in Trinidad which had many parallels to Guyana. There are, however, many important differences. The political history of Trinidad and its route through independence has been far less problematic. It has also been fortunate in that oil has given it comparative wealth for most of this century and incomparable wealth during part of the recent past. These and other fortuitous historical factors mean than the relationship between contemporary Trinidadians and modernity is likely to be rather less mediated by colonial discourses than is the case in Guyana (see Miller forthcoming).

As with class the degree of change may be measured against the best available baseline which was the survey in the 1950s by Braithwaite (1975). This work is certainly weakest when it comes to the treatment of Indians, but much of the discrepancy between the way he represents Trinidad and what would seem obvious today may be a result of the actual dynamism of Trinidadian society itself. More particularly, I would argue that the prime location for ascribing difference within Trinidadian society has itself shifted during the subsequent three decades. This would imply a remarkably rapid shift in the objective circumstance and also the self-perception of this society, but there is good evidence for precisely such dynamism, particularly if we consider the recent history of the Indian community.

For those who visit Trinidad today, one of the most surprising set of statistics to confront is the characterisation of the Indian population after the Second World war. At that period, when it is clear that the ex-slave population is already extremely distant from its ancestry in slavery and fast developing within the modern world, the Indians seem to be only just emerging out of the period of indentured labour and to represent a remnant peasantry, as far removed as any population in the Caribbean from the appropriation of these new possibilities. Most of the population was officially illegitimate since it was only at this period (1946) that Hindu marriage was legally recognised. Caste was seen as a sign of primitive backwardness with which the Muslim community would disparage the Hindus as one of a variety of fissionable elements within the Indian community. It was only at this time that the population disparity between the two sexes, which began with the differential importation of men as indentured labourers, had finally disappeared. The figures for education are among the most striking in that the 1946 Census of the British West Indies shows the Indians of Trinidad as having the highest level of illiteracy of any ethnic community in any of the islands: that is 50.6 per cent compared to the Black population of Trinidad with only 9.5 per cent (Smith 1974: 306). In general the community would at that time have been characterised as the most deprived and least developed in the area.

The oral history of local Indians reflects the same picture, with most people living in dwellings of traditional materials, using a traditional South Asian style of hearth. Chaguanas was then a slow, sleepy, larger village with cricket played in its main street. The orientation of the community was essentially rural with the distant 'other' being Port of Spain. In St Pauls the traditional *panchayat* was only just losing its authority and identity related to caste position, including lower castes such as *dom* or *chamar*, were still of major significance. The one major disruption to this sense of sloth was the impact of an American airbase situated a short distance to the south of Chaguanas, and the increasing impact of images from the United States representing a 'bright' modern world as against the colonial legacy of the British.

Although a powerful presence in oral history, the American influence is not so evident in the abundant descriptive ethnography available for this area, in particular from the monograph by Klass (1961), set in a village close to Chaguanas during 1957–8, but in other respects there is a close fit. In this book Klass devotes considerable attention to the discussion of Hindi kinship terminology (ibid: 94–108); there is a powerful legacy of traditional untouchability echoed in spatial segregation within the village, a work pattern almost completely dominated by the sugar estates, and a system of early marriage which is only then moving from arranged to approved. The tone of such academic reports emphasises a continuity with traditions derived from South Asia, although there is some acknowledgement (particularly in a similar study by Niehoff and Niehoff 1960) of the changes in house construction, the introduction of cars and so forth.

The next generation of fieldworkers show markedly different concerns. Nevadosmky (1982, 1983) returning to study the same site as Klass, defines himself by opposition. He emphasises change, including new freedoms in the organisation of marriage, the rise of consumer goods and the dominance of the nuclear family (for which see also Schwartz 1965), arguing for the construction of tradition rather than actual retention. Clarke (1986), working in urban San Fernando as well as in the rural context, agrees with the evidence for rapid change and a decline in distinctive social structures, but notes the maintenance of institutional and political separation despite spatial proximity.

By the late 1980s the pace of change in the Indian community seems to have accelerated, assisted, no doubt, by the oil-boom that took place subsequent to Clarke's main fieldwork period. While at the beginning of the decade Africans still enjoyed a significantly higher average income to Indians (Harewood and Henry 1985), the oil-boom almost certainly saw a reversal of this distinction. By 1988, in the Chaguanas area, it was not only arranged marriage and dowry that had essentially disappeared, but also the links to the sugar estates. Where Clarke found Hindi to be reasonably common in use, I found an expectation that one would have to hunt hard among the elderly or deeply religious to find anyone capable of speaking more than a few words of Hindi. Very few informants had a clear idea of their caste origins and the entire contents of Klass's (1961) chapter on Hindi kinship had become historical. These and other changes are confirmed by Klass himself during a recent return visit to Trinidad (Klass 1991: 45–68).

Perhaps most important in terms of marking change is the general shift in the self-conception of the Indian community from being a backward-looking peasantry to becoming the vanguard of Trinidadian society. Today the Indians are more likely to affirm that, out of all the ethnic groups in the old British West Indies, they are the best-educated, best-connected with metropolitan regions and most successful entrepreneurially. There is a sense of a community which has outgrown its own foundations, from which it feels a strong sense of alienation. So that, despite long-awaited political success in 1986, it had become evident by 1988 that many members of this community felt literally ready to move on – in this case to Canada. The year 1988 was a problematic time to characterise such a rise in fortunes, given the deepening of the recession, but community values had been forged during a decade of oil-boom and, at least in the early stages of fieldwork, this still dominated the self-representation of the community.

In the 1950s the Indian community might well have looked as though it was moving into the kind of ethnic-class hierarchy portrayed by Braithwaite (1975). Contrary to M. G. Smith's model of pluralism, which assumes a disparity of internal-organisation principles between different communities, and, more specifically, that the Indians did not use this colour criteria for internal segmentation (1974: 323–4), there is plenty of evidence that the Indians might have fitted comfortably within Braithwaite's single status emulation complex. The Indians' amalgamation of southern and darker Madrassi Indians as a virtual new untouchable class within Trinidad was based on traditional South Asian associations between caste and colour, but fitted well into this new context. By 1988, Indians are fully integrated into the continuance of this more general gradation, in so far as it is the lighter-skinned among the Indians who are most often found in the same banking and media work as light-skinned Africans. In addition, it is today probably the Indians who most often make explicit statements expressing positive emulation of whites. However, largely as a result of the changes in Trinidad which were accentuated by the oil-boom, the possibilities for ordering by class have been increasingly subordinated to a dominant ethnically based classification.

This process is well-exemplified in the fictional texts which have previously been used to illustrate contemporary Trinidadian ideologies. The key protagonists of *The House for Mr Biswas* and *The Dragon Can't Dance* are ethnically distinct, but not merely so.

When examined more closely they may be found to provide a quintessential picture of ethnicity which firmly grounds dualism in ethnic terms. Biswas (modelled on Naipaul's own father) is not just a representative of the Indian community. He is a Brahmin and as such a member of that group which was most concerned with the self-designation of the Indian as a specific entity within Trinidad, and which has dominated the leadership and expressive roles within the Hindu community at least. But then Biswas is not even a typical Brahmin: the house which dominates much of the book is the house in Chaguanas in which the leader of the political opposition was brought up. However unflatteringly portrayed by Naipaul, he was to become the semi-formal figurehead for the Indian community as a whole. Furthermore, even at this time Chaguanas had emerged as the best candidate for an alternative ethnic capital within Trinidad, as the site, for example, for the controversy over the *Arya-Samaj*. The world of this novel is almost exclusively Indian and high-caste. There are several dark references to Indians of lower caste living in much more humble conditions, with sexual liaisons with persons of other races. Indeed, throughout the book there is a general sense of the negro and sexuality as another world, kept as far as possible away from the kind of environment in which Biswas is portrayed.

A clear symmetry arises with Lovelace's main protagonist. Aldryck is not merely of African descent, but is situated up on a hill. This hill lyrically described within the novel will have immediate resonance as Laventille. It is Laventille rather than Port of Spain which is the undisputed capital of African culture in Trinidad, and as such is celebrated as the symbol of authenticity in the culture of Carnival, steelband and calypso. In the lyrics of contemporary calypso (e.g. David Rudder) Laventille is the wellspring where the best bards and musicians should ideally have become imbued with a sense of rhythm which emanates from the place itself. It is no coincidence that in a question as to which would be the worst place in Trinidad to live, the people of Newtown chose Laventille far more often than any other location. Thus by choosing Laventille Lovelace focuses not on the typical but on the quintessential. Lovelace seems to be working hard to portray Indian culture sympathetically within the novel in the figure of Pariag. Nevertheless, Pariag clearly embodies a certain sense of both family and property which lies in opposition to the dominant culture of the hill. This is portrayed by an incident over a bicycle which is seen as threatening to the basic ethos of egalitarian poverty, and then later in the novel through the expectations of Pariag's own family and finally in his role as shopkeeper (1981: 140–7, 206–12).

Both these novels express sentiments and expectations which are held much more widely in Trinidad today and, as such, they echo the close articulation between the values of transience and transcendence with that of ethnicity. Both novels also have texts which would emphasise the relation to class. Lovelace provides an alternative oppositional model in the kind of residential area to which the calypsonian Philo eventually migrates, while Biswas' struggle for respectability through property and his children's education suggests an increasingly important role for discrimination by comparative success. Similarly, both could be analysed on gender lines, since in Aldryck's relation to Sylvia, and equally in Biswas' relation to his wife, there is a consistent representation of the female as occupying a domestic space which men must resist in order to find authenticity and freedom. Nevertheless, because of the spatial and social location of both of the two protagonists, and because the two novels need to be seen in relation to each other as emergent from the same culture, it is ethnicity which emerges as the fundamental dimension of contrast, and this is a true reflection of that which would be found in most Trinidadian's conversational accounts.

Recent decades in Trindad have seen two related but, at first, paradoxical movements. The first is the growth of actual syncretism of the Indian and African populations; the second is the increasing tendency to define them in terms of a dualistic polarity. On many occasions during the previous chapters I have both described material in terms of ethnic contrast but also cautioned against the interpretation of other evidence in ethnic terms. There are areas in which ethnicity can be discerned in cultural distinctions, but both communities have historical backgrounds which can account for the particular relationship to property, for example, and the survey of house interiors showed remarkably little evidence of ethnic distinction.

Africans discussing the Indian population constantly referred to the rapidity of change among Indians and especially Indian women. There was, however, virtually no mention of an Indianisation to balance what was assumed to be a process of Creolisation. The assumption that Trinidadian and African culture were synonymous and that it was a question of whether an alien group would finally be assimilated, was one of the ideological constructions which most offended Indians, who saw this representation as government policy. As the media noted: 'most Indians had come to see the PNM as giving only token respect to Indian culture, while quietly trying to force a *callalloo* culture based on steelband, calypso and carnival' (*Guardian*, 31 January 1988).

The evidence from Chaguanas certainly suggests a two-way process, rather than a simple Creolisation. One of the best examples of Indianisation was a family in Newtown whose origins had been in the south of the country. When their son was born they asserted the custom of not cutting his hair until he reached a certain age; during the christening they handed round a plate for offerings of money from those who were attending. These are practices which are clearly Indian in origin, and caused some confusion, in the case of the christening, to a man who had come from Port of Spain and was completely unfamiliar with the idea of a plate being passed around for monetary donations. Many of their sayings and beliefs were also recognised by Indians as of South Asian origin. The family concerned would, however, be mortified at the suggestion that they were following practices of Indian as opposed to traditionally African custom. The further south one goes, the more evident this feature becomes. Bell, for example, noted that African women in the south seemed to marry later than in those in the north and he (and also Clarke 1986) appreciates that there has been an 'Indianisation' of social structure in this area.

The evidence for Creolisation is more widely acknowledged. At the level of explicit symbolic behaviour, the increasing presence of Indians, and especially Indian women at Carnival is evident, though this is not yet the case for professional steel-band performance. One of the most prominent calypsonians at the 1988 and 1989 Carnival season was an Indian female, Drupatee, whose songs with titles such as 'Hotter than a *Chulah*' and 'Pepper Pepper' promoted an Indian version of soca that became highly successful and is taking over from an older tradition of syncretic 'chutney' music. The development of the weekly newspapers was also important here, since these tended to be Indian-owned, as opposed to the dominance of Africans over the established daily papers. With their racy content, the weeklies projected an image of Indian life and scantily clad Indian women which placed them in the centre of that terrain which Indians had previously projected as being exclusively African. With the oil-boom money, Indians could enter into the clubs, the fashions and direct contact with metropolitan areas which were conceptually the centres of modern style.

Rather than seeing such shifts in terms of Indianisation or Creolisation, however, they may both be part of a larger syncretic pattern which is reducing the significance of ethnic contrasts in relation to a wide range of social and cultural practices. Most significant here is the evidence for homogenisation of social behaviour discussed in Chapter 4. Whether we look to age at marriage, nature of mating arrangement, size and form of family or virtually any other characterisation of social structure the evidence is for increasing similarity of practice. At the level of the upper classes there has emerged a consensual group based on international canons fostered in university education abroad and the same devotion to imported goods and the project of becoming 'sophisticated'. I recall how a group of these highly educated younger Indian women could gather at a cocktail party and note with feigned shock and evident pride that none of them were able to cook *roti*. An equally strong case could be made for syncretism among low-class religious practices centred around 'problem-solving' rituals related to Kalimai temples, the use of experts in *Obeah*, and increasing Indian influence in areas such as the Shango cult (Mahabir and Maharaj 1989) and Spiritual Baptist churches (Glazier 1983).

The growing cultural similarities between the two numerically dominant ethnic groups coexists with a number of factors which have led to the preservation, if not the enhancement, of a separate ethnic consciousness and continued ethnic antipathy. Most Trinidadians seeking to account for an ethnic rivalry which, while avoiding violent conflict in recent decades, is clearly manifest in everyday conversation, tend to lay the blame squarely on the impact of politics.

Oral history in St Pauls continually asserts that there had once been a time when the ethnic communities were increasingly sharing cultural festivals such as Christmas, Carnival and Hosay and that this was leading to a more general sense of integration, but that this trend went sharply into reverse with the advent of democratic politics, after which the division between Indians and the rest became increasingly entrenched. For example, an Indian taxi driver noted: 'Politics is responsible for everything (good-will) dwindling away. I myself was hurt, when I say hurt, I did taxi work here for 14 years and when election came I had to take a side and I took the Indian side for that matter, and the negros didn't travel with me, so I had to give up the taxi and go look for work.' This contention is echoed in the writings of Naipaul who portrays the ethnically divisive effects of vote securing in his book *The Suffrage of Elvira* (1958).

Clarke (1986:3), quoting from Naipaul to this effect, argues within a general pluralistic model that politics acts to transform what are already constituted as corporate categories into clear corporate groups (ibid: 141), though noting the complexities of class and religion which cross-cut this picture. The context for this debate over the impact of politics is the dominance of the PNM for thirty years, and the litany of complaints by Indians that Eric Williams' government systematically marginalised their interests, for example, in the preference of industry to agriculture (Hintzen 1989: 73–7, 198), the closure of the railway system, the allocation of educational scholarships and many others examples. The local *cause célèbre* was the failure of the government to support the Divali Nagar as the festival of Indian culture which has become established as an annual event in Chaguanas.

Indians who supported and enjoyed the patronage of the PNM are presumed to include only particular groups. One would be élites sympathetic to the government's suppression of the Black Power movement of 1970, to which few Indians felt affiliated. Another would be Christians and Muslims using politics to express traditional divisions within the Indian community. Thus Ryan (1991b 127–9) argues that voting patterns are less tied to ethnicity among Indians than among Africans.

The resulting sense of alienation was evident in a sometimes ambiguous identity as in the anecdote heard from several Muslims about someone returning from a Pakistan v. West Indies cricket match to announce, 'We won, I mean we lost'. To offset this mar-ginalisation, Indians have promoted their own cultural projects and also attempted to revitalise their religious traditions, using, as Vertovec has noted (1992: 162–97), the proceeds of the oil-boom.

The complaints by Indians find their symmetry in the growth of accusations directed against them, though in this case it is other sources of power, mainly economic, which are held to be abused. Most Africans welcome the individual Indian as a liming partner or companion, but argue that it is the Indian community in general, with its avarice and power, that is putting too much pressure on the poor Black population. From the less circumspect emerge much wider conspiracy-theory-style 'anecdotes', such as about Indian doctors only recommending hysterectomies for Blacks and priding themselves on the number of 'nigger wombs' they have removed. Trotman (1989) argues that calypsos provide an historical account of African derogatory stereotypes of other groups. In 1988 the Dimanche Gras calypso Monarch competition was won with two songs, one of which was called, 'Corruption in Common Entrance', is an explicit accusation of preference given in the education system to Indians or at least against Africans. A recent book titled *Eight East Indian Immigrants* (de Verteuil 1989) fully illustrates the stereotype which has emerged. The first chapter is called 'Coming in search of money', and the final chapter is called 'The curse of too much money'. It is worth recalling that this is directed at a community which until recently was among the most impoverished in the Caribbean!

De Verteuil demonstrates the use of a highly selective history in the emergence of the new stereotypes (for a more critical approach to modern stereotypes see Ryan 1991c). To construct the massive shift from the trajectory portrayed by Braithwaite based on the symbolism of the white community to the emergence of ethnic dualism today has necessitated a very specific use of history to construct the origin myths of both the main communities, which then match the portraits presented in the two novels discussed above. The history of the African becomes simplified in a number of ways. First, it is homogenised as based solidly in slavery, although much of the evidence suggests that the sheer number of alternative sources of immigration – ranging from free immigrants from Africa to demobilised American soldiers – probably make the direct descendants from Trindadian slaves a minority within the African population overall. Second, there is a great stress on the development of an urban-based population directed towards emancipation and the cosmopolitan. What is increasingly neglected are the traditions of African property-based and descent-orientated social structure which formed the foundation for that element of West Indian kinship which is not that typified in the debates about 'West Indian Kinship'. This includes the so-called cocoa peasantry, which established a strong agrarian base and might well have provided the kind of conservative but entrepreneurial peasantry found in neighbouring Barbados (Shepherd 1932; Ryan 1991c: 171–4).

Amongst the evidence in refutation of the developing assumptions about 'African' patterns, is the work of Macdonald and Macdonald (1973) whose studies demonstrate the problems with the supposed 'culture of poverty' argument, and also the assumption that Africans are entirely sundered from their traditions while Indians represent pure continuity. Among their most telling evidence are the statistics which indicate that in Tobago, where a small-holding peasantry managed to establish itself, the subsequent patterns of kinship are in many respects closer to those associated with Indians in Trinidad than with Africans in Trinidad (ibid: 177). Popular history prefers to remember Africans as refusing to have anything to do with the land after emancipation. This was partly fostered by the records of the contemporary landholders themselves who may well have exaggerated this antipathy to agriculture in order to argue for a new scheme of indentured labour to replace slavery.

The history of the Indian becomes then the inverse of that of the African. Indians are seen as almost exclusively agrarian until recent times and the stress is constantly on continuity with ancient South Asian traditions. The population is again homogenised, such that differences which grew up between, for example, the sugar-plantation labourers and those based in citrus or cocoa areas are largely ignored. Just as new historical evidence is revealing greater continuity among the African population of the Caribbean than was once thought (Mintz and Price 1976) so recent work on the Indian population is showing a greater degree of rupture and constructed homogenisation in the late nineteenth-century (Vertovec 1992: 92–127).

To conclude from this survey, it must be admitted that, on this issue at least, the perspective from Chaguanas is a particular one, and would probably not accord with fieldwork based, for example, in Port of Spain. In the capital, the white population has a much greater presence and the trajectory implied by Braithwaite might still appear of considerable importance. My expectation would be, however, that the ethnic dynamics portrayed above, which have made ethnicity the key vehicle for the objectification of dualism, is spreading to all parts of Trinidad.

There is some contingency here, as much will depend upon the particular political developments, since as Eriksen (1991) has pointed out in comparing the situation to Mauritius, ethnicity can develop in a quite different and less dualistic manner. Once contingency can be admitted, the assumed direction of linkage between ethnicity and dualism may be challenged. As with gender and class, we can stop looking to ethnicity as the cause of dualism, and instead investigate why ethnicity is emerging in the form of opposed stereotypes at exactly the same time as historically we find considerable syncretism.

This perspective allows for a re-examination of the recent study of inter-ethnic relations by Clarke in order to draw rather different conclusions. As a geographer Clarke was particularly interested in spatial interaction and studied an area where spatial integration is pronounced, that is the second largest town of San Fernando. His main conclusion is that: 'Spatial proximity does not necessarily make for social integration or reduce social separation in other spheres of life, contrary to popular belief: household structural similarities do not imply commonality let alone intimacy' (1986 i). All this is certainly justified by his research results, and would also be supported by the evidence from Chaguanas, where there is also formal inter-ethnic visiting during festivals such as Christmas but, in general, the dominant pattern is intra-ethnic sociality.

Clarke sees this lack of social interaction as evidence for the continuity of the type of pluralism analysed by M. G. Smith. In order to do so, he has to agree that social proximity is not the key variable which determines the nature of inter-ethnic relations. But he moves from downplaying proximity to privileging social interaction, which itself becomes the key variable and the basis for a description of the actual relations between ethnic groups. Yet Clarke's general findings could equally well support the evidence presented above for the increasing fusion between the two communities at the level of cultural and social practices. Clarke provides considerable evidence for homogenisation, including upper-class social structure, where both African and Indians are taken as emulating the Creole and colonial family, also through the tendency of Christian Indians to emulate Creole cultural patterns and towards syncretism of lower-class cultural customs (Clarke 1986: 84–5, 110, 133).

Clarke is thereby faced with a paradox. He states that: 'The experience of San Fernando's Christian Indians shows that even if Hinduism and Islam were lost and objective cultural distinctions became nil, racial boundaries would probably remain intact and provide the basis for social segmentation and political alignment' (Clarke 1986: 150). This is certainly borne out by the circumstances of Northern Ireland, where the degree of political conflict is hardly matched by any strong cultural distinctions between Catholics and Protestants. It is the same paradox which is found in juxtaposing the increasing evidence for cultural syncretism with the persistence of political division.

The focusing upon dualism, rather than pluralism, suggests that the use of ethnicity, in this case to construct difference, is best understood comparatively, for example, in relation to the use of gender or class elsewhere in the Caribbean. In Trinidad ethnicity appears to dominate class. The African middle-class would certainly wish to project themselves in terms quite opposed to the stereotypical 'African' as evident in their contempt for Laventille. They remain more extensive than the Indian middle class, and clearly dominant in the capital Port of Spain. The problem, however, for this group is the rapid rise in the fortunes of the Indians in the last three decades, and the focus of attention on what that might presage. This has led to a shifting of the larger stereotypes, and the suppression of other divisions in so far as they have become inconsistent with the increasingly dominant ethnic distinction. Many values which the African middle class see as their own are thereby becoming Indianised. The new polarity grants the Indian the mantle of entrepreneurial achievement/greed, and renders Africans as feckless but free. In contrast then to the nation-of-retailers image which Greenfield (1966) paints for Barbados, the African population of Trinidad is increasingly seen as having neither the inclination not aptitude for such work, and their success in this domain, as also in management, is ignored.

It is clearly ethnicity where dualism as an explicit discourse is most clearly acknowledged in Trinidadian life, and it is the domain through which dualism is represented and argued through. The lengthy descriptions which are given of people who live only for the event, spend their money out, emphasise style but know how to enjoy life, or equally those who can plan and save, but are mean and oppressive, who can be true to their family but exclude others, all these are presented as ethnicity. The impact of dualism is therefore increasingly to make each ethnic group perceive itself as a polarity within a structure. Thus when Clarke (1986) notes that: 'Indians in San Fernando have forged a sense of identity more in opposition to Creole dominance than with reference to their own receding past' (79), I take this to be not the cause but the consequence of dualism. This discourse refuses to acknowledge many of the changes in society and culture which can actually be observed: the vast movement of Indian men into the culture of liming, fêting and the event, the increasing power of Evangelical Christianity and strident domesticity and thrift which characterise many African families. The kind of evidence put forward in Chapter 6 for the homogenisation of the living-room would generally be denied. A 'real' Trinidadian could tell the difference, as they could instantly recognise the ethnicity of the person they encounter. Even the briefest acquaintance with discussions of Orientalism or anti-Semitism would establish the point on a comparative basis, but it is remarkably hard when living within Trinidad to escape from the pervasive sense (pervasive equally in the frequency with which it is vehemently denied by the media in the interests of giving a positive profile to the country) that ethnicity really is 'it'.

This dualistic discourse also increasingly plays down the significance of all other ethnic groups in Trindad. At one time the White population was the pivotal point from which other ethnic generalisations were generated. In Trinidad, as in Belize (Wilk 1990), television has rendered the Whites' previous knowledge of metropolitan styles redundant. Today they are increasingly anomalous themselves, as having the resources and power of transcendence while being often overtly irreligious and immodest. In a sense their shift away from the limelight has suited them very well as they have shifted the basis of their power from political control to the dominance of economic institutions, as is evident when one goes into the the managerial offices of almost any large Port of Spain-based enterprise, from the advertising industry through to manufacturing.

Other ethnicities which complicate any attempt to project a simple dualism include the Chinese who have played an important role in the Chaguanas area, and the Syrians, a group with powerful business interests in the capital but who are virtually unrepresented in Chaguanas. Much more important is the general question of mixed or Creolised populations. As noted in the Introduction it is often the 'red' or the *dougla* who seem to suffer the most opprobrium, but there is also a sense that the potential of the mixed population to provide a model for the authenticity of the new Caribbean is also starting to emerge, as, for example, in the incorporation of images of the Spanish in Christmas noted in Chapter 3, though as yet there is nothing that amounts to the kind of celebration of the cultural potential of the Mestizo which is found in radical Latin America.

Conclusion

As noted at the beginning of this chapter, the problem is not that it is hard to find an explanation for the observations of the previous chapters, but rather there are simply too many convincing and plausible 'causes' for any particular trait. Transience could come from almost anywhere. There is the concept of rupture, which now looks as though it could be applied to the Indian as well as the African population. There is the influence of both a popular culture and social structure in England and, more especialy in France, which now looks very different from the kind of nuclear family and model domesticity which was once supposed to be the colonial model. There has been the impact of colonial interests and prejudices which, as Williams (1991) shows for Guyana, can become the crucial ingredient in the formation of local but enduring cultural categories. There are also the external influences which range from the stereotype of the Black analysed by Fanon, to the influence of the American soldiers during the war, to the recent oil-boom.

Trinidad has never been short of origins, and if the result today was merely a pluralistic cacophony of different voices and experiences – the kind of postmodern portrait which current academic fashions wish to project onto all parts of the world – then there would be little problem in accounting for this result. But Trinidad today, for all its Creolised origins, is anything but a cacophony. The analysis of Christmas in Chapter 3 revealed a highly normative ritual creating a sense of a specific and rooted national culture, in clear structural tension (as exemplified in the rituals of Old Year's Night) with an equally specific variant of global culture: that is Trinidadian Carnival. It matters very little that historical sources show that virtually every trait which today is now seen as typified by Carnival was once objectified most fully by Christmas. The dualism expressed in the festivals was also found, in subsequent chapters, to provide the foundation for social organisation and the appropriation of mass consumption. Clearly, then, there remains something to be accounted for. Histories are continually being 'revised' in order to provide legitimations for quite specific social alignments which seem to act as the objectification of basic cultural contradictions.

This conclusion also provides the basis for a comparative question, in which Trinidad is understood in the context of the anthropology of the Caribbean. If dualism is not an imposition reflective of fashion in the discipline of anthropology, but a particular characteristic of the region, then it seems to be objectified distinctly in the various islands. Assuming that most of the accounts one reads are reasonable for their particular islands, then gender is the key domain in Providencia, class is the dominant dimension of difference in Jamaica, and it is certainly clear that in contemporary Trinidad ethnicity is *primus inter pares*.

Other social dimensions could have served. To take one more example, an earlier ethnography of nearby Barbados by Greenfield (1966), provides an excellent counterpoint to Trinidad. Once again there is a quite distinct dualism, which for Greenfield is based in the lifecycle. The shift between two opposing value systems is represented as a temporal shift activated by when a man can afford a wedding and his own house. At this point he may firmly reject many of the values with which had had previously been associated and adopt those which he had hitherto denigrated. The same phenomenon has been noted for Trinidad, especially in Newtown, but in Trinidad this is subservient to ethnicity. As noted above, virtually all the main characteristics and values which Greenfield describes as African for Barbados are described as Indian for Trinidad. The African of Barbados is stereotyped as highly entrepreneurial with a particular emphasis on retailing, and focused upon educational advancement. At one point it would have seemed that the same could have been said for Trinidad, but the way things are going it seems there will soon come a point at which it will be forgotten that retailing and educational achievement could ever have been a distinctly African ambition.

The point of a comparative context is that it moves the goal of interpretation from highly specific historical trajectories and current tensions to more general concerns. Once they are considered in relation to other Caribbean studies it becomes evident that, although the study of ethnicity, age, gender and class in any particular island all have their place, there are also grounds for asking some further questions. Although Wilson (1973) has been criticised, in this chapter, for his particular interpretations of gender, the question this led to, as to whether there was a particular dialectic to Caribbean societies (ibid: 220–3), remains pertinent.

It is then the conclusion to this chapter which provides one of the main justifications for the title of this book. What has been argued is a repudiation of the dominant attempts to explain the main characteristics of Trinidadian and possibly some wider Caribbean social relations. Others have tried to privilege one or other of the sociological parameters described here as providing the underlying explanation for more general aspects of social life. Of course, the forms and patterns of social intercourse have to be understood within the specific and particular histories and often contingent events. But this specificity does not prevent the drawing of analogies and comparisons in order to attempt analytical characterisation of certain key contradictions which may be common to a number of such instances.

One aim of the present project is simply to refine our views of modernity by subjecting them to ethnographic illustration. But the other aim, which emerges from this chapter, is that the foundational and consistent feature found in recent ethnographic accounts may itself be better appreciated if it is referred back to a theoretical debate about the nature of modernity which could at least account for the existence of this dualism and why it should be pervasive in this particular time and region. This depends in turn on the argument in the first chapter that the Caribbean has indeed claims to be a particularly likely region for the manifestation of certain key components and traits associated with the condition of modernity. In the final chapter I want to return to the argument that this dialectic finds its source in the intrinsic contradictions of modernity, but as a particular, unpredictable and contingent manifestation.

Notes

1. The phrase 'real cornflakes' became central to the internal debate on this issue. A reporter for a daily newspaper wrote a farewell to Trinidad letter in the paper before emigrating. She gave the inability to find 'real conflakes' any more as one example of her need to move. This point was taken up in a number of letters and articles which followed in the press discussing the grounds for the current wave of emigration.

Chapter 7

Modernity as a Specific Condition

Modernity is more often evoked than described. A particular scene in a film, a political event and its global transmission. These are the kind of 'illustrations' provided to the otherwise largely theoretical debates about the nature of modernity. In this book, by contrast, the intention has been to employ a series of traits and expectations derived from this general literature as the background frame through which a more sustained description of contemporary Trinidad is to be viewed. The general literature on modernity is only now returned to the foreground in order to help account for that dualism which the last chapter suggested more conventional sociological and anthropological approaches fail convincingly to encompass.

This final chapter has three main aims. The first is to consider the dualism which features so strongly in the previous chapters. The argument is that dualism should be understood as manifesting, within this specific context, contradictions which are inherent in modernity. But this is not to argue any necessity by which contradictions of modernity have to be manifested as dualism. Having established this point it is then possible to consider more generally the contribution which theories of modernity make to the understanding of contemporary Trinidad. Finally, the argument is reversed to consider the contribution that an ethnography which is inevitably of a specific situation can make to the literature on modernity as a general condition. This is attempted in two parts, first by drawing out the implication of relativism and second by arguing that consumption itself has become the critical process by which the link between modernity as general theory and modernity as specific case-study can be drawn. 'Can' be drawn, but also 'should' be drawn since this emphasis upon consumption provides the condition for self-respect which may aid in rejecting the 'mimic men' attitude to which all countries, otherwise designated as 'peripheral', are subjected by the dominant perception of modernity. As such the deliberate juxtaposition of theory and ethnography may not only enhance theoretical debate but also mediate in the colloquial 'consumption' of such theories.

The arguments for the particular suitability of Trinidad to the ethnographic study of modernity were given in Chapter 1. After a birth in the extreme alienation of slavery and indentured labour, followed by a century of complex immigration and emigration, this highly Creolised island had, by the period of fieldwork, experienced an alternative state of relative self-confidence reflected in the oil-boom stories about lavish holidays abroad, and the echo of previous dependency and oppression which returned with the current recession. The argument is not that Trinidadians are unable to overcome their historical legacy. Many instances have been given of their ability to appropriate imported forms and images. Rather, history has given Trinidadians a rapid education in the fluctuating fortunes of the international economy and subsequent possibilities of both appropriation and oppression which make the issues of modernity particularly pertinent. In short, history demonstrates the fragility of the condition of self-creation, where identity may be positively constructed, but against a background awareness of the possibility of this other consciousness, one saturated in the sense of alienation and insignificance.

The experience of this legacy of Creolisation, internal oppression and external degradation is not merely theorised here; its actuality has been thrown into the foreground by Trinidad's best-known novelist. The title of one of V. S. Naipaul's books *The Mimic Men* (1967) is commonly employed in Trinidadians' self-deprecating descriptions of themselves as a people who can do nothing but emulate, though few would go as far as Naipaul's savage indictment found in *The Middle Passage* (1962: 40–85), where he argued that given the brutality of its historical origins nothing could ever be created in Trinidad. Naipaul specifically associated Trinidad with the sense of (flawed) modernity which means: 'constant alertness, a willingness to change, a readiness to accept anything which films, magazines and comic strips indicate as American, beauty queens and fashion parades are modern' (ibid: 46), 'but modernity in Trinidad, then, turns out to be the extreme susceptibility of a people who are unsure of themselves, and having no taste or style of their own, are eager for instruction' (ibid: 47). The point is not that these comments have turned out to be sustainable as a characterisation but that they represent a constant possibility for self-characterisation, as a people who can never be 'themselves', only second-rate versions of someone else. What does indeed make Trinidadians modern is the fragility of their self-creation. Even the best-loved of its cultural emblems, such as Carnival, can and have been dismissed by the kind of self-deprecating scorn which Naipaul expresses.

Trinidad is clearly a society which potentially has a strong sense of rupture, a radicalisation of the present with the concomitant effect that it cannot rely on a clear sense of custom or a morality that is defended as mere custom emergent from 'roots' in the land. It thereby meets the first criteria defined by Habermas from Hegel. There is little danger here of what Hegel saw as *sittlichkeit* deadened by positivity. There are, however, clear differences between the historical trajectory leading to the experience of modernity in Trinidad and that which leads to modern Europe. Indeed, it would be hard to find comparable examples of unremitting rupture, alienation or the denigration of custom in Europe. This would imply that in so far as there is commensurability between the concept of modernity as applied in the two regions, the experiences and consequences in the Caribbean are likely to be that much more extreme. In Europe, the processes which evolve into modernity are diluted by the much slower transformations of deeply conservative social orders such as the peasantry and class structure. This may account for a number of the findings of the present ethnography. What emerges as ambivalence (but framed by disparate material culture such that it does not become confrontation) in seventeenth-century Amsterdam may become a powerful dualism in the Caribbean, based on identities defined by contrast. A general debate in Europe about freedom, most fully realised in a small élite or bohemian avant-garde, may become a much more potent experience of radical freedom in the Caribbean which is evident as a possibility pervading everyday life. The search for roots in painfully constructed ethnic identities and the development of Protestantism in Europe may become a much more assertive proselytising religiosity and assertion of roots in the Caribbean.

There is a danger here of a return to the more mechanistic grounding of comparative analysis. The differences which exist between Europe and the Caribbean arise not because they are two different stages of a unilineal evolutionary process but because of many contingent, unpredictable historical events and forces which happen to have occurred and were not necessarily part of some anticipated stream. I do not want to suggest that Trinidad is more 'truly' modern than some other society or region, or that it represents some quintessence of modernity. Rather, the intention is to open the way towards an anthropological analysis of comparative modernities informed by ethnographic detail. As was evident in the previous chapter I have chosen to focus upon a particular approach to modernity which may assist in comprehending particular observations about Trinidadian society. There are many alternative approaches to modernity that have not been highlighted here.

The implication of this reading of Trinidadian history and contemporary society is that a particular attempt to consider some of the implications of abstract principles of culture by Hegel and Habermas, seems pertinent to the findings of ethnography. This may be related to the degree of historical rupture and present fragility in Trinidadian culture and its exposure to difference, without implying historical necessity. Much of the clarity of this relationship has only emerged through the effects of the oil-boom, the coming of which has absolutely nothing to do with the previous history of the country or any characteristic of its varied population, but is entirely fortuitous.

Objections to Dualism

Neither of the two main terms I have used in the description of Trinidadian culture, that is 'transience' and 'transcendence', are much used in Trinidad, and where they are used they may not have the connotations which they have been given here. I have, however, preferred them to the use of a local term such as 'bacchanal' since I suspect that a different effect is achieved by the use of a local, as opposed to an imported, terminology, in such circumstances. My intention in using terms, which are clearly impositions, is to highlight the process of academic mediation in attempting something which would not normally be undertaken by local participants.

To consider these terms as analytical abstractions is not to imply that they are not well grounded in Trinidadian life and experience. On the contrary, they are intended to satisfy the verification criteria of the qualitative social sciences, by accounting for certain observable phenomena more convincingly than other forms of representation might have done. While there have been no pretensions to positivistic hypothesis testing or any assumption that the descriptive account is ultimately 'objective' outside the influence of my presumptions or intentions, I assume that the account is constantly moulded by observations which constraint it. What is imposed as academic is the constant imperative to provide an understanding of the experiences of fieldwork at a level of abstraction and generality which may be of limited immediate interest to those who are primarily concerned with practical issues arising from their specific circumstance. This imperative comes from the desire to comprehend and teach about comparative cultural studies, common to academics inside and outside the Caribbean.

The plausibility of the dualism itself comes from the weight of the descriptive material which it can encompass. In chapter three it was the existence of the two festivals, their centrality to Trinidadian life and the evidence for their systemic opposition. In the following chapter it was the simultaneity of two apparently opposed ways of organising and conceiving of family life and the evidence for a systematic opposition between two media of objectification, that is property and sexuality. Later on, the evidence comes from the manner in which consumer goods were being appropriated and the particular nature of ethnicity as ideology in Trinidad. I would expect that most (though of course by no means all) Trinidadians, from that social fraction relevant to any specific section of my account, would recognise and affirm the descriptive details.

This does not mean that there are not alternative explanations or relevant approaches for many of these same phenomena. To an extent I have played down domains such as religion and politics simply because they are so fully covered in previous academic accounts and in a wide range of recent books on Trinidad. I have also made little use of the material on commerce and power since these will be more fully explored in a subsequent volume. The perspective taken here is not intended as comprehensive, but is selected and organised in a manner which allows the Trinidadian material to be rendered within a comparative argument about the nature of modernity.

Nor should the use of analytical anthropology be opposed to ethnographic realism. It has certainly been my intention in the previous chapters to evoke something of the 'spirit' of Christmas or bacchanal, the depth of feelings about ethnicity, the emotive violence of inheritance disputes and so forth. Any failure here would be one of my own writing ability and style. Indeed, this is one of the reasons I have used Trinidadian novelists: to exemplify themes which I observed, but felt I was ill-equipped to transmit, in comparison to the eloquence of Trinidadian writers.

Another objection to an emphasis upon dualism might derive from the nature of dualism itself as an organisational principle. At one level it is so simple as to appear universal, the basis of the binary system and so forth. This would imply that it is merely banal. Yet the argument here is that dualism operates in a manner in Trinidad which is not commonly found. It is not fundamental to most class or caste systems. For this reason no implications are drawn from dualism as cognitive tendency or ability. Rather, it is the specific use of dualism as a normative order which is at issue.

This distinction may be illustrated by a comparison between the typical perspective which emanates from the transcendent and the transient respectively. Transcendence itself does tend to the dualistic, where, for example, it creates radical splits between the categories of family verses non-family, or moral and immoral. By contrast, there is nothing dualistic about transience as a perspective. Transience tends to construct as gradation, for example, degree of ethnicity or relative inclusion within family membership. The approach developed by Douglas (1966) towards category formation and the avoidance of ambiguity would fit very well within transcendence, but would be quite inappropriate when applied to transience. The latter is a perspective which seems to thrive on ambiguity and employ it for stylistic creativity.

The terms transience and transcendence are not direct translations of any Trinidadian term or concept, nor should we expect any individual or group of people to be consistent with respect to the set of values which are homogenised by the use of such terms. These terms are applied with the intention of what Bourdieu called a: 'methodological objectivism, a necessary moment in all research, by the break with primary experience and the construction of objective relations which it accomplishes, demands its own supersession' (1977: 72). Dualism does simplify in the interests of explanation, and Trinidadian society is as diverse and unpredictable as any other. The method is justified in that through abstraction we can account for that consistency which can be observed in the minutiae of everyday life, from a minor ritual such as 'sticking the cake', to the grand gestures represented by the existence of Carnival.

I do not want to give the impression that dualism is itself closely linked to modernity in general, although I have certainly argued that it provides the primary form of modernity for Trinidad. This does not mean, however, that all modern societies are dualist or all dualisms are modern. Dualism is much too simple a principle to be claimed for historical specificity. I would affirm, as argued in Chapter 2, the centrality of contradiction to modernity, but dualism is only one of many possible outcomes of this. The same applies to the content of this dualism. The local equivalent to transience may occupy only a highly marginal position, if that, in some other region of the world.

Dualism should therefore not be the focus of attention, it is primarily an instrument of order for my academic presentation of Trinidadian modernity. I cannot say what place it has in the subjectivities of Trinidadians except as it is manifested in particular discourses such as ethnicity. Of much greater importance is the content, the particular traits and values, which are the subject of this ordering into oppositions. It is, however, worth concluding this discussion of ordering principles by clarifying the relationship between individuals and that which is implied by the use of two generalised terms. This may be accomplished in part by reference to what has become the best-established attempt to create an anthropological perspective on the mechanisms which link subjectivity to order: that is the concept of 'habitus' as used by Bourdieu (1977).

There has been considerable debate about the degree of fixity which readers of Bourdieu perceive the habitus to possess as a model of the inculcation of generative order through the socialisation of individuals in society. Bourdieu is at pains to argue for flexibility and strategy in the manner by which individuals in their practices translate habitus into action, but in the main, habitus itself is described through the structural homologies between the different domains upon which everyday taxonomies are inscribed.

In Chapter 6 an example of such structural homologies was given in the homologies between dualism as expressed in gender, class and ethnicity, but the point was made that this was not because they reflected the habitus of people but rather because people were objectified as an expression of dualism. If the starting point was the individual then the model of habitus becomes problematic. There are indeed certain individuals who consistently inhabit one of the two extreme poles and it makes sense to talk of them as 'transient' or 'transcendent' people. But most Trinidadians have affinity with both of these sets of values, such that one might refer rather to 'habiti' than 'habitus', or at least to a habitus based upon contradiction.

It is noticeable that many of the best exemplifications of habitus presented by Bourdieu in, for example, his description of the Kabyle house or distinctions in French taste, come from the analysis of material culture. The implication of this was rendered explicit in Chapter 5 where it was argued that arrays and orders of objects were not a secondary manifestation of subjectivities but were more properly conceived as the primary objectification of values and orders, in which groups of people as, in effect, arrays of objects are then also incorporated. If we reject the romantic notion that the increasing importance of commodities is necessarily a diminution in the humanity of the people who use them, this has the advantage that, while we sometimes become disturbed by the inconsistencies and partial commitments of people, it is less problematic to find contradiction and ambivalence signified in objects.

At this point the tendency to structure in Bourdieu's work might be contrasted with the tendency to 'anti-structure' in the recent work of anthropologists such as Strathern (1991). Strathern is attempting to describe or at least evoke the more complex world which follows from an emphasis less on order than on 'partial connections,' sometimes linked, sometimes disconnected or transformed into alternative domains of objectification, often again utilising arrays of objects. Strathern notes that our perception of order is constantly dependent upon the focus of our analysis moving from micro to macro concerns. This suggests an habitus of bits and pieces, of partial evocations each apparently specific to its own level of perception but also partly evocative of some larger but again partial order. Identity is formed through such partial connections and differences which echo across the timescale of observation. The distinction between transience and transcendence is thus at one moment represented as the ethos of the day versus that of the night, but at another moment in this book it is a seasonal difference, represented by Christmas v. Carnival. It may be a key lifecycle contrast as people are seen to flip from the values of their youth to the values of parents, but this also evokes a major part of the understanding of social distinction essentialised as gender or ethnicity. Rarely are these found in the complete or abstract form as painted in this volume: they are experienced as partial orders, partial commitments to being a certain kind of person, and very often as ambivalence.

The idea that dualism is better explored as found within the habitus of individuals rather than expressing a contrast between individuals, and is composed of partially ordered evocations of other partial orderings is quite compatible with the suggestion that Schama's historical ethnography of Amsterdam provides a precursor to the present project. Indeed, it is worth repeating in full the quotation given in Chapter 2: 'As in many other departments of Dutch culture, opposite impulses were harmoniously reconciled in practice ... Nor did it take any lofty wisdom to see that the world was not torn asunder between abstinence and indulgence. Any fool could see that the *same people* embodied, at different times, in different places, the values appropriate to their impermanent role' (Schama 1987: 371). With respect to Trinidad the same point may be illustrated by a return to the person whom most Trinidadians would regard as the funniest figure in Trinidadian fiction, that is Tanti Merle, with the implication that the fictional figure is a close pastiche of elements found in many real Trinidadians. Reports of Paul Keens-Douglas' superb performances of his own material almost always start by invoking their 'truth' to life.

Most of the stories which involve Tanti Merle have the same basic structure in which she arrives as the symbol of respectability denouncing the wickedness she encounters, but then becomes drawn into the event in such a manner that she becomes the instrument for collapsing everything into utter chaos and disorder (a fact which she, of course, never recognises). For example, in 'Party Nice' (Keens-Douglas 1979: 87–95) the author portrays himself as intending a very small quiet birthday celebration which gets expanded by his friends into a full-scale party. When Tanti Merle unexpectedly arrives:

> She stop in de doorway an' survey de scene,
> Den she take over.
> She say, 'Turn down de music it too loud

Where all yu tink yu is, in de market?

After a few drinks, however, Tanti Merle becomes the life and soul of the party with a very different talk:

Don't dig nutten, we gotta keep ah clean scene
Ah am de cool fool with de live jive

The party ends with Tanti Merle falling through the floor and the arrival of the police. Similarly in 'Tanti at de Oval' (Keens-Douglas 1976: 26–32), she is taken to an important cricket match, arriving with a pink parasol and a huge basket of food, but 'Dat same Tanti Merle dat look as if butter can't melt in she mout' starts 'cussing out' the umpire and finally leads a pitch invasion.

Tanti Merle captures the spirit of bacchanal precisely because of her pretensions to something quite different, her desire to emulate a lifestyle and set of values which can, for her, only be a façade which will collapse at any moment to reveal the true nature of honest disorder. Of course, Tanti Merle is never a true picture of transcendence, this is only her pretension to that kind of order, nor is she a good model of transience which is only her 'failing'. She partially inhabits both, desperately attempting to hide one beneath the other but finding it constantly slipping back into view. Here academic debates about structure and anti-structure are seen reflected in the same dilemma for identity construction, and answered as so often in Trinidad by ambivalence and humour.

To conclude: dualism is used both by myself and by Trinidadians on occasion with clarity as a firm opposition through which values are conceived and expressed. The analysis of the festivals would be a case in point. Elsewhere dualism becomes a partial evocation across scales and through homologies between arrays of the qualities of objects or persons, pertinent in some cultural domains, almost irrelevant in others. An abstract dualism will not help make Tanti Merle funny (alas, the opposite may be the case), but it may help to explain why Tanti Merle is so funny.

The Contribution of Theories of Modernity to Understanding Contemporary Trinidad

The conclusion of Chapter 6, that it was more helpful to see social groups as the objectification of dualism than to understand cultural orders as merely symbolic manifestations of social relations, still leaves us with the problem of accounting for the stark nature of certain fundamental oppositions as presented ethnographically. In Chapter 2 various approaches to modernity were discussed with an emphasis on one which seemed to have clear affinities with the major attributes of contemporary Trinidadian society. The implication which may be drawn is that Trinidadian people, and in some respects the Caribbean more generally, develop their values and cultural forms in some measure in response to the problematic posed by the self-consciousness of modernity. This then illustrates in more detailed mode the general point made in the beginning of this book and of this chapter about the likely immediacy of modernity for Caribbean peoples as a result of their historical rupture. These relationships have formed in different ways, as in the different histories of Guyana and Trinidad which make Williams' (1991) account much more plausible for one context than the other.

The various attributes theorised as modern in Chapter 2 have been undoubtedly instrumental in the process of interpretation and representation which results in an ethnography. Inevitably one is involved in a constant comparison between the society being studied and the society from which the ethnographer emanates. At times I identified transcendence and transience as almost a diurnal rhythm. For much of the day my family would be enjoying the immense hospitality of Trinidadian families, the degree of acceptance, the subsequent expectations of sharing and reciprocity. This degree of involvement in the collectivity was immensely attractive. The warm embrace of this intensive sociality allowed one to relax one's own individuality and dissolve it into the group. It was impossible not to feel positive about the sheer generosity and affection involved in the construction of these ties. Having a child born in Trinidad was to take part in a social phenomenon quite unparalleled by our previous experience of this event in England (largely restricted to one's more immediate circle of family and friends). This experience certainly helped to clarify the same sentimentality which I have experienced in relation to such expressions of sociality and community within my own society and employed in positive affirmations of other domains, such as left-wing politics.

As the baby grew, and thanks in no small measure to my wife, I was (and later – given the relative ease of child care – we were) also able to explore a very different fieldwork experience. In Ford, and to a lesser extent in other areas, it had been evident that what I had seen during the day was viewed almost as a respite from the site of 'real' living which took place at night. As I became part of a culture of fêting, I experienced again a tremendous sense of attraction. In many ways this took me back to activities which I had enjoyed as a student but been weaned off by the sense of the seriousness and responsibility of parental life. But student parties were anyway never going to match a Trini fête. The sheer exhilaration and excitement, the intensity of the dance, the degree to which one could become lost in its energy and physicality, and the surrounding aura of spontaneity and freedom were a revelation. Again it was an experience I could relate to, but more as a half-formulated, half-experienced ideal. Some Trinidadians seemed to live in only one or other of these two domains; others travelled, as we did, between them during the course of twenty-four hours.

It follows that the fact I found Trinidad so immensely attractive was based less upon some sense of its exotic nature and rather more on the manner by which it seemed to allow desires already nascent to become realised. Part of this sense of commensurability must derive from the actual common culture of modern life. Many of my Trinidadian friends watched the same television programmes and went through a similar educational system to myself, and in some cases had relatives in England. But there was also a sense that in Trinidad these experiences achieved a clarity, as though inhabiting the logic of some imperative of desire, which was muddied by the much more compromised/ hypocritical and reticent/hidden environment which are often thought of as stereotypical to British cultural traditions.

There have been major transformations in modern life which pertain to both areas and contribute to the sense of the commensurate. In Britain there is also increasing concern to keep a dialectic between a sense of roots and internal identity and the freedom of individualised voluntaristic personhood. In Britain this is particularly constructed as a dualism of the values represented by town versus those represented by the country (Williams 1973). In general, this dualism is overlain by others such as class and does not realise itself with the same overarching force as in Trinidad. It is noteworthy, therefore, when, on occasion, it does emerge with comparable clarity. For example, in a recent project on the use of technology in the home, the anthropologist Hirsch investigated a family living in North London (1992 and personal communication). This family lives a double life. The first is centred upon their London home which is open-planned and full of the latest technology. The stress is on the individual freedom of the members of the family and their ability to utilise all the possibilities of metropolitan London within what they define as a humane and moral perspective. As a result they tend to be so busy that they are summoned for meals by a home telecommunications system and may be forced to meet by appointment. By contrast, the same family own a second home in Cornwall which has minimal technology, not even a telephone. This home is the centre for a family life which is characterised as quiet and unhurried and in direct contrast to their London existence, based around boating and enjoying the pleasures of traditional country living. The family are quite explicit about their desire for both of these modes of existence, and view those friends who have settled in the country as having 'opted out'.

This family may be viewed as merely clarifying in extreme a dualism which is otherwise evident in British society but usually buried and muddied by being cross-cut by a variety of other dimensions and compromised positions. They have used their wealth and resources to make this opposition fundamental and clear. The distinction between town and country in Britain is not the same as that between transience and transcendence in Trinidad but may be one of its closest translations into British cultural terms, as I believe it derives in good measure from related contradictions in the modern condition. In Britain there is also a perception of modernity as allowing for an unprecedented degree of freedom and speed, but at the same time a desire for images of stability and tradition. The relationship is also evident in Naipaul's (1987) 'pilgrimage' to Stonehenge.

I fully appreciate that there are moral questions posed by this experience. Given my own background, both middle-class and inclined to social-democratic forms of socialism, my sympathies are ultimately with transcendence and not transience. I am looking for emancipation, not radicalism, for Hegel's ethical freedom not his absolute freedom. I am content to enjoy transience as an event, within framed moments such as going dancing, but outside of that the limits of transience are those posed by the novelist Lovelace. It is better at negating than constructing, and my own ambitions tend to the long term. To that extent my sympathies are with the left-leaning Trinidadian politicians and religious leaders who have to compromise between pragmatism and ideals rather than the simpler imperative of escaping 'pressure' which may be sympathetically viewed when it emerges from lack of opportunity but can become the enemy of any more painstaking historical construction of ethical freedom.

In discussion with Trinidadians I have often found a strong antipathy to the foreigners' desire to romanticise the culture of 'bacchanal' as, for example, anti-colonial or anti-capitalist resistance, which they castigate as a racist projection of European desires, where Black people as 'resistance' become one with Black people as naturally 'musical' or as 'stylish'. My attempt to comprehend ethnographic observations leads me to the belief that it makes little sense to try and view either transience or transcendence as intrinsically more or less authentic, or more or less progressive. Either may be situated in either camp depending upon political circumstances. My hope is that an insistence that the polarities of both are authentic to Trinidad and constructed in historical relation to colonial moralities may assist in the development of a more mature and less essentialist understanding of 'difference.'

This sense of commensurability and yet difference between England and Trinidad is, I submit, an aid rather than a barrier to interpretation, providing that this is employed to create a comparative perspective by an articulation through theory. In this case the abstract generalities which have been argued pertain to accounts of modernity. This is justified where it is argued that it is indeed modernity that provides for those elements of commensurability but also difference which emerge through the ethnographic account. In this case I suggest that the specific forms of transcendence and transience are in part understandable precisely as forms of temporal consciousness which emerge out of the historical encounter of this Caribbean people with rupture, and then the struggle for criteria by which to live. These are not constructed in abstract polarity but in forms such as festivals, kinship and mass consumption where they are objectified and thereby understood as a dynamic cosmology.

This shift in consciousness, as described in Habermas' account of Hegel, with respect to Europe's emergence into modernity, was not historically unique: a similar argument could be made, for example, with respect to the development of 'liberal' attitudes in Athens of the fifth century BC, or to the development of conservative Christianity in relation to the sense of loss of tradition in the Roman Empire of the fourth century AD. But it is given unprecedented consequence by a commensurate shift in industrial and communicative possibilities and the rise of secularisation. These lead an increasing number of people to conclude that much of culture is not to be derived simply from custom but that we ourselves create the criteria by which we judge ourselves. This realisation is associated with a new and heightened sense of temporality in which the present is rendered apart from the past and becomes part of a triumvirate with the future of increasingly autonomous locations for human experience, each to be considered in their own terms. In many modern societies, such as in West Africa (Rowlands forthcoming), this may be emerging as an extreme distinction between a passionate commitment to the future and an equally resolute determination to live according to custom. This is not the case in Trinidad where the rupture to custom was much greater. Rather we find a struggle to objectify the event held against a sense of longer temporal concern projected both to the past and the future.

With respect to each consequential trait, Trinidad has emerged with a recognisable variant which may be related to, but is also distinct from the generalisations found in the literature on modernity. There is certainly that sense of excitement and change, of fragmentation and fluidity that Berman (1982) illustrates through the work of modernist writing and which is closely connected to the search for and desire for freedom, but it has a particular immediacy in Trinidad which is not subsumed by any one of Berman's own examples. In conjunction with this explicit evocation of modernity, there develops an increasingly explicit sense of moral foundations and encompassing ideals, which are transformed by their conscious opposition to other modernist qualities, although they may also seek to affirm certain emancipatory principles. As such they may become 'that which calls itself custom'. But, as others have noted, this is certainly not the same as custom, or even as the explicit notion of 'Kastom' found in contemporary Melanesia (Jolly and Thomas 1992). There is a considerable difference, for example, between a cosmology which defends itself through a mere assumption of the customary and a tradition of descent, as against a religion which places the burden of ritual observance upon the knowledgeable and voluntaristic individual – a religion which comprehends itself as existing in the teeth of secularisation. There is a new consciousness of who creates morality. One needs to know who has provided the criteria by which one lives, and if the answer is God then God may well have a presence that is relatively speaking unmediated as compared to merely customary religious practice.

There is no one response to the conditional factors which define modernity, and I would strongly assert, contrary to most authorities, that the modern condition is just as varied and plural as the non-modern. There is no global homogenisation except in the most superficial sense. Nor is this condition necessarily fixed itself in temporality: elements of it may have been the problematic of a ninth-century chiefdom in East Africa, while it may pertain but little to some section of Europe which is presently reconstructing itself around the rigid nationalism of its 'forebears'. Without such acknowledgment of historical contingency the term lapses into simple primitivism, as argued by Fabian (1983). On the other hand, the combination of these changes in historical consciousness, together with the effects of technological and scientific revolutions (or according to many approaches the specific nature of capitalism), may lead to the increase in those elements of modernity which may be regarded as unprecedented.

The reason why Trinidad, and quite possibly the Caribbean more generally, provides a clarity in its reaction to the central contradictions of modernity is likely to derive from those aspects of its history which have been often pointed out by James (1980), Mintz (1985b) and others. In a sense, the burden that the Caribbean carries today is less that of slavery, which is a century and a half old, but that of freedom which may become increasingly burdensome as time goes on. A desire to objectify freedom, that is to construct forms in which and through which the sense of freedom is constructed and experienced, is hardly coincidental with an experience of slavery, but slavery is an historical condition, while the problematics of freedom are contemporary. Today's contradictions may be as authentically manifested in the tensions over property and respectability as over peer-group egalitarianism or Carnival wining as absolute freedom. This is because the quest for freedom is much more than a simple quest for liberation, and is better understood within the larger contradictions and burdens of the self-consciousness of modernity. Many well-intentioned politicians in Trinidad look ruefully to the difficulty in constructing a state based on the identification of its members, in a society within which a core element seems so suspicious of any kind of constraint or authority or supra-identity, and only celebratory of its own sense of spontaneity and pragmatism, leading to what Lovelace portrayed as the politics of a dragon dance. In this looser, more generalised model of the burden of freedom, it matters little if the individual Trinidadian can find direct roots in ancestral slavery. Today, the descendants of slave owners may internalise a sense of freedom which has emerged from the collective legacy of the experience of being a slave, a relationship which was anyway always of dialectical form.

History allows for contingency rather than dictating a logic of unfolding events, and there was no necessity by which the desire for freedom should manifest itself in particular idioms or structures. The specific role for sexuality and property may be understandable in historical terms and their evolution plotted, but only by virtue of the *déjà vu* of the contemporary perspective, not as predictable. Historical trajectories are commonly quirky: if one recalls with Schama (1987: 350–66) that in the seventeenth-century Dutch confrontation with modernity one of the most conspicuous consequences was an the obsession with tulips, who knows what the Dutch would have done with car upholstery? This argument for the relevance of modernity need not therefore impinge very much on the significance of other factors. The importance of income differentials, or the particular articulation between ethnicity and voting patterns and such factors remain equally present in accounting for the specificity of Trinidadian modernity.

Given these loose, semi-causal links there are likely to be particular affinities between Trinidad and the other legacies of slavery in the New World. For example, there are no Trinidadian novels (except perhaps James (1936) in *Minty Alley*) which explore the direct relation between transience and transcendence. Most seem to exemplify either one or the other. A better exploration of this theme would probably be found in the novel *Dona Flor and Her Two Husbands* by the Brazilian novelist Jorge Amado (1986), where the two cultural projects are embodied literally in the figures of the two husbands, one pure Carnivalesque devoted to sexuality and the event, the other pure respectability. Amado's descriptions and construction of these idealised values for Bahia work extremely well when applied to Trinidadian society. Trinidadians certainly recognise the affinities with Bahia (for example, in David Rudder's calypso *Bahia Girl*), while any visitor from each would also note many specific qualities which are not held in common.

Trinidad is not, however, some 'inverse transformation' of Jamaica or Bahia. To understand the similarities and differences we have to have ideas about the processes which create them. We also have to appreciate the common historical legacies, for example, the direct transference of aspects of habitus from parts of Africa to places such as Jamaica, Trinidad and Bahia (Mintz and Price 1976). But there are many contingent factors, ranging from the particular individuality of an Eric Williams or Michael Manley, to the astonishing dynamic of Trinidadian Indians in the last thirty years, which made ethnicity rather than class the main medium of dualism as ideology today. For these reasons an ethnography cannot finally teach us what modernity is, but it provides many illustrations as to what modernity has been made into.

The Contribution of Ethnography to an Understanding of Modernity

The project of comparative modernity is well overdue. There have of course been many previous demands for and attempts at such a project; writers on, for example, China or the Middle East constantly bemoan the hegemony of European and North American experience in writing about modernity. Nevertheless, as the survey given in Chapter 2 demonstrates, these complaints have as yet had little effect. Indeed, the assertions of global change, such as surround the use of the term postmodernism, serve to buffer the theorist against having to consider any particular instance too closely. It is worth therefore indicating explicitly the implications of the particular study for the general literature at the same theoretical level at which the main debates about modernity are pitched. As might be expected, the main initial contribution of an ethnography is relativism. Throughout this ethnography the particularity of Trinidad stands out, such that it should be abundantly clear that a consideration of Trinidad within comparative theory does not render it homogenised to some global form. One of the main concerns in Chapter 5 was to document the very processes by which international forms were rendered specific to the region. In this section two cases will be given to illustrate the more general argument for relativism, by demonstrating the insensitivity of the current literature on modernity. These are the use of the term 'individualism', and the relationship between 'style' and 'superficiality'.

The growth of individualism has been one of the most common clichés of the literature on modernity. On the whole the characterisation of the modern subject has been dominated by North American models. It tends to assume a typical 'capitalist' subject, as intensely competitive for status as it is individualistic. Counter-examples of very different versions of individualism, as might be derived from capitalist societies in East Asian or Scandinavia, are rarely evoked (though see Abercrombie *et al.* 1986). Giddens, for example, is much concerned with the reflexive project of the self 'which consists in the sustaining of coherent, yet continuously revised biographical narratives' (1991: 5), and much of his recent book is about attempts to sustain this project in difficult conditions or the use of therapies which purport to 'patch up' one's autobiography. There is certainly ethnographic evidence for the importance of the trait he defines. The book *Habits of the Heart* (Bellah *et al.* 1985) provides an ethnographically informed, careful construction of how precisely this individualism operates. What such studies reveal is an ideology of individualism with its focus upon personal biography, the individualism of liberalism and of the artist. It is the same individualism which has been the subject of intensive critique by the theorists of post-structuralism. For all these approaches the individual is assumed to be the life project, the core imperative to which the individual devotes him or herself, the auto-development which produces what has been called the culture of narcissism. Such individualism is primarily concerned with internalisation and with a long-term project that ends only with death.

What the ethnography of Trinidad reveals is that there may be radically modern subjectivities which are quite distinct from narrative autobiography. Here individualism has to be constantly recreated at each event, in each relationship, and has few accretive properties. Its opposition to institutionalisation is therefore continued through to a refusal to institutionalise the individual, even as biography. The dude therefore cannot develop the narcissism of the dandy. For many it is only with the switch to a dominant transcendence, coming with the simultaneous move into property, marriage and religiosity that the individual becomes a life project almost immediately subsumed into the family, the ethnic group, the politics of development or some other superordinate phenomenon. Similarly, reciprocity in the transient mode has very little in common with the principles identified by Mauss in his writings on the gift, with its emphasis on the inalienable and on long-term obligations that defined the relationship between, for example, two societies. Here, by contrast, the instruments of reciprocity, such as sexuality, are selected precisely for their alienability, which is why money is often the preferred mode of exchange, even between couples, where in many other societies this would be seen as quite inappropriate if not demeaning. The opposition to formal kinship and to institutionalisation is precisely that these diminish the possibilities of transience.

A similar problem arises when using the term style to understand the foundations of transient values. One immediately comes up against the assumption of both philosophical and colloquial discourse. When we use concepts such as 'being' and 'ontology' these usually elicit a general sense of permanency and depth. Their profundity is established precisely by their opposition to the literal meaning of the term superficial. They refer to foundational elements hardly concerned with, or affected by, the day-to-day contingencies of life; they are utterly serious, authentic and constant, the place where any certainties or uncertainties of existence should be argued and resolved.

In such a context the demands of style, the desire to keep things on the surface, and a preference for constant change may very easily become elided with a sense of the superficial and the trivial. This is precisely the way in which transient values are derided by those serious institutions which oppose them within Trinidad, in particular, the church, the education system and the politicians (both establishment and radical). What may be retained, however, from a concern with ontology is the existential sense that we require continual confirmation of existence and some leverage on our experience and sense of being in the world. This poses a problem for the practitioners of transience, since if one is constantly trying to keep things on the surface then it follows that the inside is kept empty. There is no deep and constant core which gives rise to the sense even of identity, there is no social status or agreed position to give placement. The ontological mechanism has to be derived from the articulation with surface.

This is precisely the significance of style. The strategy

employed, then, is one of display and response. In going to a fête or forming a relationship, the individual usually aims high, attempting the best style, the wittiest verbal agility and if possible the most prestigious partner. From the response of the day, such as the judgements made upon what one is wearing, or from this particular and assumed transient activity, one finds who one is. It is the event itself that gives judgement, that acts as a kind of reverse omen-taking which establishes also who one has been (compare Strathern 1988: 268–305 for Melanesia). However, this is only a specific event or relationship, there is no accretive value. Its implications hardly carry beyond the event itself, so that the position has to be recovered again on the next occasion. It is in this manner that an identity is constructed that is free, that is minimally subject to control. In this strategy style plays a vital role, since it is the ability to change which renders one specific to the event.

The concept of superficial is entirely inappropriate here. Certainly things are kept on the surface, and it is style rather than content which counts, as a bartender noted to Manning (1973: 62–3) in Bermuda: 'no conversation around here is boring until you stop and listen to it'. This is because the surface is precisely where 'being' is located. It is the European philosophical tradition, and in particular the ultra-conservatism of philosophers such as Heidegger, for whom being and rootedness are effectively synonymous, that make it difficult to understand how the very possibilities of modernist speed and ephemera can become the vehicle for both viable and authentic existence. As made clear in novels such as *The Dragon Can't Dance*, style is based on emptying the self into a transient externality.[1] In such a context the current debates about postmodernism become merely parochial and irrelevant. The idea that Trinidadians might lose their authenticity in Baudrillard's reversal of the sign where the person comes to signify the commodity is clearly nonsense, where one starts with a struggle to escape from depth.

There is no limit to the number of ways in which the problematics of modernity may be 'lived through' and influence cultural patterns. Contradiction can lead to single or plural responses as well as to dualism. An assumption that modernity is homogenising would be on a level with an argument that most societies have in the past been similar in so far as they have been mostly hierarchical. A trait as basic as hierarchy says little about the diversity of hierarchical forms which human history has thrown up. Both the United States and Trinidad may be characterised by individualism but it seems that these two kinds of individualism could hardly be more distinct. Arguing for a commensurability arising out of comparable historical contradictions does not necessarily imply growing homogeneity. Future societies are as likely to astonish as historical ones in their pluralism and creativity.

This is one of the reasons why ethnographic accounts of modernity are likely to be more fruitful than purely theoretical accounts. Ethnography has the additional advantage in that there are fewer questions posed as to the feasibility of a particular cultural mode, and is therefore likely to be much more optimistic in its conclusions than the baleful tone of much theoretical work. In theoretical accounts one is often left wondering whether any society could actually exist in such a manner; with ethnography it is evident that at least one can and does. In turn, an ethnography of modernity has positive effects upon the discipline of anthropology. Up to now that discipline has largely derived its *raison d'être* from the idea of diversity as given by history. Anthropology studied varied social forms and cultural orders which arise from the spatial diversity of 'cultures'. In debates over the terms the 'local' and the 'global' some attempts are being made to confront the implications of modernity; although the initial tendency is still to safeguard the relevance of anthropology by looking to structural continuity (in the Pacific – Friedman 1990; Sahlins 1988; Thomas 1991), these same anthropologists are increasingly coming to see these terms more as a dialectical pair and less as alternative stages in history. The debates on postmodernism seem to extend the worst parochialisms of the previous discussions of modernity. Non-European or North American societies are invoked but as tokens of difference or homogenisation. There remains a central model which is the experience of the core. Cultural distinction itself becomes merely a trait and thereby almost an irrelevance. Anthropology is mainly employed outside the discipline to evoke lost worlds and the inauthenticity of the present.

This implies the necessity for an extraordinary turnaround for the practice and implications of anthropology. Up to now legitimacy has been drawn almost exclusively from the 'a priori' – the diverse origins of diverse customs and people. It has been evident for some time now that this attitude to the world would render the discipline merely a branch of history, as societies increasingly construct themselves through the consumption of familiar commodities and ideologies, from coca-cola to feminism. What an ethnography of modernity demonstrates, however, is that the same imported commodity forms may, as acts of consumption, become the very instruments by which a culture defines itself as specific. It is through these means that, notwithstanding economic dependency and the transnational family, Trinidadians have an ever stronger sense of the 'true true Trini'. As long as anthropologists are prepared to acknowledge the authenticity of the a posteriori instead of only the a priori then the world made in consumption continues to require ethnography. There is the additional advantage to this new anthropology that the metropolitan regions become just as exotic as anywhere else and anthropology finally loses its primitivist bias. We are all equal when it comes to the bizarre world of re-enchanted commodities.

This provides also the conclusion to this book, a uniting of its theme and sub-theme. What has been rejected is the juxtaposition of theories of modernity alongside ethnography with a sense of replacement of the 'traditional' with the modern. Part of the advantage of basing the ethnography in Trinidad is that this was a society artificially created in relation to the vanguard of the modern economy. There never was a tradition to be replaced. The absorbtion of capitalism within prior cultural orders is of itself of considerable importance and interest (Sahlins 1988) but it leaves open the temptation to render this lesson of relativism, the diversity of modernity, as the legacy of the a priori. In Trinidad, by contrast, the act of consumption is not to be seen as a secondary transformation of an entity whose authenticity derives from production, but as the creative dynamic of modernity.

This is why the earlier chapters on festivals and kinship are as much about consumption and modernity as the chapter on material culture. With mass consumption the processes of consumption as the forging of Trinidadian 'partial' orders is evident, but this allows us to turn back to areas such as family structure and comprehend them in the same light as striving for modern expression rather than mere legacies from South Asian caste or West African kinship. Nevertheless, it is in the consumption of industrial material culture that Trinidad most clearly manifests modernity as a specific condition, and it is therefore the specificity of material culture as mass consumption which provides a conclusion to this study.

Conclusion: Forging Trinidad

In Trinidad the foundation of any equivalent to 'habitus' appears to be contradiction. In some cases this emerges as ambivalence, but equally common is the coexistence of incompatible beliefs and behaviours which are organised by levels and contexts to emerge according to appropriate circumstance. Integral to this ability to utilise 'framing' (Goffman 1975) devices are object taxonomies and arrays. Objects operate according to a wide variety of mechanisms. Style is quite distinct in its implications from fashion or from the juxtaposition of objects within the living-room. The distinction between objects and subjects becomes far harder to define when persons identify their subjectivity closely with the impression made by clothing, and refuse an image of depth ontology, or when through ethnicity persons become themselves the array of objects which are used to objectify fundamental cultural traits.

The context for interpreting the appropriation of mass consumption in Trinidad is the legacy of the oil-boom, which saw a substantial shift in the sheer quantity of goods available in that country. As Simmel argued for Europe, at the turn of the century, there is a sense in which such a quantitative increase must be examined for the qualitative shift it may represent for society at large. The currently most popular interpretation of this shift at a global level may be swiftly disposed of. According to writers such as Baudrillard (1981) and Jameson (1984), the condition of post-modernity which is associated with late capitalism and cultures swamped by mass commodity forms is one in which previous values have become submerged within a new superficiality, in which a global homogenisation of culture renders all responses of little consequence. Social beings become mere mannequins wearing the lifestyles which are manufactured with the goods they use.

It is not just that this use of 'superficiality' has been found to be untenable. In Trinidad the main expressive effect of mass consumption (that quintessence of inauthenticity) is first to refine projects previously formulated largely through the medium of kinship (that quintessence of authenticity) and ethnicity. The dominant dualism which has been analysed here did not begin with mass consumption and is well-represented in books such as *Crab Antics* (Wilson 1973), based on societies with a relative paucity of material culture. In Trinidad, I would argue, mass consumption starts by completing and clarifying the tendency towards dualism but the shift in the mode of objectification invariably also implies a shift in that which is the subject/object of objectification. Once again, the study of Amsterdam by Schama (1987) suggests a similar role for a clearly expansive material culture, which becomes evident because of Schama's unusual attention to the detail and expressive import of material and visual images.

The ability of mass consumption to extend and clarify these projects depends on properties possessed by this very efflorescence of goods. Material culture does indeed possess certain properties which come into play in such circumstances. Despite being a highly visible element of our external environment, objects seem very quickly to pass below the focus of vision to take their place as mere background to what are regarded as significant events. As such, their ability to express as material taxonomies important ordering principles, in the manner detailed by Bourdieu (1977), may go largely unnoticed. Unlike the explicit self-representation of people in speech, material culture often inhabits a 'taken for granted' and relatively inconspicuous position as the environment of social life, and is often regarded as trivial. But this very trivialisation of material culture, what I have elsewhere (Miller 1987: 99–108) called 'the humility of objects' may allow them to express values in a manner which would not be possible in areas of explicit contest such as politics, religion or ethnicity. This attribute also accounts for the tendency of material culture to play the role of frames or cues, which lead people to adjust their behaviour and expectations seen as appropriate to particular circumstance or place, without this becoming apparent or having to pass through explicit consciousness. In recent years the simple dichotomy of the home and the street is extended by a series of new 'frames', such as the car, which extend and shape previous distinctions.

In one respect those who debate about postmodernism are quite correct. This is their contention: that consumer objects and images are increasingly taking over from people as the objectification of human values. However, this has quite contrary implications to those argued by such authors. It is very probable that since the oil-boom Trinidadian people have made increasing use of images such as those provided by soap opera, or the arrays of objects as found in the living-room, as the media by which their ideals are formulated and their problems argued through. As

Wilk (1990) has argued for Belize, consumer goods may become the means by which a variety of alternative 'futures' posed by the problems of development are expressed and argued over. Thereby mass consumption has helped shift the embodiment of values from their objectification in persons to their objectification in things. The arguments of Chapter 6 demonstrate that there may be a generally unregarded positive implication to such a change. As found when studying ethnicity and gender, there is a sense in which persons make not only imperfect media of objectification as against material culture, but from the perspective of the moralities associated with modernity they make quite problematic forms of objectification assisting the formation of essentialism.

A similar error is made by those who debate over postmodernism with respect to the nature of contradiction. The ability of material culture to act increasingly effectively as frames allows for the increasing ability of social actors to take on a variety of partial identities which might be seen as contradictory and in conflict if put in direct relation to one another. It has therefore become easier for Trinidadians to exhibit contradictory responses, with less anxiety as to the implications of this lack of consistency. At the very least this means in Trinidad the clarification and elaboration of dualism within the identity of most contemporary Trinidadians, although when ethnicity, politics and religion – that is, domains which have been relatively neglected in this book – are taken into account, the term pluralism may be more appropriate. This pluralism, however, does not render the subject less authentic simply by reason of its diversity; indeed, in many respects, the development of multi-faceted forms of identity is the most appropriate response to a modernity which has contradiction as an intrinsic condition.

Many of the points so far argued may be brought together in a concluding consideration of the effects of the oil-boom. Trinidad in 1988 often seemed as close as one might get to a country suffering from a hangover. In considering consumption I am concerned with both the narrower definition of the term – the incorporation of the imports which followed the oil-boom – but also the larger sense of consumption as appropriation in response to the sheer dependence of Trinidad upon external influences and forces. I have previously argued (Miller 1987) that this latter use of consumption is one of the most important developments of the last two centuries. Whereas writers in the nineteenth-century (and by no means Marx alone), took production relations as the natural site for the self-construction of value, there is a sense in which for many societies the place of work has become reduced to a necessary but relatively unimportant component in the formation of identity. What remains from the earlier critique are the inequalities of resource allocation and the differential rewards of work. It is increasingly as consumers that the mass population take from the products of mass production and forge strategies of self-construction.

In facing the issue in Trinidad it should be clear that consumption pertains to much more than simply the individual Trinidadian going shopping, confronted by the massive display of modern goods. What is of concern here is the extent to which the self-construction of society is based upon resources and images which were not originally created by that society. In the case of a small island nation-state emerging from colonialism and with a fluctuating economic strength, it is Trinidad itself that has to face up to the centrality of consumption, since so much of what is important to it, from historical influences, media images and actual consumption goods are derived from the outside. Thus the problematic posed by the new importance of consumption can be posed at the level of the nation-state as usefully as at the level of the individual member of that state. What is produced by consumption is Trinidad itself.

To understand the role of consumption, we can start by translating the abstractions of the philosophical position on modernity into the actual experiences of contemporary Trinidadians. The temporal consciousness which is seen as specific to modernity emerges with the loss of faith in custom as the basis for legitimation. Trinidad and the Caribbean generally does have a peculiar relation to its own history. Although there may be generalised attempts to locate roots in Mother Africa or Mother India, it is clear that the one place where it is difficult to locate such roots is within Trinidad itself.

The land of present occupancy evokes first the conditions of humiliation and alienation which were the circumstance of settlement. This initial condition of alienation is compounded by the fact that the environment of degradation did not end with emancipation or the abolition of indentured labour. Trinidad merely continued with a class structure based on racism which continued to alienate the majority population to such an extent that one sees the kind of self-denigration (and chauvinism) of Black and Indian peoples which was analysed by Fanon (1967) the psychotherapist. This abiding legacy of colonialist and imperialist conditions of power continues even after independence, with the growing sense of peripheral status and economic dependence. The oil-boom represented a real change with Trinidad asserting control over its own resources, but by 1988 the government quite visibly had had to negate its oil-boom claims and was in the position of virtually begging foreign investors back into the land through the typical constructions of the economic periphery such as export-processing zones. Even where the oil-boom brought some economic power it severely decreased the use of internal products and made Trinidadians increasingly dependent upon foreign products and images. Producing little except oil which is not much more tangible than currency, Trinidadians continued to see themselves as living lifestyles literally purchased off the shelf from outside, and evoked in imported commodities such as Johnny Walker Black whisky or a passion for American soap opera. There could be few better candidates for a 'mimic men' state rooted only in the inauthentic and ambivalent, a state based upon alienation.

This makes consumption in a sense the key justification for appropriating the model of modernity given in Chapter 2. For writers such as Hegel and Habermas, the primary concern is a transformation in consciousness, a radicalisation of the present by virtue of its rupture from the past. Although Habermas lives within a world of mass consumption this is not central to his understanding of these changes. In the case of Trinidad, however, it is precisely mass consumption that finally forecloses any simple return to unreflective roots and a sense of continuity with the past. Mass consumption becomes crucial to modernity in Trinidad because the sense of alienation is most powerfully expressed in this condition of 'mimic men', but at the same time I would argue that it is mass consumption which provides the means by which this condition is dialectically transcended in an act of forgery.

Many counter-instances have been provided in previous chapters to the 'mimic men' portrait, and what they have in common is that they are based on a process of consumption, which emerges not as the instrument of postmodern pastiche, but as the only domain which seems to provide a genuine field for self-construction. Trinidad is blessed with the archetype example of consumption as transformation in the steel-band. Although Carnival is vital to the sense of Trinidadian identity, perhaps the best loved of all cultural forms among the most oppressed sectors of Trinidad's population is steelband. As is constantly pointed out, the construction of this often very large orchestra, literally out of the detritus of the oil industry, and the forging of rhythm out of the least 'disciplined' and most spontaneous social elements, is almost a paradigm of the possibilities of popular appropriation.

It would be easy enough to extend this example throughout the arts for which Trinidad has a significant international reputation, whether in literature or Carnival costume, but the arts have a relatively privileged place and is perhaps too obvious a candidate here. More important are the parallels amidst the mundane, amidst the ugly and ordinary facets of life. One of the main themes which snakes through the previous chapters is the specificity of Trinidadian culture. There may be parallels to the sense of bacchanal in other countries, dualisms throughout the Caribbean, but there is nothing quite the same as the configuration of cultural dimensions which may be found in Trinidad. Trinidad is not becoming more like anywhere else, except in the most superficial sense that it is using products of the global economy.

It is consumption as a process which is the instrument creating this specificity, consumption which takes the imported goods and gives them meaning in relation to local debates and symbolic struggles. This was the clear lesson of the material from Chapter 2. Christmas could be condemned as 'decking the malls', or a 'tropical snowscape', yet paradoxically it is the single most important institution in creating a specific sense of the land of Trinidad itself, a Creole 'Spanish' identity rooted in local traditions, subsuming all differences in an intensive celebration of the land that culminates in the feeling that 'Trini Christmas is the best'. Ironically, given the assumptions made by Wilson and others, in so far as Christmas is more genuinely inclusive than Carnival, it is the cult of domesticity and respectability rather than of spontaneity and display which is most effective at countering colonial dependency and creating the sense of inalienable association. Furthermore, in contrast to one of the most common assumptions made about consumption, it was found that so far from being individualising, the process of consumption represented by Christmas is one of gradual but increasing incorporation of the community.

A Trinidadian anthropologist remarked in conversation on the sight of Trinidadians falling over themselves to obtain trays of apples when the ban was lifted on their import in 1990. The commentator noted that the strange thing was that many of these same people had within the last few months been in places such as New York where cheaper and better apples were readily available. The point is that these people are not after apples as symbols of their dependency, they are passionately concerned that they can once again obtain one of the key symbols of the specificity of their own Christmas. After all, the British would be much affronted if the raisins necessary for Christmas pudding were banned in order to save on foreign exchange. Notwithstanding that raisins are not a British fruit, notwithstanding that the equivalent of Christmas pudding might be found in many other nations, as far as the British are concerned a Christmas without Christmas pudding is no Christmas. It is the consumption of apples and grapes, not their production, nor their origins, which defines what they are.

The same point may be repeated for each domain of material culture which has been considered. There is nothing quite like the Trinidadian tradition of car upholstery because it relates to the specific local contradictions of Trinidadian cultural forms. Fashion is found throughout the modern world as it relates to the cycles of capitalist production, but the particular consumption of fashion as style in Trinidad is organised according to a sense of the self and loci of identity is very different from that in the countries from which many of these fashions originate. Similarly, home decoration turns out to be an oasis of the normative where it might have been expected to be competitive.

In all these examples consumption takes promiscuously from historical and contemporary objects and images, and fashions both the sense of being Trinidadian, and the sense that one can always 'Spot the Trini'. Indeed, the more knowledge people have of other societies, the more specific their own appears to be. There is a tremendous irony here for anthropology. In recent decades anthropologists have been critical of their previous use of the term 'culture' and most especially when the term is used in the plural sense of 'cultures'. It is certainly the case that anthropologists have misapplied the concept of culture to regions elsewhere, ignoring the actual heterogeneity of society and the degree of contact or influence with external forces. But just as anthropologists are abandoning the concept of 'culture' as an anachronistic artefact of their own making, they discover 'culture' renewing itself as an object of analysis, with normative traits and endogamous tendencies. It is only when one comes across the unlikely case of Trinidad with its exceptional internal pluralism and international links, that the concept of plural cultures seems appropriate, because one can actually watch, in activities such as Christmas, the deliberate self-creation of a specific entity with normative tendencies out of this bricolage. Precisely because Trinidad seems at first the worst possible candidate for reconstructing this outmoded anthropological concept, it becomes the best exemplar of a Hegelian[2] sense of true 'culture', ideally stripped of 'positivity', a process of self-construction by an inseparable combination of national identity and citizenship.

The attempt to transform our conception of the term consumption with regard to supra-individual cultural processes, may be summarised with reference to the two meanings of the term forged. In the first place forged is intended to connote the process by which intractable materials are, in the forge, turned into something new, both useful, solid and fine. But the term forged is also a verb pertaining to the act of forgery as an act of faking. It seems to me that this is a most felicitous pun, because as such it condenses a key paradox in modernity. In most discourses we see forged in the first sense as the essence of authenticity, while in the second sense it is the very definition of the inauthentic. I have argued that these aesthetic assumptions need to be disregarded since in modernity the two meanings in fact combine. Authenticity is created out of fakery. Once again steelband seems to provide an almost overly literal example of how this can be, something which at first glance does not seem to be an authentic musical instrument, but which in fact forges, in both senses of the word, as fine a sense of inalienable culture as one could wish for. Culture as an act of forgery remains aloof from those criticisms which have led contemporary anthropologists to argue for the abandonment of the term culture itself.

This is entirely resonant with the sense of culture which emerges from the Hegelian attempt to construct a philosophy of specifically modern culture. Trinidad has authentic culture for precisely the reasons that most people deny its presence as culture. It is because culture is knowingly forged with a sense of struggle and fragility, a sense that it could be otherwise and a constant fear that it is otherwise, that makes it modern culture. This works equally well for Carnival, where this sense is in its triumphant mode, as for Christmas where it suffuses into quiet achievement. A culture which is self-constructed, in full knowledge that it is in fact self-constructed, seems to be the logical conclusion of Hegel and Habermas' modern condition. Nothing can be taken for granted any more; identity, like liberty, is intrinsically an act of forgery.

An ethnography based in Trinidad leads into very different terrain from the politics of despair found in the tradition of Horkheimer and Adorno (1979). I would argue there are positive consequences for the advent of mass consumption and plural cultures, wealth in materials and in imagery. This conclusion goes against the traditions of Western aesthetics which has been a baneful influence upon current trends. To argue that culture's authenticity derives from the fact that it has no roots, that it is Creolised, that it is based upon mass consumption, and that it rests on dualist contradiction is in a sense also to give hope to the experience of modernity itself. Given the inevitability of that condition today, the ethnographic exploration of the strategies by which contradiction can be lived and culture appropriated may have some advantages over an endless dialectic of nihilism. One such advantage, which derives from ethnography as academic practice, is that it goes beyond the abstract solutions of philosophical or political programmes, to encounter these struggles in the compromised pragmatics of everyday life, and, if a model does arise from such conditions, it is one which offers some prospect of feasible emulation. In this task Trinidad has a great deal to offer.

Notes

1. For a further elaboration about this point see Miller in press. For an alternative working out of the implications (and historical foundations) of style see the concept of Signifyin(g) as developed by Gates (1988).

2. In using this term 'Hegelian' I appreciate there are a multitude of interpretations of Hegel. In this instance I am largely following that given in Wood 1990.

Bibliography

Abdullah, N., 'Structure of the Population: Demographic Developments in the Independence Years', in S. Ryan (ed.), *Trinidad and Tobago: The Independence Experience 1962–1987*, St Augustine, University of West Indies, 1988, pp. 437–70

Abercrombie, N., Hill, S. and Turner, B., *Sovereign Individuals of Capitalism*. London, Allen and Unwin, 1986

Abrahams, R. *The Man of Words in the West Indies: Performance and the Emergence of Creole Culture*. Baltimore, John Hopkins Press, 1983

Abrahams, R. and Szwed, J. (eds), *After Africa*, New Haven, Yale University Press, 1983

Alexander, J., 'Love, Race, Slavery and Sexuality in Jamaican Images of the Family', in R. T. Smith (ed.), *Kinship Ideology and Practice in Latin America*, University of North Carolina Press, 1984, pp. 147–80

Alleyne, D., 'Petroleum and Development (1962–1987)', in S. Ryan (ed.), *Trinidad and Tobago: The Independence Experience 1962–1987*, St Augustine, University of West Indies, 1988, pp. 19–26

Amado, J., *Dona Flor and her Two Husbands*, London, Serpent's Tail, 1986

Anderson, B., *Imagined Communities*, Verso, London, 1983

Anderson, P., 'Modernity and Revolution', *New Left Review*, London, 1984, pp. 96–113

Appadurai, A., 'Disjuncture and difference in the global cultural economy', *Theory Culture and Society*, 7, 1990, pp. 295–310

Austin, D., 'Culture and Ideology in the English Speaking Caribbean, A view from Jamaica', *American Ethnologist*, 10, 1983, pp. 223–39

Austin, D., *Urban Life in Kingston, Jamaica*, New York, Gordon and Breach, 1984

Austin, R., 'Understanding Calypso Content: A Critique and an Alternative Explanation', *Caribbean Quarterly*, XXII, 1976, pp. 74–83

Auty, R. and Gelb, A., 'Oil Windfalls in a Small Parliamentary Democracy: Their Impact on Trinidad and Tobago', *World Development*, 14, 1986, pp. 1161–75

Bakhtin, M., *Rabelais and his World*, Massachusetts, MIT Press, 1968

Banton, M., *Ethnic and Racial Competition*, Cambridge University Press, 1983

Baptiste, O. (ed.), *Women in Mas*, Port of Spain, Imprint Caribbean, 1988

Barrow, C., 'Male Images of Women in Barbados', in J. Massiah (ed.), 'Women in the Caribbean', part 2, *Social and Economic Studies*, 35, 1986a, pp. 51–64

Barrow, C., 'Finding the Support: Strategies for Survival', in J. Massiah (ed.), 'Women in the Caribbean', part 1, *Social and Economic Studies*, 35, 1986b, 131–76

Barrow, C., 'Anthropology, the Family and Women in the Caribbean', in P. Mohammed and. C. Shepherd (eds), *Gender in Caribbean Development*, Mona, University of the West Indies, 1988, pp. 156–69

Barthes, R., 'The Death of the Author', in *Image-Music-Text*, London, Fontana, 1977, 142–8

Baudrillard, J., *For a Critique of the Political Economy of the Sign*, St Louis, Telos Press, 1981

Bell, R., 'Marriage and family differences amongst lower class Negro and East Indian women in Trinidad', *Race*, 12, 1970, pp. 59–74

Bellah, R. *et al.*, *Habits of the Heart*, New York, Harper and Row, 1985

Bellow, S. and Amis, M., 'The Moronic Inferno', in B. Bourne U. Eichler and D. Herman (eds), *Modernity and its Discontents*, Nottingham, Spokesman, 1987

Benjamin, W., *Charles Baudelaire. A Lyric Poet in the Era of High Capitalism*, London, Verso, 1983

Berman, M., *All That is Solid Melts into Air*, New York, Simon and Schuster, 1982

Besson, J. and Momsen, J. (eds), *Land and Development in the Caribbean*, London, Macmillan, 1987

de Boissiere, R., *Rum and Coca-cola*, Melbourne, Australasian Book Society, 1956

Bourdieu, P., *Outline of a Theory of Practice*, Cambridge, Cambridge University Press, 1977

Bourdieu, P., *Distinction: A Social Critique of the Judgement of Taste*, London, Routledge and Kegan Paul, 1984

Braithwaite, L., *Social Stratification in Trinidad*, Mona, Institute of Social and Economic Research, 1975 (1953)

Braudel, F., *The Structures of Everyday Life*, London, Collins, 1981

Brereton, B., 'The Trinidad Carnival 1870–1900', *Savacou*, 11, 1975

Brereton, B., *A History of Modern Trinidad 1783–1962*, Kingston, Heinemann, 1981

Bush, B., *Slave Women in Caribbean Society 1650–1838*, Bloomington, Indiana University Press, 1990

Campbell, C., *The Romantic Ethic and the Spirit of Modern Consumerism*, Oxford, Blackwell, 1987

Cantor, M. and Pingree, S., *The Soap Opera*, Beverly Hills, Sage, 1983

Carmichael, A. C., *Domestic Manners and Social Condition of the White, Coloured, and Negro Population on the West Indies*, New York, Negro University Press, 1969 (1833)

Carrithers, M., Collins, S. and Lukes, S. (eds), *The Category of the Person*, Cambridge, Cambridge University Press, 1985

Clarke, C., *East Indians in a West Indian Town*, London, Allen and Unwin, 1986

Clarke, D., *Analytical Archaeology*, London, Methuen, 1968

Clarke, E., *My Mother who Fathered Me*, London, Allen and Unwin, 1957

Cohen, A., 'A Polyethnic London Carnival as a Contested Cultural Performance', *Ethnic and Racial Studies*, 5, 1982, pp. 23–42

Coward, R., *The Whole Truth*, London, Faber and Faber, 1989

Crowley, D., 'Plural and Differential Acculturation in Trinidad', *American Anthropologist*, 59, 1956, pp. 817–24

Da Matta, R., 'Constraint and Licence: a Preliminary Study of Two Brazilian National Rituals', in S. Moore and B. Meyerhoff (eds), *Secular Rituals*, Assen, Van Gorcum, 1977, pp. 244–64

Davidoff, L. and Hall, C., *Family Fortunes*, London, Hutchinson, 1987

Deosaran, R., 'The Caribbean Man, a Study of the Pyschology of Perception and the Media', in D. Dabydeen and B. Samaroo (eds), *India in the Caribbean*, London, Hansib, 1987, pp. 81–117

Dirks, R., *The Black Saturnalia: Conflict and its Ritual Expression on British West Indian Slave Plantations*, Gainsville, University of Florida Press, 1987

Douglas, M., *Purity and Danger*, London, Routledge and Kegan Paul, 1966

Du Boulay, J., *Portrait of a Greek Mountain Village*, Clarendon Press, Oxford, 1974

Eagleton, T., *The Ideology of the Aesthetic*, Oxford, Blackwell, 1990

Eco, U., 'The frames of comic freedom', in U. Eco, V. Ivanov and M. Rector (eds), *Carnival*, Berlin, Mouton, 1984

Elder, J., 'The Male/Female Conflict in Calypso', *Caribbean Quarterly*, 14, 1968, pp. 23–41

Eriksen, T., 'Liming in Trinidad: The art of doing nothing', *Folk*, 32, 1990, 23–43

Eriksen, T., 'Ethnicity versus Nationalism', *Journal of Peace Research*, 28, 1991, pp. 261–78

Fabian, J., *Time and the Other*, New York, Columbia University Press, 1983

Fagerberg, I., Cappelen, A., Mjoset, L. and Skarstein, R., 'The decline of Social-Democratic State Capitalism in Norway', *New Left Review*, 181, 1990, pp. 60–94

Fanon, F., *The Wretched of the Earth*, Harmondsworth, Penguin, 1967

Fanon, F., *Black Skin White Masks*, London, Pluto, 1986 (1967)

Flandrin, J-F., *Families in Former Times*, Cambridge, Cambridge Univerity Press, 1979

Forbes, R., 'Arya Samaj in Trinidad', unpublished PhD thesis, University of Miami University, 1984

Forrest, J., *Lord I'm Coming Home*, Ithaca, Cornell University Press, 1988

Foucault, M., 'What is an author', in *Language, Counter-Memory, Practice*, Oxford, Basil Blackwell, 1977, pp. 113–38

Foucault, M., *The History of Sexuality*, vol. 1, London, Allen Lane, 1979

Freilich, M., 'Cultural Diversity among Trinidadian Peasants', unpublished PhD thesis, University of Columbia, 1960

Freilich, M., 'Sex, Secrets and Systems', in S. Gerber (ed.), *The Family in the Caribbean*, Rio Piedras, Institute of Caribbean Studies, 1968

Friedman, J., 'The Political Economy of Elegance', *Culture and History 7*, 1990, pp. 101–25

Friedman, J., 'Narcissism, Roots and Postmodernity', in S. Lash and J. Friedman (eds), *Modernity and Identity*, Oxford, Blackwell, 1992

Frosh, S., *Identity Crisis*, London, Macmillan, 1991

Gates, H. L., *The Signifying Monkey*, Oxford, Oxford University Press, 1988

Geertz. C., 'Thick Description', in *The Interpretation of Cultures*, New York, Basic Books, 1973

Giddens, A., *A Contemporary Critique of Historical Materialism*, London, Macmillan, 1981

Giddens, A., *The Consequences of Modernity*, Cambridge, Polity Press, 1990

Giddens, A., *Modernity and Self-Identity*, Cambridge, Polity Press, 1991

Glazier, S., *Marchin' the Pilgrims Home: Leadership and Decision Making in an Afro-Caribbean Faith*, Westport, Greenwood Press, 1983

Goffman, E., *Frame Analaysis*, Harmondsworth, Penguin, 1975

Gonzalez, N., 'Rethinking the Consanguineal Household and Matrifocality', *Ethnology*, 13, 1984, pp. 1–12

Goody, E and Groothues, C., 'The West Africans: the quest for education', in J. Watson. (ed.), *Between Two Cultures*, Oxford, Blackwell, 1977

Greenfield, S., *English Rustics in a Black Skin*, New Haven, College and University Press, 1966

Gudeman, S. and Rivera, A., *Conversations in Columbia*, Cambridge, Cambridge University Press, 1990

Guss, D., *To Weave and to Sing*, Berkeley, University of California Press, 1989

Gutman, H., *The Black Family in Slavery and Freedom 1750–1925*, Oxford, Basil Blackwell, 1976

Habermas, J., 'Technology and Science as Ideology', in *Towards a Rational Society*, Boston, Beacon Press, 1970

Habermas, J., *The Philosophical Discourse of Modernity*, Cambridge, MIT Press, 1987

Handler, J. and Frisbie, C., 'Aspects of slave life in Barbados: music and its cultural context', *Caribbean Studies*, 11, 4, 1972, pp. 6–43

Hanley, E., 'The Guyanese Rice Industry and Development Planning', in J. Besson and J. Momsen (eds), *Land and Development in the Caribbean*, London, Macmillan, 1987

Harewood, J., *Mating and Fertility: Results from three WFS Surveys in Guyana, Jamaica and Trinidad and Tobago*, WFS Scientific Reports no 67. Voorburg, Netherlands, International Statistical Institute, 1984

Harewood, J. and Henry, R., *Inequality in Postcolonial Society: Trinidad and*

Tobago 1956–1981, St Augustine, Institute of Social and Economic Research, 1985

Harrison, D., 'Social relations in a Trinidadian village', unpublished PhD thesis, University of London, 1975

Harrison, D., 'The Culture of Poverty in Coconut Village, Trinidad; a critique', *Sociological Review*, 24, 1976, pp. 831–58

Hart, K. (ed.), *Women and the Sexual Division of Labour in the Caribbean*, Mona, Consortium Graduate School of Social Sciences, 1989

Harvey, D., *The Condition of Postmodernity*, Oxford, Basil Blackwell, 1989

Hebdige, D., *Hiding in the Light*, London, Routledge, 1988

Henriques, F., *Family and Colour in Jamaica*, London, Eyre and Spottiswoode, 1953

Henry, R., 'The State and Income Distribution in an Independent Trinidad and Tobago', in S. Ryan (ed.), *Trinidad and Tobago – The Independence Experience 1962–1987*, St Augustine, Univerity of West Indies, 1988, pp. 471–93

Herskovits, M. J. and F. S., *Trinidad Village*, New York, Alfred and Knopf, 1947

Higham. B. W., 'African and Creole Slave Patterns in Trinidad', in M. Crahan and F. Knight (eds), *Africa and the Caribbean*, Baltimore, John Hopkins Press, 1979, pp. 41–64

Hill, E., *The Trinidad Carnival: Mandate for a National Theatre*, Austin, University of Texas Press, 1972

Hill, E., 'Traditional Figures in Carnival: their Preservation, Development and Interpretation', *Caribbean Quarterly*, 31, 1985, pp. 14–34

Hintzen, P., *The Costs of Regime Survival*, Cambridge, Cambridge University Press, 1989

Hirsch, E., 'The Long Term and the Short Term of Domestic Consumption: an Ethnographic Case Study', in R. Silverstone and E. Hirsch (eds), *Consuming Technologies*, 1992, pp. 208–26

Horkheimer, M. and Adorno, T., *Dialectic of Enlightenment*, Harmondsworth, Penguin, 1979

James, C. L. R., *Minty Alley*, London, Secker and Warburg, 1936

James C. L. R., *Party Politics in the West Indies*, San Juan, Vedic Press, 1962

James, C. L. R., *Spheres of Existence*, London, Allison and Busby, 1980

Jameson, F. (ed.), *Aesthetics and Politics*, London, New Left Books, 1977

Jameson, F., 'Postmodernism, the Cultural Logic of Late Capitalism', *New Left Review* 146, 1984, pp. 53–92

Jameson, F., *Postmodernism or the Cultural Logic of Late Capitalism*, London, Verso, 1991

Jolly, M. and Thomas, N., 'The Politics of Tradition in the Pacific', *Oceania*, 62, 1992, p. 4

Keens-Douglas, P., *When Moon Shine*, Port of Spain, College Press, 1975

Keens-Douglas, P., *Tell Me Again*, Port of Spain, Keensdee Productions Ltd., 1979

Kelly, J., 'From Holi to Diwali in Fiji: An Essay on Ritual and History', *Man*, 23, 40–55, 1988

King, A. (ed.), *Culture, Globalization and the World-System*, London, Macmillan, 1991

Klass, M., *East Indians in Trinidad*, New York, Columbia University Press, 1961

Klass, M., *Singing with Sai Baba: The Politics of Revitalization in Trinidad*, Boulder, Westview Press, 1991

Kuper, A., *Changing Jamaica*, London, Routledge and Kegan Paul, 1976

Le Roy Ladurie, E., *Carnival in Romans*, Harmondsworth, Penguin, 1981

LaGuerre, J. G., 'Race Relations in Trinidad and Tobago', in S. Ryan (ed.), *Trinidad and Tobago – The Independence Experience 1962–1987*, St Augustine, Univerity of West Indies, 1988, pp. 193–206

Lasch, C., *The Culture of Narcissism*, New York, Norton and Co, 1979

Lash, S. and Friedman, J. (eds), *Modernity and Identity*, Oxford, Blackwell, 1992

Levin, D., 'Susu and Investment', unpublished MA thesis, Fletcher school of diplomacy, 1973

Lieber, M., *Street Life: Afro-American Culture in Urban Trinidad*, Boston, G.K. Hall and Co, 1981

Littlewood, R., 'An Indigenous Conceptualization of Reactive Depression in Trinidad', *Psychological Medicine* 15, 1985, pp. 275–81

Lovelace, E., *The Dragon Can't Dance*, London, Longman, 1981

Lovelace, E., 'The on-going values of our indigenous traditions', in S. Ryan (ed.), *Trinidad and Tobago – The Independence Experience 1962–1987*, St Augustine, University of West Indies, 1988, pp. 335–44

Lowenthal, D., *West Indian Societies*, Oxford University Press, 1972

Lukacs, G., 'Reification and the consciousness of the proletariat', in *History and Class Consciousness*, London, Merlin Press, 1971

McCracken, G., "Homeyness': a Cultural Account of One Constellation of Consumer Goods and Meanings', in E. Hirschman (ed.), *Interpretive Consumer Research*, Provo, UT, Association for Consumer Research, 1989

McKendrick, N., Brewer, J and Plumb, J., The Birth of a Consumer Society, London, Hutchinson, 1983

Macdonald, J. S. and L. D., 'Transformations of African and Indian Family Traditions in the Southern Caribbean', *Comparative Studies in Society and History*, 15, 1973, pp. 151–98

Macdonald J. S., *Trinidad and Tobago*, Praeger, New York, 1986

Magid, A., *Urban Nationalism: a Study of Political Development in Trinidad*, University Press of Florida, 1989

Mahabir, N. and Maharaj, A., 'Hindu elements in the Shango/Orisha cult of Trinidad', in F. Birbalsingh (ed.), *Indenture and Exile*, Toronto, TSAR, 1989, 191–201

Malik, Y. K., *East Indians in Trinidad; a Study in Minority Politics*, Oxford, Oxford University Press, 1971

Mandle, J. R. and Mandle, J. D., *Grass Roots Commitment : Basketball and Society in Trinidad and Tobago*, Pakersburg, Caribbean Books, 1988

Manning, F., *Black Clubs in Bermuda*, Ithaca, Cornell University Press, 1973

Manning, F., 'Nicknames and Number Plates in the British West Indies', *American Folklore*, 87, 1974, pp. 123–32

Massiah, J., *Women as Heads of Households in the Caribbean; Family Structure and Feminine Status*, Unesco, 1983

Massiah, J., (ed.), 'Women in the Caribbean', *Social and Economic Studies*, 35, 1986

Massiah, J., 'Researching Women's Work: 1985 and Beyond', in P. Mohammed and C. Shepherd (eds), *Gender in Caribbean Development*, Mona, University of the West Indies, 1988, pp. 206–31

Mathura, M., *The Coup*, Play performed at National Theatre, London, 1991

Meyer, J., 'Illegitimates and Foundlings in Pre–Industrial France', in P. Laslett, K. Oosterveen and R. M. Smith (eds), *Bastardy and its Comparative History*, London, Edward Arnold, 1980 pp. 249–63

Miller, D., 'Modernism and suburbia as material ideology', in D. Miller and C. Tilley (eds), *Ideology, Power and Prehistory*, Cambridge, Cambridge University Press, 1984

Miller D., *Material Culture and Mass Consumption*, Oxford, Basil Blackwell, 1987

Miller, D., 'Appropriating the State on the Council Estate', *Man*, 23, 1988, pp. 353–72

Miller, D., 'Absolute Freedom in Trinidad', *Man*, 26, 1991, pp. 323–41

Miller, D., 'The Young and the Restless in Trinidad: A Case of the Local and the Global in Mass Consumption', in R. Silverstone and E. Hirsch (eds), *Consuming Technology*, London, Routledge, 1992, pp. 163–82

Miller, D., 'Christmas and Materialism in Trinidad,' in D. Miller (ed.), *Unwrapping Christmas*, Oxford, Oxford University Press, 1993

Miller, D., 'Style and Ontology', in J. Friedman, (ed.), *Consumption and Cultural Strategies*, London, Harwood, in press

Miller, D., 'Spot the Trini', in U. Hannerz and O. Lofgren (eds), volume on *Nationalism*, forthcoming

Mintz, S., *Sweetness and Power*, New York, Viking, 1985a

Mintz, S., 'From Plantations to Peasantries', in S. Mintz and S. Price (eds), *Caribbean Contours*, Baltimore, John Hopkins University Press, 1985b, pp. 127–53

Mintz. S. and Price, R., 'An Anthropological Approach to the Afro-American Past: a Caribbean Perspective', *Occasional Papers in Social Change*, Philadelphia, Institute for Study of Human Issues, 1976

Mohammed, P., 'The 'Creolisation' of Indian women in Trinidad', in S. Ryan, (ed.), *Trinidad and Tobago – The Independence Experience 1962–1987*, St Augustine, University of West Indies, 1988, pp. 381–98

Mohammed, S., 'Carribbean Studies Project', Library, University of West Indies, 1987

Mukerji, C., *From Graven Images*, New York, Columbia University Press, 1983

Naipaul, V. S., *The Suffrage of Elvira*, London, André Deutsch, 1958

Naipaul, V. S., *A House for Mr Biswas*, London, André Deutsch, 1961

Naipaul, V. S., *The Middle Passage*, London, André Deutsch, 1962

Naipaul, V. S., *The Mimic Men*, London, André Deutsch, 1967

Naipaul, V. S., *The Enigma of Arrival*, London, Viking, 1987

Naipaul, V. S., *India. A Million Mutinies Now*, London, Heinemann, 1990

Nevadomsky J., 'Social Change and the East Indians in Rural Trinidad; a Critique of Methodologies', *Social and Economic Studies*, 31 (1), 1982, pp. 90–126

Nevadomsky, J., 'Economic Organisation, Social Mobility, and Changing Social Status Among East Indians in Rural Trinidad', *Ethnology*, 22, 1983, pp. 63–79

Niehoff, A. and J., *East Indians in the West Indies*, Milwaukee, Milwaukee Public Museum Publications in Anthropology, 6, 1960

Olwig. K. F., *Global Culture, Island Identity: Continuity and Change in the Afro-Caribbean Commuity of Nevis*, forthcoming

Orvell, M., *The Real Thing*, University of North Carolina Press, 1989

Oxaal, I., *Black Intellectuals and the Dilemmas of Race and Class in Trinidad*, Cambridge, Mass., Schenkman, 1982

Parker, R., *The Subversive Stitch*, London, Women's Press, 1984

Patterson, O., *Slavery and Social Death*, Cambridge, Harvard University Press, 1982

Pearse, A. (ed.), *Trinidad Carnival*, Port of Spain, Paria Publishing, 1988 (1956)

Powrie, B., 'The Changing Attitude of the Coloured Middle Class towards Carnival', in A. Pearse. (ed.), *Trinidad Carnival*, Port of Spain, Paria Publishing, 1988 (1956)

Price, N., *Behind the Planter's Back*, London, Macmillan, 1988

Rampersad F., 'The Development Experience-Reflections', in S. Ryan (ed.), *Trinidad and Tobago –The Independence Experience 1962–1987*, St Augustine, Univerity of West Indies, 1988, pp. 3–18

Rodman, H., *Lower Class Families: the Culture of Poverty in Negro Trinidad*, New York, Oxford University Press, 1971

Rohlehr, G., 'Sparrow and the Language of Calypso', *Savacou*, 2, 1970, pp. 87–99

Rohlehr, G., 'Images of Men and Women in the 1930's Calypsoes: the Sociology of Food Acquisition in the Context of Survivalism', in P. Mohammed and C. Shepherd (eds), *Gender in Caribbean Development*, Mona, University of West Indies, 1988, pp. 232–306

Rohlehr, G., *Calypso and Society in Pre-Independence Trinidad*, Port of Spain, Gordon Rohlehr, 1990

Rowlands, M., 'The material culture of success', in J. Friedman (ed.), *Consumption and Cultural Strategies*, London, Harwood, forthcoming

Rubenstein, H., 'Folk and Mainstream Systems of Land Tenure and use in St Vincent', in J. Besson and J. Momsen (eds), *Land and Development in the Caribbean*, London, Macmillan, 1987

Ryan, S. (ed.), *Trinidad and Tobago: The Independence Experience 1962–1987*, St Augustine, Institute for Social and Economic Research, 1988

Ryan, S., 'Popular Attitudes Towards Independence, Race Relations and the Peoples National Movement', in S. Ryan (ed.), *Trinidad and Tobago – The Independence Experience 1962–1987*, St Augustine, University of West Indies, 1988, pp. 217–28

Ryan, S. (ed.), *Social and Occupational Stratification in Contemporary Trinidad and Tobago*. St Augustine, Institute for Social and Economic Research, 1991

Ryan, S., 'Social Stratification in Trinidad and Tobago, Lloyd Braithwaite revisited', in S. Ryan (ed.), *Social and Occupational Stratification in Contemporary Trinidad and Tobago*, St Augustine, Institute for Social and Economic Research, 1991a, pp. 58–79

Ryan, S., 'Social and Ethnic Stratification and Voting Behaviour in Trinidad and Tobago: 1956–1990', in S. Ryan (ed.), *Social and Occupational Stratification in Contemporary Trinidad and Tobago*, St Augustine, Institute for Social and Economic Research, 1991b, pp. 113–44

Ryan, S., 'Race and Occupational Stratification in Trinidad and Tobago', in S. Ryan (ed.), *Social and Occupational Stratification in Contemporary Trinidad and Tobago*, St Augustine, Institute for Social and Economic Research, 1991c, 166–90

Sacks, C., 'Sex Roles and Survival Strategies in an Urban Black Community', in Rosaldo, M. and Lamphere, L. (eds), *Woman, Culture and Society*, Stanford, Stanford University Press, 1974, pp. 113–28

Sahlins, M., 'Cosmologies of Capitalism: The Trans-Pacific Sector of 'The World System'', *Procedeedings of the British Academy*. LXXIV, 1988, pp. 1–51

Schama, S., *The Embarrassment of Riches*, London, Fontana, 1987

Schwartz, B., 'Patterns of East Indian Family Organisation in Trinidad', *Caribbean Studies*, 5, 1965, pp. 23–36

Segal. D., 'Nationalism in a Colonial State', unpublished PhD thesis, University of Chicago, 1989

Senior, O., *Working Miracles: Women's Lives in the English–Speaking Caribbean*, London, James Currey, 1991

Sennett, R., *The Fall of Public Man*, London, Faber and Faber, 1977

Shepherd, C.Y., *The Cacao Industry in Trinidad*, Port of Spain, Government Printery, 1932

Simmel, G., 'Fashion', *American Journal of Sociology*, 62, 1957, pp. 541–58

Simmel, G., *The Philosophy of Money*, London, Routledge and Kegan Paul, 1978

Singh, C., *Multinationals, the State and the Management of Economic Nationalism: the Case of Trinidad and Tobago*, New York, Praeger, 1989

Smith, M. G., *West Indian Family Structure*, Seattle, University of Washington Press, 1962

Smith, M. G., *Corporations and Society*, London, Duckworth, 1974

Smith, R. T., *The Negro Family in British Guiana: Family Structure and Social Status in the Villages*, London, Routledge and Kegan Paul, 1956

Smith, R. T., 'Introduction in R. T. Smith, (ed.), *Kinship Ideology and Practice in Latin America*, University of North Carolina Press, 1984

Smith, R. T., 'The Matrifocal Family', in J. Goody (ed.), *The Character of Kinship*, Cambridge, Cambridge University Press, 1973

Smith, R. T., 'The Family and the Modern World System: Some Observations from the Caribbean', *Journal of Family History*, 3, 1978, pp. 337–60

Smith, R. T., 'Hierarchy and the dual marriage system in West Indian society', in J. Collier and S Yanagisako (eds), *Gender and Kinship – Essays Towards a Unified Analysis*, Stanford, Stanford University press, 1987

Smith, R. T., *Kinship and Class in the West Indies*, Cambridge, Cambridge University Press, 1988

Stewart, J., 'Patronage and Control in the Trinidad Carnival', in V. Turner and E. Bruner (eds), *The Anthropology of Experience*, Urbana, University of Illinois Press, 1986, pp. 289–315

Stewart, J. O., *Drinkers, Drummers, and Decent Folk*, Albany, State University of New York, 1989

Strathern, M., *The Gender of the Gift*, Berkeley, University of California Press, 1988

Strathern, M., *Partial Connections*, Savage, Rowman and Littlefield, 1991

Taylor, S., *Parang in Trinidad*, Port of Spain, National Cultural Council, 1977

Thomas, N., *Entangled Objects*, Cambridge, Mass, Harvard University Press, 1991

Trotman, D., *Crime in Trinidad*, Knoxville, University of Tennessee Press, 1986

Trotman, D., 'The Image of Indians in Calypso: Trinidad 1946–1986', in F. Birbalsingh (ed.), *Indenture and Exile*, Toronto, TSAR, 1989, 176–90

de Verteuil, A., *Eight East Indian Immigrants*, Port of Spain, Paria Publishing, 1989

Vertovec, S., *Hindu Trinidad*, London, Macmillan, 1992

Warner, K., *Kaiso/The Trinidad Calypso: A Study of Calypso as Oral Literature*, Washington, Three Continents Press, 1982

Wilk, R., 'Consumer Goods as a Dialogue about Development', *Culture and History*, 7, 1990, 79–100

Williams, B., *Stains on My Name, War in My Veins*, Durham, Duke University Press, 1991

Williams, R., 'Advertising: the Magic System', in *Problems in Materialism and Culture*, London, Verso, 1980, pp. 170–95

Williams, R., *The Country and the City*, London, Chatto and Windus, 1973

Wilson, P., *Crab Antics: The Social Anthropology of English Speaking Negro Societies of the Caribbean*, New Haven, Yale University Press, 1973

Winer, L. and Aguilar, E., 'Spanish Influence in the Lexicon of Trinidadian Creole', *Nieuwe West-Indische Gids/New West Indian Guide*, 65, 1991, pp. 153–91

Wood, A., *Hegel's Ethical Thought*, Cambridge, Cambridge University Press, 1990

Yelvington, K., 'Gender and ethnicity at work in a Trinidadian factory', in J. Momsen (ed.), *Caribbean Women*, London, Macmillan, forthcoming

Yelvington, K., 'Trinidad and Tobago 1988–89', in J. Malloy and E. A. Gamarra (eds), *Latin American and Caribbean Contemporary Record*, vol. 8, New York, Holmes and Meier, 1991

Young, V., 'Household Structure in a West Indian Society', *Social and Economic Studies*, 39, 1990, pp. 147–79

Index